Instrumentalists and Renaissance

This innovative and multilayered study of the music and culture of Renaissance instrumentalists spans the early institutionalization of instrumental music from c.1420 to the rise of the basso continuo and newer roles for players around 1600. Employing a broad cultural narrative interwoven with detailed case studies, close readings of eighteen essential musical sources, and analysis of musical images, Victor Coelho and Keith Polk show that instrumental music formed a vital and dynamic element in the artistic landscape, from rote function to creative fantasy. Instrumentalists occupied a central role in courtly ceremonies and private social rituals during the Renaissance, as banquets, dances, processions, religious celebrations, and weddings all required their participation – regardless of social class. Instrumental genres were highly diverse artistic creations, from polyphonic repertoires revealing knowledge of notated styles, to improvisation and flexible practices. Understanding the contributions of instrumentalists is essential for any accurate assessment of Renaissance culture.

VICTOR COELHO is Professor of Music and Director of the Center for Early Music Studies at Boston University, a fellow of Villa I Tatti, the Harvard University Center for Italian Renaissance Studies in Florence, and a lutenist and guitarist. His books include *Music and Science in the Age of Galileo, The Manuscript Sources of Seventeenth-Century Italian Lute Music, Performance on Lute, Guitar, and Vihuela*, and *The Cambridge Companion to the Guitar*. In 2000 he received the Noah Greenberg Award given by the American Musicological Society for outstanding contributions to the performance of early music, resulting in a recording (with Alan Curtis) that won a Prelude Classical Award in 2004. His recordings as lutenist and director appear on the Stradivarius, Toccata Classics, and Teldec labels: http://people.bu.edu/blues/.

KEITH POLK is Professor Emeritus, University of New Hampshire, and has also taught at Brandeis University; the New England Conservatory, and Regents College, London. He is one of the foremost authorities on

Renaissance instrumental music, and has produced numerous articles and several books on the subject, including *German Instrumental Music of the Late Middle Ages* (Cambridge University Press, 1992). He is also a professional player of the French horn, having performed with the San Diego Symphony, the Amsterdam Concertgebouw Orchestra, Boston Baroque, and the Smithsonian Chamber Players. His *Festschrift, Instruments, Ensembles, and Repertory, 1300–1600*, ed. Timothy McGee & Stewart Carter, was published in 2013.

Instrumentalists and Renaissance Culture, 1420–1600

Players of Function and Fantasy

VICTOR COELHO
Boston University

and

KEITH POLK
University of New Hampshire

CAMBRIDGE
UNIVERSITY PRESS

University Printing House, Cambridge CB2 8BS, United Kingdom

One Liberty Plaza, 20th Floor, New York, NY 10006, USA

477 Williamstown Road, Port Melbourne, VIC 3207, Australia

314-321, 3rd Floor, Plot 3, Splendor Forum, Jasola District Centre, New Delhi - 110025, India

79 Anson Road, #06-04/06, Singapore 079906

Cambridge University Press is part of the University of Cambridge.

It furthers the University's mission by disseminating knowledge in the pursuit of education, learning and research at the highest international levels of excellence.

www.cambridge.org
Information on this title: www.cambridge.org/9781316509203

© Victor Coelho and Keith Polk 2016

This publication is in copyright. Subject to statutory exception and to the provisions of relevant collective licensing agreements, no reproduction of any part may take place without the written permission of Cambridge University Press.

First published 2016
First paperback edition 2018

A catalogue record for this publication is available from the British Library

Library of Congress Cataloging in Publication data
Coelho, Victor, author. | Polk, Keith, author.
Instrumentalists and Renaissance culture, 1420–1600 : players of function and fantasy / Victor Coelho and Keith Polk.
Cambridge, United Kingdom : Cambridge University Press, 2016. | Includes bibliographical references and index.
LCCN 2015042964 | ISBN 9781107145801
LCSH: Instrumentalists – Social conditions. | Renaissance. | Instrumental music – 15th century – History and criticism. | Instrumental music – 16th century – History and criticism.
LCC ML3795 .C635 2016 | DDC 784.09/031–dc23
LC record available at http://lccn.loc.gov/2015042964

ISBN 978-1-107-14580-1 Hardback
ISBN 978-1-316-50920-3 Paperback

Cambridge University Press has no responsibility for the persistence or accuracy of URLs for external or third-party internet websites referred to in this publication, and does not guarantee that any content on such websites is, or will remain, accurate or appropriate.

For Brita
For Janet

Contents

List of figures [*page* xi]
Preface and acknowledgments [xiv]
List of abbreviations [xvii]

Prologue: The culture of Renaissance instrumental music [1]
Patronage, population, and printing [3]
Perspectives on Renaissance sound and context [5]
The combination of voices and instruments [7]
Case study 1: Josquin in the instrumental repertory of the Renaissance [8]
Renaissance instrumental music and periodization [14]

1 Renaissance instrumental music and its patrons [17]
Patrons and professionals [17]
Burgundy: the model of power – 1400–77 [18]
Case study 2: Magnificent Burgundy: instrumental music during the reign of Philip the Good [19]
The Burgundian model expands – 1480–1520 [22]
Maximilian I – Ercole d'Este – Henry VII [25]
The Burgundian model transcended – 1520–50 [27]
Case study 3: Patronage runs rampant: instrumental music at the court of Henry VIII [28]
Francis I – Charles V [32]
A new model of power: Bavaria – 1550–1600 [34]
Church patronage of instrumental music [36]
The fifteenth century: instrumental music through back alleys [37]
The sixteenth century: doors open to instrumental music [41]
Case study 4: Renaissance instrumentalists in the New World and cross-cultural encounters [42]
Civic patronage in the fifteenth century [49]
Germany and Italy – Flanders and England – France and Spain [50]
Civic patronage in the sixteenth century [55]
Case study 5: Players and politics: Tielman Susato and the Antwerp Band, c.1550 [55]
Size matters [58]

2 A source-based history of Renaissance instrumental music [62]
1) A variable repertory for instrumentalists: Faenza, Biblioteca comunale 117 (c.1380–1426) – *Faenza* [64]

2) Zorzi Trombetta and a watershed moment for ensemble instrumental music: London, British Library, Cotton MS Titus A. xxvi (c.1440) – *Zorzi*   [66]

3) A compendium of fifteenth-century keyboard techniques: The Buxheim Organ Book, Munich, Bayerische Staatsbibliothek, Cim. 352b (formerly Mus.ms. 3725), (c.1460–70) – *Buxheim*   [69]

4) Ensemble instrumental music moves to center stage: Rome, Biblioteca Casanatense, MS 2856 (c.1481–90?) – *Casanatense*   [71]

5) A tipping point for instrumental music: Petrucci's *Harmonice musices Odhecaton A* (Venice, 1501_1) – *Odhecaton*   [76]

6) The end of the beginning of lute music: Francesco Spinacino, *Intabulatura de Lauto Libro primo/Libro secondo* (Venice, 1507_2) – *Spinacino*   [78]

7) The chanson tradition challenged: Augsburg, Staats- und Stadtbibliothek MS 2^0 142a (c.1510) – *Augsburg*   [85]

8) Introducing the *tre corone* of Renaissance lute music: Giovanni Antonio Casteliono, *Intabolatura di leuto de diversi autori* (Milan, 1536_9) – *Casteliono*   [89]

9) Professionals at work: Copenhagen, Det kongelige Bibliotek, Gl.Kgl.Sml. 1872-4° (c.1545) – *Copenhagen*   [94]

10) Alonso Mudarra, *Tres libros de música en cifras para vihuela* (Seville, 1546_{14}) – *Tres libros*   [97]

11) Dances for musical recreation: Tielman Susato's *Het derde musyck boexken... danserye* (Antwerp, 1551_8) – *Danserye*   [100]

12) Practice meets theory: Vincenzo Galilei's *Intavolature de lauto* (Rome, 1563_7) and *Fronimo Dialogo* (Venice, $1568_2/1584_5$)   [104]

13) Keyboard music in Venice: Claudio Merulo, *Ricercari d'intavolatura d'organo* (Venice, 1567_2) – *Ricercari*   [109]

14) International repertory on the periphery: Lerma, Archivo de San Pedro, MS. Mus. 1 (c.1590) – *Lerma 1*   [113]

15) *Per sonare, non cantare*: Giovanni Gabrieli, *Sacrae symphoniae* (Venice, 1597_5)   [116]

16) Viols, voices, and instrumental music in Elizabethan England: William Byrd, *Psalmes, Sonets, & songs... made into Musicke of five parts* (London, 1588_2)   [120]

17) Insular genius at work: Fitzwilliam Virginal Book, Cambridge, Fitzwilliam Museum, Music MS 168 (c.1615–20) – *Fitzwilliam*   [123]

18) The magnificent close: Robert Dowland, *A Varietie of Lute Lessons* (London, 1610) – *Varietie*   [126]

3 The players   [131]
  The daily life of an instrumentalist: conditions of work   [132]
  Income and benefits   [134]
  Guilds and education   [139]
  Case study 6: An artist in his own words: Benvenuto Cellini on the training and early career of an instrumentalist   [141]

Recruiting professionals [146]
Professional players and their origins [148]
Case study 7: The *cieco miracoloso:* Conrad Paumann [150]
Female instrumentalists [154]
Amateurs [156]
Case study 8: Two Renaissance playlists: the lutebooks of Raffaello Cavalcanti (*Cavalcanti*) and Emanuel Wurstisen (*Wurstisen*) [159]

4 Instrumental music for celebration and ceremony [164]
Festivals [165]
Case study 9: Music and political ceremony: the ritual granting of privileges and forgiveness, Bruges, 16 May 1488 [166]
The wedding as festival [169]
Case study 10: Taste and magnificence entwined: the Bavarian wedding of 1568 [169]
Processions [171]
Instrumental music and banquets [173]
Case study 11: Pressing the boundaries of extravagance: the Feast of the Pheasant – Lille, 1454 [174]
Dance and its context [177]
Music in the theater [180]
Instrumental music in sacred celebrations [184]

5 The instrumentalist's workshop: pedagogy, intabulation, and compositional process [189]
Instruction, composition, and performance in the fifteenth century [191]
Permanence and evanescence in fifteenth-century composition [193]
Case study 12: The theorist speaks: Tinctoris on counterpoint, *res facta*, and singing *super librum* [196]
Learning the basics [199]
Acquiring skill on an instrument [203]
Performing the repertory [204]
Performance practice and instrumentalists, 1400–1500 [205]
Instruction, composition, and performance in the sixteenth century [208]
Learning the basics [209]
Composition and arrangement [212]
Intabulations and the musical text [213]
Renaissance translations [217]
Case study 13: Intabulations as translations: Etienne Dolet's *De la manière de bien traduire d'une langue en autre* (1540) [220]
Convergence of instrumentalist and composer [224]

6 Renaissance instruments: images and realities [226]
Challenges to invention [227]
Economics, distribution, and ownership [228]
An image-based history [232]
  I. Plucked-string instruments [233]

x   Contents

             Gittern   [234]
             Lute: fifteenth century   [237]
             Lute: sixteenth century   [239]
             Vihuela   [242]
             Renaissance guitar   [245]
             Harp   [247]
             Psaltery and dulcimer   [250]
    II.   Bowed string instruments   [252]
             Fiddle   [252]
             Rebec   [254]
             Viols   [255]
             Violins   [258]
    III.1   Keyboard instruments   [261]
             Organ   [261]
             Portative organ   [263]
             Positive organ   [264]
             Regal   [265]
    III.2   Keyboard string instruments   [266]
             Clavichord   [267]
             Harpsichord   [269]
             Virginals and other string keyboards   [272]
    IV.   Wind instruments   [273]
             Shawm and bombard: early fifteenth century   [273]
             A slide trumpet?   [275]
             The bagpipe, pipe and tabor, and douçaine   [276]
             The wind band *c.*1500   [278]
             Cornetts and trombones   [279]
             Recorders   [281]
             Crumhorns   [282]
             Flute   [283]
             Wind band with shawms: late sixteenth century   [285]
             Trumpets: early fifteenth century   [286]
             Trumpets: sixteenth century   [289]

Epilogue: function and fantasy   [292]

Bibliography   [296]
Index of primary sources   [318]
General index   [322]

Figures

6.1 Gittern: *Coronation of the Virgin* (detail), Fra Angelico, c.1450–3. Paris, Musée du Louvre. ©RMN-Grand Palais/Art Resource, New York   [*page* 235]

6.2 Three-string lute (or gittern): Francesco del Cossa, detail from *The Triumph of Apollo, the Month of May* (1469–70), Ferrara, Palazzo Schifanoia. Scala/Art Resource, New York   [236]

6.3 Fifteenth-century lute: *Concert*, Lorenzo Costa (c.1485–95). London, National Gallery/Art Resource, New York   [239]

6.4 Seven-course lute: Annibale Carracci, *Portrait of the lute player, Giulio Mascheroni*, c.1593–4, Dresden, Staatliche Kunstsammlungen/Art Resource, New York   [241]

6.5 Vihuela: frontispiece to Luys Milán, *El Maestro* (Valencia, 1536)   [244]

6.6 Renaissance guitar: frontispiece to Guillaume Morlaye, *Le premier livre de chansons, gaillardes, pavanes ... reduictz en tabulature de Guiterne* (Paris, 1552)   [246]

6.7 Harp, fiddle, and positive organ: Jan and Hubert van Eyck, detail from *Ghent Altarpiece,* 1432. Ghent, Cathedral of St. Bavo. Scala/Art Resource, New York   [248]

6.8 Psaltery from Sebastian Virdung, *Musica getutscht* (Basel, 1511), sig. B2v   [251]

6.9 Dulcimer: Hans Memling, *Angel Musicians*, c.1480, Antwerp, Koninklijk Museum voor Schone Kunsten. Scala/Art Resource, New York   [252]

6.10 Rebec: Gerard David, *Virgin among the Virgins* (detail), c.1509, Rouen, Musée des Beaux-Arts. Erich Lessing/Art Resource, New York   [255]

6.11 Viol: Silvestro di Ganassi, frontispiece to *Regola Rubertina* (Venice, 1542–3)   [256]

6.12 Violin: anonymous, Marguerite de Valois ("La Reine Margot"), 1553–1615, dancing *la Volta* at the Valois Court, late sixteenth century. Rennes, Musée des Beaux-Arts. Erich Lessing/Art Resource, New York   [259]

6.13 Violins playing for a banquet, from Hanns Wagner, *Kurtze doch gegründte Beschreibung* [of the Munich Court Wedding, 1568] (Munich, 1568)   [260]

6.14 Portative organ: Marcellus Coffermans, *Maria with Child*, c.1560. Antwerp, Museum Mayer van den Bergh, MM. 0021   [264]

6.15 Regal organ: Martin Agricola, *Musica instrumentalis deudsch* (Wittemberg, 1529), fol. 18v, sig. C2v   [265]

6.16 Clavichord: Italian, end of the sixteenth or early seventeenth century, Boston, Museum of Fine Arts, Lesley Lindsey Mason Collection, 17.1796   [268]

6.17 Harpsichord: Neapolitan, c.1550, Boston, Museum of Fine Arts, Arthur Tracy Cabot Fund, 1986.518   [271]

6.18 Virginals, title page from *Parthenia* (1612)   [272]

6.19 Courtly dancing with wind band of shawm, bombard, and slide trumpet: Bible of Borso d'Este, executed under the direction of Taddeo Crivelli, 1455–61, Modena, Biblioteca Estense, Ms. VG 12 lat. 422-3, fol. 280 (detail). Alfredo Dagli Orti/Art Resource, New York   [274]

6.20 Peasants dancing to bagpipes: Pieter Brueghel the Elder (1568), Vienna, Kunsthistorisches Museum. Erich Lessing/Art Resource, New York   [277]

6.21 Ceremony with wind band of shawm, bombard, and trombone: coronation of Pope Pius III, Bernardino Pinturicchio (c.1504), Siena, Libreria Piccolomini. Scala/Art Resource, New York   [278]

6.22 Cornett and trombone with vocal ensemble: Hans Burgkmair and others, *The Triumph of Maximilian I*, c.1518, plate 26   [280]

6.23 Recorder: detail from *The Three Ages of Man*, Titian, c.1512–14, Edinburgh, National Galleries of Scotland. Erich Lessing/Art Resource, New York   [281]

6.24 Consort of crumhorns: Hans Burgkmair and others, *The Triumph of Maximilian I*, c.1518, plate 20   [283]

6.25 Flute, with lute and singer: Master of the Female Half Lengths, first half of the sixteenth century, St. Petersburg, the Hermitage Museum. Scala/Art Resource, New York   [284]

6.26 Wind band with shawms, trombone, cornett, and curtal: procession in Brussels in Honor of Archduchess Isabella (1615), Denijs Alsloot, 1616, Madrid, Prado Museum. Album/Art Resource, New York   [286]

6.27   Trumpets heading a procession of nobles: the Limbourg brothers, 1412–16, "May" from the *Très Riches Heures du Duc de Berry*, Ms. 65, fol. 5v (detail). Chantilly, Musée Condé. ©RMN-Grand Palais/Art Resource, New York   [287]

6.28   Trumpets in procession: Hans Burgkmair and others, *The Triumph of Maximilian I*, c.1518, plate 117   [289]

Preface and acknowledgments

Renaissance instrumental music is a vast, sprawling repertory of written and unwritten contributions, original and arranged compositions, and source types in several notations and many formats intended for instruments in an accelerated stage of development. We could never have negotiated this varied and often uncharted musical landscape without the generosity, guidance, and assistance of many colleagues. The chapters on patrons and players build on the foundational documentary and source work by Lewis Lockwood, Bonnie Blackburn, Frank D'Accone, Timothy McGee, and Bill Prizer; for German sources, that of Walter Salmen and Franz Krautwurst; and for those in the Low Countries, that of Reinhard Strohm, Craig Wright, Godelieve Spiessens, and Kris Forney. Scholars working with English sources have been ever helpful, particularly Andrew Ashbee, David Lasocki, and Richard Rastall, while work with French material has been significantly aided by the recent work of David Fiala and Gretchen Peters. Every one of these scholars has provided material either before publication or in addition to what they have committed to print.

For our work on musical sources and repertories, we must recognize the impact of a particularly brilliant cohort of four scholars. First among these is the late Howard Mayer Brown, who was a mentor as well as a friend to us, as he was to so many. The others are David Fallows, Joshua Rifkin, and, again, Reinhard Strohm, all of whom have been unfailingly generous in lending their support. We must mention here, too, the help, vision, and long friendship over many years of the late Jean-Michel Vaccaro. Not only was his remarkable work on lute music of the Renaissance unusually perceptive, his vision for the future of research on this repertory at the Centre d'Etudes Supérieures de la Renaissance in Tours through conferences, editions, and digital projects – a dream that has become a reality through the work of Philippe Vendrix and his team at the CESR – guided our work and that of many others. Those studying individual sources, composers, and repertories over the years have also been openhanded; these include Armin Brinzing, Philippe Canguilhem, Tim Crawford, Dario del Puppo, Dinko Fabris, Kenneth Gouwens, Stefano

Graziano, John Griffiths, Douglas Kirk, Martin Kirnbauer, Ralph Maier, Arthur J. Ness, Franco Pavan, Peter Urquhart, Lorenz Welker, and Blake Wilson. Many friends and colleagues read and commented on the manuscript (or, just, commented) as it evolved over close to a decade, and we especially thank John Kmetz for his detailed reading of the entire book at an intermediate stage, as well as Mike Beckerman and Thomas Peattie.

The topics of pedagogy and performance have attracted a fascinating array of talent. Our ideas concerning music theory have been formed particularly by the efforts of Klaus-Jürgen Sachs and Bonnie Blackburn. Our treatment of performance issues, similarly, is indebted to the research and recordings of a remarkable set of scholars, performers, and scholar-performers, including Paul Beier, the late Alan Curtis, David Dolata, Ross Duffin, Randall Cook, Adam Gilbert, Paul O'Dette, Hopkinson Smith, Crawford Young, the late Robert Spencer, and the late James Tyler. When we turn to the study of individual instruments our list of debts expands even further. One person we have turned to time and again is Herb Myers, who has always willingly put his vast knowledge at our disposal. Also helpful have been Ross Duffin concerning winds, Stewart Carter and Trevor Herbert concerning brasses, the lute maker Grant Tomlinson, and Peter Holman and Ian Woodfield concerning strings.

One of the great pleasures in completing a book of this kind is to be able to recognize the contributions of all of these colleagues. Naturally, of course, we also recognize that any errors remain our responsibility, not theirs.

We would like to thank the many archives, libraries, and digital repositories that have provided access to their holdings and granted permission to use them. We give particular thanks to the Mugar Music Library, the School of Music, and the Office of the Provost at Boston University for material and research support. We are extremely thankful for support from the Martin Picker Endowment of the American Musicological Society, funded in part by the National Endowment for the Humanities and the Andrew W. Mellon Foundation. Lastly, profound thanks must be given to all of the fellows, staff, and directors at Villa I Tatti, the Harvard University Center for Italian Renaissance Studies in Florence, for many years of supporting and facilitating this research.

We are deeply grateful to Vicki Cooper, former Senior Commissioning Editor, Music and Theatre, at Cambridge University Press for helping us conceive of this book and for the many hours of counsel, and, of course, to Kate Brett, Publisher, Music and Theatre, at the Press for seeing it through its final stages. Finally, it is a pleasure to acknowledge the careful editorial work, creative solutions, and good spirits throughout of Aishwariya Ravi.

This book has been a joint effort, and another pleasure for both of us is the opportunity to recognize the unfailing encouragement and warm support we have received from our wives Brita and Janet – to whom we dedicate this volume.

Boston, July 2015

Abbreviations

1507_1	Date followed by a subscript refers to the print and inventory as listed in Howard Mayer Brown, *Instrumental Music Printed Before 1600* (Cambridge, MA, 1965)
20r/20v	Refers to manuscript foliation: 20 recto/20 verso
c.	*circa*
CS 1	Refers to the case studies that appear throughout the book
SBS 1	Refers to one of the source-based studies contained in Chapter 2

Journals and editions

AcM	*Acta Musicologica*
AM	*Analecta Musicologica*
AMw	*Archiv für Musikwissenschaft*
BJhM	*Basler Jahrbuch für historischen Musikpraxis*
Brown, *1600*	Howard Mayer Brown, *Instrumental Music Printed Before 1600* (Cambridge, MA, 1965)
EM	*Early Music*
EMH	*Early Music History*
GSJ	*Galpin Society Journal*
HBSJ	*Historic Brass Society Journal*
JAMS	*Journal of the American Musicological Society*
JLSA	*Journal of the Lute Society of America*
JMR	*Journal of Musicological Research*
JSCM	*Journal of Seventeenth-Century Music*
LSJ	*Lute Society Journal*
MB	*Musica Brittanica*
MD	*Musica Disciplina*
ML	*Music & Letters*
MQ	*Musical Quarterly*
New Grove	*The New Grove Dictionary of Music and Musicians*. 29 vols., 2nd Ed. Stanley Sadie. London, 2001.
PRMA	*Proceedings of the Royal Music Society*

RIM	Rivista Italiana di Musicologia
TVNM	Tijdschrift van de Vereniging voor Nederlandse Muziekgeschiedenis

Sources frequently cited

Augsburg	Augsburg, Staats- und Stadtbibliothek MS 142a
Buxheim	Munich, Bayerische Staatsbibliothek, Cim. 352b
Capirola	Chicago, Newberry Library, Case MS -VM 140 C 25
Casanatense	Rome, Biblioteca Casanatense, MS 2856
Casteliono	Giovanni Antonio Casteliono, *Intabolatura di leuto de diversi autori* (Milan, 1536_9)
Cavalcanti	Brussels, Bibliothèque Royale de Belgique, MS II 275
Copenhagen	Copenhagen, Det Kongelige Bibliotek, Gl.Kgl.Sml. 1872-4°
Copenhagen 1873	Copenhagen, Det Kongelige Bibliotek, Gl.Kgl.Sml. 1873-4°
Danserye	Tielman Susato: *Het derde musyck boexken ... danserye* (Antwerp, 1551_8)
Faenza	Faenza, Biblioteca comunale 117
Fitzwilliam	Cambridge, Fitzwilliam Museum, Music MS 168
Florence 176	Florence, Biblioteca Nazionale Centrale, MS Magl. xix. 176
Florence 229	Florence, Biblioteca Nazionale Centrale, MS Banco Rari 229
Fronimo	Vincenzo Galilei, *Fronimo Dialogo* (Venice, 1568_2/1584_5)
Galilei 1584	Florence, Biblioteca Nazionale Centrale: Fondo Anteriori di Galilei 6
Lerma 1	Lerma, Archivo de San Pedro, MS. Mus. 1
Lerma 2	Utrecht, Universiteitsbiblioteek MS 3.L.16
Lochamer	Berlin, Staatsbibliothek Preussischer Kulturbesitz, Mus.ms.40613 (*olim* Wernigerode, Fürstlich Stolbergsche Bibliothek, Zb 14) [Lochamer Liederbuch]
Odhecaton	Ottaviano Petrucci, *Harmonice musices Odhecaton A* (Venice, 1501_1)
Pesaro	Pesaro, Biblioteca Oliveriana, Ms. 1144
Pixérécourt	Paris, Bibliothèque Nationale de France, f.fr 15123

Ricercari	Claudio Merulo, *Ricercari d'intavolatura d'organo* (Venice, 1567$_2$)
Sacrae symphoniae	Giovanni Gabrieli, *Sacrae symphoniae* (Venice, 1597$_5$)
Spinacino	Francesco Spinacino, *Intabulatura de Lauto Libro primo/Libro secondo* (Venice, 1507$_1$/1507$_2$)
Tres libros	Mudarra, *Tres libros de música en cifras para vihuela* (Seville, 1546$_{14}$)
Varietie	Robert Dowland, *A Varietie of Lute Lessons* (London, 1610)
Windsheim	Berlin, Staatsbibliothek theol. lat. quart. 290
Wurstisen	Basel, Universitätsbibliothek, F IX 70
Zorzi	London, British Library, Cotton MS Titus A. xxvi

Pitch registers are indicated by the Helmholtz system, as follows:

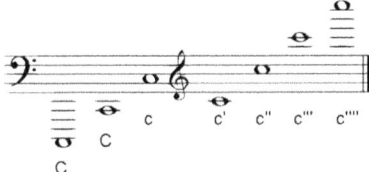

Prologue: The culture of Renaissance instrumental music

In Renaissance courts and cities, instrumental music was deeply woven into the fabric and function of everyday life, and was accessible to a wide, demographically diverse swath of the populace. Domestic entertainment, civic and village events, courtly ritual, and the functional, clockwork activities of a city, court, or militia, all demanded the contributions of instrumentalists. The wide diversity of these events involved players of an extraordinary range of backgrounds and training. This set of variables – a heterogeneous talent pool of players with a wide stylistic bandwith – has proved challenging for music historians seeking to present a cohesive history of this sprawling repertory. As opposed to vocal music of the Renaissance, which was a predominantly notated tradition that circulated in print and in manuscript, instrumental music was executed and transmitted through more diverse means and techniques. To be sure, much of the sixteenth-century lute, ensemble, and keyboard repertory is preserved in printed books and, to a lesser degree, in manuscript. However, this is balanced by an incalculable unwritten body of music that instrumentalists improvised, executed from memory, or adapted *ex tempore* from preexisting vocal works and melodies. The result was a transitory and highly volatile repertory, which in turn led to its neglect in modern historical commentary. This neglect would have seemed unthinkable for those who experienced the soundscape of the time. The clamor and calm of instruments during the Renaissance – what Kendrick has called "The sonic articulation of urban space"[1] – were both widely public and inescapable, marking off virtually all important social events: civic wind players announced the hours of work and rest; trumpeters – probably the most frequently mentioned performers in any sampling of source documents – proclaimed the arrival of visitors into the gates, or signaled from ships or castle and city towers; lutes and viols performed during intervals at banquets and were the preferred instruments in the home; drums could be heard leading military formations, and along with shawms and sackbuts also charted the progress of the innumerable civic processions. Of course,

---

[1] Robert L. Kendrick, *The Sounds of Milan, 1585–1650* (Oxford, 2002), 373.

dancing, by far the most important social entertainment of the age, was in essence impossible without the participation of instrumentalists, whether it is the elegant shawm band playing for a courtly dance or the hefty player of the pipes in Brueghel's village scenes.

But despite the wealth of detailed and general studies on Renaissance music, patronage, and its sources produced over the last half-century, our knowledge of instrumental music of this period remains underdeveloped and incomplete. In his indispensable bibliography of printed sixteenth-century instrumental music from 1965, Howard Mayer Brown could cite Joseph W. Wasielewski's *Geschichte der Instrumentalmusik im XVI. Jahrhundert* of 1878 as the only attempt at a book-length survey of the subject. Today, Brown's observation remains unchanged, despite his own pioneering contributions to the field: our understanding of European music from about 1420 to 1600 is still almost entirely founded on the history of vocal genres in which instruments appear as accessories. The enormous and diverse printed repertory that exists for ensemble, lute, and keyboard – Brown's bibliography alone lists several hundred items that appeared between 1500 and 1600 – attests to the incompleteness of this scenario.

That so much Renaissance instrumental music was not committed to notation has made the investigation of this repertory, at least for the fifteenth century, understandably difficult. But there are ways around this problem, as we will map out in the following chapters. The reality is that any history of this music will need to develop a broader conceptual and methodological focus than we have used until now in order to include the contributions of players that were neither committed exclusively to notation, nor bound to an authorized text or style of performance. Renaissance instrumental music is the product of autonomous composition and the result of arrangement, often resulting in many extant versions of the same piece. At the textual level, the derivative versions made by many types of musicians confront the critical and philological methods that have generally blueprinted how Renaissance music history has been studied. Thus, in examining this music, one must resist the temptation to prioritize repertories – and particular versions – since so many of them are tightly interwoven with culture and function across class. The notion of redacting a single *Urtext* that can be traced back to the original composer is almost beside the point in the study of instrumental music. We must remember that so much of the vocal music was arranged by instrumentalists and popularized in notated instrumental versions. For many listeners of the Renaissance these instrumental arrangements were both the initial and most frequent contact with this vocal repertory. In addition, through their use of many well-known dance tunes or songs and their frequent roles as musicians hired by the city, instrumentalists were also part of the popular culture of their day, an area that remains unrecognized in music scholarship of the period.[2]

Patronage, population, and printing

As a repertory that is social, institutional, ceremonial, functional, and highly adaptable, instrumental music was an essential ingredient in the daily rituals of Renaissance courts and cities. At the level of civic patronage, population and economic might were important determinants for the sustained presence of instrumentalists. Bologna, a city of only middling rank in Italy, boasted of a civic ensemble in the 1520s of six wind players called *pifferi*. By 1550, this group had grown into an ensemble of eight *musici*, a newer designation for musicians that recognized their broader training and technical skill, and also demonstrating that instrumentalists had achieved more or less equal status to the composer of vocal music.[3] By contrast, contemporary Nuremberg and Augsburg, the largest and most important cities in Southern Germany and only half the size of Bologna, accordingly supported groups of roughly half that size – a reminder that the urban centers of Italy were, in fact, consistently much larger than those of the north and replete with funding for music. Unfortunately, it is difficult to produce anything like a pie chart showing the relative expenditures of a town like Nuremberg on musicians. However, for a small city such as Windsheim, we can estimate that instrumental music absorbed nearly 20% of the city's yearly budget.[4]

Along with economics and population size, patronage strategies played an important role in the flourishing culture of instrumentalists. From the

---

[2] An excellent starting point is Peter Burke, *Popular Culture in Early Modern Europe*, 3rd ed. (Aldershot, 2009). Rebecca Oettinger's *Music as Propaganda in the German Reformation* (Aldershot, 2001), 137–70, is relevant to how the instrumental repertory circulated through popular culture through her discussion of alternate methods of transmission – oral, pamphlet, broadside – and through the use of popular melodies. For a study dealing with an analogous area, youth culture, see Victor Coelho, "Bronzino's *Lute Player:* Music and Youth Culture in Renaissance Florence." In *Renaissance Studies in Honor of Joseph Connors*, ed. Machtelt Israëls and Louis A. Waldman, I Tatti Studies in the Renaissance (Milan, 2013), 650–59 & 734–35.
[3] See Osvaldo Gambassi, *Il Concerto Palatino della Signoria di Bologna* (Florence, 1989), 614–21.
[4] See Keith Polk, *German Instrumental Music of the Late Middle Ages: Players, Patrons and Performance Practice* (Cambridge, 1992), 257.

fifteenth to well into the sixteenth centuries, Italian cities and courts recruited German instrumentalists for many of the most prominent ensembles – Florence and Ferrara are cases in point – because these imports were judged to be of a much higher caliber than the respective indigenous performers. In a telling Medici document from 1443, all four members of the *pifferi* ensemble, three of them Italians, were abruptly dismissed, initiating a policy that subsequent members of the *pifferi* were to be "non-Florentine and born elsewhere."[5] Clearly, Italian centers in the fifteenth century, with increased opportunities, higher salaries, and greater prestige, provided a stimulating cultural environment, but still had to draw upon the distinctly smaller German cities for the best instrumental talent. An index of the importance placed on attracting only the finest musicians is Lorenzo the Magnificent's personal involvement in the recruiting of trombonist Bartolomeo Tromboncino and Michel Schubinger, a member of the *pifferi* at the Ferrarese Court. Although Lorenzo was unable to employ either musician, the fact that both musicians communicated with Lorenzo directly confirms that the hiring of musicians was a concern at the highest administrative levels.[6] It should be noted, however, that while German players were preeminent in the late fifteenth century, after 1500 the recruitment channels had shifted direction. The first notice of this came with Italians reclaiming prized positions in Italian centers. Indeed, the roster of Medici-employed instrumentalists under Cosimo I (1543–60), Francesco (1564–86), and Ferdinando I (1588–1608) consisted almost entirely of Italian musicians.[7] And in a clear reversal of the flow of talent, by about 1550 Italian instrumentalists began to flood into the ensembles north of the Alps. Almost all the players in the ensembles in Munich under the leadership of Orlando di Lasso, for example, were Italians.[8]

The sheer amount of surviving instrumental music of the Renaissance is, of course, the direct result of the advent of music printing, which draws a convenient historical line of demarcation with Francesco Spinacino's *Intabulatura di Lauto*, the first explicitly instrumental book published by Petrucci in 1507_1. A statistical analysis of this enormous repertory offers only very general evidence of the relative popularity, regional preferences, or cultural standing of particular instruments, but it is difficult to ignore

---

[5] Quoted in Timothy McGee, *The Ceremonial Musicians of Late Medieval Florence* (Bloomington, 2009), 162–63.
[6] See ibid., 184–5, for a summary of these documents.
[7] See the detailed fold-out chart of musicians appended to Warren Kirkendale, *The Court Musicians in Florence during the Principate of the Medici* (Florence, 1993), n.pag.
[8] On the musicians in Munich, see chapter 1, n. 19.

the fundamental relationship between printed books and the demands of the market.[9] Around two dozen instruments are represented in the almost 500 books of instrumental music printed during the sixteenth century, of which solo lute and ensemble music – the latter showing a clear preference for music of four parts – are the most popular performing media, comprising almost half of the total output, followed by works for solo keyboard. The raw data also provides some information about general trends in instrumental music production during the sixteenth century. Owing to the crucial compositional shift from improvisation to written notation, combined with the technological learning curve faced by printers and the highly regulated environment in granting printing licenses, it takes almost fifty years after 1500 to reach the milestone of 100 printed instrumental books. The next 100 prints, however, appear by around 1560, and the 100 after that appear by the mid-1570s. With printing, the entire production of instrumental music – building, playing, teaching, composing, collecting, consuming – has become dramatically augmented and visible.

Perspectives on Renaissance sound and context

While instrumental music is the product of natural human ability, it is also dependent on the sonic capacities of assembled materials. In fact, for most of the Renaissance, "sound" – loud or soft, plucked, picked, bowed, or blown, solo or in combination of like and unlike instruments – was one of the most important determinants for the context of instrumental music. The development of instruments in tandem with stylistic changes is thus crucial in mapping the changing soundscape of Renaissance instrumental music that occurred over approximately two centuries. Audiences and musicians of the fifteenth century viewed instruments as generally falling into the two classes of loud (*haut*) and soft (*bas*), distinguished by timbre, and in general, occupying defined roles in context. The loud category included trumpets, shawms and other winds (exclusive of recorder), trombone, and bagpipes. Instruments for soft music consisted of organs and other stringed-keyboard instruments (like clavichords and harpsichords), lutes and other plucked strings, all bowed-string instruments, and recorder. These categories, though, were not exclusive, as professional musicians

---

[9] For an excellent introduction to the commercial dynamics of music publishing and its supporting infrastructure, see Jane A. Bernstein, *Music Printing in Renaissance Venice: The Scotto Press (1539–1572)* (New York and Oxford, 1998), 11–28.

were constantly pressed to be flexible.[10] The blind German musician Conrad Paumann, who began his career in the 1440s, was a superb organist and lutenist (both of them instruments in the soft group), but was evidently capable of playing such loud instruments as shawm and bagpipe. Also, loud players consistently included recorders in their performance options and were known in some instances to be competent on bowed strings or even the lute. Still, in general, players of soft instruments formed one distinctive class, those of loud ones another.

Loud and soft categories persisted through the sixteenth century at the functional level: outdoor, festive, and most civic events called for loud instruments, while for intimate gatherings, domestic settings, private courtly music, and accompanying the voice, the soft cohort of solo or a small ensemble of instruments was preferred. A characteristic difference in the instrumentation of sixteenth-century ensembles was the preference for families of instruments – consorts of recorders or viols, for instance, sometimes even lutes – representing distinct voice ranges from soprano to bass. This type of ensemble was ideal for the new imitative textures of sixteenth-century music. The resulting sound quality was one of balance, cohesion, and symmetry, and instrumental music, like vocal music of this period, operated within a remarkably well-defined pitch range of around three octaves, from bass to soprano, that is consistent with the natural playing range of a conventional sixteenth-century lute.

Fundamental to understanding instrumental music in the Renaissance is connection between sound and context. Our modern perspective is skewed in that for us, the "concert" is a central musical experience. At the beginning of the fifteenth century, on the other hand, very little music was dedicated for focused listening only. Players provided the characteristics of rhythms and melodies for dancing, or provided a suitable atmosphere of sound for processions or banquets. Instrumentalists might play from a balcony or around a table, but their purpose in any case was to enhance whatever was being choreographed below or in front of them. In the city, little if any of the functional music was intended for qualitative discrimination. To be sure, we have accounts of élite musicians playing in private settings for the delectation of a select group, but throughout the entire

---

[10] The classic study of this subject remains that of Edmond Bowles, "Haut and Bas: the Grouping of Musical Instruments in the Middle Ages," *MD* 8 (1954), 115–40; see also Polk, *German Instrumental Music*, 13–86. In terms of terminology, the two categories, loud and soft, are most clearly distinguished in French sources, where the words *haut* and *bas* occur with some frequency. The terms are less common in English documents, and rare in those from Germany and the Low Countries.

Renaissance, most of the activity of professional instrumentalists was devoted to providing a soundtrack to one kind of event or another. In fact, throughout most of the Renaissance, the term "concert" simply didn't exist. When the word *concerto* began to appear in Italy late in the sixteenth century it had a meaning quite different – namely, instruments *in consort* – from what it means today.

The combination of voices and instruments

While it has been generally assumed that in most sacred contexts and many secular ones vocal and instrumental forces were not combined, in fact, voices and instruments interacted constantly throughout the Renaissance. The extent of this interaction has been difficult to gauge, especially in the fifteenth century, as musical sources then almost never indicated which performance forces might be called for. The issue is further complicated in that the interaction should be viewed as taking place on two levels. The first concerns the relatively straightforward question of establishing performance contexts when voices and instruments might have combined. The second is the more essential consideration. A vast swath of the music of the era was a shared repertory, for which distinctions between what might be vocal or instrumental, whether or not the work had text, are quite beside the point.

Concerning the first, the general outlines now seem reasonably clear. In fifteenth-century sacred music, voices and instruments (with the exception of the organ) were only very rarely combined. This sharp divide broke down late in the century, and soon after 1500 instrumental ensembles often performed with voices in sacred celebrations. In secular music, on the other hand, throughout the Renaissance a range of options was available. Performances of chansons (a key item of the repertory throughout the era) could be purely vocal, purely instrumental, or a combination of voices and instruments.[11]

---

[11] For a balanced overview of the views on performance by voices and/or instruments, see David Fallows, "The Early History of the Tenorlied and its Ensembles." In *Le Concert des voix et des instruments à la Renaissance*, ed. Jean-Michel Vaccaro (Paris, 1995), 199–201. More recently, see Christopher Page, "David Fallows and the Performance of Medieval Music." In *Essays on Renaissance Music in Honour of David Fallows: Bon jour, bon mois et bonne estrenne*, ed. Fabrice Fitch and Jacobijn Kiel (Woodbridge, Suffolk, 2011), 2–8. For a study advocating instrumental participation, see Peter Urquhart and Heather de Savage, "Evidence Contrary to the *a cappella* Hypothesis for the 15th-Century Chanson," *EM* 39 (2011), 359–78.

With the second level we introduce what will be a predominant theme throughout this volume and a fundamental point regarding Renaissance instrumental music. For the entire Renaissance much of the music was a shared repertory between singers and players. Manuscript sources of the chansons of Dufay, for example, indicate that, according to the context, these songs could be performed across a spectrum, from purely vocal at one end to purely instrumental – with everything in between possible, depending on the demands or desires of the moment. Around 1500 as sacred music became less rigid in terms of performance options, yet another expansive band of repertory opened up for collaborative or adaptive options. There is no better example of the fundamental affinity between voices and instruments than the instrumental arrangements of the music of Josquin des Prez (c.1450–1521), the preeminent composer of the High Renaissance. Accordingly, our first case study will provide a template of the close, dependent relationship between vocal and instrumental music during the Renaissance, and the manner in which instrumentalists adapted the vocal repertory.

Case study 1

Josquin in the instrumental repertory of the Renaissance

For good foreign music to intabulate, do not forget the music of the great musician, Josquin [with which] music began.[1]

Josquin seems to have composed only a few pieces that were explicitly intended for instrumental performance, but his music became a cornerstone of the sixteenth-century instrumental repertory and continued to resonate in printed and non-printed repertories for many years. Instrumentalists began to be drawn to his music around 1480 and continued to adapt, transcribe, and arrange it until the 1590s, leaving behind well over 250 arrangements that are stylistically and culturally diverse.[2] Surviving instrumental sources reveal in particular a brilliant afterglow of Josquin's music in the 1540s and 1550s, reflected in a range of adaptations – literal and decorated – for lute, vihuela, keyboard, viol, winds, and accompanied song. Amateur and professionals drew upon the full breadth of his music, secular and sacred, and from all genres, Mass, motet, and chanson. As instrumental adaptations of vocal music transcended the divisions of geography, language, and even religion, Josquin's reach extended to players throughout Europe, from the perimeter of

Stockholm and Seville and the traditional centers of Venice and Paris, to Protestant England and Germany, of which the latter had a particular attraction to his music.[3] In short, an understanding of how Josquin's music was adapted for instrumental performance underscores a central theme in the complex interactions of players, singers, and composers in the Renaissance; namely, that musicians did not view vocal and instrumental repertories as separate and distinct, but as a single, central body of work in which vocal music could be arranged and translated for a range of abilities, uses, and contexts.

Two distinct profiles, solo and ensemble, characterize the instrumental source types, and they reveal that the players of each approached Josquin's music quite differently. Only a few collections for solo instruments exist prior to 1500, but none of them contain music by Josquin, and we are on safe ground in asserting that the earliest instrumental arrangements were for ensemble.[4] *Casanatense*, containing the repertory of court musicians in Ferrara from the early 1480s, includes around a half dozen of his songs out of a total of 123 pieces. Similarly, the massive chansonnier *Florence 229*, dating from the early 1490s, and the first printed collection of polyphonic music, Petrucci's *Odhecaton* of 1501, contain around six Josquin pieces each. All of these works appear in the sources without text, suggesting that they were to be performed instrumentally; their titles, however (e.g. "Adieu mes amours," "La plus des plus"), are evocative of the chanson repertory, and thus raise the equal possibility that they were not originally conceived for instruments and that their *status nascendi* was vocal.[5] Only "La Bernardina," a three-part work that first appears in Petrucci's *Canti C* of 1504, seems securely rooted as an instrumental work for reasons of its non-chanson title and through-composed formal structure.

The absence of Josquin from the few extant solo sources from this period should not suggest, however, that the solo (or duo) repertory was Josquin-free. Prior to 1500 and before tablature notation became firmly established during the first quarter of the sixteenth century, solo instrumentalists did not generally write their pieces down. The first solo source containing music by Josquin is also the first printed book of instrumental music, Petrucci's *Spinacino* of 1507, which, given the retrospective stylistic nature of this landmark publication, strongly indicates that Josquin was part of the soloistic repertory earlier.[6] Furthermore, more than a quarter of the twenty-one song arrangements in *Spinacino* are by Josquin (three are specifically indicated in the print, while three others have been attributed through concordances in other sources) marking, for the first time, Josquin as the most popular composer in an instrumental collection. To be sure, instrumentalists during these years clearly drew on the more copious chanson repertoire, but evidence shows that they also performed motets. Unfortunately, we have nothing to indicate that Josquin's were then part of the instrumental repertory. In fact, the sources reveal that prior to 1500, instrumentalists drew upon a surprisingly small group of pieces by Josquin – all secular and only about a dozen in all. More familiar to them were the works by Agricola, Compère, and Busnoys, which vastly outnumber those by Josquin in chansonniers prepared between about 1480 and 1500.

In the decades after 1500, a much wider selection of Josquin's music becomes available and subsequently incorporated into the instrumental repertory. The advent of printing undoubtedly played a crucial role in Josquin's music becoming more widely known to instrumentalists, but manuscript transmission remained an important process through which instrumentalists could keep abreast of Josquin's most recent work. The Capirola Lute Book, dated c.1517, contains two intabulations from Josquin's *Missa Pange Lingua*, showing that its compiler had some privileged access to the sources – or the composer – of this Mass more than twenty years before it was published, making *Capirola* one of the earliest versions of the work.

Through their characteristically swift response to the new music being made available through prints, and remaining within the loop of internal manuscript circulation, instrumentalists at the beginning of the sixteenth century provided through their arrangements increased opportunities for hearing Josquin's music, especially his Masses and motets, in new demographic and geographic settings. Seven of the ten Josquin pieces in *Copenhagen* (c.1540) are motets, and while these works amount to only 6% of the manuscript's inventory (10 out of 163 pieces), the fact that they vastly exceed the total number of pieces by all other composers of his generation is important. Lute and keyboard players were also drawn to his motets; their arrangements of *Ave Maria, Pater noster, Stabat Mater*, and *Benedicta es* helped make these works extremely popular during the sixteenth century, and through the efforts of printers and sub-arrangers they were kept in a continuous rotation for almost fifty years. *Benedicta es*, for example, appears in versions for lute from Italy, the Low Countries, Germany, and France; it was also arranged for vihuela in Spain, for keyboard in Spain and Germany, and for ensemble in Copenhagen, Germany, and Spain. The stature of the piece was such that it was selected as the opening piece both in Newsidler's lute collection of 1574[5] and Paix's keyboard publication, 1589[6].

In addition to the motets, arrangements of Josquin's Mass movements were particularly favored by Spanish vihuelists: Narváez (1538_1) included five; Mudarra (1546_{14}), six; and Valderrábano (1547_5) arranged eight. If these nineteen individual Mass arrangements attest to the profound veneration of Josquin's music in Spain, the intabulation of eight *complete* Josquin Masses by the vihuelist Diego Pisador in 1552_7 could be regarded as a devotional obsession with the composer.[7] Through the way they defer to or "emulate," in the words of Howard Brown, authoritative models, intabulations constituted a sp̄⎯⎯⎯⎯ry in Spanish Renaissance music, and their relationship to "n⎯⎯⎯⎯ly underlined by Spanish theorist Juan Bermudo⎯⎯⎯⎯*laraçion de instrumentos musicales*, entitled "Ho⎯⎯⎯⎯Bermudo identifies four composers whose works⎯⎯⎯⎯huelists to imitate: Juan Vásquez (particularly his⎯⎯⎯⎯rales (whose works will make the arranger "not ⎯⎯⎯⎯evout"), Josquin ("who started [is the father of] m⎯⎯⎯⎯er is experienced, "the excellent" Nicolas Gombe⎯⎯⎯⎯as a Northerner, but worked in Spain as master⎯⎯⎯⎯Chapel between 1526 and 1540.[8] For Bermudo – ⎯⎯⎯⎯hirty years later – the arranging of masterful voca⎯⎯⎯⎯stitutes a systematic pedagogical practice for n⎯⎯⎯⎯terpoint, repudiate inferior musical styles, and a⎯⎯⎯⎯sitional techniques of the great composers. As a ⎯⎯⎯⎯ential in bestowing canonical status on Josquin a⎯⎯⎯⎯posers he held in high esteem, and he clearly reg⎯⎯⎯⎯e process through which to "read" these works o⎯⎯⎯⎯dition, Bermudo saw the art of intabulation as a⎯⎯⎯⎯le technique for the composing of fantasias, cle⎯⎯⎯⎯cal relationship between vocal polyphony, their ⎯⎯⎯⎯nd autonomous fantasia composition. In the end⎯⎯⎯⎯ the apex of Josquin's appeal to instrumentalists in the 1550s, and, by extension, the years of Josquin's greatest popularity. Instrumentalists continued to arrange his now "classic" works to the end of the century, the increase in arrangements by organists testifying even further to a certain institutional and canonic status.[9] In the 1590s, three of Josquin motets were copied into the first of the Lerma codices, and these certainly extended the hearing of Josquin's music well into the seventeenth century.

Turning to style considerations, a fundamental difference exists between ensemble and solo arrangements. Ensemble arrangements, such as those in *Copenhagen*, essentially duplicate their vocal models but with the texts omitted. Solo arrangements and lute duos, on the other hand, frequently alter the originals, often quite substantially in the case of Mass and motet arrangements. In the solo and duo arrangements of Josquin's "La Bernardina" contained in *Spinacino*, the original framework is maintained but vastly stretched out, with intricate layers of decorative figures or diminutions inserted, sometimes so profusely that the original can be difficult to discern. In general, the soloistic approach to vocal models called for more originality and modification, and these arrangements are illustrative of both the creative genius and the technical abilities of their arrangers. Vaccaro has usefully delineated four categories of arrangement relating to the "increasing degrees of freedom of imagination on the part of a composer/instrumentalist," as follows: (1) "The strict setting of a vocal model ... just as it appeared in its own notation"; (2) "The intabulation of a vocal model enriched by more or less dense and imaginative ornamentation ..."; (3) The *Fantasia sopra*, in which the composer "transforms [the original model] into an entirely new polyphonic work" (discussed below); and (4) "The free fantasia or ricercar in which all of the compositional elements are newly invented."[10] In some cases, they may even capture some of the spontaneous accretions performers added in performance. Using Albert de Rippe's intabulation of Josquin's *Benedicta es* published in 1558_6 as an example, the original counterpoint is retained but with many added decorations in the middle voice, added scales in the outer voices when the original superius or bassus either drops out or proceeds in long notes, and repeated notes in the spaces created by long notes that the instrument cannot sustain.[11]

A more sophisticated approach to arranging involves the reworking of material from the model in more autonomous ways as suggested by Bermudo. The so-called *fantasia sopra* ... – that is, a fantasia built upon a polyphonic vocal model – is a genre of this kind, involving the creation of a non-literal, seemingly autonomous piece that is related in style to parody procedure.[12] Exceeding the complexity involved in the literal and conventionally decorated arrangements, this type of fantasia demands far more originality than the straightforward intabulation, and the process of combining the original material with new composition speaks to a particular reverence to the model and the creativity of its composer. Some of Enrique de Valderrábano's fantasias in his *Silva de Sirenas* of 1546 fall into this category. Fantasia 19 (fol. 73v), for instance, draws on the second Kyrie from Josquin's *Missa de Beata Virgine*. It is essentially a parody of Josquin's original that makes an extensive use of quotation, generally from original voice entries, that is interspersed with new material by the composer "that makes little reference to Josquin's work."[13] Another parody work of this kind is his vihuela duet on *Obsecro te Domina*, a work that is ascribed to Josquin by Valderrábano, but for which no vocal model exists.[14]

As a spokesman for musicians of the 1470s, Tinctoris famously wrote that "Now (what cannot astonish me enough) does there exist anything that was composed more than forty years ago which was deemed, by those who are trained, to be worthy of the hearing."[15] This statement has been widely interpreted as an observation that something novel in the musical vocabulary had developed about 1420, but in fact the forty-year limitation held as a general rule of thumb for the life span of a Renaissance composer's output. The secular pieces of Dufay and Busnoys, for example, staples of the repertory when Tinctoris expressed his view, were almost unknown in instrumental collections after about 1510 (the last piece by either in printed music occurs in Spinacino's *Libro secondo* of 1507). The contrasting endurance of Josquin is thus remarkable as instrumentalists continued to perform his music into the early seventeenth century. In fact, highly unusual in the era, many of his pieces, validated by both musicians and theorists on qualitative and structural grounds, achieved a masterwork status that was recognized by virtually all instrumentalists of the sixteenth century. Thus, instrumental music helps to map the larger historical trajectory and reception of a composer's output, and neutralizes style change as a sole determinant of historical progress in music.

Notes

1 Juan Bermudo, *Declaración de instrumentos musicales* (Osuna, 1555), IV, "De tañer vihuela," Ch. 71. For a translation, see Dawn Astrid Espinosa, "Juan Bermudo: 'On Playing the Vihuela ("De tañer vihuela")'," *JLSA* 28–29 (1995–96), 65–66.

2 Of these, 235 are for plucked strings or keyboard. See Willem Elders, *Josquin des Prez and His Musical Legacy: An Introductory Guide* (Leuven, 2013), 53–54. On instrumental arrangements of Josquin's music, the logical place to begin remains Kwee Him Yong, "Sixteenth-Century Printed Instrumental Arrangements of Works by Josquin des Prez. An Inventory," *TVNM* 22 (1971), 43–52, 54–66.

3 See Kerry McCarthy, "Josquin in England: an unexpected sighting," *EM* 43 (2015), 449–54.

4 For a description of manuscript sources between about 1480 and 1500 that contain Josquin's secular music, see Louise Litterick, "Performing

Franco-Netherlandish Secular Music of the Late Fifteenth Century," *EM* 8 (1980), 484–85. See also David Fallows, *A Catalogue of Polyphonic Songs 1415-1480* (Oxford, 1999), 5–52.

5 Fallows has recently argued that even "Ile fantazies de Joskin" in *Casanatense*, long thought to be instrumental, is almost certainly vocal in origin; see his *Josquin* (Turnhout, 2009), 45–46.

6 On Spinacino, see *SBS* 6.

7 On Pisador's Mass arrangements and borrowing practices in the vihuela repertory, see Ralph Maier, "Josquin's Mass Settings for Vihuela, with a Critical Edition of Diego Pisador's Intabulations of *Faysant regretz* (1552)," PhD diss., University of Calgary (2011).

8 The translations are from Espinosa, "Juan Bermudo," 65–66.

9 See Kwee Him Yong, "Sixteenth-Century Printed Instrumental Arrangements," 51–52; on Lerma, see *SBS* 14. For a selected edition and introduction of Josquin's music arranged for keyboard in sixteenth-century sources, see Thomas Warburton, ed., *Keyboard Intabulations of Music by Josquin des Prez*. Recent Researches in the Music of the Renaissance 34 (Madison, 1980).

10 See Jean-Michel Vaccaro, "The *Fantasia sopra* ... in the Works of Jean-Paul Paladin," *JLSA* 23 (1990), 35.

11 See Jean-Michel Vaccaro, ed., *Œuvres d'Albert de Rippe: II. Motets/Chansons* (Paris, 1974), 64–82.

12 For a detailed analysis of the *fantasia sopra* in the works of the lutenist Jean-Paul Paladin and a well-conceived theoretical foundation for understanding the stylistic breadth performers had in adapting a model, see Vaccaro, "The *Fantasia sopra*," 18–36.

13 See John Griffiths, "The Vihuela Fantasia: A Comparative Study of Forms and Styles," PhD diss., Monash University (1983), 264–73.

14 For a discussion and transcription of this work, see Victor Coelho, "Revisiting the Workshop of Howard Mayer Brown: [Josquin's] *Obsecro te Domina* and the Context of Arrangement." In *"La musique de tous les passetemps le plus beau": Hommage à Jean- Michel Vaccaro*, ed. H. Vanhulst and F. Lesure (Paris, 1998), 47–65.

15 Quoted and translated by Rob C. Wegman, "A Renaissance in Music," in *Renaissance? Perceptions of Continuity and Discontinuity in Europe, c.1300–c.1550*, ed. Pit Péporté and Harry Schnitke (Leiden, 2010), 130.

Renaissance instrumental music and periodization

In several instances above, as well as in our title, we draw on the term "Renaissance" to define the chronological outer limits of this study with the apparent assumptions that (1) the term conveys a well-defined time span, and (2) that this definition finds general agreement across a variety of scholarly disciplines. Alas, neither of those assumptions is true. Our point of departure is that important changes in instrumental music become clear in the last decade or two of the fourteenth century. The next two centuries were a period of constant tension between firmly held traditions versus a cascading series of innovations. During these two centuries, however, musicians were generally able to accommodate novel ideas by folding them into their practices without major turmoil. About 1600, however, arrived a completely disruptive challenge, one that had been simmering in the accompanied lute-song repertory for decades: negotiating the change from an essentially contrapuntal musical texture based on combining several strands of melody at one time, to a practice that was based on a single melodic line, supported by a bass line (from which a supporting harmonic structure might be inserted).[12] Our book, therefore, spans the period of the early institutionalization of instrumental music at the Burgundian Court on the one side, and the rise of the basso continuo and newer accompanimental roles for instruments on the other.

We recognize that scholars discussing terminal dates for periods in which there is little consistency between disciplines can sometimes resemble the game that children play in their sand boxes, drawing lines and then arguing when those sacred markers are violated. Given that many of these disputes seem more about how one makes the point than the point itself, we are not inclined to press our case with any vigor. We fully acknowledge the futility in attributing everything "renaissance" to a concept of "rebirth." Indeed, one of our major premises is that instrumental music challenges these notions: what is striking and in fact characteristic of Europe in this era in general (and in music as well) is that completely new ways of thinking resulted in entirely original phenomena. The world had never before heard an instrument remotely like the sixteenth-century harpsichord, nor the musical structure of imitation, in which one melodic idea flowed through several parts in a musical texture. To refer to these developments as some kind of "rebirth" is utterly inaccurate. We face the further complication that for some aspects of our subject we can make fairly clear divisions between fifteenth-century practices and

---

[12] On the relationship of the lute-song repertory to both the development of monody and of basso continuo, see Kevin Mason, "*Per cantare e sonare:* Accompanying Italian Lute Song of the Late Sixteenth Century." In *Performance on Lute*, ed. Victor Coelho, 72–107, and Victor Coelho, "The Players of Florentine Monody in Context and in History, and a Newly Recognized Source for *Le Nuove Musiche*," *JSCM* 9 (2003), 48–67. http://sscm-jscm.press.uiuc.edu/jscm/v9/no1/Coelho.html.

those that followed. For the former one might easily apply the term "Late Medieval," and "Early Modern" for the latter. In the end, we see more logic in considering the span from around 1420 to 1600 as a unit for which we need a convenient descriptive tag. To refer to a "late medieval and early modern lute" (for example) strikes us as hopelessly cumbersome; we choose "the Renaissance lute" with all its admitted flaws.

This book brings together an array of disparate and diverse topics – patronage, source studies, performance, pedagogy, translation, instruments, improvisation, historiography, and the music of both Brueghel's villagers and Fra Angelico's angels – under the umbrella title of "instrumental music." The result is that several options present themselves for executing a plan to organize this material. We have chosen to emphasize internal coherence within each chapter, but allow each chapter to stand alone. Detailed consideration of individual instruments, for example, appears as the final chapter, rather than threaded throughout the fabric of the book. Thus, one can read the individual chapters in any order that one might wish, or, for example, use Chapter 2 by itself as a self-contained source-based history of the topic or as a supplement to other studies. Similarly, thirteen case studies – focused and instructive profiles about performers, patrons, repertories, and events – are embedded within the chapters, and while tightly written to be relevant to the main topic, these self-contained essays may also be read independently.

Finally, since instrumental music is so deeply immersed within cultural activities of the Renaissance, one prominent ambition of the authors is that the book succeeds in communicating to a wide readership of Renaissance scholars and early music performers. It is not designed to appeal only to music specialists. Accordingly, even though much of the book is concerned with the music and sources themselves, the discussion does not rely on musical examples. An art historian should be as comfortable with this book as a skilled performer on the lute.

1 | Renaissance instrumental music and its patrons

Patrons and professionals

To begin, let us examine the infrastructure of Renaissance instrumental music from the two perspectives of the players and the patronage networks that supported them. Of the two, it was the patrons who provided the contextual and, by extension, the explicit and implicit stylistic parameters for performance, and it was those frameworks that provided the compensation – very often, being the only information we possess concerning performers in this period – that supported almost all outstanding instrumentalists. This fundamental relationship, evolving but steady, engendered the creation of musical genres, styles, and even the new varieties of instruments that appeared during this era. It is appropriate, then, that our discussion departs from the role of the patrons, which divides into four distinct categories: courtly, church, civic, and private.

Although instrumental music was widely – and during the sixteenth century, even primarily – cultivated in the private, nonprofessional environment, it was the courts that throughout the age of our coverage remained the defining unit of style and innovation. The courtly calendar, similar to the church calendar for the chapel choir, determined the regular events for which instrumental music was to be provided, and the court was where new trends could be explored and standards could be set. The court patrons paid the bills and hired the musicians, and for them, the musicians needed to have the flexibility, range of repertory, and sense of role (talented but silent) of a modern-day studio musician. Courtly appointments had higher prestige than civic employment, usually distinctly higher salaries to which were often added allotments of wine, wheat, or land, and, of course, then, as now, talent was not indifferent to pecuniary considerations.

Most performances were tied to regular, sometimes specific, courtly function which could form part of public and private ceremonies – Galilei rants that cornetts and trombones played "on the fences of public squares for the satisfaction of the common people and the public and, against any right, in the choruses and on the organs of the sacred temples for solemn feast days."[1] Unlike sacred music, which operated within the specific ritual of church services or private devotion, instrumental music, being devoid of text or calendar obligations, was not conceived as function-specific. Rather, the connection between instrumental music and courtly ritual is most safely approached through the choice of genres, style, and the selection of instruments, rather than through individual pieces. For example, dancing, a social ritual that was a central activity at many courtly events, generally called for wind bands (part of the category of "loud" instruments). Their repertory consisted of arrangements of popular melodies, pieces with sectional contrasts (like French chansons), and works chained in a succession of slow and fast dances. At the other end of the spectrum was contemplative music for small private audiences, for which "soft" category instruments like lutes and viols (sometimes together) were appropriate. For such occasions in the fifteenth century, the chosen repertory included lute solos or duos featuring ornamented arrangements of songs and melodies; in the sixteenth century, more discursive contrapuntal works were used, such as the *fantasia* (or *ricercar*) or a brilliant solo arrangement of a vocal work. With these categories as general guidelines, let us now turn to a closer examination of the relationship among professional player, patron, and context.

Burgundy: the model of power – 1400–77

Political institutions, built on the forging of alliances and the mutability of succession, were notoriously unstable in the Renaissance, especially in the fifteenth century. Through the several decades just after 1400, the French king was intermittently insane and at best hardly able to function, and much of France, including Paris itself, had slipped from his grasp. In England, Henry IV, Edward IV, Richard III, and Henry VII, were usurpers who gambled all on a desperate grab for the crown – even Henry VIII was so unsure of his claim to the throne that he engaged spies, including two musicians, to keep track of potential pretenders – one was the scribe Petrus Alamire whose workshop produced the most dazzling musical manuscripts of the time. The tale of the Burgundian state under the Valois can serve as a metaphor for the times: assembled

---

[1] Vincenzo Galilei, *Dialogue on Ancient and Modern Music,* translated and edited by Claude Palisca (New Haven and London, 2003), 353.

patiently – and ruthlessly – over almost 100 years from bits and pieces of political units (a duchy here, a county there), it reached its high tide about 1450. But it vanished in an instant with the death of Charles the Bold in 1477.[2]

With this instability and the stakes involved, the nobility engaged in a variety of strategies to shore up their positions. One of these was to develop a sense of "magnificence."[3] A contemporary view was that a powerful means of aggrandizing one's status was through the way music helped create that image; thus, the support of stables of musicians came to be viewed as an essential component for the nobility. The Duchy of Burgundy provides an apt example for aristocratic patronage of instrumental music in the fifteenth century – apt, because no court was more conscious of the imperative of "image" than the Valois. They had risen from a minor duchy in the late fourteenth century to a position of immense power and wealth by 1450, but with prestige reined in by its theoretical status as a vassal to the French king.

Case study 2

Magnificent Burgundy: instrumental music during the reign of Philip the Good

In the years between about 1420 and 1460 Philip the Good had relatively stable control over extensive territories including not only his duchy of Burgundy but much of present-day Belgium and the Netherlands as well. The economic activity of the cities in the Low Countries gave him access to vast wealth, and with his ample financial resources and relatively secure political structures he occupied a stronger position than either of his rivals, the kings of France and England. Still, he was only a duke, and they were kings. This undoubtedly impelled him to place great emphasis on shoring up his position as he assembled around him a wide range of the trappings that would make unmistakable the stature of Burgundy. Included was the complete stable of instrumental music that was expected of a member of the highest nobility.[1]

---

[2] Concerning the two musicians who acted as spies for Henry VIII, see Bruno Bouckaert and Eugeen Schreurs, "Hans Nagel, Performer and Spy in England and Flanders (c.1490–1531)." In *Tielman Susato*, ed. Keith Polk (Hillsdale, NY), 63–102. On the rise and fall of the house of Burgundy, see Richard Vaughan. *Valois Burgundy* (London, 1975), 14–31, 194–227.

[3] A.D. Fraser Jenkins, "Cosimo de'Medici's Patronage of Art and the Theory of Magnificence," *Journal of the Warburg and Courtauld Institutes* 33 (1970), 162–70.

The Burgundian stable of instrumental musicians was divided into three groups. The first, and most important for ceremonial image, were the trumpets. In about 1400, two trumpeters were on the ducal payrolls, but this number increased to five or six by 1450, though as many as twelve could be called upon for special occasions. Dressed in gorgeous livery and playing beautifully wrought silver instruments that were decorated with Burgundian banners, the function of trumpets was to provide appropriate prestigious clamor. As was the case with monarchs and others of the very highest nobility, the court trumpeters preceded their lord at formal entries, provided fanfares at important celebrations and feasts, and were dispatched to various cities to dramatize the announcement of important events and decisions. The Renaissance trumpets, like the modern bugle, were not equipped with valves, and therefore they could play only a few notes. In fact, their musical qualities were quite limited; but the sound of trumpets became one of the most powerful aural symbols of high station of the era.

The second group was a wind band. Up to about 1420 this had consisted of a combination of double-reed shawms, basically in two sizes, the shawm proper playing in the discant range and the larger shawm, usually called a bombard, filling out the lower range. The Burgundian accounts starting about 1420 provide the earliest consistent evidence of the arrival of a new instrument, the early trombone, in this wind ensemble, which provided a valued extension into the lower register. The band was highly prized for its ability to satisfy needs for music in a wide variety of contexts. The group was effective outdoors in playing for processions and entries, and was especially useful, as we have already noted, in accompanying that most popular of social entertainments, dancing. Since this ensemble consisted of professional musicians, they were also capable of doubling on other instruments, such as recorders. They could also provide "softer" music at indoor occasions, like elegant banquets.

The third group was more a category than a specific type of ensemble. This included the performers, sometimes called "chamber" musicians, who played on softer-timbered instruments such as lutes, fiddles, harps, and small organs. At the Burgundian court in the 1430s and 1440s this category usually included three players: a harpist (who was a soloist, or performed with singers), along with what was one of the most renowned duos of the era, two players known as Fernandez and Cordoval, both of whom were equally competent on lute or fiddle.[2] They seem to have always performed together (though they could perform occasionally with a singer), and it was at about this time that the chamber duo, especially when performing on lute, became the rage throughout Europe – and again, the Burgundian accounts provide the earliest consistent documentation of the prominence of this combination. The quality of their performances was evidently stunning. Martin Le Franc, a highly sophisticated courtier, observed that both Binchois and Dufay, the leading composers of the time, had heard the pair and were chagrined because they couldn't match aspects of the music heard when the duo performed.[3] The notable feature was not that important concepts originated within the circle of the Burgundian court. Cordoval and Fernandez, after all, were imports (evidently from Spain), just as the mechanism for the early trombone was certainly not developed within a court workshop. What is significant, however, is that the patronage by Philip the Good provided the environment where such new concepts could flourish – and, just as significant, anything happening at the Burgundian court was soon broadcast abroad and provided the model to be followed elsewhere in other cultural centers throughout early Renaissance Europe.

Notes

1 On the musicians supported by Philip the Good, see Jeanne Marix, *Histoire de la Musique et des Musiciens de la Cour de Bourgogne sous le règne de Philippe le Bon* (Strasbourg, 1939; reprint, Geneva, 1972); for a chronological listing of musicians from 1420 to 1468, see 264–74. While Philip the Good expanded the support of instrumentalists, the structure of his patronage followed the patterns established by his father and grandfather; see Craig Wright, *Music at the Court of Burgundy* (Henryville-Ottawa-Binningen, 1979), 23–53.
2 Marix, *Histoire*, 267–73.
3 For a recent discussion of Le Franc's well-known text, see Margaret Bent, "The Musical Stanzas in Martin Le Franc's *Le Champion des Dames*." In *Music and Medieval Manuscripts, Paleography and Performance: Essays Dedicated to Andrew Hughes*, ed. John Haines and Randall Rosenfeld (Aldershot/Burlington, 2004), 91–127.

Throughout Europe the higher nobility supported instrumentalists along the lines of the three-part framework as seen at the court of Burgundy. The Count of Holland early in the century and the courts of Ferrara and Bavaria/Munich at around 1450 are but a few of numerous courts that in general matched, or at least imitated, the Burgundian model. These examples highlight a consistent feature of aristocratic patronage to which we have already alluded: the aggressive international recruitment of musicians. The house of Aragon at about 1400 maintained instrumentalists in patterns much like those elsewhere. Spanish courts put a premium on staying current with mainstream developments by importing foreign musicians, who, in the case of wind players, were most often German. This could work in both directions, as the two renowned blind minstrels of the court of Burgundy were evidently from the Iberian Peninsula. The Count (later Duke) of Savoy was another noble who availed himself freely of foreign talent.[4]

Given that the higher nobility frequently intermarried, international musical connections probably reflected political realities as much as any pure musical taste *per se*. The Queen of France *c*.1400 was German, as was the Duchess of Burgundy (the Count of Holland at this time was also German), and wives and husbands were sought for Italian nobility in France and Germany. These connections resulted in multiple levels of international influence. Foreign nobility could bring musicians with them, as did the Queen of France and the Count of Holland – and these could represent a relatively permanent presence. Just as important was the incessant international traffic: court diplomats negotiating possible marriages, assemblies to celebrate betrothals, and then assemblies yet again to celebrate the actual weddings. All of these events demanded extensive rounds of official display, including formal processions, banquets, outdoor gatherings and activities (such as a *chasse*), and, invariably, of dancing. Instrumental music formed a central element in all of these – even the *chasse* called for the use of a hunting horn – involving both a foreign audience and international sets of musicians. The importance of these varied points of contact on such matters as performance practice and repertory is incalculable. And this is why we find Burgundian dances in German manuscripts, French tunes in Dutch sources, or German ones in Italian collections.

The Burgundian model expands – 1480–1520

We have noted that much of the first half of the fifteenth century is characterized by a weakness of central authority. From about midcentury onward, though, the situation changed. The French monarchy

---

[4] On the court in Holland, see Antheunis Janse, "Het Muziekleven aan het Hof van Albrecht van Beieren (1358–1404)," *TVNM* 36 (1986), 136–57; for Ferrara, see Lewis Lockwood, *Music in Renaissance Ferrara 1400–1505* (Cambridge, MA, 1984); for Bavaria, see Polk, *German Instrumental Music*, 99–101; for Spain, see María del Carmen Gómez Muntané, "El manuscrito M 971 de la Biblioteca de Catalunya (Misa de Barcelona)," *Butlletí de la Biblioteca de Catalunya* 10 (1982–4) [1986], 159–317; concerning the court of Savoy, see Robert John Bradley, "Musical Life and Culture at Savoy, 1420–1450," PhD diss., City University of New York (1992).

recovered its cohesion, regained its lost territories, and with the reign of Edward IV beginning in 1462, England, too, was again under able leadership. The rising power of the monarchies was symbolized by the fall of Burgundy with the death of Charles the Bold on the battlefield of Nancy in 1477. Ironically, this event introduced the third major player on the scene, as the subsequent marriage of Maximilian I with Mary of Burgundy (Charles's only surviving child) set in motion the forces that brought the Habsburgs into power sufficient to challenge France and England for European supremacy.

In 1450, however, this was all in the future, and the court of Burgundy remained the patronage model for its European contemporaries. In terms of instrumental music, this meant a sustaining of the three-part structure that had been in place for decades. The ceremonial trumpets took prominence, as recognized both in the ordinances and in the payment lists. The Burgundian ordinances of 1474 called for twelve trumpets – but the financial reality was that the dukes provided funds for only between four and six (Duke Charles was notoriously short of funds due to exorbitant expenses from his constant military campaigns).[5] The membership of the second group, the wind band, adhered more closely to the stipulation of the ordinances, which called for "six haulx menestrels," in that there were usually four or five players on the salary lists. The third unit within the Burgundian court included the "soft" minstrels, and may well be the most fascinating group. Undoubtedly central to the music life of the court, their presence is nevertheless veiled and ill-defined. The date 1433 provides a key; this was shortly after Duke Philip married Isabel of Portugal, and in fact the minstrel pair of Cordoval and Fernandez were included in the entourage of the duchess, not the duke. In any case, in 1434 the payments for both indicated that they were musicians "de Mme la duchesse," just as in 1441 and 1448 the musician Jehan de la Court was indicated as "harpeur de Madame."[6] This indicates that while the court overall divided the musical forces into three groups (trumpets, wind band, and soft minstrels) the first two of those were primarily associated with the duke, and the third, the soft players, were to some extent under the wing of the duchess, which

---

[5] For the ordinances, see Brussels, Algemeen Rijksarchief, Mss divers, 795, fol. 2; see also Marix, *Histoire*, 273–4.

[6] Marix, *Histoire*, 267 and 123, notes that in 1439, Perrinet Thierry was paid as "harpeur de Mgr. De Charrolais," that is, to the future Charles the Bold. On the Castilian origins of Fernandez and Cordoval, see David Fiala, "Les musiciens étrangers de la cour de Bourgogne à la fin du XVe siècle," *Revue du nord* 345–6 (2002), 17.

explains their equivocal place in the salary lists and in the official ordinances.

The prestige of Burgundy was far-reaching, with long-running contacts in Germany and in Italy. A landmark event was the visit of the Duke of Burgundy to Regensburg in 1454, with important interactions with prominent cities and courts. The Burgundian party heard civic musicians from, among others, Basel, Ulm, and Regensburg. Most of the important courts in southern Germany were also involved. One Duke of Bavaria took a leading role as host, and we can only imagine the quality of the interchange that may have taken place between the two blind chamber musicians of Burgundy and the also blind lutenist and organist Conrad Paumann (see CS 7), who had recently joined the Bavarian staff. In addition to Paumann, there were two other lutenists, a wind band of four (undoubtedly superbly qualified), and a trumpet ensemble of six. In both numbers and in ability, the Munich musicians matched those of Philip the Good. But other distinguished stables were also part of the elaborate festivities surrounding this visit. These included the Margrave of Brandenburg, the Count (and soon-to-be-Duke) of Württemberg, and the Duke of Austria, all of which had musical retinues matching in quantity (and probably quality) with those of Bavaria and Burgundy. All supported chamber musicians, shawm bands, and trumpets. The Burgundian accounts reveal one aspect of aristocratic patronage in the region that must have been particularly impressive to the visitors: the copious resourcing of lute pairs by German courts both large and small. Time after time, payments were made to one, two, or three lutes.[7] Duos of chamber musicians (in Germany almost always identified as lutenists), which were present in all the larger courts of the mid- to late fifteenth century, became a kind of cultural trademark of some of the smaller noble households, many, in fact, identified with a female patron.[8]

Although ties between Burgundy and Ferrara were particularly close, in Ferrara, instrumental music seems to have been more than able to stand on its own as well – or, at least, was certainly in no way dependent on Burgundy as a model. Among the chamber musicians, the lutenist Pietrobono (with his tenorist) was one of the most spectacular performers

---

[7] Marix, *Histoire*, 68–74.

[8] Polk, *German Instrumental Music*, 25–30. The lute pairs active in Biberach, Henneberg, Hessen, Pappenheim, and Weinsberg, as well as the bishoprics Mainz and Würzburg, provide a sampling of duos that were identified in German accounts of the mid- and late fifteenth century. Lute pairs in Weinsberg, as well as of the larger courts of Berg, Cleve, Jülich, and Saxony, were tied to women patrons.

of the century. Pietrobono was a native Italian as were the members of the Della Viola clan, Andrea being the first at court, appearing in the lists of 1466. But in 1450 the harpist at the court was English (described in pay records as "Giovanni dall'arpa Inglese"), as was a remarkable chamber singer in 1465 ("Anna cantarina Anglica"). An organist in 1476 was "Rudolfo da Frisia" – more accurately identified as Rudolph Agricola of Groningen, who became one of the more prominent humanists of the age. One of the most distinguished of Pietrobono's colleagues was German, Niccolo Tedesco "cantor et pulsator [lutenist]." Niccolo was, in fact, Nicholas Krumsdorfer, later a central figure in the chapel of the Duke of Austria. The German influence was most pronounced in the wind contingent, as "Corrado d'Alemagna piffaro" was for years the highest-paid musician of any kind in Ferrara. Among his German colleagues was Michele Tedesco (Michel Schubinger), of the extremely gifted Augsburg family. One of the wind players from 1472–82 was Stefano "da Savoia," adding still more to the international mix. While Ferrara evidently took talent from where it could be found, the trumpeters remained exclusively Italian. But even here the recruiting net was wide, as men were drawn from such diverse locations as Arezzo, Assisi, Bologna, Faenza, and Montepulciano. To sum up, the Ferrarese court musicians can be divided into the same three categories as elsewhere: chamber musicians, a shawm band, and a corps of trumpeters.

Maximilian I – Ercole d'Este – Henry VII

From about 1480 onward the general economic conditions in Europe improved and populations were increasing. At the same time the great monarchies of Europe were moving toward greater internal control, and with more stability and increased prosperity, monarchies had significantly more resources to allocate for display and ceremonies. The clearest examples are those of the courts of Maximilian I and Henry VII (unfortunately, the records of the French royal court at this time are too sparse to yield a coherent picture).

The lavish display of Maximilian is well known to many with interests in Renaissance culture through the remarkable set of illustrations of *The Triumph of Maximilian I* (see Figures 6.22, 6.24, and 6.28). These images were designed and executed under close supervision from Maximilian himself. They purport to show what Maximilian hoped his contemporaries would expect of a procession in which the full panoply of the Imperial court was on display. As such, they represent a spectacular example of propaganda. More than eighty musicians are shown to be associated with the emperor's court, which vastly exceed the numbers (in truth, about thirty) that Maximilian routinely had on his payroll. The blatant exaggeration itself underlines the priority that this ruler placed on music when it came time to present an impressive image to the hostile world. Hyperbole aside, Maximilian's stable was nonetheless almost double in number than that of the Duke of Burgundy just two or three decades earlier: the trumpet ensemble expanded to ten or more players, plus kettledrums, and the shawm band, numbering about five, could expand to seven or even eight. The players included Hans Neuschel and Georg Stewdlin on trombone, and the fabled Augustine Schubinger on cornett. Among the "chamber" contingent were the brilliant organist and composer Paul Hofhaimer, two exceptionally fine lutenists, and ultimately a new grouping, an ensemble of four viols. A drummer and one or two "fifers" (transverse flutes), often referred to as a "Swiss Pair," were also a regular part of the court entourage. Though perhaps stretched to the breaking point, Maximilian's instrumental forces did, in fact, continue the traditional three-part division, that is, a military group (trumpets, tympani, drums, and the Swiss Pair), a wind band, and the chamber musicians. However inflated the image presented by the *Triumph* might be, the fact remains that Maximilian was a spectacular success as a patron of instrumental music. The quality of his performers was unmatched by any other court of the day.[9]

The intense rivalry between courts meant that competition was close on Maximilian's heels. One remarkably successful patron was Ercole d'Este (reigned 1470–1505) at the far smaller, but artistically bountiful, court of Ferrara. In terms of composers, Ercole actually outbid Maximilian through his ability to employ at various times Johannes Martini, Jacob Obrecht, Antoine Brumel, and Josquin des Prez, while Maximilian could boast of only one composer, Isaac, of equal prestige. Even in instrumental music, Ercole dug deep into his treasury. In most years he provided for a trumpet ensemble of about ten, and an even larger number of chamber musicians, including two players "della Viola" (i.e., of bowed stringed instruments), a lute pair (which included Pietrobono well into the 1490s), a harpist,

---

[9] On the instrumental forces at the court of Maximilian, see Polk, *German Instrumental Music*, 91–4; on the woodcuts of *The Triumphs of Maximilian I*, see Rolf Damman, "Die Musik im Triumphzug Maximilians I," *AfM* 36 (1974), 245–89, and Uta Henning, *Musica Maximiliana. Die Musikgraphiken in den bibliophilen Unternehmungen Kaiser Maximilians I* (Neu-Ulm, 1987).

organist, and a fine wind band of about five members. While Ferrara might not have matched the total quality of the northern court at the height of Maximilian's reign (between about 1500–15), it provides nonetheless a stunning example of what could be accomplished by a discerning individual patron.[10]

In England, Henry VII earned a reputation for being tight-fisted, with a more dour personality than his ebullient son, Henry VIII. But while Henry VII was a far more prudent financial (and political) manager than Maximilian, he, too, provided generous funding for instrumental music.[11] The numbers fluctuated from year to year, but the core size was on the order of nine trumpets, a wind band of five, and three "string minstrels." To these numbers should be added a pipe-and-tabor player, and minstrels of the queen and of the prince.[12] Henry VII was also able to recruit first-rate talent, through his hiring of Hans Nagel and John de Peler as part of his retinue of sackbut players. Hans was apparently German and later closely associated with Petrus Alamire in the Low Countries, while de Peler was apparently an import from Flanders. It should be noted that the numbers of musicians had already begun to expand under Edward IV, but increased still more under Henry VII.

The Burgundian model transcended – 1520–50

The intense rivalry among the three major patrons of the period, Charles V (the Habsburg emperor), Francis I of France, and Henry VIII, played out at all levels, including music, as none of them dared present a lesser image of magnificence. Whenever any of them would meet, opulent ceremonial

---

[10] For a general discussion of the musicians in the service of Ercole, see Lockwood, *Music in Renaissance Ferrara*, 121–84; for year-by-year listings of Ercole's instrumentalists, see ibid., 318–28.

[11] On the musicians at the English court, see Richard Rastall, "The Minstrels of the English Royal Households, 25 Edward 1–1 Henry VIII: An Inventory," *R.M.A. Research Chronicle* 4 (1964), 1–41; see also Trevor Herbert, "Susato's Colleagues: the Trombonists of the Tudor Court." In *Tielman Susato and the Music of His Time*, ed. Keith Polk, 117–32. A recent work, valuable for the international perspective, is Theodor Dimutrescu, *The Early Tudor Court and International Relations* (Aldershot, Hampshire and Burlington, Vermont, 2007).

[12] In some accounts from about 1496 through the reign of Henry VIII (which began in 1509), payments are recorded to a rather mysterious group of "still minstrels" – usually eight in number (if numbers are specified) and apparently all English. See Eileen Sharpe Pearsall, "Tudor Court Musicians, 1485–1547: Their Number, Status and Function," PhD diss., New York University (1986), vol. 2, 14. For varied payment listings to the still minstrels, see Andrew Ashbee, ed., *Records of English Court Music*, vii: 1485–1558 (Aldershot, 1993), 21–289.

arrangements would follow, as demonstrated in the meeting of Francis I and Henry VIII in 1520 – an occasion so grand that it has become known as the Field of the Cloth of Gold. Intense competitive pressures between Henry, Francis, and Charles were reflected in vastly expanded expenditures for instrumental music. Of the three crowned heads, the most complete documentation of patronage is that of the English court.

Case study 3

Patronage runs rampant: instrumental music at the court of Henry VIII

One dismal contrast in the Renaissance is that of the young Henry VIII at the start of his reign in 1509 versus the same man at his death in 1547. The strong, well-proportioned youth was a brilliant conversationalist, a gifted athlete, and could also play well on lute, keyboard instruments, and recorders. He was an utterly charming companion who relished "pastimes in good company." By the time he turned fifty he was grossly overweight, frequently hobbled by chronic leg infections, and, much worse, proved to be a vicious player of the Renaissance game of politics.

However dodgy (from a modern viewpoint, of course) Henry's moral standards might have been, he was a stunning patron of instrumental music. Contrary to the thumbnail sketch of his life given above, he seems at first to have been conservative, following closely the patronage model of his father, Henry VII, and only slowly initiated significant expansion. The framework for the first few years after 1509 remained exactly the same as previously: "loud" players in two groups (trumpets on the one hand and a wind band of shawms and trombones on the other); a small group of chamber players (lutenists and keyboard players); plus, evidently somewhat on the periphery, a group of "still minstrels." The latter group, eight in number, had been a unique aspect of the English court for some decades. Generally, they appeared only in the lists of gifts presented at the New Year, and were not given a place in the regular payroll as salaried musicians. Almost all of the musicians in all categories in the early years had, in fact, been on the payroll before the accession of Henry VIII.[1] This underlines an essential feature of English court music: it was part of a very large bureaucratic machine that tended to grind away on its own regardless of changes at the top. A particularly telling example of this occurred after the death of Richard III and the seizure of the throne by Henry VII. At the upper levels, surviving courtiers who had been loyal to Richard were eliminated and replaced by those loyal to the new king. Change at lower levels was another matter. As an example, the court musicians in almost all categories remained the same.[2] They simply transferred their allegiance to the new sovereign. They might well shout "long live the king" – whoever that might be.

No instrumental group was more important to a Renaissance monarch than trumpets, and after 1509 it would appear on first glance that Henry VIII authorized an expansion from nine, as they had been under his father, to about fifteen. On closer examination, however, the increase was inconsequential; before 1509 there had been nine trumpets "of the king" and several associated with the crown prince (the young Henry after the death of his elder brother Arthur in 1502). As there was no crown prince in 1509 (Henry having not yet fathered a son to fit that role) the men previously associated with the prince were added to an expanded "king's trumpets."[3] From then on until 1549 the number remained almost static at about fifteen, some years a bit more, some a bit less. Henry VIII seemed to have been of two minds concerning his trumpets. He wanted to be sure they would be available to support court pageantry, but beyond that he seems to have vested little interest in them. Almost all the trumpeters, for example, were English while most of the other groups were regularly infused with foreigners – Flemish, French, and Italian, particularly.

A clearer barometer of Henry's shifting tastes can be seen with his wind bands. From at least 1502 a group of Flemings had been engaged as "sackbuts and shawms," and a peculiarity of English court terminology is that from this time onward the wind players were identified in the pay records simply as "sackbuts" when it is clear from instrumental purchases that they remained a mixed band including shawms (with, of course, doublings on other instruments as well). The presence of Flemings continued under Henry VIII, almost certainly because they could provide both the dance music fashionable at the turn of the century, as well as the Franco-Flemish secular music also in vogue at this time, as reflected in the so-called Henry VIII manuscript.[4] New currents rippled through the English court, however, as rivalries with Francis I and Charles V intensified. The influence of the French court was perhaps clearest, for not only was there a new kind of French music coming into vogue (seen clearly in the chansons of Claudin de Sermisy) but Francis I also embarked on a campaign to recruit Italian artists of all kinds, including musicians. The musical imports, primarily instrumentalists, brought with them new vocal and dance repertories. Ever the sophisticate, Henry quickly matched the competition. By at least 1525 (records for these years are inconsistent), five Italian wind players were added, ultimately termed the "new sackbuts" as the Flemish band remained in service (as the "old sackbuts"). The Italian contingent enlarged further with the arrival of the Bassano family first, evidently in 1531 on a short term, then permanently in 1539 when five Bassanos were assigned places within the court. Lasocki has proposed that these musicians were specialists on the recorder, but it is almost certain that while they may have focused their efforts on wind instruments, they were omnibus musicians, capable of performing on a variety of instruments as desired, including bowed strings.[5]

Viol ensembles were known in Italian courts (particularly Ferrara and Mantua) in the 1490s, and Maximilian I engaged an ensemble of professionals on the instrument by about 1515. Henry VIII lagged slightly in this regard, as the first two players of "vialls" were hired only in 1525 (keeping in mind that no pay records survive between 1521 and 1525); a third player was added in 1531.[6] These early string musicians were either Flemish or German, but the wave of Italians continued, as five imports arrived from Italy in 1541; by 1543 they expanded to six, and were termed "the new viols." Henry VIII may have been slightly behind the curve in support of viols because he had in fact a small ensemble of bowed stringed instruments, rebecs, from perhaps 1514 (with the appointment of Thomas Evans), and certainly from 1518 when John Severnake, from France, was recruited as a court minstrel to join with Evans. A third player, John Pyrot, also French, joined them by 1525. That Severnake and Pyrot were French is revealing since the reason for their presence was to provide music for dancing in the French fashion that had considerable vogue during these years. The fretted viol was certainly limited in the volume it could produce, but the unfretted rebec could certainly provide enough sound to cut through the distracting noise that was created by the movements of dancers.

Henry VIII performed well on both lute and keyboard instruments, and according to an inventory he may be the first known owner of the four-course Renaissance guitar in England.[7] While the numbers of players in the category of "chamber musicians" did not increase as dramatically as in others, Henry supported superb lutenists, organists, and harpsichordists throughout his reign, from Anthony Dewes (probably French) and Dionysius Memo (Italian) early on, to Philip van Wilder (from French Flanders), who served the court from at least 1525 to well after Henry had passed from the scene. These musicians were the ones that played for Henry, and at times with him, in his private apartments. They were an international group and undoubtedly served as a conduit for the latest information on the musical scene. Though few in number they served as a defining influence in the court's music.

In summary, if we put the trumpets and the rather odd "still minstrels" aside (the numbers in both these categories remained static), the court music increased from about a dozen instrumentalists in 1509 to over thirty by 1547. Moreover, the older medieval division into essentially three categories (trumpets, a wind band, and chamber players) had disappeared, replaced by a much more complex and subtle organization. This change was in large part due to the involvement of Henry himself. We should also bear in mind that after the death of Henry V, the English Crown lost any real pretense of control over French territories. At the same time, England had not yet moved into the role of leader in world trade and exploration. It was an island on the periphery of Europe and might well have become insular and disconnected from developments at the center of European culture. In music, at least, this did not happen, and in fact in the 1540s no court in Europe could match the range or the sophistication of the instrumental music that came into being under the very personal patronage of Henry VIII.

Notes

1 All the relevant payment listings for music at the Tudor court for this period are in Ashbee, *Records*, an essential volume for study of the topic. Also see Pearsall, "Tudor Court Musicians."
2 Listings of musicians under Richard III are in Rastall, "Minstrels," 34–5; for a sampling of those in the early years under Henry VII, see Ashbee, *Records*, 2.
3 For listings of trumpets under Henry VII, see Ashbee, *Records*, 189; for the first year under Henry VIII, see ibid., 190.
4 The Henry VIII manuscript, London, British Library, Additional MS 31922, is available in John Stevens, ed., *Music at the Court of Henry VIII*, Musica Britannica, XVII (London, 2nd rev. ed., 1969). The presence of a foreigner is particularly clear in the trombonist at court; see Herbert, "Susato's Colleagues," 117–32.
5 David Lasocki, *The Bassanos: Venetian Musicians and Instrument Makers in England, 1531–1665* (Aldershot, 1995), 3–16.
6 For payroll listings for the string players at court, see Ashbee, *Records*, with listing given chronologically. For a well-informed discussion of the string musicians under royal patronage, see Peter Holman, *Four and Twenty Fiddlers: The Violin at the English Court 1540–1690* (Oxford, 1993), 60–77.
7 See Christopher Page, *The Guitar in Tudor England: A Social and Musical History* (Cambridge, 2015), 36.

Francis I – Charles V

Widespread destruction of documents during the French Revolution frustrates any attempt at a detailed study of music at the French court, and only a few archival records remain relating to music at the court of Francis I. These are at least sufficient, however, to show that the general outlines of patronage were probably quite similar to those in England, though it must be said that of the two courts the French was the more influential, especially in embracing the vogue for things Italian. As early as 1502, Louis XII had imported an entire wind band from Milan, this when northern musicians were still firmly entrenched at the English court (Henry VIII did not begin to recruit Italian ensemble players until almost two decades later).[13] The preference for southern wind players continued during the reign of Francis I with the significant addition of two cornett players. This is an early sign of the preeminence of Italian cornettists, who became an increasing feature of late Renaissance practice. Besides the wind players, Francis engaged several lutenists, including another Italian virtuoso, the Mantuan lutenist Alberto da Ripa (Albert de Rippe), a prolific composer who must be considered as one of the most extraordinary instrumentalists of the Renaissance.[14] As in England, a band of string musicians, identified as players of violin (though they almost certainly also played viols), was added to the court entourage probably by about 1520, but in contrast to the inclination of Henry VIII, the French court players were all French, and remained so throughout Francis's reign. Figures for the trumpet ensemble are vague, but this group undoubtedly matched that of Henry VIII.[15]

Charles V was potentially the most powerful of the three monarchs. In 1519 he was elected Holy Roman Emperor, becoming not only Emperor, but holding title to a vast patchwork of territory that included the Kingdom of Spain (which at that point also included Naples), most of the Low Countries, the traditional Habsburg Austrian lands, and a rapidly expanding New World empire. His attempts to create an integrated governing structure consumed him throughout his reign, and his support of music was interwoven with those efforts. In 1516, as Charles moved to assert his authority in Spain, he authorized two households: one Burgundian, preserving a tradition running back to his great grandfather, Charles the Bold, and the other Castilian to help smooth relations in Spain. Both were

---

[13] Christelle Cazaux, *La musique à la cour de François Ier* (Paris, 2002), 44.
[14] For an accessible and detailed account of Albert de Rippe, see Lyle Nordstrom, "Albert de Rippe: *Joueur de luth du Roy*," *EM* 7 (1989), 378–85.
[15] Cazaux, *La musique à la cour*, 108–16.

fully staffed with instrumental musicians.[16] The Burgundian instrumental forces (all northerners initially) included ten trumpets, a fine wind band of six, including Hans Nagel and Jan van Winkel, a pipe and tabor, and a fife and drum pair. The Castilian stable contained a trumpet and kettledrum group of about ten, and a wind band of seven, all Spanish. Both ensembles were customized for ceremony. Neither the Burgundian nor the Castilian payrolls included chamber musicians at this point, but organists were available, though officially attached to their respective chapel choirs. The total then was about forty instrumentalists. Though records of the Burgundian household are scanty thereafter, the general outlines are clear. The Burgundian musicians (including the renowned Capilla Flamenca) were the ones that moved with Charles V during his almost incessant travels; the Castilian instrumentalists usually remained in Spain. After establishing the framework, the number of Flemish musicians gradually dwindled. By 1532 the wind band had practically ceased to exist, and by 1543 the Flemish trumpet band had been replaced by one consisting of Italians.[17] The Castilian stable, on the other hand, expanded; the trumpets and tympani soon included up to fifteen, and by 1530 the wind band in some years had ten players available. A small contingent of chamber players, including Antonio de Cabezón, was also added.[18] A consistent feature of Charles's approach was to relocate the players to where they were needed; the entire Castilian stable, for example, including, apparently, both the Spanish and the Italian trumpet bands, accompanied Philip II on his lengthy stay in England and the Low Countries in 1554–6.

In the last years of Charles's reign the general outline of his patronage of instrumentalists was quite similar to before, comprising two bands of trumpets (some twenty in all), about twelve wind players, and three or four chamber players, including Cabezón. One new ensemble was the group of about five bowed-string instrumentalists. The number varied from four to six, and most of them were of German origin, in contrast to

---

[16] On the decision to maintain both households, see Mary Tiffany Ferer, *Music and Ceremony at the Court of Charles V: The Capilla Flamenca and the Art of Political Promotion* (Woodbridge, 2012), 72–3.

[17] Charles did, however, continue to maintain the *Capilla Flamenca*, which at times included such composers as Gombert and Crecquillon.

[18] On the Burgundian forces, see Ferer, *Music and Ceremony*, especially the tables on 65, 69, 78, and 100. Concerning Charles V's Castilian performers, the classic work is Higinio Anglés, *La Música en la corte de Carlos V* (Barcelona, 1944, rev. ed., 1965), which has been updated by Luís Robledo Estaire, Tess Knighton, Cristina Bordas Ibáñez & Juan José Carreras, *Aspectos de la Cultura musical en la corte de Felipe II* (Madrid, 2000); see especially Robledo Estaire, "La estructuración de las casas reales: Felipe II como punto de encuentro y punto de partida," 1–34.

those in the French and English courts, who were Italian. If Charles had any real enthusiasm for music it was evidently for the singers of his exceptionally fine Flemish Chapel. His attitude toward instrumental music seems altogether functional. While Charles certainly maintained a large number of players, their effect was, of course, diluted, with some musicians accompanying him on the road, while others remained in Spain. The demands of ceremony might have been met, but there is little evidence of the enthusiastic personal interest shown by Henry VIII.

A new model of power: Bavaria – 1550–1600

During the second half of the sixteenth century, it was the patronage of the high nobility that best reveals the directions of stylistic development – but not necessarily popularity – in instrumental music. An apt example is provided by the varied groups of musicians maintained by the Duke of Bavaria in Munich. This house had unified the varied ducal branches early in the sixteenth century and had entered into a long period of stability and marked economic prosperity. Albert V succeeded to the title in 1550, and while his extravagant support of the arts led to considerable political turmoil, his patronage of music was both clever and remarkably successful. In 1556 he attracted the young Orlando di Lasso, who was soon elevated to the position of chapel master in 1563. Lasso served as a virtual magnet for talent, with composers such as Andrea and Giovanni Gabrieli, and brilliant instrumentalists, organists, lutenists, violinists, and wind players rotating constantly in and out of Munich.[19]

A vivid description of Albert's enthusiastic patronage and the guidance of the musical household by Lasso was given by Massimo Troiano concerning the court wedding in Munich in 1568.[20] Troiano is particularly valuable as a witness because he was a singer and composer, as well as a literary figure. This commentary will be given in detail in Chapter 2, but suffice to say here that it reveals the tensions between tradition and innovation at the court in Munich. The strength of tradition in instrumental music is shown in that yet again the instrumental forces were divided much the same as those 100 years earlier at the Burgundian

---

[19] See Hans-Joachim Nösselt, *Ein ältest Orchester 1530–1980. 450 Jahre Bayerisches Hof- und Staatsorchester* (Munich, 1980), and the still useful Adolf Sandberger, *Beiträge zur Geschichte der bayerischen Hofkapelle unter Orlando di Lasso* (Leipzig, 1894–5).

[20] [Massimo Troiano], *Die Münchner Fürstenhochzeit von 1568; Massimo Troiano: Dialoge*, ed. Horst Leuchtmann (Munich-Salzburg, 1980).

court: a group of chamber musicians (three organists and a lutenist), a trumpet corps (for the festivities, twelve, including tympani), and a wind band (now increased to seven or eight). But to this framework was added an additional ensemble, a group of seven string players – all Italian – representing a new wave of fashion. The leading organist in Munich at this time was Gioseffo Guami, also Italian, and both Andrea and Giovanni Gabrieli were at times in the city as well. Even the wind players were Italian, which overwhelmed long-standing conventions. German wind instrumentalists had been preeminent in Europe until the early decades of the sixteenth century, and at the Bavarian court the wind players had been German into the 1560s. Fine players from such families as the Hurlachers, Rauchs, and Schnitzers representing several generations of tradition were now brushed aside, which must have aroused intense antagonism from the local players.[21] German civic ensembles, on the other hand, remained firmly resistant to any outside threats as foreign instrumentalists were completely excluded.

The opposing thrusts of "new" versus "old" also played out in the ways in which instruments were combined in Munich. Much of the sixteenth century was dominated by what Howard Brown characterized as the "consort principle," that is, the idea of playing instruments in families of like instruments, such as groups of four recorders or viols covering all voice ranges from soprano to bass.[22] This approach ran throughout the wedding banquet in 1568, as in the first course, with six trombones, and in the fifth, with six viols, six trombones, and six singers. The almost gravitational pull toward consorts is clear with the wind component. Often the trombone choir, lacking a soprano instrument, would substitute the cornett, an instrument that has the ability to match quite closely the tone quality of the trombone, so that the cornett and trombone ensemble was actually considered a kind of whole consort. In any case, as shown in Troiano's text, violins, violas, flutes, and trombones were normally played in consorts – as were recorders and crumhorns, though these played no role in this particular series of performances. Of course, sixteenth-century musicians were certainly aware of the potential advantages of contrast, and the notion of consorts was never exclusive. Contrast nonetheless played a role at that

---

[21] For a survey of instrumentalists in German courts, see Martin Ruhnke, *Beiträge zu einer Geschichte der deutschen Hofmusikkollegien im 16. Jahrhundert* (Berlin, 1963). One lone German carryover among the instrumentalists in Munich was the lutenist Hans Kolmann, who Troiano indicated was "a great virtuoso."

[22] Howard Mayer Brown, *Sixteenth-Century Instrumentation: The Music of the Florentine Intermedii* (Rome, 1973), 78.

event, as seen in the ensemble to accompany the sixth course, which involved "cembalo, trombone, recorder, lute, crumhorn, a still cornett, a viol and a flute" (this particular grouping of instruments became almost a standard combination, as it is similar to the "broken consort" favored in England at the end of the century). Perhaps the most striking reflection of innovation in Troiano's description lies in the way the instruments were combined in a twelve-part piece played with the third course, which included a consort of six violins, a wind consort of five trombones and cornett, supported by a regal (i.e., a small organ). Brown observed that the most important new approach in the later sixteenth century was the development of the "foundation principle," by which he meant the addition of an instrument or instruments that would underlie and support the bass line, as well as (in the case of the regal) filling out the harmony.[23] Evidently the foundation principle was already an established fact in Munich in 1568.

In the second half of the sixteenth century, the patronage frameworks of the higher nobility throughout Europe seemed in general to mirror the Munich model. The royal courts in France and England, for example, continued to organize musicians into four groups: trumpets, an assemblage of chamber musicians (lute and keyboard players), a wind band, and a string band. Not all high nobles had either the inclination or the resources for such expansive support, and some northern courts arrived at a logical way to reduce costs quite substantially. At the Danish court around 1550, for example, a surprisingly simple strategy of consolidation was devised. Given that playing the trumpet for most required purposes was not particularly complex, instead of having two separate groups (one of trumpets the other the wind band), both functions were rolled into one. In fact, it seems likely that these players might have been expected to perform on stringed instruments as well, creating, in short, only a single group, but one capable of providing the same musical functions that were accomplished by three at the Munich and English courts.

Church patronage of instrumental music

A theme throughout this book is that in the Renaissance, instrumental music was interwoven tightly with contemporary institutions. Relations

---

[23] Brown, *Sixteenth-Century Instrumentation*, 81. For the description of the music that accompanied the banquet, see *Die Münchner Fürstenhochzeit*, 122–67.

with the church offer one partial exception in that the place of music in religion, especially when instruments are involved, has always been a contentious issue. The debate as to whether music contributes to an intensification of faith, or whether it acts as an unworthy distraction, has raged throughout the ages, with sometimes one view, sometimes the other holding prominence. The Second Vatican Council (1962–5) largely provided a new context of inclusion, with the result that many styles of music, especially folk genres, are used in services. During the Renaissance, at least in relation to instrumental music, a conservative view prevailed, particularly in the fifteenth century, when instruments (other than the organ) were only exceptionally heard within church services. A gradual change took place beginning about 1470 with instruments beginning to take part in the liturgy by about 1500; but in most regions of Europe, only after 1550 did the church begin to assume an active role as a patron.

The fifteenth century: instrumental music through back alleys

During the decades following the Great Schism (1378–1415), the Roman church reestablished itself as the Papacy gradually reasserted central control from Rome, first through the successful reunification that resulted from the Council of Constance (1414–18), then through survival of the challenge of the Council of Basle (1431–49). When items of the liturgy, such as the parts of the Mass, were provided with music in the fifteenth century, the performances were by singers – and occasionally in *cantus alternatim* with organ variations through the genre known as the "Organ Mass," of which one of the earliest sources is *Faenza*, copied around 1400.[24] Ensemble instruments were excluded from the liturgy and instrumental performers, too, were unsupported by the fifteenth-century church.

Nonetheless, instrumental music was welcomed in some contexts within church institutions. Many of the princes of the church maintained musical ensembles. The higher positions in the Roman church were almost invariably drawn from the nobility, and their patronage reflected that of their class. The Bishops of Utrecht at various times engaged bands of trumpets, wind bands, and small chamber ensembles, using the same framework as that of secular nobles such as the Duke of Burgundy. It seems somewhat curious to the modern observer that one of the consistent favorites among

---

[24] See Pedro Memelsdorff, "New Music in the Codex Faenza 117," *Plainsong and Medieval Music* 13 (2004), 141–61. For further information on this manuscript, see *SBS* 1.

German bishops through most of the fifteenth century was the wind band, given that much of the utility of such ensembles was for distinctly secular activities such as dancing. These same bishops from time to time also supported small groups of lutes and fiddles. The function of such patronage, however, seems to have been that of providing music of recreation or of supporting the bishop's image – not that of contributing to sacred services.[25]

Music evidently played an important role in the cultural life of monasteries and convents, though hard evidence is very uneven. We have ample records of the great abbeys and convents in England, for example, but very little for much of the Continent. The English houses unequivocally provided substantial support for visiting musicians throughout the late Middle Ages and Renaissance. At the Fountains Abbey during the years 1456–9, for example, no less than sixty-seven separate payments were made to various minstrels – some from noble houses, and some to civic or independent musicians.[26] Most payments from these establishments were for participation of minstrels in the festivals of the church, such as for Christmas, Easter, and for dedication days of the respective houses. While the performance contexts are never spelled out, the minstrels were almost certainly brought in to enliven the festivities associated with these occasions. They were not performing within the religious services themselves. Most of the evidence concerning the Continent is indirect as records are sparse and have been little studied for what they might tell us about music performed. A few manuscripts also testify to the active interest in instrumental music among some members of religious communities. The Glogauer Part Books, for example, seem to have been associated with such a community. This collection is dominated by motets, but it also contains pieces that were certainly included to be performed by instruments. *Buxheim*, too, appears to have been associated in some way with monastic life.[27] But while payments to minstrels, ownership of instruments, and the presence of musical manuscripts all testify to the importance of music to life in religious communities, there is no link to sacred services themselves.

---

[25] On the support of music by the German bishops, see Polk, *German Instrumental Music*, 104–7; for the situation in England see Rosalind Conklin, "Medieval English Minstrels, 1216–1485," PhD diss., University of Chicago (1964), 149–68, which is supplemented by Richard Rastall, "Secular Musicians in Late Medieval England," PhD diss., Manchester University (1968), 60–87.

[26] Conklin, "Medieval English Minstrels," 158.

[27] On the Glogauer Part Books and the Buxheim manuscript, see *SBS* 3.

One context, however, did provide such a link, though this was rather through a back alley. That is, as the conservative structure of the church firmly guarded the front entry by defending the purity of the official liturgy of the church, popular enthusiasm could not be suppressed and kept finding a way past the barriers. One of these back-door approaches was tied to the enormous enthusiasm for Marian services in the late Middle Ages, which reached a peak at the end of the fifteenth century. A clear example is that of the *Salve* (or *Lof*) celebrations in the Low Countries. These were para-liturgical in nature, and held in the late afternoon or early evening. In Kampen, a document from about 1474 directed that the newly hired civic ensemble was to perform "the *lof* in honor of the Virgin Mary every Saturday evening." The authorities in Bruges authorized payment of similar services in 1483, and in 1484 Nicasius de Brauwere, succentor of St. Saviour's church in Bruges, had been compensated by the city for preparing a set of motets for the Bruges civic ensemble. One use for these motets would certainly have been for the *Lof* performances. In 1488, a chronicler in Bruges noted that the civic ensemble there had performed "in honor of Our Lady" and named the pieces played – *Ave regina celorum*, as well as *Salve regina* (these two motets might have been drawn from the de Brauwere manuscript, though of course the players may have also improvised their own versions based on these well-known Gregorian melodies). In the same vein, when the civic band was reestablished in Utrecht in 1489 (the ensemble had been disbanded some years earlier due to financial crises), they were directed to play on "Holy days in the evening ... a motet" ("Alle heylige dagen 'savonds ... een Motet spelen").[28] That performance of motets was taking place in the south at about the same time is revealed by a letter from Giovanni Alvise, evidently a member of the Venetian civic ensemble, to Francesco Gonzaga in Mantua in 1494. Alvise stated that he was sending a motet by Obrecht originally written for four voices, in an arrangement that he had prepared in a six-part version. He also sent an arrangement for five parts of a four-part motet of Busnois.[29] Alvise said nothing about the context for the performance of his transcriptions, but clearly by about 1480 civic wind bands in the Low Countries were regularly taking part in the Salve services and playing appropriate

---

[28] This practice in Utrecht was, in fact, resuming "the old custom" (*naar ouder gewoonten*); see Polk, *German Instrumental Music*, 135.

[29] For the Alvise letter, see Dietrich Kämper, "Studien zur instrumentalen Ensemblemusik des 16. Jahrhunderts in Italien," *AM* 10 (1970), 53. Kämper, following earlier sources, gave the date incorrectly as 1495; see Polk, *German Instrumental Music*, 85.

repertory, that is, instrumental versions of motets, often with optional (*si placet*), added parts.[30] At first, the musicians played these pieces from the balconies outside the church, but gradually they moved inside, and bit by bit their connection with the service itself became closer. By the early sixteenth century, they were not only inside the church, but began to play within the liturgy.[31]

Another phenomenon associated with popular piety that introduced instruments into religious celebrations was the participation of fifteenth-century citizens in the confraternities. A telling example is that of the Confraternity of Our Lady of the Snow in Bruges, which expanded rapidly in the second half of the fifteenth century. The confraternity celebrated its main feast day with a Mass, two celebrations of Vespers, a procession, and a banquet. The group hired the town ensemble, at first, apparently, just for the procession and the banquet, but by the end of the century, the confraternity records indicate that the instruments were actually performing within the celebration of the Mass itself.[32]

In both the incorporation of instruments into the Salve service and in the services sponsored by confraternities, we see further examples of instrumental music reflecting contemporary conditions. In these cases, popular sentiment proposed that music could have a valuable place in religious services – a sentiment that the Roman church, in its rigidity, did not find acceptable (note that in the above instances it was either the city or the citizenry that provided the support for instrumentalists, not the church itself). In sum, despite the enthusiastic cultivation of instrumental activity by monastic institutions (or the rather marginal support of the princes of the church), the barrier against instrumental participation in liturgical services themselves remained firmly in place to the end of the fifteenth century. The Church itself did not offer direct patronage to instrumental ensembles. Still, the strength of the barrier was weakening in the face of challenges from multiple alternative sources of patronage. During wedding celebrations of the high nobility, bands of trumpets would be brought in to

---

[30] For a different context for Alvise's details about performance flexibility and *si placet* parts, see William F. Prizer,"Instrumental Music/Instrumentally Performed Music ca. 1500: The Genres of Paris, Bibliothèque Nationale, Ms Rés.Vm.[7] 676." In *Le concert des voix et des instruments*, ed. Jean-Michel Vaccaro, 185–7.

[31] No fifteenth-century collections of motets assembled for instrumental use have survived. The clearest discussion of the *Lof* performances in relation to instrumental music is Reinhard Strohm, *Music in Late Medieval Bruges* (Oxford, 1985), 85–6; on the background of these services see Barbara Haggh, "Music, Liturgy, and Ceremony in Brussels, 1350–1500," PhD diss., University of Illinois (1988), 397–419; see also Polk, *German Instrumental Music*, 121–2.

[32] Strohm, *Music in Late Medieval Bruges*, 47–8.

add brilliant sound embellishment at several points in the wedding Mass – as preludes and postludes, for example, and at the Elevation of the Host. These trumpets fanfares were considered as supplementary decoration; they were not part of Mass liturgy itself. But the striking impression made by trumpets revealed that instruments could have an effective role in a sacred service.[33] In fact, a more deeply rooted alternative support came from the many confraternities established in cities throughout Europe in the late Middle Ages as a result of a surge of popular piety. These confraternities and their music will be taken up later in this chapter.

The sixteenth century: doors open to instrumental music

The sixteenth century was dominated by the revolts originating in England and Germany that staggered the centralized Catholic Church. Partly in response to the political and social upheavals, but also simply the result of ideas that had been developing on their own, a new place was carved out for instrumental music in religious life. Beginning with isolated instances around 1500, the pace of change quickened, and by about 1550 instrumentalists were heard performing with singers within church services throughout Europe. Still, this feature just illuminated the larger realities of the time. One characteristic of the religious conflicts was that each region arrived at its own solution – that is, there were distinct regional differences in how accommodations were made, or not, to the new beliefs. Incorporation of music, and its support (or lack thereof) by the church clearly reflected those differences.

Italy, France, and Spain remained within the faith; Italy was relatively less severe, while Spain adhered firmly to its Catholic allegiance. In fact, Spanish officials looked to their religion as a means of extending their authority as they attempted to control the vast territories that Spain acquired subsequent to the explorations that began in 1492. France, too, after years of civil unrest, ultimately resolved decisively to stay with the traditional church. The rest of Europe was a patchwork. Parts of Germany remained Catholic while others took the side of reform, but various versions held sway in various locations, as was the case throughout the north. It is hardly surprising then, that there was little uniformity in the way music found a new place for itself. One element was consistent, which

---

[33] On the use of trumpets in the Mass, see Andrew Kirkman, *The Cultural Life of the Early Polyphonic Mass: Medieval Context to Modern Revival* (Cambridge, 2010), 230–1.

was that instruments began to take a more direct role in church services. What varied was how this was accomplished.

Case study 4

Renaissance instrumentalists in the New World and cross-cultural encounters

In 1963, a young Maryknoll missionary assigned to the parish of San Miguel Acatán in the remote highlands of northwestern Guatemala stumbled on a box containing a number of bound volumes in the attic of the village church. The volumes, and others that were found in subsequent searches, turned out to be manuscript collections of music of the late sixteenth and early seventeenth centuries, including a substantial body of music by leading European composers (Isaac, Mouton, Josquin, and Morales, among others) copied for the use of native musicians for performances in local churches. Among the pieces, some were evidently intended for performance by indigenous instrumentalists. The chance discovery provided an unexpected and fascinating perspective into the very complex interactions between the Spanish Crown and native musical cultures during the Renaissance, and between secular and sacred authority in the New World.[1]

When Spanish explorers – and the military units that followed – encountered the New World they soon enmeshed themselves in conflicts that aimed at domination, or if necessary, destruction of the existing political structures. The stakes were very high on both sides. The locals knew that their basic institutions were threatened, and the small Spanish armies in turn realized that if they were defeated, there would be no honorable surrender – they knew from vivid experience that when Aztec warriors captured any of the despised foreigners that they quite literally butchered them. In general, success for the colonizers came relatively quickly, as the "discovery" was essentially a military occupation, and much of present-day Mexico, Central America, and a northern strip of South America was under firm Spanish control by the mid-sixteenth century. Often compromises were brokered in which local elites retained some element of authority, at least in the early decades of conquest, but one consistent means of control was religion through evangelization and conversion, as Catholicism was introduced and enforced everywhere.

Two aspects conditioned the introduction of the sacred element into this environment. One was that the relationship between secular and sacred authorities was often quite troubled, especially as the Spanish elements in control of the political and economic machinery – in their desire to extract maximum personal gain – were often extraordinarily harsh in their treatment of the indigenous population. Churchmen and even some Jesuits would occasionally push back, speaking out in defense of the natives. This caused tensions that in one dramatic instance led to the murder of the outspoken bishop of Nicaragua in 1550. A second aspect was that the "Catholicism" established in the New World was modeled along current practice in Spain, and instrumental music thrived in the Spanish church from the early sixteenth century onward. In most other urban regions of Europe – Flanders, England, and Italy, for example – the primary patrons of wind ensembles were the cities themselves. When churches in these regions needed cornetts and sackbuts to reinforce their services they would often simply draw upon the civic groups. In Spain, the situation was quite different. Though the picture of Spanish civic patronage of music remains rather shadowed, cities there evidently did not include wind ensembles on their regular payrolls. Major Spanish churches, on the other hand, began from the early sixteenth century to add small wind ensembles to their permanent musical staffs, which became a standard feature by about 1540, just as colonial churches were becoming well organized.

The force and organizational skill with which Catholicism was introduced remains impressive to this day as directives soon came from Rome to organize the structure of the church in the colonies. A bishop was named for Mexico City by 1527, and the construction of a cathedral began soon after. This was followed by similar moves throughout the regions under Spanish control. Two Episcopal Sees were established in the greater territory of Guatemala in 1534, with a third in 1539. In Mexico, Oaxaca was added in 1535, with Guadalajara in 1541. The workhorses of all this frenetic activity were the members of the monastic orders, especially the Dominicans, Franciscans, and, after 1540, the Jesuits. The vigor with which they pursued their calling was striking, as churches and monastic communities sprang up throughout the territories where they were active, including into such remote native villages as Ixcoy (San Juan Ixcoy), Ixtatán (San Mateo Ixtatán), and Santa Eulalia in the Guatemalan highlands. And as the Spanish friars went about their tasks of inculcating what was for the locals a new religion, in many areas they met one happy accident. Indigenous societies existed in considerable variety, from the Aztecs in central and southern Mexico to the Incas on the west coast of

South America, but in general their structures had similarities. They were all dominated by a ruling nobility. Often this dominance was supported by a class of priests who possessed considerable influence and status. Within this stratum, significantly, were often included players of musical instruments whose function was to support religious ceremony. Because of their association with the caste of priests, these musicians, too, were well placed in society. As their traditional societies collapsed, with a vast majority of the local populations reduced to servile status, many of these musicians realized that if they transferred their allegiance to the new religion, and the new music, they, as musicians within the church, could retain some remnant of status.

Transfer of allegiance was one thing, transfer of skills, though, was quite another matter. Here, however, we are left with little hard information. In early sixteenth-century Spain, as in the rest of Europe, a young man would begin to learn an instrument at about ten years of age and enter into an apprenticeship with a master that would last for several years. In this span, the apprentice learned to play a variety of instruments, to read music, and acquired the basic principles of improvisation and counterpoint (bear in mind that the careful balance of consonance and dissonance that characterized the harmonic system of the sixteenth century had developed over several centuries). The young musicians would learn as well a substantial repertory, much of this from memory. In sum, the master would not only teach present-day repertory and techniques, but also impart traditions of the craft that stretched far back into previous eras. Training was completely dependent on face-to-face contact – there were no method books written for budding professionals.

It appears that the native musicians in the New World quickly took up European instruments, as from the very beginning the players associated with church performances were local, not Spanish imports. The first reference to instrumentalists in the cathedral in Mexico City, in 1543, notes specifically that they were "menestriles yndios." In fact several years earlier, in 1539, in a formal entry of the Duke of Medina into Seville, the account reveals the presence there of "eight 'Indian' minstrels... playing shawms and sackbuts, who were praised for the sweetness of their playing."[2] It appears that almost from the first years of church music in the New World, the singers and organists were by preference drawn from Spain, but instrumental music was the province of the locals. The nagging question remains – how did the native musicians acquire their skills? We know from accounts of the Portuguese Asian missions that musical training was supplied by the Jesuits – in Goa, India, it was the College of St. Paul, founded in 1542 by Francis Xavier. Surviving records from Guatemala reveal that a variety of musical instruments were imported, but if there were any master instrumentalists drawn from the old country, no record of them is known to this study. Organists probably had some general knowledge of wind instruments, and professional singers apparently often played lutes and viols; perhaps they were able to pass on basic rudiments.

The intriguing set of manuscripts uncovered in Guatemala in 1963 may shed some light on this matter. The majority of the works included in these manuscripts are sacred, many provided with texts. A group of secular pieces, French and Spanish, is also included – the French pieces are without text and most likely these were to be used by the local instrumentalists. There is also a smaller group of pieces identified by title only, frequently of uncertain meaning, without texts and also probably intended for instrumental performance.

This last group is especially relevant in that these pieces contain numerous passages in which peculiar effects – peculiar to European ears, but likely imitations of indigenous practices – seem explicit. In some pieces parallel perfect intervals occur in quite distinct contexts. In Manuscript 8, fols. 53v–54r, in a piece ascribed to Alonzo de Avila, the tenor moves in parallel fifths above the bass in dotted rhythms, ascending and descending, while the alto, also following exactly the same pattern, is written an octave above the bass. (A similar example occurs in the same manuscript on fols. 37v–38r.) The effect, to sophisticated Old World ears of the sixteenth century, would have been almost unbearably crude. Curious dissonances abound. In Manuscript 6, fol. 7r, in an incompletely preserved piece titled *Zuanella*, the tenor sounds a drone on middle C in dotted rhythms throughout. The bass below this alternates between the G below, descending to D, returning to G, and sounds this throughout the piece; the D, of course, will be especially grating against the C. Meanwhile, the alto part duplicates the bass an octave higher. The pattern is repeated five times – that is, this seems to be positively the intent of the scribe. The curious aspects of the manuscript occur too often to be ascribed to simple errors in copying. They seem to represent the clear local practices of the indigenous musicians, a true native style adapted to a European context.[3] What we have in these manuscripts may of course also be described as evidence of an incomplete transfer of European concepts that may have been due in part to the lack of sufficient teachers or a systematic pedagogy. On the other hand, a later New World instrumental manuscript from Puebla, Mexico, dating to the 1670s, contains a very retrospective repertory (it could just as well have been written about 1590) that is completely conventional in all musical aspects with none of the oddities of the Guatemalan collections. One interpretation could be that with time local instrumentalists learned to conform to European standards, ushering in a "musical" colonization – that blanched all indigenous traits gradually.[4]

In sum, the Spanish, through vastly superior military technology and by means of shrewd, if duplicitous, diplomacy, were able to overwhelm the indigenous nations in the New World. Within a short time those with Spanish blood essentially held all-important positions in political, economic, and cultural arenas throughout the territory they termed New Spain. One small chink in this wall of Spanish domination was in instrumental music in the church, where native performers held sway. Analogies can be found in Europe; German musicians were preeminent in Italian courts and cities in the late fifteenth century just as (in a delicious irony) Italians dominated in German courts a century later. Yet, the rapid assimilation of native musicians into the otherwise Spanish-dominated church structures presents an even more dramatic example of the ability of music to transcend otherwise rigid cultural barriers.

Notes

1 Bloomington, Indiana University, Libby Library, Santa Eulalia M. Md. 6 & M. Md. 8. See Paul Borg, "The Polyphonic Music in the Guatemalan Music Manuscripts of the Lilly Library," PhD diss., Indiana University (1985). The manuscripts were first described by Robert M. Stevenson, "European Music in 16th-Century Guatemala," *MQ* 50 (1964), 341–52.
2 Juan Ruiz Jiménez, "Power and Musical Exchange: the Dukes of Medina Sidonia in Renaissance Seville," *EM* 37 (2009), 408.
3 All the pieces in the Guatemalan sources are transcribed in Borg, "The Polyphonic Music." A selection of pieces from Ms. 8 was made available in Sharon Girard, ed., *Renaissance Wind Band Music of Guatemala* (Berkeley, CA, 1981).
4 Kenneth Kreitner, "The Repertory of the Spanish Cathedral Bands," *EM* 37 (2009), 267–86, discusses the background of Spanish instrumental music and also provides a brief discussion with inventory of Puebla, Archivo de Música Sacra de la Catedral, Ms. XIX. The manuscript is also discussed by Douglas Kirk, "Rediscovered Works of Philippe Rogier in Spanish and Mexican Instrumental Manuscripts." In *Encomium Musicæ: Essays in Memory of Robert J. Snow*, ed. David Crawford and Grayson G. Wagstaff (Hillsdale, NY, 2002), 47–74. On musical contacts and instrumental exchange in this period between Europeans and Asia, see Victor Coelho, "Old Worlds and New." In *The Cambridge History of Seventeenth-Century Music*, ed. Tim Carter and John Butt (Cambridge, 2005), 88–110.

Italian cities were early to adopt what was to become a common and expedient strategy. They simply added religious duties to the functions of their town musicians. In Bologna, for example, a town document from 1556 specifies that the civic musicians are now to play "at mass at all the principal feasts," a directive that was repeated in later documents to the end of the century. In Siena, too, the civic ensemble was required to play "on holy days... when Mass was celebrated at the chapel in the Palace... at the Elevation of the Host." In both of these instances it was the entire ensemble that performed. Some cities brought in individual players from their ensembles, rather than all, to perform in religious services, as was evidently the case in Bergamo beginning in 1542.[34] Only after mid-century, and then only sporadically, did churches in Italy begin to hire their own players. The most significant example of this was at San Marco in Venice, which initiated the practice in 1568 with the hiring of an ensemble that included the eminent cornettist Girolamo Dalla Casa. At San Petronio, the main church of Bologna, the church also acquired its own musicians. In 1560 they hired a trombonist, then, by 1574, they had added a cornettist as well. By the 1590s the group had grown to an ensemble of three trombones, a cornettist, and a violinist.[35]

North of the Alps, each strand of Reformation thought placed its own value on the participation of instruments in their liturgy. In the German city of Ulm, the earliest reformed leadership was under the influence of Zwingli, and as a result instruments were not welcomed. By 1571, however, the Lutheran element had gained prominence, and the *Stadtpfeifer* ("city shawms") were then made part of the religious services. Generally, where the cities were Lutheran, the involvement of the *Stadtpfeifer* ensemble was common, as for example in Braunschweig, Lüneburg, and Leipzig. Still, in

---

[34] Gambassi, *Il Concerto Palatino*, 154; concerning Siena, see Frank A. D'Accone, *The Civic Muse: Music and Musicians in Siena during the Middle Ages and the Renaissance* (Chicago & London, 1997), 583–4; concerning Bergamo, see Gary Towne, "*Tubatori e Piffari*: Civic Wind Players in Medieval and Renaissance Bergamo," *HBSJ* 9 (1997), 184 and 192, n. 43.

[35] On musicians in Venice, see Eleanor Selfridge-Field, *Venetian Instrumental Music from Gabrieli to Vivaldi* (Oxford, 1975), 14–15. She notes, however, that the Doge's ensemble (in effect the civic ensemble of Venice) would also perform on some occasions in San Marco, though Giulio Ongaro, in his extensive survey of practices in San Marco into the 1560s, reported no instances of performances in San Marco by ensembles either from the city or as musicians of the church itself; see Giulio Ongaro, "The Chapel of St Mark's at the Time of Adrian Willaert (1527–62): A Documentary Study," PhD diss., University of North Carolina (1986). Ongaro also notes that later one musician was both a member of the Doge's ensemble and also employed as a cornettist at San Marco. See Giulio Ongaro, "Sixteenth-Century Venetian Wind Instrument Makers and their Clients," *EM* 13 (1985), 392 and 395, n. 17; on Bologna, see Osvaldo Gambassi, *La cappella musicale de S. Petronio* (Florence, 1987), 83–96.

these instances, it was the city, not the church, that was ultimately the patron.[36] The same tended to be true in the Low Countries. In 1546, the city of Haarlem paid one of the civic musicians, playing cornett, to support the singers of the city's church in the performance of the *Lof*. By 1559 his duties had been expanded to include performance during the Mass on all Sundays and Holy days. Similarly, in Mechelen and in Bergen op Zoom, it was the city musicians, paid from city accounts, who performed with church singers in various religious celebrations. Even when the musicians were paid from church funds, or perhaps by religious confraternities, the musician were still in most cases the official players of the city.[37]

England followed its own twisted path: first with the break from the Roman church under Henry VIII (continued in the brief reign of Edward VI), followed by the short period of Catholic restoration under Mary, then finally (for the sixteenth century) settling again on the Anglican rite during the long reign of Elizabeth I. The reversals created social turbulence, but in terms of attitudes toward music, what can be said is that the more extreme reforms demanded by Calvin and Zwingli never gained ascendance, the result being that the more elaborate forms of music were not excluded from the liturgy. In terms of patronage of instrumentalists, however, the pattern in England was similar to that of the Low Countries. Only after 1550 did instrumental support of sacred music by sackbuts and cornetts become more general, but even then in the cathedrals in England it was apparently the professional civic musicians (the town waits) who were called upon, as for example in Canterbury, Durham, and Worcester. In one remarkable turn of events, in Norwich, four of the town waits were actually joined with the

---

[36] On the shift in Ulm, with the city authorities specifying the participation of the city musicians in the church services, see Steffen Schure, *Die Geschichte des Stadtmusikantentums in Ulm (1388–1840)* (Ulm and Stuttgart, 2007), 71. For information on Braunschweig, see Werner Greve, *Braunschweiger Stadtmusikanten* (Braunschweig, 1991); for Lüneburg see Walter Horst, *Musikgeschichte der Stadt Lüneburg* (Tutzing, 1967); for Leipzig during the Renaissance, still of great value is Rudolf Wustmann, *Musikgeschichte Leipzigs*, vol. 1: *Bis zur Mitte des 17. Jahrhunderts* (Leipzig and Berlin, 1909).

[37] On sources in Haarlem, see Maarten Albert Vente, ed., *Bouwstenen voor een geschiedenis der toonkunst in de Nederlanden*, 3 (Utrecht and Amsterdam, 1980), 176 & 180. For a discussion of instrumentalists in Mechelen and Bergen op Zoom, see Keith Polk, "Susato and Instrumental Music in Flanders in the 16th Century." In *Tielman Susato*, ed. Keith Polk, 90–92. Note that the organ was somewhat insulated from any antagonism from reformists as seen in the continued presence of organs in churches throughout Germany and the Low Countries, whichever brand of reform was adopted.

professional choristers in the Norwich cathedral; they were evidently performing both as instrumentalists and as singers.[38]

Spain was the one region in which the church itself engaged professional ensembles, which, in fact, began quite early. The church authorities in Seville appointed a five-part ensemble in 1526 consisting of three shawms and two trombones to perform for services in the cathedral. Wind ensembles were subsequently absorbed with great enthusiasm in churches and cathedrals throughout Spain, with generous support from the church, and wherever Spain established colonies, wind bands followed.[39] In a tragic irony of sorts, as the repressive regime of Philip II crushed the musical culture of the Low Countries, Spain was engendering a rich local musical culture reflected in such musical manuscripts as the two Lerma Codices, which were assembled specifically to allow for the use by instrumentalists within the liturgy.[40] Spain was an exception, however, and in most regions, the church (either in its Catholic or reformed versions) did not itself provide vigorous patronage of instrumental music until late in the Renaissance. This is perhaps beside the point, however, for after 1500 resistance within church leadership gradually dissolved and a more hospitable attitude led to far greater participation of instruments within church services throughout Europe.

Civic patronage in the fifteenth century

Civic account books are quite ample in revealing that most European cities supported instrumental music in some form through official patronage. The earliest documents reveal that by 1300 most cities provided for watchmen who played various kinds of horns; sometimes associated with these watchmen might be small groups of shawms and perhaps a drummer. The presence of such watchmen is especially clear in strategic Italian cities

---

[38] Trevor Herbert, *The Trombone* (New Haven and London, 2006), 103; see also Carole Ann Janssen, "The Waytes of Norwich in Medieval and Renaissance Civic Pageantry," PhD diss., University of New Brunswick (1977), 71–3.

[39] Spanish churches also provided enthusiastic support of organists and developed talent of the first order. Cabezón, though attached from an early age to the court of Charles V, was a product of that artistic environment.

[40] On the initiation of civic support for wind bands in local cathedrals and churches in Spain, see Kenneth Kreitner, "Minstrels in Spanish Churches, 1400–1600," *EM* 20 (1992), 533–46; on the wind bands and the links to the two Lerma codices, see Douglas K. Kirk, "Churching the Shawms in Renaissance Spain: Lerma, Archivo de San Pedro Ms. Mus. 1," PhD diss., McGill University (1993).

such as Bologna, Florence, and Siena. In many cases, it was through an expansion of the watchmen function that groups with a more musical focus were engaged. Indications of more diverse musical ensembles first come from German regions, where many cities had initiated groups called the *Stadtpfeifer* by about 1380.[41] Similar groups in Italian cities came slightly later, with Florence defining a new civic group, the city *pifferi*, in 1386.[42] Soon afterwards, initiation of similar patronage took place in Bologna and Siena. It is clear that by the early fifteenth century in both Germany and Italy, civic patronage and targeted funding of a shawm group as a primarily *musical* ensemble was a general feature. This evolution from function to finesse played out in most regions of Europe, but with distinctive variations within each locale.

Germany and Italy – Flanders and England – France and Spain

German cities were at the forefront of developments in instrumental music. By 1400 cities large (Cologne, Strasbourg, and Nuremberg) and small (Deventer, Dinkelsbühl, and Windsheim) from throughout German-speaking regions were supporting civic ensembles. Moreover, German musicians were prized imports into the cities of Italy as well as courts in Spain, France, and the Low Countries. German cities in the north also appear to be the earliest to have incorporated a slide instrument into their ensembles, this occurring shortly after 1400. This vigor continued throughout the century. Early on larger cities generally supported three musicians (by about 1420 the configuration was discant shawm, tenor shawm, and trombone), but by the end of the century these cities expanded to four, or in a few cases, to five players. A striking feature of German patronage was that very small cities such as Windsheim would find the means to support an ensemble, often just two. This was undoubtedly related to the political realities of the region. Many of these cities were "Imperial cities" – that is, they owed allegiance directly to the emperor and were thus independent of their local lord. The civic ensembles, dressed in livery in the colors of the city, wearing medallions displaying the city coat of arms, were a visible and aural mark of their independence.[43]

Italian cities in 1400 were also free from any effective central control, as their nominal overlord, the Holy Roman emperor, was unable to exert any

---

[41] Heinrich W. Schwab, *Die Anfänge des weltlichen Berufsmusikertums in der mittelalterlichen Stadt. Kieler Schriften zur Musikwissenschaft* 24 (Kassel, 1982); see also Polk, *German Instrumental Music*, 108–12.
[42] McGee, *Ceremonial Musicians*, 131–3. [43] See Polk, *German Instrumental Music*, 108–31.

real authority. They were, furthermore, much larger than German cities, with vast discretionary funding available. Still, their relative autonomy did not lead to peaceful conditions as constant frictions led to numerous wars large and small. In short, for Italian cities, too, came the necessity of maintaining an image of strength and grandeur. They poured money into supporting ensembles on a scale unmatched anywhere in Europe. Florence in the early fifteenth century funded a wind band of three, a band of ceremonial trumpets, and an additional group of trumpeter/ messengers – roughly five times the number of players as found in Augsburg at this time. Florence was hardly alone, as Bologna, Siena, and most likely Venice, fielded similar numbers. Concerning developments within the wind bands (the most important units in terms of music), Italian and German ensembles were in fact quite similar. As in Nuremberg, the wind ensemble in Florence increased to four by about mid-century and to five by c.1500. Similarities are hardly surprising, though, as many of the musicians in the Italian ensembles were German; the four-man group in Florence in 1444 was entirely German.[44] The imports were undoubtedly fine performers, but German performers were also seen as lending prestige, thus contributing to the image of the city. When a vacancy opened in the ensemble in Florence in 1489, Lorenzo the Magnificent himself participated in the correspondence that ultimately brought the great cornettist Augustine Schubinger to the city.

By 1400, the cities of Flanders and those in neighboring Brabant had begun their long recovery from the devastations of the plagues that had swept through in the fourteenth century. The region was densely populated and had a well-developed industrial base. The cities were generally prosperous, and most had the means to provide ample support for civic musicians. An influencing factor in this regard was that the traditional freedoms enjoyed by these towns were increasingly hemmed in by the ambitious Dukes of Burgundy; Philip the Bold of Burgundy had succeeded

---

[44] On Florence, see McGee, *Ceremonial Musicians*, 158–98; concerning Siena, see D'Accone, *The Civic Muse*, 438–511 and 512–621. Information on Bologna, though with little discussion, is available in Gambassi, *Il Concerto Palatino*. Very few records for Venice remain, though a valuable outline of Venetian patronage is available in Rodolfo Baroncini, "Zorzi Trombetta and the Band of *Piffari* and Trombones of the *Serenissima*: New Documentary Evidence," trans. Hugh Ward-Perkins, *HBSJ* 14 (2002), 59–82; see also his "Zorzi Trombetta da Modon and the Founding of the Band of *Piffari* and *Tromboni* of the *Serenissima*," *HBSJ* 16 (2004), 1–17. Jeffrey Kurtzman and Linda Maria Koldau explore the sixteenth-century use of brass instruments in Venice in "*Trombe, Trombe d'argento, Trombe squarciate, Tromboni*, and *Piffari* in Venetian Processions and Ceremonies of the Sixteenth and Seventeenth Centuries," *JSCM* 8 (2002), accessed December 14, 2015. http://sscm-jscm.org/v8/no1/kurtzman.html.

to the title of Count of Holland in 1384. Support of civic ensembles was for them one of the gestures they could make to support an image of strength and some independence.

In Flanders, the link to the older tradition of calling on musicians to serve as watchmen continued longer than in Germany or Italy. At the beginning of the fifteenth century, ensembles of wind players were on the payrolls of such cities as Bruges, Ghent, and Mechelen, but they were usually termed "watchmen," and they were, in fact, actually called upon to fulfill the watch function. Not until about 1450 did the terminology change from "watchmen of the city" to "minstrels of the city," indicating a shift to a more purely musical function. In any case, the transition from watchmen to musicians is unusually clear in Flemish accounts. These accounts also reveal the impact of troubled economic and political conditions. In the 1480s much of Flanders rose in revolt against the policies of their new overlord, Maximilian of Habsburg, who had succeeded Charles the Bold through a hasty marriage to Mary of Burgundy following the death of Charles in 1477. Trade was seriously disrupted and economies deteriorated severely. A clear measure of the severity was that in several cities the fall in revenues was drastic enough that subsidies for civic ensembles were suspended. On the other hand, as the period of crisis ended, trade quickly revived and cities soon brought back their musicians. In short, support of music can serve as a barometer of both good times and bad.

England offers another clear vista of Renaissance patronage. It suffered the usual round of plagues, the vicious conflicts between the houses of York and Lancaster, and the occasional disaster, such as the great 1666 fire in London, which destroyed much documentation of previous centuries. Still, in general, for English cities the years from 1400 to 1600 were a period of gradual but distinct increase in trade and prosperity, with growing populations and city councils willing to support music. Moreover, the documentation for much of England has survived in substantial quantity, and, as a further boon for our particular efforts, English sources have received extensive sifting and interpretation, with much of this work of very high quality.[45] British civic account books do not become general until well

---

[45] Study of music in English cities is immensely aided by the various volumes of the *Records of Early English Drama* [*REED*]. See also Conklin, "Medieval English Minstrels," and Rastall, "Secular Musicians in Late Medieval England." For a recent update, see Keith Polk, "English Instrumental Music in the Fifteenth Century." In *Uno Gentile et Subtile Ingenio: Studies in Renaissance Music in Honour of Bonnie J. Blackburn,* ed. Jennifer M. Bloxam, Gioia Filocamo, and Leofranc Holford-Strevens (Turnhout, 2009), 659–67.

into the fifteenth century, and without precise records, we are unable to pinpoint for most cities when civic subsidy actually began. Still, support of civic ensembles clearly took root quite early. Bristol, Cambridge, Colchester, Exeter, and London had ensembles in place shortly before 1400, with Beverly, Canterbury, Norwich, and Salisbury joining by 1410.[46] In about 1430, records document the presence of town bands essentially in every substantial town. This is perhaps slightly later than contemporary support in Germany, but occurred at about the same time as similar developments in Italy and the Low Countries. The usual term for English civic bands was "waits," hinting at some rather indistinct tie to watchmen, as was indicated by the naming of many Flemish groups as *wachters* ("watchmen" in Flemish). Still, both Rastall and Conklin emphasized that the English waits were from their beginnings as civic ensembles engaged not to watch, but to perform musical functions.[47]

The subsequent pattern of growth for English civic ensembles was similar to that on the continent. Some smaller towns began with two players, but three seems to have been viewed as a standard minimum in most locations in the early decades. By 1450 larger towns preferred to have four, with three being considered the desired minimum. London had by far the greatest population in England, but so few records have survived that it is impossible to follow the course of patronage there in detail. Some nine London waits were mentioned in a document from 1442, but this number seems highly unlikely to have referred to an exclusively musical organization. Perhaps some of these men were restricted to purely watch functions. By about 1500 the city was providing for six players, and that appears to have remained the desired number for some time thereafter.[48]

France and Spain present a kind of minority opinion concerning civic patronage of music. A recent study of French urban centers by Gretchen

---

[46] For most of these, see the appropriate *REED* volumes. The ensemble for Colchester was first noted, oddly enough, in the accounts of the court of Guelders for 1389–90, Rijksarchief in Gelderland, Arnhem, Hertogelijk Archief 220, fol. 70, "der stat pyperen van Colchester," and the first known reference to the London waits is in these same accounts; see Gerard Nijsten, *Het Hof van Gelre: Cultuur ten tijde van de hertogen uit het Guliske en Egmondse huis (1371–1473)* (2nd ed., Kampen, 1992), 124. For extensive treatment of Norwich, see Janssen, "The Waytes," which updates the still-useful George Arthur Stephen, *The Waits of the City of Norwich through Four Centuries to 1790* (Norwich, 1933). All previous work, however, should take into account the information now available in the *REED* set.
[47] See Conklin, "Medieval English Minstrels," 202–3, and Rastall, "Secular Musicians," I, 120.
[48] See Walter L. Woodfill, *Musicians in English Society from Elizabeth to Charles I* (Princeton, 1953), 33–4 and 39, which has been updated by the work of Conklin and Rastall, cited above.

Peters reveals unequivocally that in contrast to the aggressive support of instrumentalists in other regions, in most of France civic subsidies for musical ensembles were thin on the ground. Toulouse and Montpelier in the south were exceptions, but in such substantial towns as Avignon, Marseilles, Narbonne, Nîmes, and Bordeaux, only a watchman or two were on the payrolls. In the center of the country the picture is even bleaker, with such cities as Arras, Beauvais, Rouen, Orleans, and Tours also restricting their outlays to a couple of watchmen. Only Troyes, along with cities in the north such as Lille, Douai, and Tournai, were exceptions, but the economic ties of these last three were to the north, and represented a kind of extension of the situation in Flanders. Peters suggested a convincing reason for the dearth of patronage in that the French crown exerted far stronger central control than was the case in Italy, Germany – or even Flanders, for that matter. Civic ensembles elsewhere symbolized civic independence, and the French kings wanted none of it. The crown dominated city councils with royal appointments, and one result was, apparently, no subsidies for civic musicians.[49]

Spain was well connected to musical developments in the main centers of Europe in the Renaissance. Spanish courts imported German wind and string players early in the fifteenth century, and indeed had a vigorous culture that produced the renowned duo of Cordoval and Fernandez, who arrived at the Burgundian court in the early 1430s. Oddly, the notion of civic support for musical ensembles did not seem to have taken hold there. Barcelona, for example, while it could boast of considerable freelance activity by instrumentalists, apparently did not support a civic wind band. There is similarly little information concerning civic ensembles in Portugal, though it is of interest that a late sixteenth-century treatise on shawm playing, now lost, was prepared by one André de Escobar.[50] The nobility being especially powerful in Spain, perhaps the support of music in aristocratic circles served to suppress civic activity. In some senses the church stepped in to fill the gap, for Spanish churches seem to have been the earliest to install resident ensembles of wind players to support liturgical services (as discussed above). This aspect of patronage was of

---

[49] Concerning music in French cities, see Gretchen Peters, *The Musical Sounds of Medieval French Cities: Players, Patrons, and Politics* (Cambridge, 2012).

[50] On Spain, see Kenneth Kreitner, "Music in the Corpus Christi Procession of Fifteenth-Century Barcelona," *EMH* 14 (1995), 153–204. On Escobar's lost treatise, see Bernadette Nelson, "Music Treatises and 'artes para tanger' in Portugal Before the 18th Century: An Overview." In *Tratados de Arte em Portugal*, ed. Rafael Moreira and Ana Duarte Rodrigues (Lisbon, 2011), 221.

such strength that it represented a major export to the New World (as discussed in *CS* 4, above).

Civic patronage in the sixteenth century

European cities reached an apex of independence in the late fifteenth century. While many continued to prosper and expand significantly, their relative power declined gradually but inexorably after about 1500 in the face of the growing centralized power under Charles V, Francis I, and Henry VIII. No more dramatic example can be cited than that of Antwerp. This city burst into the front ranks of European cities in the early sixteenth century, reaching its height by about 1550. But for every city, fate was tied to a political component. Antwerp was a unit within the Habsburg Empire, and this was a fatal link.

Case study 5

Players and politics: Tielman Susato and the Antwerp Band, *c.*1550

Antwerp in the sixteenth century should have been a splendid environment for professional instrumentalists. Very quickly after 1500, trade routes altered as traditional overland patterns shifted in favor of sea lanes, much to the advantage of port cities with openings to the Atlantic.[1] The city boomed, easily replacing Bruges as the region's commercial center, and by 1550 it was the most dynamic urban center in northern Europe. Antwerp, however, existed within a larger and quite unstable political framework. The harsh, uncompromising religious intolerance of Charles V became ever more short-sighted under his successor, his son, Phillip II, and led to utter catastrophe. The horrific events that struck the city affected all of its citizens, bringing devastating consequences for many of the city's musicians.

But in the early years of the sixteenth century the disasters lay far in the future, and then all was bustle and growth. The details are patchy, as almost all of Antwerp's accounts books before 1530 were lost in subsequent destruction (as were many of those after 1530).[2] Still, much can be pieced together from records in other nearby cities, for the Antwerp musicians were much in demand for festivals and celebrations in other towns in the region. Records in Bergen op Zoom and Dendermonde indicate that the

Antwerp ensemble had expanded to four players by about 1480. By about 1515 the Antwerp ensemble had expanded to five.

The first sixteenth-century payroll record from Antwerp itself, from 1530 to 1531, lists five musicians as "stadt pypers." Two of these are among the outstanding wind players of the era. One was Hans Nagel, an unusually colorful character.[3] In the first explicit record of Nagel, he was noted as a trombonist at the court of Henry VII in England in 1501 (he had probably been with Henry for at least a few years before 1501, as English court accounts list only exceptionally named instrumentalists in these years). By 1504 Nagel had moved to the Low Countries to serve in the court of Philip the Fair – where he would have come in contact with Augustine Schubinger who was also serving Philip at this time, as well as the composers Alexander Agricola and Pierre de La Rue. After the death of Philip in 1506, Nagel was recruited into the town band in Mechelen in 1509–10, probably through the influence (and perhaps the patronage) of Margaret of Austria. Margaret was acting as regent in the Low Countries during the minority of Charles, and had chosen Mechelen as her primary residence. It was at this time that Nagel, along with the well-known musical scribe Petrus Alamire, became involved in espionage, providing information to the English court concerning the English exile community in the Low Countries. At some point, probably about 1520, he moved to Antwerp where he became a member of the civic ensemble. He remained in Antwerp until his death in 1531.

The other name that stands out in the 1530–1 Antwerp payroll list is that of Tielman Susato.[4] Susato described himself as "from Cologne" and was born about 1510. He probably served his apprenticeship in Cologne, and may well have been a choirboy there when very young, for his first notice in Antwerp was as a musical scribe copying sacred music for the Antwerp Confraternity of Our Lady. Training in a choir school would have provided training in written counterpoint and composition (which Susato clearly had), an education that was unusual in the training of instrumentalists during the early sixteenth century. He was obviously a brilliant young man in 1530, and at first all went well. He performed in the Antwerp ensemble on trombone and other wind instruments, and probably as well on the viol. He began his publishing ventures in 1541, first in a partnership, and then setting out on his own in 1543, continuing to publish books of chansons, instrumental music, motets, and Masses until 1561. Among his publications were a large number of his own works; his chansons and motets were particularly skillful and effective. His troubles began in 1549 when the town ensemble was dismissed *en masse*, evidently for participating in some gesture of protest during a visit of Charles V and his son (soon to be Philip II). Some of the members of the ensemble were reinstated, but Susato never regained his post – an indication that he may have been tagged as a ringleader in the protest and also probably because his strongly held Protestant views were all too well known. For a time Susato appears to have simply shifted his interests to publishing, editing, and composing, with great success, but the religious climate in Flanders became increasingly threatening as the Inquisition was loosed in an attempt by the Spanish authorities to maintain the region as Catholic. In 1561 Susato left his business in the hands of his son and made for the somewhat safer town of Alkmaar in the north of Holland. He appears to have left there in 1565, and in 1566 was involved as a courier in negotiations for a possible marriage between the Swedish king and the princess of Lorraine. The Swedish king was an extraordinarily difficult man, and when Susato had disposed of certain critical documents that were thrown overboard when his ship appeared to be in danger of falling into enemy hands, the king became infuriated. Susato managed to survive the ensuing interrogations (though his very life lay in the balance) and remained in Sweden until about 1570, after which no more is known of him. His personal tragedy was that he managed to overcome the blow of his dismissal in 1549 as well as the ire of the Swedish king, but in being forced to leave Antwerp in 1561 his creative life was essentially over.

But Susato's misfortune was just one of many as religious conflict roiled through the Low Countries. In Antwerp, two other members of the town ensemble, Segher Pelken and Gommar van Oisterwijk, were later banned, though both managed to establish themselves successfully as performers in London (Pelken with the London Waits, van Oiterwijk within the court of Elizabeth I). A grimmer fate struck one of their colleagues, Jenyn Verhoeven, who had remained in Antwerp service. Verhoeven was "foully murdered" by Spanish troops who took out their anger over hunger and lack of pay with three weeks of looting and destruction in Antwerp in 1576, known as the infamous "Spanish Fury." Between about 1550 and 1580 about half of the men who had been on the payrolls as civic musicians were lost to the city.

Antwerp was desolated and its economy in shambles. Still, the city might well have recovered – but the calamities were not yet over. As the conflicts between the Low Countries and the Spanish crown continued in subsequent decades, the Dutch managed to effectively block the sea lanes into Antwerp, which was a fatal blow. Trade shifted to other centers, especially Amsterdam and London, and Antwerp would never regain the prominence or the prosperity it had enjoyed in the early sixteenth century. Parallel with this phenomenon, the bleak experiences of Susato, Pelken, van Oisterewijik, and Verhoeven reflect the reality of the trajectory of music and musicians in the region. In 1550 Antwerp (and Flanders as a whole) was one of the major centers of musical activity in Europe. Lasso was briefly in Antwerp, for example, about that time, and his Opus 1 volume was published there – by Susato. By early in the next century the musical culture of the region had been savaged. It did not recover.

Notes

1 For the background of Antwerp in general, see the various essays in *Antwerp, Story of a Metropolis, 16th–17th Century*, ed. Jan Van der Stock (Ghent, 1993).
2 On civic music in Antwerp see Godelieve Spiessens, "De Antwerpse stadsspeellieden Deel I: 15e en 16e eeuw," *Noordgouw* 10 (1970), 1–53; this has been updated in her *De Antwerpse stadsspeellieden (c.1411–1794)* (Antwerp, 2014). A summary of her conclusions is in Polk, "Susato and Instrumental Music." In *Tielman Susato*, ed. Keith Polk, 70–75.
3 On Hans Nagel, see Bruno Bouckaert and Eugeen Schreurs, "Hans Nagel, Performer and Spy in England and Flanders (c.1490–1531)." In *Tielman Susato*, ed. K. Polk, 101–15.
4 On Susato's career, see ibid., Kristine Forney, "New Insights into the Career and Musical Contributions of Tielman Susato,", 1–10, and Ardis Grojean, "Tielman Susato and Sweden; The Swedish Evidence, 1555–1570," 45–59.

Size matters

Bologna was by no means the largest city in Italy, but it was far larger than most cities in the north. The city had supported both trumpet and shawm ensembles in the fifteenth century and expanded these forces in the sixteenth century. In about 1501, the city's musical corps comprised four trumpets, a shawm band of five, a harpist, and a drummer. By 1520 the trumpets were increased to eight and the winds to seven (five shawms, *piffari*, and two *tromboni*). The accounts of 1546 indicate change in that the terms *piffari* and *tromboni* disappear, and eight players are lumped together and listed in the higher rank of *musici*. Supplementary documents reveal that six of these musicians were primarily players of shawm, along with two of trombone, but the change of terminology probably reveals the increasing pressures for versatility; most likely these men were being called upon to play viols and violins as well as wind instruments, and the term "musician" more accurately reflected the flexibility that the city expected of them. Some further support for this suggestion comes from the fact that two of the players in the 1546 payroll list were Ganassi, that is, members of the prominent Venetian musical family of that name; Silvestro Ganassi, probably their cousin, published a tutor on recorder playing shortly before, the *Opera intitulata Fontegara* (Venice, 1535_1). Through much of the sixteenth century the framework of patronage in Bologna remained remarkably stable, with a total of nineteen musicians.[51] Siena was a smaller city with its independence limited by the political domination from nearby Florence, but nonetheless supported a large trumpet ensemble throughout the sixteenth century. Trumpeters are ubiquitous in the archival documents, pointing to their central role in all civic events.[52] In terms of regularly contracted players, Siena through most of the sixteenth century supported about eighteen musicians.

North of the Alps the thrust was similar to cities in Italy, though with some inconsistency, especially as political conflicts, rooted in revolutionary new religions, rippled through the regions. A limiting factor for cities north of the Alps was that they were distinctly smaller than those in Italy. With less ample income sources, none of the northern centers came close to matching the expansive patronage of Bologna (and Bologna was a city of only middling stature in Italy). In the German regions, Augsburg may serve as an example. As one of the most prominent of all German cities throughout the sixteenth century, the city normally supported a civic ensemble of only five wind players, though occasionally it would expand to six.[53] Even the largest German cities apparently did not, as a general rule, expand beyond five or six performers because of the prohibitive costs of maintaining large ensembles. But if the German cities could not match the regional courts in numbers, they certainly did so in quality, as they continued to provide key personnel for courtly ensembles. In the early years of the sixteenth century, the Augsburg native Augustine Schubinger was a star cornett player at the courts of Philip the Fair and Maximilian I, while his brother was serving the court in Mantua. The ducal establishment in Munich

---

[51] For the payroll listing of 1546 (which comprised eight trumpets, eight *musici*, a harpist, a lutenist, and a "naccarino"), see Gambassi, *Il Concerto Palatino*, 620, and for listings throughout the sixteenth century, see 612–37.

[52] D'Accone, *The Civic Muse*, 438–511.

[53] There is not yet a detailed survey of instrumental music in Augsburg. For the figures given here, the documents may be found in the Augsburg Stadtarchiv in the series *Baumeisterbücher*, which shows that between 1520 and 1561, the size of ensemble varied from between four and six players, briefly expanding to eight players in 1601 in order to engage Hans Leo Hassler to head the civic ensemble.

recruited Hans Rauch and Sebastian Hurlacher, both from families long active in Augsburg, while Mary of Hungary borrowed Wolff Gans and Endries Hurlacher for an extended stay at her court as regent of the Low Countries from about 1535 to 1538 (Gans and Hurlacher were contracted musicians in Augsburg, and evidently allowed to travel to Brussels on some kind of long-term leave).[54] For German cities of lesser stature, Leipzig, for example, the ensemble remained at four through most of the century. Here, and probably in other cities as well, the city would call on supernumeraries – players with a regular association with the band, without fixed contracts, and most critically, without fixed income obligations from the city – whenever additional forces were judged necessary.[55]

Civic ensembles in England closely parallel those in Germany. London, by far the dominant city, considered six as the appropriate number for its official ensemble, the Waits of London, but additional musicians were available when a larger ensemble might be desired. Norwich, similar to Leipzig as an example of a smaller, though substantial city, generally maintained four musicians through much of the sixteenth century, though the ensemble did expand to five from time to time, as in 1553.[56] Support of waits was widespread throughout England, and most cities of more modest size such as Cambridge, Coventry, Lincoln, and York, maintaining three musicians in their ensembles.[57]

Even in times of prosperity and growth, Renaissance cities in the sixteenth century could no longer sustain the numbers, nor, more crucially, the range of musical patronage of the high nobility after about 1520, when several new trends had appeared. One was the vastly increased preference for the sounds of cornett and trombone consorts. This engendered no major

---

[54] On the career of Augustine Schubinger, see Keith Polk, "Augustein Schubinger and the Zinck: Innovation in Performance Practice," *HBSJ* 1 (1989), 83–92. For Rauch and Sebastian Hurlacher at the Munich court, see Hans-Joachim Nösselt, *Ein ältest Orchester 1530–1980*, 21–30. On Gans and Endries Hurlacher in Brussels, see Glenda Goss Thompson, "Music in the Court Records of Mary of Hungary," *TVNM* 34 (1984), 139; Thompson suggests that Gans and Hurlacher were in Brussels from 1531 to 1540; but these Augsburg players were only there from 1535 to 1538; see Augsburg, Stadtarchiv, BB, 1535–6, fol. 116 (the last date they were still in Augsburg), and BB 1538–9, fol. 120v, which notes their return. This last entry also recorded the death of Hurlacher in that same year.

[55] Rudolf Wustmann, *Musikgeschichte Leipzigs*, 33 and 187–9.

[56] For discussion of the London waits, see Woodfill, *Musicians in English Society*, 33–5, and 83; for the Norwich ensemble, see Janssen, "The Waytes," 45.

[57] No comprehensive information is available for patronage in French cities during the sixteenth century – Peters, *The Musical Sounds*, ends her study at 1500; the same is true of Spanish cities.

dislocation in either courts or cities, as players could accommodate to this development by a simple shift within the existing winds ensembles. One or two of the shawmists would double on cornett, while others doubled on trombone. More destabilizing was the increasing popularity of stringed instruments. Many of the larger courts reacted by engaging string specialists as a separate group. In courts where this was the case (with Henry VIII or at the Munich court in the 1560s, for example) the result was that courts organized musicians in four distinct categories: a corps of trumpeters, a wind band, a string ensemble, and several chamber musicians. Patronage at this level was simply not an option for the cities that lacked the financial resources to compete. The solution that smaller cities found took varied forms. In Italy, as the example of Bologna has shown, a city could ask the wind players to double on strings (Bologna in addition did have trumpeters and a few chamber musicians on staff as well). Most cities to the north were unable even to match support at this level. In cities such as Antwerp, one civic ensemble was expected to provide all of the options desired; one ensemble could appear as a trumpet band, a shawm ensemble, a consort of cornetts and sackbuts, or as an ensemble of stringed instruments.

2 | A source-based history of Renaissance instrumental music

To understand how instruments were employed by Renaissance musicians and how they were deployed across an extraordinarily wide landscape of cultural settings requires different fundamentals of organization than for any later period. Prior to 1600 (and with the exception of solo music, of course) composers of instrumental music did not mandate specific instrumentation in their scores. The title pages of both the *Music nova* (1540_3) and Jacques Buus's *Recercari* (1547_1), for example, state that the pieces are intended for "organ and other instruments," though without further precision. Nor did instrumentalists even require dedicated instrumental publications since they played directly from vocal scores, the title pages of many chanson publications from the sixteenth century explicitly acknowledging vocal or instrumental performance. Pierre Attaingnant's *Vingt & sept chansons musicales a quatre parties*... of 1533_3 contains chansons that are fully texted in all of the voices, but could also be played by flute, recorder, or by both instruments.[1] Thus, because instrumentalists so frequently performed or memorized from vocal scores, Howard Brown's important bibliography of instrumental music printed before 1600 reasonably could have included *every* music book printed during the sixteenth century, a possibility he well understood:

> There is scarcely any vocal music at all [during the sixteenth century] that cannot be played on instruments and that was not so performed. In other words, the ensemble counterpart of the lute and keyboard intabulation is missing completely from the present volume; to understand what actually happened during the century the reader should remember that the instrumentalist also performed "vocal" music.[2]

In the years around 1600, composers began to indicate specific instruments in their scores, most notably by Giovanni Gabrieli (see below, *SBS* 15). They also wrote more idiomatically, taking into account the capabilities and sound of specific instruments, resulting in fewer prints intended for

---

[1] Attaingnant designates these instruments with letters – *a* for flute, *b* for recorder, and *ab* for both.
[2] Brown, *1600*, 3.

instruments of "all sorts," the rubric that is common in many sixteenth-century ensemble publications. Let us look at the change that occurred during the new century in another way. In writing a chapter on the use of the violin during the seventeenth century, one could draw upon a base of dozens of sources for which the composer expressly called for the instrument. For an analogous treatment of the fifteenth-century fiddle – an instrument certainly as common in its time as the seventeenth-century violin was in its own – the contrast could not be more stark: we do not possess a single musical source that calls for the instrument. In sum, Renaissance composers certainly knew the capabilities of instruments and expected frequent instrumental participation in performances of their music. Performers also had clear understandings about when and whether a particular piece might be sung or played, but decisions on such matters were left to conventions relating to the context of the moment and were not dictated by a score or an ideology. With the exception of music intended for solo keyboard and lute, Renaissance music *written* for specific instruments is almost non-existent; the repertory *performed* by instruments, on the other hand, is vast, drawing on literally all the genres of the era.

Thus, the decision about how to organize a history of Renaissance instrumental music can take a variety of paths. Perhaps the most efficient was that presented by Brown in his *Music in the Renaissance* (1976). Drawing upon his unparalleled knowledge of the sources and his clear advocacy for including instrumental music within the historical narrative of Renaissance music, he chose to be reductive, dividing instrumental music into distinct categories – dance music, intabulations, idiomatic pieces, and so forth. We have chosen a different approach, deciding instead to organize our history around a series of source-based studies consisting of a selection of manuscripts and prints drawn from various periods in the Renaissance, in chronological order (insofar as precise dates of non-printed sources can be ascertained). Brown's reductive approach distills instrumental music into useful, artificially clear categories by genre, but the performer's reality was messier, with constant interaction between memory, adaptation, improvisation, and increasingly through the Renaissance, performance from written scores. By following an organization around sources, rather than genre, category, or instrument, a history of instrumental music is presented neither as a deterministic, evolutionary, or theoretically anchored series of events, nor as a series of distinct categories, but as one in which old and new styles often comingle, where regional styles are as important as the ones at the traditional centers of music production, and in which revival and innovation, and amateur and professional contributions are part of the overall narrative.

The following sources thus draw on a diverse collection of manuscripts from courtly, liturgical, domestic, and urban settings as well as from the thriving commercial business of Renaissance print culture. Both the choice of the source-based approach and our particular selection of individual sources extend from the fundamental argument in this study: instrumental music was pervasive and inclusive in the Renaissance. There was no center and no periphery: as much music was heard in a small town or a tiny provincial court as in large urban centers or in the rarified lands of Philip the Good; as much music was improvised as committed to notation, and by the sixteenth century, just as much, if not more, was played by amateurs as by professionals. We have selected our sources to reflect these realities.

* * *

1) A variable repertory for instrumentalists: Faenza, Biblioteca comunale 117 (*c*.1380–1426) – *Faenza*

The numerous illustrations of instrumentalists in the early fifteenth century are unanimous on one point: minstrels, soft or loud, are never shown performing from written music. The surviving sources of music of that era largely reflect that and are almost exclusively slanted to the needs of vocal performers. However, several invaluable exceptions have survived, and these provide a reasonably clear picture – indeed, probably a retrospective one – of instrumental repertories during the fifteenth century.

The most important instrumental source that survives from the early fifteenth century is *Faenza*. Its format as a two-part score has engendered a good deal of debate about whether it was intended for solo keyboard or for an instrumental duo.[3] While the weight of current scholarly opinion favors solo performance, one quite reasonable compromise is that the codex was put to use by a performer in the mold of Conrad Paumann, an outstanding player of both organ and lute. Such a musician could have played the sacred items in church on a large fixed organ, or, perhaps, on a positive organ, and, when desired, could have played the secular items in

---

[3] The possibility that *Faenza* might be intended for lute is explored in Timothy J. McGee, "Instruments and the Faenza Codex," *EM* 14 (1986), 480–90. Roland Eberlin, however, argued against that proposal in his article "The Faenza Codex: Music for Organ or for Lute Duet?" *EM* 20 (1992), 461–6.

an ensemble, perhaps with portative organ (or fiddle) playing the soprano and lute covering the lower part.[4]

The repertory of *Faenza* includes sacred pieces, both motets and liturgical items including portions of the Mass. In this very early collection, we are reminded that all classes of minstrels consistently included sacred items in their repertories, and that all extensive collections that contained music that might have been played included at least some sacred pieces. Indeed, from very early in the fifteenth century even trumpeters and shawmists, more often involved in distinctly secular activities, were present at the most solemn liturgical celebrations. No description or source provides any specifics as to what the contemporary wind musicians actually played, but their contributions were certainly more in the line of decoration to the ceremony rather than participation in the actual items in the liturgy. *Faenza*, however, includes Kyrie and Gloria settings that are laid out for *alternatim* performance. That is, they were designed for performance within the liturgy, for an organist alternating with singers.

The secular pieces in *Faenza* include many arrangements. One group of these represent local, that is, Italian, repertory (the manuscript was compiled in northern Italy), but a majority are versions of pieces based on French models. From this earliest of sources, we see a phenomenon that characterized the entire Renaissance – the chanson formed the cornerstone of the instrumental repertory everywhere. Some of the secular pieces are reasonably current with the copying of the manuscript, yet others, such as those by Machaut, were several decades old. As we have noted earlier, the inclusion of such retrospective items is a feature we expect of instrumental music, which because of its emphasis on performance from memory, by its nature tends to retain items in repertory for some time. Interestingly, the arrangements are consistently of two parts, even when (as was most often the case) the model called for three parts. In a very few passages in the manuscript a third voice is indicated; this does not alter the fundamental

---

[4] The various views on the manuscript are summarized in Pedro Memelsdorff, "*Motti a motti*: Reflections on a Motet Intabulation of the Early Quattrocento," *Recercare* 10 (1998), 39–68. Memelsdorff offers yet another perspective on the manuscript, where he sees evidence for what he terms "interactive performance." The notation of *Faenza*, as he reads it, suggests that certain passages in the manuscript are so written to indicate that the player was to interact with other performers while in the act of reading the notation. An updated and expanded version of Memelsdorff's views is available in his "The Filiation and Transmission of Instrumental Polyphony in Late Medieval Italy: The Codex Faenza 117," PhD diss., University of Utrecht (2010). See also Pedro Memelsdorff, *The Codex Faenza 117: Instrumental Polyphony in Late Medieval Italy; Introductory Study and Facsimile Edition* (Lucca, 2013), vol. I, Introductory Study; vol. 2, Facsimile Edition.

approach in which the discant and tenor only of the original appear in *Faenza*. Also interesting are the few instances in which there occur fairly long rests in an original tenor; in these passages the arranged tenor inserts a segment drawn from the contratenor.[5] Also, as Pirrotta pointed out in the *Faenza* version of "Sotto l'imperio," the diminution "represents a composite line, taking and ornamenting whichever of the two original cantus voices is on top at a given moment."[6]

Scholars and performers have rightly focused on the highly embellished discant diminutions in *Faenza*, which provide a virtual catalogue of approaches to decoration from the early fifteenth century – skill at adding diminutions, as will be shown below, being a basic requirement of professional instrumentalists throughout the Renaissance. The tenors, on the other hand, stay much closer to the originals, with only a few restrained diminutions. As a general approach, this parallels what is found later in *Buxheim* (although the *Buxheim* intabulations include all three parts where three-part originals are the models). A few of the pieces in *Faenza* are apparently independent instrumental music, including at least two that are clearly dance settings, "Bel fiore dança" and "Biance flour," which is based on the dance tune "Colinetto." The importance of these is that they serve as a reminder of the extent to which much of *Faenza* represents music from the world of the minstrel, which is underlined in that the untitled textless piece on fol. 94v is, in fact, "Souvent m'espas," whose tenor appears twice in the Zorzi Trombetta manuscript, described below. Nothing is more significant in *Faenza* than the window it provides of the demands made of successful performers in the early Renaissance with its incessant mixture of sacred and secular and its jumble of international hits, local favorites, sacred items, and dance tunes.

2) Zorzi Trombetta and a watershed moment for ensemble instrumental music: London, British Library, Cotton MS Titus A. xxvi (*c*.1440) – *Zorzi*

In 1444, a young musician calling himself "Zorzi Trombetta" (Zorzi = Giorgio in the Venetian dialect) signed on for service on one of the

---

[5] For an example, see Dragan Plamenac, ed., *Keyboard Music of the Late Middle Ages in Codex Faenza 117* (n.p., 1972), number 30, "Aquila altera," 81, mm. 18–19.
[6] Pirrotta, quoted in Memelsdorff, "*Motti a motti*," 55; Pirrotta suggested the term "cantus continuus" for this procedure; see ibid., 54.

London, British Library, Cotton MS Titus A. xxvi (c.1440) 67

Venetian galleys plying the Flanders and England route.[7] He was not the only musician involved as there exist payment records, in addition to Zorzi, for two shawm players. This indicates that our Zorzi served a double function: he played trumpet to sound naval signals, and played a slide instrument, probably an early version of the trombone, with the wind ensemble when services of a more purely musical nature were required.

Zorzi had an inquisitive mind, as is revealed in a notebook he began to assemble in earnest in 1444. The topics run through a fascinating variety of subjects; his jottings include notes on navigational aids, astronomical items, and treatments for medical problems. Tucked in among all that is a section of landmark importance concerning the development of instrumental music: some ten pages of music spread over six folios. The section is in two main categories. The first consists of a few folios that Zorzi evidently acquired somewhere in his travels: folios 3r–5r contain four chansons (three in three parts, one for two) including the widely disseminated "Une fois avant que mourir." These were evidently copied by an unknown professional scribe sometime before 1440. Folio 6r contains the tenor and contratenor of Dunstable's "Puisque m'amour" in the hand of a second, also unknown scribe, again probably a professional. Of central importance is that the notation of the tenors takes a highly distinctive form. They are written in a simplified notation that avoids many of the complications of the mensural system. Repeated shorter notes, for example, are written instead of a long note (long notes could have either a duple or triple value in the complex mensural scheme; one had to know an elaborate set of rules to know which was appropriate). Zorzi adopted the same kind of notation in the portion of the collection that is in his own hand. This simplified approach does not conform to the notation in manuscripts prepared for the elite vocal ensembles of the period. This first section appears to be in the hands of professionals, that is, by two scribes who

---

[7] This is the date that Zorzi's association with galley service is first indicated in the manuscript. For a brief description, see Fallows, *A Catalogue of Polyphonic Song*, 26. More extensive is Daniel Leech-Wilkinson, "Il libro di appunti di un suonatore di tromba del quindecesimo secolo," *RIM* 16 (1981), 16–39; the importance of *Zorzi* in relation to instrumental performance practice is discussed by Lorenz Welker, "'Alta Capella' zur Ensemblepraxis der Blasinstrumente im 15. Jahrhundert," *BJhM* 7 (1983), 159–61. Zorzi clearly signed the manuscript, as on fol. 2r where he wrote "this book was written in the year of our Lord 1444 by Zorzi Trombetta da Modon" ("in nomine domini 1444 se fatto questo libro per zorzi trombetta da modon"). This indicates that Zorzi was from Modon, a small port city under Venetian control at the tip of the western Peloponnese peninsula in Greece. The city, though small, formed a vital link in the trade between Venice and the east.

prepared these pages either on commission or for sale. This in turn suggests that there was a kind of market for such items, but the products of this market have almost completely disappeared from view. These were evidently prepared in small sets of only a few folios, and were of a quite practical nature. They would have been carried around and seen heavy use, and, of course, after three or four decades the repertory would have been quite dated. The almost zero survival rate of such tatty pages of obsolete music indicates that when their useful life was over they ended up in a rubbish heap, and in fact Zorzi's little collection survives only because it was included within a larger manuscript of a non-musical nature.

The second section of the manuscript is of parallel importance, but for a different reason. This section was written by Zorzi himself, and can be divided into three categories. One consists of tenors of two named chansons ("En ce printemps" and "Souvent mes pas") and of a "balattina franzese." Zorzi also included one tenor evidently for dancing (with the title "gie se far danser le dames"). Finally, in perhaps the most significant section, he wrote out the tenor of Dunstable's "Puisque m'amour," and then added several efforts to provide a contratenor to go with that tenor. These are not completely successful according to conventional rules, in that there are a few raw dissonances and instances of parallel writing that would not be acceptable as sophisticated counterpoint. Still, it seems clear that Zorzi had more than a rudimentary knowledge of how to combine voices, and in fact some of the more crude effects are also present in contemporary sources as *Faenza*. The paucity of instrumental sources in this period means that caution is in order, but it would appear that instrumentalists at least up to mid-century indulged in occasional dissonances and parallelisms that were not part of the high-art style of, for example, the contemporary chansons of Dufay.

Although *Zorzi* is quite small, it does include both French chansons and dances. The inclusion of the chansons confirms that the chanson was a basic building block of the secular repertory throughout Europe in the fifteenth century – even for a young musician holding a relatively low-ranking job as a member of a ship's wind band. Still, those few pages represent a landmark moment in the history of ensemble instrumental music, for they yield a first explicit glimpse of oral musical practices that had been lying below the surface for many decades.[8]

---

[8] One further item of interest in *Zorzi* is that on fol. 55r, Zorzi inserted two drawings of what appear to be an instrument with a double slide. The drawings may be seen in Stewart Carter,

3) A compendium of fifteenth-century keyboard techniques: The Buxheim Organ Book, Munich, Bayerische Staatsbibliothek, Cim. 352b (formerly Mus.ms. 3725), (*c*.1460–70) – *Buxheim*

As Kerala Snyder has written, the organ "invites us to reflect upon matters beyond music," and its surviving early repertory and its depictions in art testify indeed to its dual role as instrument of function and of contemplation.[9] Organs, portable and fixed, are widely represented in the hands of angels in paintings of the fourteenth and fifteenth centuries, and the symbolism attached to the organ's role as providing heavenly music, or as the provider of sounds of profound devotion, was common in the early to mid-fifteenth century. By around 1450, however, it is clear that the organ repertory was broadened to include a great deal of secular music, and with this came a change in its function and in the compositional techniques of its players. While keyboard sources are infrequent in most regions in Europe, for Germany more than twenty fifteenth-century manuscripts have survived. These are enough to begin the description of one of the most important of these early keyboard sources prior to 1500, the so-called Buxheim Organ Book, one of the largest sources of any kind in the fifteenth century.[10]

Many of these sources are fragments, but the Ileborgh (1448) and Lochamer (*c*.1450) collections are ample.[11] Leaving *Buxheim* aside for the moment, the earlier sources are quite mixed in nature. Some include pedagogical material. In the case of Lochamer, this is in the form of an early version of a *Fundamentum* by Conrad Paumann. Since these are organ

---

The Trombone in the Renaissance: A History in Pictures and Documents (Hillsdale, NY, 2012), 18. These drawings suggest that when Zorzi picked up an instrument to play with his shawm-playing colleagues, that instrument was an early form of the trombone. This would seem verified by information from Zorzi's subsequent career. In 1458 a Giorgio da Modon was a player of trombone in the Doge's official wind ensemble in Venice. This was almost certainly the galley musician of the 1440s, in that it is improbable that two musicians of the same name, from the same small city, would be active in Venetian service. In any case, Zorzi's drawings are among the earliest evidence we have that an instrument with a double slide had arrived on the scene. See Baroncini, "Zorzi Trombetta," 59–82, and also his "Zorzi Trombetta da Modon," 1–17.

[9] Kerala Snyder, ed., *The Organ as a Mirror of Its Time: North European Reflections, 1610–2000* (Oxford, 2002), 1.

[10] On *Buxheim*, see Berta Antonia Wallner, ed. *Das Buxheimer Orgelbuch. Das Erbe Deutscher Musik*, vols. 37–9 (Kassel-Basel-London, 1958).

[11] The Lochamer manuscript is in Berlin, Staatsbibliothek Preußischer Kulturbesitz MS Mus. 40021. The Ileborgh tablature, formerly owned by the Curtis Institute of Music in Philadelphia, is now in a private collection.

sources, the inclusion of sacred items is hardly surprising. *Windsheim* includes a *Summum Sanctus* and *Patrem*, while *Lochamer* includes two short pieces, one titled *Magnificat sexti toni*, the other called *O clemens*, as well as a German sacred song, *Benedicte almechtiger got*.[12] What is unexpected is that a majority of the named pieces are secular songs. *Lochamer* contains, among others, German songs such as "Mit ganzem Willen" and "Des Klaffers neyden" as well as a setting of the *basse danse* tenor "Une fois avant que mourir." A few pieces titled *Preambulum* are scattered throughout the sources; these are short, unpretentious pieces, but are clearly the forerunners of the idiomatic non-imitative fantasia of the early sixteenth century. These earlier German sources are more insular than the sophisticated *Faenza*, but they contain the same general kinds of pieces. In *Windsheim*, the right hand is quite active and embellished, while the left hand is almost entirely restricted to one long note at a time. The left hand is slightly more active in the Ileborgh source, and distinctly more so in *Lochamer*, which contains far more two-part writing than is the case in *Buxheim*. Similarly, the harmonic progressions earlier are often distinctly raw, with strongly audible parallel fifths, for example, and grating dissonances on occasion. The harmonic vocabulary in *Lochamer*, in contrast, is smoother and conforms more to the norms of contemporary vocal counterpoint.

A comparison between the versions of Paumann's *Fundamentum* in *Lochamer* with those in *Buxheim* suggests that a change in style indeed occurred just after around the middle of the fifteenth century. The first of the two *Fundamenta* includes the ascription *Fundamentum organisandi Magistri Conradi Paumanns Ceci de Nüremerga Anno [14]52* – which is almost certainly the date when the manuscript was copied rather than the date when Paumann produced this early version. Paumann had left Nuremberg for service with the Duke of Bavaria in Munich in 1450. Archival sources after 1450 identify him as associated with the ducal court, not with Nuremberg. The musician who wrote out *Lochamer* probably knew Paumann personally, and, to be sure, Paumann was a native of Nuremberg. Thus, a dating of the *Lochamer* version of the *Fundamentum* at *c.*1445 seems plausible. *Buxheim* was assembled between 1460 and 1470, and the *Fundamenta* by Paumann it contains were likely produced by *c.*1455. In any case, they are more complicated. The general division of labor, with the top part carrying the embellished melody and the left hand providing harmonic support, is retained. The writing is consistently for

---

[12] *Windsheim* is also described briefly and edited in Apel, *Keyboard Music*, v–vi and 15–18.

three parts, however, and the left hand is distinctly more complicated in its contrapuntal makeup. The harmonic treatment is more sophisticated and the dissonance treatment smoother. The difference in sound is unmistakable. In fact, one German song in *Buxheim*, "Bekenne myn klag," is ascribed to Paumann, and the piece is a completely successful example of contemporary three-part writing, matching the standard of the chanson composers in the orbit of the Burgundian court.[13]

In many ways, *Buxheim* provides a northern version of *Faenza*, discussed above. In both there are sacred items, including some that could be included in the liturgy, an international repertory (French chansons), local items (Italian in *Faenza*, German in *Buxheim*), and settings of dances. *Buxheim* goes beyond *Faenza* in that it includes versions of Paumann's *Fundamenta* along with some sixteen free preludes. The manuscript itself was probably put together at some remove from Munich and the immediate circle of Conrad Paumann, but it was closely tied to him and undoubtedly reflects the type of repertory Paumann would have played as an organist and chamber musician in a noble court.

What these sources suggest is that from the early fifteenth century onward, all minstrels (chamber musicians as well as wind players) were expected to produce a wide range of music. For all active professionals, a knowledge of the international repertory (French chansons) was indispensable, as well as familiarity with local pieces. And, of course, providing music for dancing was a standard requirement for all employed instrumentalists. They would have been called on to play sacred pieces where appropriate, and while only organists actually played liturgical pieces, a great variety of minstrels did in fact perform within church services, given that chamber players and sophisticated wind musicians all performed motets.

4) Ensemble instrumental music moves to center stage: Rome, Biblioteca Casanatense, MS 2856 (*c*.1481–90?) – *Casanatense*

Between *Zorzi* and about 1480 only fragmentary sources of instrumental ensemble music survive.[14] But beginning just before 1480 a series of rapidly

---

[13] The same piece is titled *Wiplich figur* in the Schedel Liederbuch; see Fallows, *A Catalogue of Polyphonic Songs*, 493.

[14] In Peter Spörl's songbook (the so-called Mondsee Liederbuch, Vienna, Österriechische Nationalbibliothek, MS 2856, from shortly after 1450) are two pieces indicated as calling for

overlapping developments occurred, the outlines of which we can trace through the sources, both in manuscripts and (after 1501) in prints. Most of the relevant sources are Italian, but one German collection, the Glogauer manuscript from *c.*1480, contains a substantial number of unidentified textless pieces.[15] And while it has been argued that these could have provided the basis for added vernacular (German) texts, or could have been simply vocalized with neutral syllables, one common performance option was certainly that of playing the repertory using instruments.

The Italian secular sources, however, yield the clearest picture of the definitive stylistic change that was taking place. Several manuscripts are extant that were prepared in this region during the years just prior to about 1480, two of which are *Pixérécourt* and *Florence 176*. These sources contain primarily French chansons in the traditional mold, that is, courtly chansons based on one of the *formes fixes*, the *rondeau* being favored over the *ballade* and *virelai*. These manuscripts are most often provided with texts and give every indication that a primary performance option was vocal.

Definite change arrived after 1480, however, as is clearly demonstrated in *Casanatense*. Carefully written on vellum by professional scribes, this is an extensive anthology of 163 folios containing 123 pieces. The dating of the manuscript has roused a formidable debate that has involved three of the preeminent scholars of our time. Lewis Lockwood proposed a dating of 1481, identifying the manuscript with one described as "a la pifarescha" in contemporary Ferrarese court records.[16] Joshua Rifkin rejected that date, pointing to several features of the manuscript that argue for a compilation no earlier than about 1491.[17] In response, David Fallows,

---

instrumental participation. Trent 89 (Trent, Castello del Buonconsiglio, Monumenti e Collezioni Provinciali, MS 89 [now 1376]) includes, among other items, probably the earliest version (from about 1475) of Martini's "La Martinella."

[15] Cracow, Biblioteka Jagiellońska, Ms. Mus. 40098. The manuscript is actually a set of three part books – a very early example of this format. The Glogauer collection contained sacred and secular music for two, three, and four parts. For a facsimile edition, see Jessie Ann Owens, ed., *Kraków, Biblioteka Jagiellónska, Glogauer Liederbuch.*" In Renaissance Music in Facsimile, ed. Howard Mayer Brown, Frank A. D'Accone, and Jessie Ann Owens, vol. 6 (New York and London, 1986).

[16] Lockwood first presented his evidence in his *Music in Renaissance Ferrara*, 269–77. He subsequently updated his views in Lewis Lockwood, ed., *A Ferrarese Chansonnier, Roma, Biblioteca Casanatense 2856* (Lucca, 2002), XI–XXX; for his response to Joshua Rifkin, see XXXI–XXXII.

[17] Joshua Rifkin, "Munich, Milan, and a Marian Motet: Dating Josquin's *Ave Maria... virgo serena*," *JAMS* 56 (2003), 316–21. As this book was in its final stages we received word that Bonnie Blackburn has discovered letters written to the Ferrarese court from Hungary in 1486 enclosing music by Agricola and promising to send a Mass and more chansons. The fact that

while accepting some portions of Rifkin's argument, in the end, and with some reluctance, agreed with Lockwood's dating of the manuscript to the early 1480s.[18] The disagreements have raised doubts about whether *Casanatense* is indeed the actual source cited in the Ferrarese documents, and, by extension, whether it can be connected directly to the wind band at the court of Ferrara. A crucial distinction here is that the archival description in question is not "per la pifarescha" (*for* the *pifari*) but "a la pifarescha," which translates more generally as "representing the repertory (or 'in the manner') of the pifari." Whatever its actual date, *Casanatense* could certainly fit that interpretation. As Lockwood emphasized, it includes at least a dozen pieces that appear suitable for instrumental and not vocal performance. None of these pieces have texts in any of the sources that convey them, and their forms do not fit any of the conventional formal schemes of the time. It must be said, though, that the vast majority of the collection consists of French chansons. As noted above, however, this is perfectly consistent with a potentially instrumental collection, as the chanson formed the foundation of the instrumental repertory. Moreover, in about 1480 Italian scribes began to take a markedly different approach by omitting texts entirely from secular musical manuscripts. *Casanatense* was one of the first to show this, and not only was it prepared without any texts at all, many of the incipits provided are hopelessly – "hilariously," according to Fallows – garbled. Finding matching texts for a vocal performance would be very difficult. Still, there is nothing in *Casanatense* that could not be sung. One possible scenario is that the songbook could have served Isabella d'Este, after moving on to Mantua as she wed Francesco Gonzaga, as a souvenir anthology of the music she had heard played by the superb Ferrarese wind ensemble during her early youth in the 1480s.[19] In Mantua, that collection could have provided raw material for performances by winds, strings, or even voices (if appropriate texts could be found). The medium would not have been as important as the message.

If *Zorzi* can be considered a milestone in the evolution of instrumental music, *Casanatense* offers a marker of equal significance. Whether or not it is the collection of 1481, it contains several pieces by Johannes Martini that

---

Agricola's music was known in Ferrara at this date suggests that the manuscript was compiled after 1486 and removes a major objection to a dating before 1490.

[18] Both of the statements may be found in Fallows, *Josquin*, 68.

[19] The wedding was in 1490, but the betrothal ceremony had taken place ten years earlier. Lockwood proposed that the preparation of *Casanatense* was linked to the earlier event.

appear to be almost certainly composed with instrumental performance as a primary option. In his detailed analysis of Martini's "La martinella," Lockwood demonstrated that the piece was most probably conceived from the outset as instrumental.[20] Even more striking is the new compositional approach that Martini explored in a piece titled "Tout joyeux."[21] Most of the French chansons in *Casanatense* essentially represent a continuation of the courtly chanson seen in the secular works of Dufay at mid-century. Usually cast in one of the fixed forms, their structure is based on a tenor/discant duet with an added contratenor. Phrases are long, and the emphasis is on elegance and variety. Imitation appears occasionally, but is most often restricted to the tenor/discant duet. "Tout joyeux" takes a very different approach, in which all three voices share in the imitations throughout. The phrases are short with strongly profiled melodies that are easily perceived as they move from voice to voice. Cadences tend to be strongly outlined with a clear emphasis on the main tonal area of the piece. This style is ideally suited to instrumental performance. Most important is that instrumental performances of this period now conformed completely to the high art music of the time with none of the jarring dissonances or rough parallelisms that still lingered in Zorzi's counterpoint.

Casanatense was likely prepared for, and indeed probably at, the Ferrarese court. These assumptions are important in terms of linking the collection to instrumental performance, for Duke Ercole had assembled a formidable stable of players. An obvious fit for the repertory was the superb wind band, which could play pieces with combinations of shawms and trombone. The wind players were also doublers, however, and could easily have played the pieces on recorders. The two Della Violas were on staff, and on occasion played with yet another member of the family, so another option would have been performance on bowed strings, perhaps early forms of the viol (Michel Schubinger, a wind player, was also known to have played the viol, so he too could have joined the Della Violas). On at least one occasion, Pietrobono was associated with the Della Violas, so yet a further possibility was an ensemble of mixed colors, plucked lute with bowed strings. And, of course, one of the skills of Pietrobono's tenorist, Francesco Malacise,

---

[20] The pieces are listed in Lockwood, *Music in Renaissance Ferrara*, 273; for the discussion of "La Martinella" see 274–7.

[21] *Casanatense*, fol. 117v–118; for a modern edition see Edward G. Evans, ed., *Johannes Martini Secular Pieces* (Madison, 1975), 71–3.

was in adapting multiple parts into his performance. Of the many authors who praised Pietrobono's skill as a performer, Lippo Brandolino in 1473 astutely mentioned the synchronized coordination between the plectrum and his fingers, that he played English, French, Spanish, and Italian pieces, and, most interestingly, that in "the whole song he goes beyond prescribed boundaries and he continually invents new modes"; Brandolino even acknowledges Pietrobono's *tenorista*, Malacise, "who holds firm and maintains the unmoving tenor."[22]

The combination of Pietrobono and his tenorist might not have yielded ideal clarity to the contrapuntal interplay in a piece such as Martini's "Tout joyeux," but the result would have been more than satisfactory. In a few years, payroll records in Ferrara indicate the presence of two chitarrino players along with the tenorist. As for the possibility of an ensemble of three lutenists, Ferrarese court records indicate that in most years only two lutenists were on staff, one the player of chitarrino (normally Pietrobono) and the other, the tenorist.[23]

In sum, *Casanatense* is likely an example of the instrumental repertory as known at the court of Ferrara in the 1480s. As with earlier sources, the chanson formed the foundation of the repertory, with the key distinction being that the high art style had been completely assimilated by the players. A new relationship between composers, singers, and instrumentalists was now in play.

---

[22] Translated in Alberto Gallo, *Music in the Castle: Troubadours, Books, and Orators in Italian Courts of the Thirteenth, Fourteenth, and Fifteenth Centuries* (Chicago, 1996), 90–5; 125–9.

[23] Jon Banks in *The Instrumental Consort Repertory of the Late Fifteenth Century* (Aldershot/Burlington, Vermont, 2006), 36–40, argues that, in essence, the entire three-part instrumental repertory of this period could have been played by three lutes. There is a great deal of archival evidence for performances by lute soloists and lute duos, but mentions of lute trios are rare before 1500, making his suggestion unlikely, especially given the extensive references to three-part combinations of other instruments. His discussion of the musical repertory itself, however, is insightful. Note that Stefano Pio, *Viol and Lute Makers of Venice 1490–1630/Liuteria veneziana 1490–1630* (Venice, 2011), 241, has argued that a form of the viol was known in north Italy by the 1470s, a suggestion that may be supported by the recent discovery of a spectacular fresco in the cathedral of Valencia which shows a viol-playing angel painted in the 1470s by a pair of Italian artists, one of whom had worked previously at the Ferrara court. See Jordi Ballester, "An Unexpected Discovery: The Fifteenth-Century Angel Musicians of the Valencia Cathedral," *Music in Art* 33 (2008): 11–29; see also María del Carmen Pérez García, *Los ángeles músicos de la catedral de Valencia* (Valencia, 2006). On "viols" in Ferrara, see Lockwood, *Music in Renaissance Ferrara*, 318, which includes both Andrea and Zampaulo della Viola in the payroll lists for 1466; earlier, however (144), he indicated that their tenure began in 1467. In any case, the members of the Della Viola clan were resident in Ferrara at the same time as the artist of the fresco.

5) A tipping point for instrumental music: Petrucci's *Harmonice musices Odhecaton A* (Venice, 1501₁) – *Odhecaton*

Ottaviano Petrucci's landmark publication of the *Odhecaton* in 1501 served notice to the world that two fundamental aspects of music had changed.[24] The first was that a means had finally been developed for printing music, which meant new and faster access to music for a far wider public. The second aspect was that as the ninety-six pieces in the print were dispersed throughout Europe, it broadcast to musicians everywhere that the foundation of the musical vocabulary had changed.

The first clear stages of the change in musical style can be traced to two decades earlier and are most clearly seen in the secular repertory, since secular sources are more ample and provide a clearer chronological framework. These sources are primarily Italian, though the repertory is primarily French, and reveal that much of the change came about through the efforts of northern composers working in Italy. One group of extant manuscripts copied in the 1460s and 1470s yields a reliably clear picture of the style as it was practiced up into the 1470s, in which the courtly chanson style remained the model. A second group, though smaller, still gives a reasonably clear view of the situation in the early to mid-1480s, in which *Casanatense* (described above) emerges as the central source. This group of manuscripts reveals that composers, now composing in three-part textures with Martini evidently providing a kind of leadership, were exploring the potential of using consistent imitation in all parts throughout a piece.

But it is a third group of manuscripts dating from about 1490 through 1500 (including *Odhecaton*) that shows the maturation and assimilation of the new vocabulary.[25] Heinrich Isaac arrived in Florence in 1485, and he evidently became familiar with the early efforts – including those by Martini,

---

[24] The classic edition of the *Odhecaton* remains Helen Hewitt, ed., *Harmonice musices Odhecaton A* (Cambridge, MA, 1942; reprint, New York, 1978). For a performing edition with introduction and an invaluable set of notes, see David Fallows, general editor, *Harmonice Musices Odhecaton A: One Hundred Songs of Harmonic Music* (Watertown, MA, 2001, revised edition, 2003). For a discussion of the source itself in scrupulous detail, see Stanley Boorman, *Ottaviano Petrucci: Catalogue Raisonné* (Oxford and New York, 2006), 458–68.

[25] The first group of manuscripts includes *Pixérécourt* and *Florence 176*, mentioned above, as well as Florence, Biblioteca Riccardiana, MS 2356. The second includes *Florence 229, Casanatense*, Florence, Biblioteca Nazionale Centrale, MS Magl. XIX. 178, Rome, Vatican City, Biblioteca Apostolica Vaticana, Cappella Giulia, XIII.27, and Bologna, Civico Museo Bibliografico Musicale MS Q16. The third group includes Bologna, Civico Museo Bibliografico Musicale, MS Q17, and Florence, Biblioteca Riccardiana, MS 2794, as well as the printed source, *Odhecaton*.

mentioned above – at composing in the new imitative style. He quickly incorporated them into his own works and produced a string of three-part pieces, such as "La morra" and "Helas." These were soon widely circulated – both "La morra" and "Helas," for example, were included in *Odhecaton* – and served to define the new style to the wider music public. This approach was based on imitation running through all parts. Each phrase would be introduced by a short melodic motive with a clear rhythmic profile, and every phrase would come to a clear end before the next phrase began. The style was balanced, the rhythms and motives highly coherent, and the overall shape of the piece easily and naturally perceived. A visual analogy to this development might be suggested by the transition in art from the thematic and organizational disparity in triptych composition to the new cohesion and balance exhibited in single-panel paintings of the fifteenth century. After about 1485, imitation was embedded as a basic component of musical composition, initiating a long tradition that climaxes with the fugues of J.S. Bach. Note that from the beginning, with pieces such as Isaac's "La morra," the abstract nature of the pieces adapts very well to instrumental performance. "La morra" is never provided with texts in any of its Italian sources, and was certainly conceived with the possibility that it would be played by instruments. As momentous as the developments of the late 1480s might have been, Isaac continued to move on, and after about 1490 turned increasingly to working with textures of four parts. By the early 1490s, imitation in four parts became the standard texture for secular music.

Odhecaton contains ninety-six compositions, with two five-part pieces and the others roughly equally divided between those for three and for four parts. Several of the four-part versions, though, were originally written for three, with Petrucci's editor providing an alternate fourth part (indicated as *si placet*) in an attempt to modernize them for a contemporary audience. Text is provided for only the first piece, de Orto's *Ave Maria*, and even there it appears in such an erratic manner that performance of the work is most awkward. The composers are all northern. Several were active in the 1470s (Hayne, Tinctoris, and the young Compère) and are represented by three-part settings in the older courtly chanson style of the *formes fixes*. More prominent are the three-part pieces in the new popular chanson style, including the two by Isaac mentioned above, "La alphonsina" (Ghiselin), "La stangetta" (possibly by Weerbeke), and two pieces by Josquin ("Cela sans plus" and "La plus des plus"). The four-part pieces in general reveal the innovative path being taken by the composers in the 1490s, such as Isaac's "Et qui la dira." The mature Compère's interest also ran also in this direction, and his "Nous sommes de l'ordre de Saynt

Babuyn" is a charming *tour de force* using limited melodic material in repetitive patterns within highly imitative textures. Josquin provided two pieces, both of which maintain links to the fixed form tradition. His "Adieu mes amours" (based on a virelai melody) is canonic throughout, while his "Bergerette savoyene," while not strictly canonic, is riddled with short canonic interchanges. Similarly Pierre de La Rue's affecting "Por quoy non" is apparently a setting of a rondeau, but is a stunning display of the potential of combining imitative counterpoint with contrasting sections of chordal writing. The same combination of imitation with homophonic writing is found in Obrecht's delightful "Tsat een meskin," though based on a bawdy song rather than an elevated courtly melody. In sum, *Odhecaton* provides a clear snapshot of the varieties of repertory developed from the late 1480s through the late 1490s.

The question of Petrucci's intentions in terms of medium has provoked a good deal of debate. Though *Odhecaton* (except for the one piece) provides no texts, quite a number of the chansons are found elsewhere fully texted. Still, while Petrucci was probably hoping for some international success, his first priority was for sales in Italy. And here, as in the case of other sources such as *Casanatense*, it is quite unclear to what extent Italian audiences would have had French texts available. In addition, as suggested above, a distinct portion of the repertory seemed obviously designed for instrumental performance. All in all, this has led David Fallows to conclude in his edition of *Odhecaton* that this volume and the two others in the series that Petrucci soon produced "were surely intended for instruments," a view that other specialists have found persuasive.[26]

6) The end of the beginning of lute music: Francesco Spinacino, *Intabulatura de Lauto Libro primo/Libro secondo* (Venice, 1507$_2$) – *Spinacino*

Archival, visual, and manuscript evidence uniformly attests to the lute's standing as the preeminent "soft" instrument of the fifteenth century, due

---

[26] Fallows, *Harmonice Musices Odhecaton*, xiii. See also Banks, *The Instrumental Consort Repertory*, 49; Boorman came to a similar conclusion, suggesting that the lack of text "argues for a larger market that was unable to cope with French texts," though he adds the interesting proviso that while Petrucci was aiming his volume at "people who need not necessarily have known any French... [the edition] may have resulted in instrumental performance, but that was effect rather than cause" (*Ottaviano Petrucci*, 270).

mainly to its adaptability to many roles and musical contexts. Until around the middle of the century, lutenists played melodies in mixed ensembles, often in duos with portative organ or harp. After 1450, the lute–lute duo becomes more or less standardized with one lute taking on the role of providing support. In Italy this second player was often identified as a "tenorist," making this support function explicit. At about the same time a single lute was also increasingly called on to provide accompaniment for courtly song.[27] Since almost all of this music was improvised, memorized, or played from vocal scores, we possess very few notated lute sources from this period, and there is no manuscript trail at all that leads to the actual repertory of any of the great fifteenth-century exponents of the instrument, such as Pietrobono.[28] It therefore seems ironic that our most detailed look at the largely unwritten (and, therefore, unpreserved) fifteenth-century lute tradition should be through the lens of the earliest surviving manuscripts and primarily through the first *printed* books of lute music, Francesco Spinacino's *Intabulatura de Lauto Libro primo* and *Libro secondo*, published by Petrucci in 1507. Closely connected to the late fifteenth-century chanson repertory contained in Petrucci's *Odhecaton* of 1501 (described above), *Spinacino* reveals the musical choices and performance practices of fifteenth-century lute players, and the techniques they used in adapting vocal music to their instrument. Facing forward, but looking back, *Spinacino* offers a bifocal view of lute music around 1500. It opens a new chapter in the history of instrumental music as the first printed lute books of tablature; at the same time it preserves, even memorializes, the unwritten practices of a previous generation of lute players.

    A direct ancestral line to *Spinacino* is difficult to establish, but an important "dotted line" candidate is the small heart-shaped manuscript of possibly Venetian provenance that is now located in Pesaro, Biblioteca

---

[27] On the emergence of the lute duo in German music of the fifteenth century, see Polk, *German Instrumental Music*, 25–8, and Keith Polk, "Voices and Instruments: Soloists and Ensembles in the 15th Century," *EM* 18 (1990), 179–98. For a general study, see Vladimir Ivanoff, "Das Lautenduo im 15. Jahrhundert," *BJhM* 8 (1984), 147–62.

[28] For studies of fifteenth-century lute sources, see Peter Danner's (though now somewhat outdated) "Before Petrucci: The Lute in the Fifteenth Century," *JLSA* 5 (1972), 4–17; David Fallows, "15th-Century Tablatures for Plucked Instruments: A Summary, a Revision, and a Suggestion." In David Fallows, *Songs and Musicians in the Fifteenth Century* (Aldershot, 1996), XIII (also in *LSJ* 19 [1977], 7–33); and Christopher Page, "The 15th-Century Lute: New and Neglected Sources," *EM* 9 (1981), 11–21. The latest and most extensive commentary thus far is in Crawford Young and Martin Kirnbauer, ed., *Frühe Lautentabulaturen im Faksimile* (Winterthur, 2003).

Oliveriana, Ms. 1144 (*Pesaro*).[29] Copied between 1480 and 1490 by several scribes, it includes among its thirty-eight pieces (including two pieces in tablature for the *lira da braccio*) arrangements of popular chansons of the period, like Hayne van Ghizeghem's widely disseminated "De tous biens playne," of which two settings appear in *Spinacino*, and many autonomous (that is, non-derivative) pieces designated as "recercare," which resemble "frozen" improvisations, consisting of scales and sequential melodic patterns, also anticipating, though in a distinctly elementary way, the ricercars that would appear later in 1507. More importantly, *Pesaro* showcases two transformational developments that took place in lute music during the second half of the fifteenth century and helped pave the way for the eventual printing of lute music by Petrucci. First, *Pesaro* may chronicle the transition from plectrum style to finger plucking technique, a development that allowed lutenists to play more complex polyphonic textures, and which must be considered as among the most important technical advances to occur in all of Renaissance instrumental music. According to Ivanoff, in *Pesaro* both plectrum *and* finger plucking technique seem to be required, corroborating visual evidence that both styles were in simultaneous use until around 1500 and that finger plucking did not become the dominant lute technique until the very beginning of the sixteenth century.[30] In a well-known passage from Marin Sanudo's diary, the lutenist Giovan Maria Alemani (Gian Maria Giudeo) is described as (still) playing with a plectrum at a Roman banquet in 1523.[31] Second, *Pesaro* testifies to both the emergence and increasingly widespread use of tablature notation. This invention is often credited to the blind German lutenist Conrad Paumann in the 1460s, through his putative development of a system in which letters of the alphabet correspond to each individual fret on the lute's

---

[29] The first detailed description of this manuscript was in Walter Rubsamen, "The Earliest French Lute Tablature?" *JAMS* 21 (1968), 286–99. A complete study, including a paleographical and historical analysis, is in Vladimir Ivanoff, *Das Pesaro-Manuskript. Ein Beitrag zur Frühgeschichte der Lautentabulatur* (Tutzing, 1988); for a modern edition of the manuscript and diplomatic facsimile, see Vladimir Ivanoff, *Eine zentrale Quelle der frühen italienischen Lautenpraxis. Edition der Handschrift Pesaro, Biblioteca Oliveriana, Ms.1144* (Tutzing, 1988). An exquisite color facsimile of the source with commentary is in Young and Kirnbauer, ed., *Frühe Lautentabulaturen im Faksimile*, 26–157.

[30] See Vladimir Ivanoff, "An Invitation to the Fifteenth-Century Plectrum Lute: The Pesaro Manuscript." In *Performance on Lute, Guitar, and Vihuela: Historical Practice and Modern Interpretation*, ed. Victor Coelho (Cambridge, 1997), 9; see also Page, "The 15th-Century Lute," 20. Crawford Young has raised doubt that it is possible to determine, as Ivanoff has proposed, which pieces in *Pesaro* are intended for plectrum lute and which are for finger technique; see Young and Kirnbauer, ed., *Frühe Lautentabulaturen*, 138–9.

[31] See Nino Pirrotta, "Music and Cultural Tendencies in Fifteenth-Century Italy," *JAMS* 19 (1966), 157–8.

neck.[32] Soon thereafter, more logical and user-friendly systems of tablature were developed in France and Italy, with French tablature remaining in use into the eighteenth century. Regardless of the national type, tablature finally provided lutenists with a notational system that was idiomatic and visually affirmative to their instrument, since it showed finger placement, not actual notes. With this notation, lute compositions could be preserved and more widely circulated, different sizes of instrument could be used without changing finger position, and with tablature being an actual "score," in which all voice parts are mounted on a single staff, it facilitated the intabulation (= arrangements in tablature) of the new three- and four-part imitative vocal music of the late fifteenth century.

It is thus no surprise that all but two of the eighty-one pieces in the Spinacino lute books are either intabulations of vocal music, with a clear preference for the chanson, or ricercars. Furthermore, most of the vocal models for these intabulations, which include compositions by Josquin, Agricola, Brumel, Ockeghem, and Hayne, had appeared earlier in *Odhecaton*. This suggests a collaborative effort between Petrucci and Spinacino in order to capitalize on the familiarity of Petrucci's earlier published material by extending its use through arrangements for lute. This was a prescient decision, for not only do intabulations make up the bulk of sixteenth-century lute music, far outnumbering ricercars, dances, or variation sets, they changed the context of music. These published arrangements broke down the barriers of access to sacred and courtly repertories, allowing them to transcend their original function and enter into secular and domestic settings.

In terms of style, Spinacino's intabulations vary according to the model. Usually, as in his arrangement of Brumel's "Una maistres" (*Libro primo*, 9), melodic lines receive extensive decoration, and in this particular work they extend to some of the very highest registers of the lute. But there are some "literal" arrangements as well, like Spinacino's intabulation of Josquin's "Comment peult avoir joye" (*Libro secondo*, 19v-20), which adds little of significance other than filling out chords and replacing long notes in the original with smaller ones. In general, though, most intabulations are characterized by the addition of new material, such as a fairly consistent running-note texture, in which long notes in the original model are filled in with scales, combined with decorated activity that occasionally obscures the melodic contours of the parent work. The diminished and sometimes

---

[32] On Paumann, see Hiroyuki Minamino, "Conrad Paumann and the Evolution of Solo Lute Practice in the Fifteenth Century," *JMR* 6 (1986), 291–310.

formulaic ornamentation appears usually in the highest voice, and through its reliance on several common melodic figures, is reminiscent of plectrum style. Spinacino's books are, of course, unequivocally intended for finger technique, given the indications in the tablature for plucking by the thumb (absence of a dot) and index finger (presence of a dot), but the musical texture frequently betrays the plectrum lute techniques of the previous generation.

Spinacino's ricercars have been more than once described as "improvisational," writers alluding to their loose structure, the reliance on certain melodic and ornamental formulas, and frequent abrupt changes in register and texture.[33] Grouped at the ends of the two books, these works have been somewhat devalued by the assumption that they were mainly ancillary, to be played before or after an intabulation as a prelude or a postlude, matched according to mode. Two of Spinacino's ricercars do actually refer in their titles to chanson arrangements that appear earlier in the volume. From a distance, the overall style of these ricercars seem to look back to the previous century. John Griffiths, however, has recently revised the notion that these works are all derivative and old-fashioned, arguing persuasively that at least some of the ricercars are, in fact, autonomous, not dependent, pieces with nothing to hide stylistically or technically.[34] Two ricercars in particular stand out in their anticipation of future developments. The "Recercare di tutti li Toni," from the *Libro primo* (40v-42), is a multi-sectional work that cadences on the finals of all eight of the modes, the cadential points numbered clearly in the tablature by Spinacino.[35] An even more audacious work is the long ricercar that closes the *Libro primo* (53v-56), which during the course of 334 measures – a length that is Wagnerian when compared to other ricercars of the period – cadences on all twelve tones of the scale.[36] A work exhibiting unprecedented originality, impressive formal design, and, to be sure, compositional hubris, it anticipates by sixty years and more the "well tempered" manuscript lute settings in Gorzanis (1567) and *Galilei 1584*, consisting of dance and variation cycles in all twenty-four of the major and minor keys.[37]

---

[33] See, for example, Allan Atlas, *Renaissance Music: Music in Western Europe, 1400–1600* (New York, 1998), 382.

[34] See John Griffiths, "Spinacino's Twelve-Tone Experiment," *JLSA* 40 (2011), 47–76, esp. 48–53.

[35] A transcription appears in Piotr Pozniak, "Problems of Tonality in the Ricercars of Spinacino and Bossinensis," *JLSA* 23 (1990), 75–6.

[36] For an analysis, see Griffiths, "Spinacino's Twelve-Tone Experiment," 60–76.

[37] Gorzanis's cycle is contained in Munich, Bayerische Staatsbibliothek, Mus. Mss. 1511a. For an edition, see Issam El-Mallah, *Ein Tanzzyklus des 16. Jahrhunderts für Laute von Giacomo*

If these two ricercars point to Spinacino's more progressive side, the six lute duets contained in the books are loud echoes of the mid- to late fifteenth century. Apart from being excellent works, they show how lutenists from the period of Pietrobono arranged vocal models for their instruments.[38] Five of these are arrangements of French chansons (the sixth is an arrangement of Josquin's "La Bernardina," a piece that exists only in instrumental versions), in which one player, the "tenorista," plays the tenor chanson melody (or a sparse accompaniment that includes the tenor voice), while the other plays an ornamented and fast-running discant above. McGee has speculated on the similarity between Spinacino's duets and the pieces in *Faenza*, which he proposes were intended for two lutes or for lute and harp.[39]

Returning to the intabulations, given the retrospective and even moribund nature of the vocal models used in *Spinacino* – many of them were contained in *Odhecaton*, which had already become out of date for ensemble players (see *SBS* 7) – why did Petrucci decide to publish this music? In his magisterial *catalogue raisonné* of the Petrucci enterprise, Stanley Boorman downgrades the lofty standing that music histories have accorded to the first printer of music and draws an alternate profile of him as a "peripheral figure, printing what his friends and patrons supplied, or perhaps what came to hand, and having little impact on musical taste or performance elsewhere."[40] In this scenario, Petrucci would seem to have been either uninterested in or uninformed about the stylistic relevance or public interest of the repertory he was publishing. On the other hand, his decision to print lute music seems anything but uninformed. He had devoted two difficult years towards developing the means to print tablature, and acknowledging the novelty of tablature and sensitive to the changes in lute performance, he included a preface "For those who cannot sing [i.e. do not read standard notation]" that explains the rules for reading tablature and for the newer finger plucking technique, reprinting this preface in every lute book that he issued. Furthermore, Petrucci developed a smart, risk-averse business model for his release of lute music,

---

Gorzanis (Tutzing, 1979); A complete study is in Issam El-Mallah, *Die Pass'e mezzi und Saltarelli aus der Münchner Lautenhandschrift von Jacomo Gorzanis* (Tutzing, 1979).

[38] Ivanoff, "An Invitation," writes that "Francesco Spinacino's prints preserve the only extant examples of a long and important tradition of lute duets." Quoted in *Performance on Lute, Guitar, and Vihuela*, ed. Victor Coelho, 2. See also Ivanoff, "Das Lautenduo."

[39] See McGee, "Instruments and the Faenza Codex," 480–90, esp. 483–5. We find McGee's evidence (for lute duet) more persuasive than Eberlein's, who in response to McGee suggests performance on organs of different sizes. See Eberlein, "The Faenza Codex," 460–6.

[40] Boorman, *Ottaviano Petrucci*, 7.

conceiving of a four-book sequence over two years, with each volume covering a different side of the lute repertory. Spinacino's two books, containing mostly intabulations and ricercars, constitute the first half of this sequence. Fifteen months later – a time that Petrucci may have needed in order to evaluate the commercial success of *Spinacino* – he issued in 1508$_1$ his *Libro terzo* containing works by the renowned Medici lutenist Gian Maria Alemani (Gian Maria Giudeo).[41] The final book of this quartet was Joanambrosio Dalza's *Intabolatura di lauto* of 1508$_2$, which eschews intabulations in favor of dances, most of them grouped into Pavana-Saltarello-Piva "suites," along with some short ricercars paired with pre-ludial "warm-ups" entitled "Tastar de corde." The especially attractive dance settings of the Piva are based on drones, evocative, as the name suggests, of fifteenth-century rustic dances accompanied by bagpipes, and the print also contains a few highly melismatic lute duets and some purely chordal dances, both of which seem to derive from the plectrum technique tradition.[42]

In the end, Petrucci planned his initial publication of lute books carefully, but as the first printer of music, the relationship between consumer and publisher had not yet been established. Consequently, he worked within an insular, essentially closed, market, publishing music that, with just a few exceptions, drew on older stylistic models or else was provided to him by a close, probably regional circle of acquaintances and contacts. Dalza and Spinacino seem to be from a previous generation, and we know nothing more about them after 1507–8;[43] conversely, we know a great deal about the life of Gian Maria, but not a single copy of Petrucci's *Libro terzo* has ever been recovered, nor have we been able to attribute with certainty any extant works to this lutenist.[44] But Petrucci did lay the foundation for

---

[41] Ibid., 296. On Giovan Maria Alemani, see H. Colin Slim, "Gian and Gian Maria: Some Fifteenth- and Sixteenth-Century Namesakes," *MQ* 57 (1971), 562–74. On the Jewish lutenist's close relationship with the Medici, see Anthony Cummings, "Gian Maria Giudeo, *Sonatore del Liuto*, and the Medici," *FaM* 38 (1991), 312–18, and for the earlier part of his career prior to 1524, Anthony Cummings, *The Lion's Ear: Pope Leo X, the Renaissance Papacy, & Music* (Ann Arbor, MI, 2012), 102–7.

[42] This is also suggested by Paul Kieffer in his informative article "An Approach to Reconstructing the First Lute Intabulations," *Lute Society of America Quarterly* 49 (2014), 31, n. 19.

[43] The only other mention of Spinacino is in Philippo Oriolo da Bassano's puerile poem, *Il Monte Parnasso, c.*1519–22, of which the only historical interest is that he is named along with almost 100 other lutenists, composers, and theorists on Mt. Parnassus; see H. Colin Slim, "Musicians on Parnassus," *Studies in the Renaissance* 12 (1965), 134–63.

[44] We do know that a copy of this book was owned by the collector Ferdinand Columbus (1488–1539), the son of Christopher Columbus, which he purchased in Rome in 1512 at a far greater price than he paid for any of the other Petrucci lute books, all of which he owned. See Catherine Weeks Chapman, "Printed Collections of Polyphonic Music Owned by Ferdinand

a remarkable century of published music, and subsequent printers of lute music – Attaingnant, Casteliono, Marcolini, Sultzbach, Gardano, Scotto, Moderne, and Phalèse – are indebted to his crucial role in the print revolution. They were, indeed, the "Lenin," as Boorman has concluded, to Petrucci's "Marx."[45]

7) The chanson tradition challenged: Augsburg, Staats- und Stadtbibliothek MS 2^0 142a (*c*.1510) – *Augsburg*

For ensemble music, the sixteenth century opened in a promising fashion with the publication of Petrucci's *Odhecaton*, which sent ripples throughout Italy and beyond the Alps as collectors seized on the print as a source for their own manuscript collections.[46] Almost as quickly, however, another, more mundane, aspect of *Odhecaton* surfaced: that however revolutionary *Odhecaton* was as the first printed book, the actual repertory it contained – as we also noted in the discussion of *Spinacino*, above – was, in essence, already out of date. But tastes were changing rapidly and very much like a substance held too long under high pressure, all aspects of instrumental music seemed almost to explode soon after 1500 with sources (both manuscript and print), instrumental types, and genres spinning off in all directions.

Indeed, though the survival rate of sources is uneven, we have ample evidence of immense growth from almost every region. In Italy there was an outpouring of prints for lute, keyboard, and after a bit of a delay, for ensembles. In Paris during the late 1520s, Attaingnant developed a more economical way of printing music and produced a series of volumes for lute, keyboard, and ensembles with emphasis on dances and chansons; he was soon followed by other French publishers, like Fézendat, Morlaye, and Moderne. The Low Countries lagged as Susato did not begin his

---

Columbus," *JAMS* 21 (1968), 47. That a piece in *Pesaro* (the "bassada[n]za," 35) may be a composition by Gian Maria has been suggested by Crawford Young in his article "The King of Spain: 'una bassadanza troppo forte'," *Lute Society of America Quarterly* 48 (2013), 40–61.

[45] Boorman, *Ottaviano Petrucci*, 7.

[46] One notable example is the Fridolin Sicher Songbook (Sankt Gallen, Stiftsbibliothek Cod. Sang. 461), dating from about 1515; see David Fallows, ed., *The Songbook of Fridolin Sicher* (Peer, Belgium, 1996). As Fallows notes (5) "the musical readings . . . are so close as to leave no reasonable doubt that the copyist had the *Odhecaton* in front of him as he worked." Another is Maastricht, Rijksarchief van Limburg, MS without ms number – see Josef Smits van Waesberghe, "Een 15de eeuws muziekboek van de stadsministrelen van Maastricht?" In *Renaissance-Muziek 1400–1600. Donum Natalicium René Bernard Lenaerts*, ed. Jozef Robijns (Leuven, 1969), 247–73.

publication ventures until the 1540s, but at about the same time Pierre Phalèse began his printing career in Louvain with several volumes for the lute. The production of both manuscripts and prints was especially rich in German-speaking regions, and these sources provide perhaps the clearest snapshot of the expansions taking place.

That tastes were changing rapidly is clearly seen in the manuscript *Augsburg*, copied about ten years after the publication of *Odhecaton* in a city that was then a center of brilliant musical activity. Maximilian I visited Augsburg frequently, bringing with him his superb instrumentalists. Maximilian's organist, Paul Hofhaimer, in fact took up residence for a time, and the court wind player Augustine Schubinger, the preeminent cornettist of his day, was a native of the city. The civic wind band was of such quality that its membership was raided constantly, not only by Maximilian but also by the Bavarian, Ferrarese, and Mantuan courts when they were in search of first-rate talent. That interest in music extended beyond court and professional circles to amateurs resident in the city is clearly revealed in our manuscript.

Augsburg has a convoluted history. The date of 1513 is written on the inside back cover, which is corroborated by watermark analysis of the main part of the manuscript. Dating is complicated in that there are at least three distinctly different sections to the manuscript. Moreover, none of the contents need be dated more than a few years either before or after 1513, so that date can serve as a rough chronological marker. A hand-written scribble on fol. 24r that mentions "the honorable and wise Jacob, *Stadtpfeifer*" ("der ersam und weisen Jacob stat pfeyfer") links the manuscript unmistakably to Augsburg, for a Jacob Hurlacher was a city shawmist there from 1492 to 1529.[47] In addition, an *ex libris* on the inside front cover reveals that the manuscript was later in the collection of Heinrich Herwart, a member of a prominent patrician family of Augsburg, further tightening the connection to the city.

The main portion of *Augsburg* is actually in two parts, one at the beginning, the other at the end. Both these parts, mostly in the hand of the main scribe, contain primarily German songs.[48] The collection is an

---

[47] The information in Adolf Layer, *Musik und Musiker der Fuggerzeit* (Augsburg, 1959), 50, is slightly incomplete. The first reference to Jacob Hurlacher is in 1492, not 1495 as Layer states (Augsburg, Stadtarchiv, Steuerbuch 1492, fol. 12; evidently Layer did not have the tax records available).

[48] Concerning the scribes in the manuscript see Armin Brinzing, *Studien zur instrumentalen Ensemblemusik im deutschsprachigen Raum des 16. Jahrhunderts, Abhandlungen zur Musikgeschichte*, ed. Martin Staehelin (Göttingen, 1998), I, 137–40.

important source for the music of Hofhaimer and Senfl, but contains only a single song by Isaac, curious in that just prior to these years Isaac had been Maximilian's court composer. One fascinating grouping comes toward the end (from numbers 69 through 78, with some breaks), which was copied directly from the *Aus sonderer künstlicher Art*, a book of German songs printed by Öglin in Augsburg in 1512. As noted earlier, another German manuscript from almost exactly the same time, copied by Fridolin Sicher, also borrowed heavily from the *Odhecaton*.[49] Apparently the availability of relatively inexpensive printed music did not dim the enthusiasm of collectors preparing their own manuscript versions. *Augsburg* contains very little three-part music, thus none of the seemingly idiomatic pieces such as Isaac's "La morra" are included, and in fact no pieces here reveal idiomatic character. As we shall see, this apparent lack of an ensemble repertory with distinctive instrumental traits is a puzzling feature of ensemble manuscripts into the late sixteenth century.

The second substantial segment of the manuscript was placed in the middle, but portions appear in scrambled order.[50] The scribe concentrated on just two composers, Josquin and Agricola. Between folios 36v and 45r he included three pieces that are credited to Josquin, and two others that can be ascribed to him on the basis of concordances. One other piece within this set, a setting of "Fors seulement," has also been suggested as being by Josquin.[51] The set opens with a motet, and the remainder consists of chansons. One of the pieces (the chanson "Faulte d'argent") is for five parts, the others are all for four. In the next portion of this segment, with seven pieces, the scribe named Agricola as the composer for two, and four others can again be established as his on the basis of concordances.[52] Again, one of Agricola's pieces is a motet, the rest chansons. And again, all pieces are for four parts save one, "Fortuna desperata," that is for six. One piece, known elsewhere as *Dulces exuviae*, is inserted within this

---

[49] See Fallows, *The Songbook of Fridolin Sicher*, 5–13.

[50] The knotted complexities of the manuscript's order have been untangled by Joshua Rifkin, "Franco-Netherlandish Repertory in an Early 16th-Century German Manuscript," unpublished paper presented at the New England Chapter Meeting of the American Musicological Society, Yale University, 10 April 1971; an updated study that also summarizes Rifkin's findings is in Fabrice Fitch, "'Virtual' Ascriptions in Ms. AugS 142a: A Window on Agricola's Late Style," *JAF* 4 (2012), 114–38.

[51] Louise Litterick, "Chansons for Three and Four Voices." In *The Josquin Companion*, ed. Richard Sherr (Oxford, 2000), 377–9.

[52] The order of this segment is problematic, as noted by Rifkin, "The Franco-Netherlandish Repertory," 4–6.

Agricola grouping, suggesting that the scribe believed this piece also to be by that composer.[53]

The third segment of *Augsburg* is much smaller, comprising just four folios, 18v – 21v). These are all dances of Italian origin, and in a hand distinct from others in the manuscript. While the script is clear enough, something is seriously awry here. Clefs are incorrect or missing entirely, and no amount of effort can make these versions work as they are written.[54] While the appearance of these pages is that of a practical script, it would have been impossible to have these pieces performed from the pages presented. Fortunately versions of most of these dances are available in concordant versions.[55] One other dance piece slightly earlier in the manuscript (fol. 13r) is providentially in the hand of the first scribe, and in fact could have been played as written.

Augsburg was assembled by an amateur, probably from a prosperous Augsburg merchant family. As is the case with *Zorzi*, *Augsburg* carries on the tradition of transmission by small packets of music, as seen in both the second and third sections described above. Clearly, the nature of the repertory has shifted. While chansons are included, a majority of the works are German songs. This shift to de-emphasize the chanson continues throughout the sixteenth century. The inclusion of a discrete section of dances represents something new as well, and is another harbinger of what became a flood of ensemble dance music collections later in the century.

In approaching the question of performance medium intended, the fact that only three pieces in the entire collection appear with text – two motets at the beginning, and one lone German song at the very end – is conditioned by the fact that sophisticated German musicians, amateurs included, by the early sixteenth century were clearly capable of providing texts to familiar German songs even if untexted in the source.[56] Still, the

---

[53] Rifkin, ibid., 6, reported that Edward Lerner, the editor of Agricola's collected works, felt that the piece seemed "wholly typical of Agricola."

[54] Unfortunately Luise Jonas, ed., *Das Augsburger Liederbuch*, Berliner musikwissenschaftliche Arbeiten, vol. 21. (Munich-Salzburg, 1983), 63–8, published faulty versions. For a reliable modern edition of these dances, see Brinzing, *Studien*, II, 11–17.

[55] Ibid., I, 148–9.

[56] See John Kmetz, "Singing Texted Sounds from Untexted Songbooks: The Evidence of the Basel Liederhandschriften." In *Le Concert des voix et des instruments*, ed. Jean-Michel Vaccaro, 121–43; see also Brinzing, *Studien*, I, 36–60, Armin Brinzing, "Zum Problem textloser Überlieferung in deutschen Quellen aus der ersten Hälfte des 16. Jahrhunderts." In *Heinrich Isaac und Paul Hofhaimer im Umfeld von Kaiser Maximilian I*, ed. Walter Salmen (Innsbruck, 1997), 43–56, and Litterick, "Performing Franco-Netherlandish Secular Music," 474–85.
A more cautious approach was suggested by Howard Mayer Brown, *A Florentine Chansonnier*

dance pieces and the untexted chansons were more likely played instrumentally, and the folio with the reference to Jacob Hurlacher contains a German song. In short, some of the repertory in *Augsburg* may have been sung, but all of it could have been played as well, and we should classify it as predominantly an instrumental source.

8) Introducing the *tre corone* of Renaissance lute music: Giovanni Antonio Casteliono, *Intabolatura di leuto de diversi autori* (Milan, 1536$_9$) – *Casteliono*

By the 1520s, the dissemination of lute music had reached international coverage, with publications by Attaingnant in Paris and by the lutenists Gerle and Judenkünig in Germany and Vienna, validating contemporary practices and showcasing national styles of repertory and notation. Ironically, it was the home of printing, Italy, that actually saw a steep decline in printed lute books during this period: of the seventeen printed sources containing lute music that appeared between 1508 and 1536, all but two were published outside of the country.[57]

Why the path of Italian lute music after *Spinacino* is difficult to follow is not easily explained. We have already noted the crucial absence of Petrucci's third lute book of 1508, containing music by the Medici court lutenist Gian Maria Alemani – the only one of Petrucci's lutenists for whom we can confirm a professional status. A few years earlier, in 1505, the lutenist Marco dall'Aquila successfully petitioned to publish lute music in Venice, but there is no evidence that he ever exercised this privilege. Some ricercars appear in Petrucci's arrangements of frottole for voice and lute in 1509$_1$ and 1511$_1$, but these too, like Spinacino's ricercars, are mainly echoes of a plectrum and improvisatory tradition and they are probably not contemporary compositions. We are left to conclude that in the more than two decades after Petrucci brought out his last works for lute in 1511, the publication of lute music was both economically prohibitive and technologically daunting. The printer Francesco Marcolini alludes precisely to this situation in a letter "to the musicians" that prefaces his *Intabolatura di*

---

from the Time of Lorenzo the Magnificent. Florence, Biblioteca Nazionale Centrale MS Banco Rari 229 (Chicago, 1983), I, 141–2.

[57] See the useful analysis and table of lute publications between 1507 and 1540 in Dinko Fabris, "Le prime intavolature italiane per liuto: 1500–1540." In *Venezia 1501: Petrucci e la stampa musicale/Venice 1501: Petrucci, Music, Print and Publishing*, ed. Giulio Cattin and Patrizia Dalla Vecchia (Venice, 2005), 485–6.

liuto (1536₃), one of the earliest publications devoted to the work of Francesco da Milano. After praising the efforts of Petrucci for making lute music available, now "the accommodation has been lacking, the accommodation which Fossombrone [the city where Petrucci moved his operation after 1509, as well as his birthplace] knew how to provide, since no one knew how to find the way used by him. The numbers and notes of the sound were carved in copper and in wood with great loss of time and much expense."[58] Furthermore, it appears that lutenists adapted only slowly (and warily) to this technology. Committing to print would require a fundamental change in compositional process, a quick replacing of improvisation with a notation-based tradition at a time when imitative polyphonic models were just becoming widely available to imitate. In short, there was probably just not much notated (or notatable) lute music available to print.

What remains from these years is a collection of only about seven manuscripts of uneven quality spanning the period from around 1510–40.[59] The most important of these is a beautifully prepared tablature known as the "Capirola Lute Book" (*Capirola*) dating from around 1517.[60] Containing 42 (total) ricercars, dances, and arrangements by the Brescian nobleman Vincenzo Capirola and compiled in Venice by his student, the painter Vitale, the manuscript traces the evolution, clearly evident in the broad and texturally diverse ricercars, from the improvisatory formulas codified in *Spinacino* to a more contrapuntal and sophisticated stage of composition that characterizes the works in *Casteliono*. *Capirola* also contains valuable performance instructions about execution, notation, fingering, tuning, and stringing, revealing many stylistic and pedagogical subtleties of lute performance from around the second decade of the sixteenth century. It is useful to think of *Capirola* as a pool between the first trickle of lute music in 1507 and the torrent that floods the markets in 1546. These thirty years can be viewed as a time of profound stylistic and

---

[58] Quoted and translated in Arthur J. Ness, "The Herwarth Lute Manuscripts at the Bavarian State Library, Munich: A Bibliographical Study with Emphasis on the Works of Marco dall'Aquila and Melchior Newsidler." PhD diss., 2 vols. New York University (1984), vol. 1, 346–7; see also the analysis of Marcolini's statement by Boorman, *Ottaviano Petrucci*, 61–2.

[59] For a list of these manuscript sources, see Fabris, "Le prime intavolature." In *Venezia 1501*, ed. Giulio Cattin and Patrizia Dalla Vecchia, 483–4.

[60] The foundational study of *Capirola* is in Otto Gombosi, ed. *Compostione di Meser Vincenzo Capirola: Lute-Book (circa 1517)* (Neuilly-sur-Seine, 1955). Capirola's detailed preface is translated in Federico Marincola, "The Instructions From Vincenzo Capirola's Lute Book: A New Translation," *The Lute* 23, pt. 2 (1982), 23–8.

technical change, and represent, perhaps, the most stylistically fertile period for the instrument during the Italian Renaissance.

Entering the market after a twenty-five year publishing drought (or, indeed, monopoly) in Italian lute music, *Casteliono* is one of five Italian lute publications to appear in 1536. Four of these are devoted entirely to music by papal lutenist Francesco da Milano (1497–1543), one of the most famous musicians of the sixteenth century.[61] Francesco's works continue to appear in Italian and non-Italian sources until well into the seventeenth century largely due to the circulation of these prints and the concordances derived from them. Outside of Italy, the same year also witnesses the first publication of music for the Spanish vihuela, Luys Milan's *El Maestro*, and the first two books by the German lutenist Hans Newsidler. The appearance of so much lute music in a single year (with much of Francesco's work duplicated among his four books) supports Boorman's contention that this is when the printed market for music finally displayed signs of real competition.[62] For the publisher Casteliono, too, the time seemed right. Rather than focus on the work of a single composer as the other printers that year had done, Casteliono produced a diversified selection of music by several of the most famous lutenists of the period, making it the first important lute anthology of the sixteenth century.

The historical importance of *Casteliono* lies in its early canonization of three great contemporary lutenists – indeed, the *tre corone* – of the first half of the sixteenth century: Francesco da Milano, Marco dall'Aquila (*c.*1470–1537), and Alberto da Ripa (da Mantova) (*c.*1500–51).[63] Francesco, referred to by Casteliono as "Il Divino," held the position of lutenist to three successive popes, Leo X Medici, Clement VII Medici (whose

---

[61] See Arthur J. Ness, *The Lute Music of Francesco Canova da Milano, 1497–1543* (Cambridge, MA, 1970). For a short but detailed biography, see Victor Coelho, "Francesco Canova da Milano." In *Die Musik in Geschichte und Gegenwart*, Personenteil 6, ed. Ludwig Finscher (Kassel, 1994), 1571–5. For a full documentary study, see Franco Pavan, "Francesco da Milano, 1497–1543," Tesi di Laurea, University of Milan (1996–7); on the relationship between Francesco's music and papal patronage, see Victor Coelho, "Papal Tastes and Musical Genres: Francesco da Milano 'Il Divino' (1497–1543) and the Clementine Aesthetic." In *The Pontificate of Clement VII: History, Politics, Culture*, ed. Kenneth Gouwens and Sheryl Reiss (Aldershot, 2005), 277–92.

[62] Boorman, *Ottaviano Petrucci*, 400, 390.

[63] Casteliono was not alone in his judgment of the eminence of these three lutenists; Marcolini's 1536 preface, alluded to earlier (see above, n. 58), praises "the tenderness of the sound which is born of the lute when played by Francesco Milanese, Alberto da Mantua, and Marco da l'Aquila, by making it felt in the soul, moves the senses of him who hears it." The entire preface is given in Ness, "The Herwarth Lute Manuscripts," 346–7.

own "Il Divino," Michelangelo, was one of Francesco's contemporaries), and Pope Paul III Farnese, and his large surviving body of work, disseminated throughout Europe, quickly became classicized as the repertory to learn and imitate.[64] The older Marco, as we have noted earlier, must have reached a point of musical maturity already by 1505, when he received permission to print music. Alberto was raised in the splendor of the Mantuan Court and may have worked there prior to his appointment to the French court of Francis I in 1528.

The three lutenists are seminal in their cultivation, already by the third decade of the sixteenth century, of the imitative fantasia, or ricercar, which in their hands became a complex polyphonic and discursive work that resembled a piece of musical literature – a motet *senza parole*. Leaving behind the older Franco-Flemish models of the Petrucci generation, these *tre corone* instead amalgamated the rhythmic verve and attractive sectional contrasts of the new Parisian chanson, the rhetorical form, smooth counterpoint, and elegant melodies of recent madrigals by Arcadelt and Verdelot, and the point-of-imitation technique and formal balance of the Mass and motet repertories of the Josquin generation. Benefitting from the new circulation of printed music, these lutenists were exposed rapidly and comprehensively to these foreign and domestic styles, and they skillfully absorbed their musical qualities, combining them into a fluid, complex, and thoroughly idiomatic framework.

As editor, Casteliono appears to have had a preferential line to the previously unpublished music of all three composers, and the book is the first to introduce them as a group to the public, marking their earliest appearance in print. Accordingly, the lutenists are given a place of distinction. The book opens with three long fantasias by each of the three lutenists (in the order Francesco–Albert–Marco, fols. 3–8v), with another section of three fantasias in the same order occupying the middle of the book fols. 25–30v, along with a fantasia by the German lutenist resident in Milan, Jacob Albutio [Giovanni Albuzio] (31–32v), and another by the Milanese lutenist, Pietro Paolo Borrono (33–34v). Completing this formal plan, *Casteliono* closes with four more fantasias in the same order by the three lutenists, inserting another fantasia by Albutio as the penultimate work, leaving Francesco to close the book.[65]

---

[64] On the cultural context and classic status of Francesco's music, see Coelho, "Papal Tastes." In *The Pontificate of Clement* VII, ed. Kenneth Gouwens and Sheryl Reiss, 277–89.

[65] The fantasia in this section by Albert (*Fantaisie XXI* in Vaccaro's edition [see n. 67, below]) is attributed in the *Tabula* (fol. 2v) to Francesco ("Fantasia del ditto," referring to his authorship [Francesco] of the previous work. Albert's fantasia was published in a much-corrected and

The opening works already carve out a stylistic profile of Francesco, Albert, and Marco. Francesco's fantasia that opens the print, one of his longest works, is the most formally sophisticated, with an arching rhetorical quality.[66] Beginning slowly with a series of long orational chords over pedals, it gradually opens into several sections of more fluid and transparent imitative textures that conclude with an exciting dialogue section in broken style textures. Albert de Rippe proceeds in a more organic fashion: beginning with a single note that becomes the germ of a chord, the piece similarly unfolds over long pedals, comprising a large opening section that takes up one fifth of the piece.[67] Less consistently imitative than Francesco or Marco and more conservative rhythmically, this, like many of Albert's works, seems more closely allied to vocal models or intabulations through the often dense chordal textures, the parallel movement in sixths, and particularly his fondness for closely spaced lower voices. Of the three lutenists, the older Marco is the most resolute composer of imitative fantasias in *Casteliono*. Without a declamatory introduction, as with the previous two fantasias by Francesco and Albert, Marco immediately develops an imitative subject, and the work continues uninterrupted in this manner, with steady rhythmic motion, until broken up with a cadential sequence a third of the way through. If Francesco and Albert's fantasias are more architecturally planned, Marco's reveal his crucial historical importance as one of the earliest composers of the thoroughly imitative fantasia.

To these *tre corone*, we might add a fourth *coroncina* that appears prominently in the print, at least in order to recognize his important connections with the other lutenists and his contributions to dance music: Pietro Paolo Borrono (*c*.1490/95–1563?), another Milanese, who is, in fact, the most frequently represented composer in the book. Borrono's dances, featuring attractive melodies and crisp, gently syncopated rhythms, are usually arranged in mini-suites beginning with a duple-meter Pavana followed by a faster triple-meter Saltarello based on the same melodic material and harmonic stamp. Most of these settings contain fluid, written-out ornamented repeats. This is the same pairing that is found in *Dalza*, and which becomes standard in dance music of the sixteenth century.

musically superior version in his *Quart livre de tabulature de luth* of 1553_9, published by Le Roy & Ballard.
[66] The work appears as Fantasia 20 in Ness, ed., *The Lute Music of Francesco Canova da Milano*, 73–6.
[67] Albert's fantasia appears as no. XII in Jean-Michel Vaccaro, ed., *Œuvres d'Albert de Rippe: I. Fantaisies* (Paris, 1972), 77–82; see also ibid., 171–7, for a comparison of the *Casteliono* reading of this fantasia with a concordant version published twenty-six years later in Paris by Le Roy & Ballard (1562_{11}).

Well aware of the strength of the repertoire he was publishing and the keen competition among printers for recent music, Casteliono specifies on his title page that the works are "newly published" (which they were) and "which no others can print or have printed [by a third party] for ten years under penalty of 100 Scudi...." While this fairly boilerplate language is frequently encountered – but usually ignored – in prints of this period, there appears to be considerable compliance in the case of *Casteliono*. Of the five pieces attributed to Francesco in the book – four fantasias and a "Tochata" – none of them appear in any of the other books printed that year containing Francesco's music;[68] they do not start appearing again in print until exactly the end of the "embargo" in 1546. Similarly, the works in *Casteliono* by Albert de Rippe do not start reappearing in print until 1552, while the pieces by Marco dall'Aquila are among the only printed works of his in the sixteenth century.

By any account, the year 1536 represents a major point of arrival for both the music printing industry and the history of lute music. *Casteliono* is testimony to the evolution in lute technique and composition, and is a critically important source through its collection of fantasias by the three greatest lutenists of the period. One can say that the change in lute playing was now complete, so much so that the repertory of the *tre corone* became the standard against which all subsequent players of the Renaissance measured their works.

9) Professionals at work: Copenhagen, Det kongelige Bibliotek, Gl.Kgl.Sml.1872-4° (c.1545) – *Copenhagen*

Augsburg is just one example of the relationship between the German public's increasing appetite for music as social entertainment during the first half of the sixteenth century and an outpouring of prints and manuscripts. Some of these sources were intended for a particular medium: the Wiltzell manuscript (D-Mu, 4o Cod. ms. 718), for example, was assembled for players of viol, while in Gerle's *Musica Teusch* of 1532_2 some sections were for viol, with others for lute. Still other collections like Forster's *Frische teutsche Liedlein* (1539) indicated that the music was "For all kinds of instruments." More often, however, printed and manuscript

---

[68] These are 1536_3 and the virtually identical $154?_4$ (undated, but which probably dates to 1536 at the latest – see Ness, ed. *The Lute Music of Francesco Canova da Milano*, 12), and the two books published by Johannes Sultzbach, *Intavolatura de viola o vero Lauto... Libro Primo della Fortuna e Libro Secondo* (Naples, 1536 [not listed in Brown *1600*]).

collections were intended for either singers or players, with the understanding that the presence of text does not necessarily mean that a piece was sung, and the absence of text does not imply that the piece was to be played. As Brinzing pointed out, even a source like Formschneider's *Trium vocum carmina* (1538_2), which appeared without any texts at all, contains much that was certainly sung.[69] Most of the German sources contained songs, and enthusiastic singers could easily have recalled from memory the texts to well-known pieces. There was, moreover, a long tradition among German musicians of adding new texts to imported pieces. Still, the inclusion of dance settings alongside song repertories, as seen in at least two manuscripts, further points to the dual-purpose nature of German "song" collections.[70] Formschneider's print (cited above) included pieces such as Martini's "La martinella" and the setting of "La stangetta" from *Odhecaton*, works that were far more appropriate to playing than singing – not because they were idiomatic, but because finding a text to fit their structure would be hopelessly complicated.

The repertories included in these German sources are quite varied, but in general most follow the general model of *Augsburg*. Franco/Flemish composers continue to appear, but the sources in the 1520s and 1530s seem conservative in this regard, with little influence of, for example, the Parisian chansons of Sermisy. With few exceptions, German songs formed the core of the repertory, and remarkably we see no sign of any truly idiomatic forms developing for instrumental ensembles to match the many fantasias written for lute and keyboard.

This expanding culture of instrumental music during the early sixteenth century is amply chronicled by the detailed theoretical and illustrated descriptions by, among others, Sebastian Virdung and Martin Agricola. Archival sources, too, document the larger number of players in musical ensembles (as discussed in Chapter 1), though, ironically, contemporary manuscripts and prints – that is, the music itself – offer surprisingly little to corroborate any such expansion. Almost all the music for ensembles in these sources remains restricted to four parts with only occasional increase to five or six parts. This changes quite emphatically with *Copenhagen* and its sister manuscripts.[71]

---

[69] Brinzing, *Studien*, I, 45–9.
[70] These manuscripts are Basel, Universitätsbibliothek, F X 5–9, and Munich, Bayerische Staatsbibliothek, Mus. MS 1516.
[71] The main source is Copenhagen, Kongelige Bibliotek, Gl.Kgl.Sml.1872-4°. Another in the family is Copenhagen, Kongelige Bibliotek, Gl.Kgl.Sml.1873-4° (hereafter *Copenhagen 1873*). A modern edition of *Copenhagen* is in Henrik Glahn, ed. *Music from the Time of Christian III*. Dania Sonans, vols. IV–V (Copenhagen, 1978–86).

Copenhagen consists of seven part books compiled by a member of the instrumental ensemble at the Danish royal court in about 1545. Most of the pieces are either for five or six parts, but there are several for seven or eight and a few works call for as many as twelve or sixteen parts. There are even indications about instrumentation: crumhorns in no. 24; in no. 89, "Auff pusaun und krumhorn" for a six-part setting of Senfl's original four-part "Ich klag denn tag"; and for no. 158, four cornetts and four trombones for an anonymous *Laudate Dominum*. The number of parts and the instruments specified reveal how far instrumental music had traveled between the late fifteenth century and 1550. A manuscript like *Casanatense*, with its rubric that the contents are "in the fashion of the wind band," contained music for only three or four parts, and with every indication that a wide range of performance options was available. The music made no technical demands beyond the capabilities of a skilled amateur. The sixteen-part *Laudate Dominum* in *Copenhagen*, however, not only demanded professionals, but was even further restricted in that only ensembles of very large courts (and with deep pockets) could assemble the forces necessary. A fissure had emerged in the relationship between the rising class of non-professional instrumentalists and the demands of the repertory, given that a significant portion of this music was not only beyond the reach of all amateurs technically, but was a stretch as well for even the largest civic ensembles.

Copenhagen also reveals a shift in the choices made by instrumentalists. Over half of the pieces are based on sacred models (mostly either Latin motets or German sacred songs), reflecting the increasing involvement of professional instrumental ensembles in sacred services. Since the compiler of the manuscript was German, as were most of the court ensemble performers, German secular songs are well represented, but the manuscript also contains a dozen French chansons, and, in anticipation of what was to come, two Italian madrigals. There are only two dances in the inventory, one of them being a "Passemeza." While the manuscript has a slightly retrospective nature – not unusual for an instrumental collection – given the inclusion of ten pieces by Josquin, fourteen by Senfl, and one by Isaac, the emphasis is clearly on more contemporary composers, including Arcadelt, Gombert, and Willaert, along with a group of German composers of more local reputation. *Copenhagen 1873*, dating only about ten years later, strikes a different balance by containing a few more secular rather than sacred pieces, as well as a very large number of chansons (fifty-two). It also includes some twenty-five dances in contrast to only two in *Copenhagen*. The choice of composers is distinctly more international and up-to-date, with Clemens, Crecquillon, and Lasso figuring prominently. Still, even with the relative prominence of chansons, the presence of some 69 sacred pieces again serves to underline the fact that instrumental performance in religious services was now a routine expectation.

10) Alonso Mudarra, *Tres libros de música en cifras para vihuela* (Seville, 1546$_{14}$) – *Tres libros*

The musical product of a Spanish culture characterized by "the solemnity of faith, the might of empire and the excitement of discovery," the vihuela repertory reveals a parallel mix of Catholic devotion, a scholastic deference to canonical authors on the one hand, and an embracing of Italian humanism and the image of the *cortesano* on the other.[72] Almost all of the music for vihuela appears in seven tablature books published between 1536 and 1576. While these comprise only a tiny fraction of the approximately 300 books of instrumental music printed during the sixteenth century, they transmit a large and diverse repertory of almost 700 pieces, including intabulations, fantasias, variation settings, duos, works for the Renaissance guitar, and a large selection of accompanied songs set to Spanish, Italian, Portuguese, and Latin texts, demonstrating a deep knowledge of Classical sources. The stylistic range of these works, many of them highly sophisticated compositions with others assuming a didactic function, allowed these books to reach an astoundingly wide demographic, from professional to amateur, and noble to bourgeois, clearly justifying the print runs of 1,000 or more copies that have been documented for some of these sources.[73] Commensurate with their audience, the vihuelists themselves came from a range of backgrounds. Luys Milán (1536$_5$) was a courtier, while Luis de Narváez (1538$_1$), Mudarra (1546$_{14}$), and the blind Miguel de Fuenllana (1554$_3$) had professional duties as musicians. Almost nothing is known of Enríquez de Valderrábano (1547$_5$), but he may have been an amateur, as is certainly the case with Diego Pisador (1552$_7$), who is, paradoxically, the most compulsive intabulator of the seven authors (see *CS* 1). Little is

---

[72] John Griffiths, "At Court and at Home with the *Vihuela de mano*: Current Perspectives on the Instrument, its Music and its World," *JLSA* 22 (1989), 7.

[73] On the printing history of the vihuela repertory, see John Griffiths, "Printing the Art of Orpheus: Vihuela Tablatures in Sixteenth-Century Spain." In *Early Music Printing and Publishing in the Iberian World*, ed. Iain Fenlon and Tess Knighton (Kassel, 2006), 181–214. All of the vihuela books were known in Portugal as well, and there are references to several sixteenth-century Portuguese vihuela treatises, cited in Nelson, "Music Treatises," 210–11.

known about the impecunious author of the last vihuela book to be published, Esteban Daza (1576$_1$), other than that he was a university student from a well-to-do family who died in poverty.

Among the vihuelist authors, Mudarra, along with Narváez, stands out as perhaps most representative of both the art of the vihuelists and their cultural context in sixteenth-century Spain. Moreover, Mudarra's *Tres libros* has the added appeal of containing some of the finest music for a solo instrument in the entire sixteenth century.[74] As we learn from the brief biographical remarks in the preface to his book, Mudarra was raised in the opulent household of the third and fourth Mendoza Dukes of the Infantando, where he was exposed to music and musicians of quality. Mudarra took priestly orders, and in 1546 became canon and, later, majordomo, at Seville Cathedral, where he remained for the rest of his life, heavily involved with the cathedral's musical programs and other administration.

One of the most visible differences between vihuela publications and lute books from elsewhere in Europe has to do with their size. Italian and French publishers normally issued the work of a lutenist or guitarist through a succession of prints (*Libro primo…/Premier livre…, Libro secondo…*, etc.) over the course of several years, sometimes followed by reissues. All of the vihuelists, on the other hand (as seen in the *Tres Libros*), assembled their work into a single, large publication that was divided internally into "books" dedicated respectively to fantasias, intabulations, and songs – dance settings are infrequent – and very often organized by mode. They are multi-purpose anthologies that appealed to a variety of potential users, including beginners, given the frequent inclusion of elementary theory and in the overall organization, in which pieces are sometimes graded in terms of difficulty.

In the *Tres Libros*, the first book is devoted to fantasias, variation and dance settings, some intabulations of Josquin, and the first works ever published for the 4-course Renaissance guitar. An unstated but clear didactic intent of the opening works is evident by Mudarra's rubric that these are fantasias "of long runs to develop the hands" (*Fantasía de pasos largos para desenbolver las manos*), or by the inclusion of the word "easy" in the title (*Fantasia facil*). Unlike the more complex fantasias that appear in Book Two, these works, though hardly elementary, are devoid of borrowed

---

[74] For a facsimile of the *Tres libros*, see Alonso Mudarra, *Tres Libros de musica en cifras para vihuela* (1546), facsimile edition with an introduction by James Tyler (Monaco, 1980). A modern edition is in *Monumentos de la musica espanola* VII, ed. Emilio Pujol (Barcelona, 1949).

material from vocal music. They combine long passages of scales, specified in the tablature to be executed with two fingers or with the index finger alone (*dedillo*), and short interludes of thirds and two-voice counterpoint.[75] This section also contains (fol. 13) one of the most unique fantasias in the entire lute or vihuela repertory, the Fantasia "that imitates the harp in the manner of Ludovico" (*que contrahaze la harpa en la manera de Ludovico*), who can be securely identified with the great Ludovico el del Arpe, the harpist who served Christopher Columbus's patron, Ferdinand II of Aragon. As we know from Bermudo and others, this Ludovico was able to create the semitones needed at cadences by pressing the harp string with his finger.[76] On the surface, this extraordinary work – one that remains popular with modern classical guitarists – is but a set of variations on a well-known Renaissance chordal scheme known as the *Folia*. But to imitate the chromatic technique of Ludovico, Mudarra uses a cross-stringing effect to create bold semitone dissonances in the final section, which is appended with the printed warning that "From here to the end there are some dissonances [but] played well they do not sound badly" (*Desde aqui fasta açerca del final ay Algunas falsas tañiendose bien no pareçen mal*). Anticipating the startled reaction by players encountering this passage, and also by the work's unconventional style of what was then understood by *fantasia*, Mudarra's title admits that the piece is "difficult until it is understood" (*. . . es difficil hasta ser entendida*).

This unique fantasia builds on Mudarra's reverence for the past in order to pay homage to a great musician from a former era, and it is difficult to think of another work in the Renaissance that explicitly imitates a specific improvised technique by a known performer. Rounding out the first book are two intabulations from Josquin's *Missa faysan regres*, the first published works for the four-course "Renaissance" guitar, and two exquisite sets of variations, one on the Romanesca chordal scheme with the other being one of Mudarra's most beautiful compositions, the twelve variations (*diferencias*) on the six-measure *Conde Claros* melody. Beginning with a simple chordal statement of the scheme, Mudarra displays the lyricism that pervades all of his music by expanding the theme melodically, decoratively, and contrapuntally throughout the registers of the vihuela, creating a gradual arc towards a climax in variation 11.

---

[75] On vihuela technique, see John Griffiths, "The Vihuela: Performance Practice, Style, and Context." In *Performance on Lute, Guitar, and Vihuela*, ed. Victor Coelho, 168–9; see also Maier, "Josquin's Mass Settings for Vihuela," 254–67.

[76] See John Griffiths, "La 'Fantasía que contrahaze la harpa' de Alonso Mudarra: estudio histórico-analítico," *Revista de Musicología* 9 (1986), 31.

Book Two is organized into eight "suites" by mode, each beginning with a preludial *Tiento* followed by a *Fantasia*, and concluding with an intabulation of a vocal work in which Mudarra at various points interpolates *glosas*, or passages consisting of his own material, within the intabulation. These fascinating works reveal how vocal models are at the root of instrumental composition, not only through intabulations and fantasias derived from intabulations, but how new material draws from and extends the original work, almost like a commentary rather than a parody. Book Three is devoted entirely to songs with vihuela accompaniment, many of them evoking the humanist spirit of courtly life through their settings of Virgil, Ovid, and Petrarch, along with those of many Spanish poets.[77] Spain in the sixteenth century produced absolutely first-rate composers of vocal music as seen in the works of Morales, Victoria, and Guerrero; the panorama revealed in the *Tres Libros* demonstrates that Mudarra and his vihuelist colleagues produced instrumental works of equal quality.

11) Dances for musical recreation: Tielman Susato's *Het derde musyck boexken... danserye* (Antwerp, 1551_8) – *Danserye*

Regardless of class, age, or gender (and maybe even skill), Renaissance men, women, and children reveled in dancing; for them it was the pre-eminent social entertainment of their time and one that is closely aligned to class, social function, and context. The mania for dancing is reflected in the flood of printed dance music for lute, keyboard, and ensembles throughout the sixteenth century, beginning with Dalza's *Intabulatura* of 1508_2, and of which Susato's *Danserye* acts as an accurate stylistic barometer of this development at mid-century.

The popularity of dancing was, of course, consistent throughout the entire era covered by this study. During the fifteenth century, however, sources are far fewer than those after 1500. For the earlier period several Italian dance manuals give detailed instructions concerning steps appropriate to various types of dances, but when they do provide music, only

---

[77] For a study of Mudarra's songs dealing in particular with the improvised background of these pieces, see John Griffiths, "Improvisation and Composition in the Vihuela Songs of Luis Milán and Alonso Mudarra." In *Gesäng zur Laute. Trossinger Jahrbuch für Renaissancemusik* 2, ed. Nicole Schwindt (Kassel, 2002), 111–32.

single-line melodies are given.[78] Similarly, two large collections of fifteenth-century French courtly dances survive, one manuscript and one *incunabulum*, once again, with detailed choreographies, but containing melodies alone.[79] In fact, the purpose of these Italian and French sources was to provide information for the dancers; they were not intended for the performers who provided the music. Accompanying dancing in the fifteenth century was a task reserved for professionals, who improvised counterpoints around the dance tunes. This was an aural and ephemeral repertory that has almost completely vanished from our view. However, a small handful of written settings of dance tunes have survived that give us some hint of how players then would approach their assignment. Two settings of the *spagna* basse dance tune, a melody known throughout Europe, provide especially apt examples, one for two parts, titled "Falla con misuras," the other for three by Francisco de la Torre, titled "Alta."[80]

Much changed in the sixteenth century, however, as is clearly seen in *Danserye*. One obvious change has to do with the fact that a clear majority of publications for instruments were either devoted to or included a substantial repertory of dance music, with this content usually recognized in the title of the volume. Most important concerning these sources, the nature of the dance types was modified with new and quite different dances appearing regularly, such as the pavane, saltarello, gagliarda, and various subcategories of branles. Earlier the emphasis was on complex dances that demanded extensive training; this was clearly an activity designed for the "1%" and served to distinguished people of elite status from lesser mortals. Courtly dancing became much more accessible in the sixteenth century, with printed treatises by Arbeau, Caroso, and Negri circulating widely,

---

[78] For an extensive discussion of Italian dance forms, their sources, and their contexts, see Jennifer Nevile, *The Eloquent Body: Dance and Humanist Culture in Fifteenth-Century Italy* (Bloomington, 2004). The central sources are Domenico da Piacenza, *De arte saltandi* (c.1450), Guglielmo Ebreo da Pesaro, *Trattato della danza* (c.1460) and *De pratica sue arte* (1463), and Antonio Cornazano, *Libro dell' arte dell danzare* (c.1460).

[79] The two sources are the Brussels basse dance manuscript, Brussels, Bibliothèque Royale de Belgique 9085, and Michel de Toulouse, *L'art et instruction de bien dancer* (Paris, 1488-96 [Brown 148?$_1$]). On the sources of the French *basse dance*, see Frederick Crane, *Materials for the Study of the Fifteenth-Century Basse Dance* (Brooklyn, 1968); for context, see Daniel Heartz, "The Basse Dance, Its Evolution circa 1450 to 1550," *AnnM* 6 (1958–63), 287–340.

[80] The source of the two-part version is Perugia, Biblioteca Comunale Augusta, MS 431, fol. 95v-96r; the one in three-parts is in Madrid, Biblioteca de Palacio Real, MS II-1335, fol. 223r. For information on the concordant manuscripts and editions of the pieces, see Fallows, *A Catalogue of Polyphonic Songs*, 529.

given the large number of melodic and tablature concordances between pieces in these collections and amateur lute books of the late sixteenth and early seventeenth centuries.

The trajectory of the basse dance provides a revealing example of the evolving "democracy" of dancing. In the fifteenth century each basse dance was individual, made up of a long string of steps in intricate patterns that had to be carefully memorized and flawlessly executed for each dance. In contrast, by the early sixteenth century those complicated constructs fell out of fashion, and the basse dance was essentially reduced to the one basic pattern known as the *basse dance commune*. The main portion of this dance was in triple meter and consisted of a choreography fixed at twenty steps, which could be achieved by combining four and eight musical phrases in a variety of ways.[81] In dancing the complete *basse dance commune* the main dance was followed by a middle section, called variously the *moitié, retour* (or *recoupe*), or something similar, with a standard form of twelve steps, and was concluded by a *da capo* return of the main dance. This in turn was followed by the faster *tourdion*, also in triple meter, but more variable in structure and consisting of two or three strains of eight measures each. In all sections the four-measure unit formed the basic structure (sometimes achieved by repeating two-measure units).[82]

If *Danserye* represents a last gasp of the basse dance, the tradition expires with Phalèse's *Leviorum Carminum* of two decades later, which contains none at all even though it otherwise draws heavily on Susato. Its state of decline is clear from the fact that Susato included only one piece of his total of fifty-seven that is identified as a basse dance (number 10 in his print); moreover, that one piece is in duple, rather than triple, meter, and it does not conform to the twenty-step structure. Instead, the *Danserye* begins with four pieces titled "Bergerette." Whereas Attaingnant's publications always present the basse dances first, in a position of honor, Susato considered his Bergerettes as the equivalent of basse dances, and the second of his group, the "Bergerette Sans roch," does, in fact, match all the criteria for the *basse*

---

[81] For a discussion of the musical features of the basse dance, see Daniel Heartz, *Preludes, Chansons and Dances for Lute* (Neuilly-sur-Seine, 1964), xxxi–xxxviii; for a useful and concise description of the *basse dance commune*, see David R. Wilson, "The Basse Dance c.1445–c.1545." In *Dance, Spectacle, and the Body Politick, 1250–1750*, ed. Jennifer Nevile (Bloomington, 2008), 174–8.

[82] For an example of a complete basse danse, see "Basse dance Saint Roch" from the *Dixhuit basses dances* published by Attaingnant in Paris in 1530, in Heartz, *Preludes, Chansons and Dances*, 64–6.

dance commune.[83] The other Begerettes, though, cannot be made to fit the twenty-measure structure, and the fourth Bergerette is, like number ten, in duple meter. The lack of conformity seems puzzling, but one obvious explanation lies with the intended market for Susato's part books. The prospective buyers were wealthy amateurs, not professionals, and the music was intended for musical recreation, not to be played on the dance floor. Even if a piece conveyed only the atmosphere or rhythmic characteristic of a particular dance, that would have been entirely satisfactory; designed for a broad public of diverse backgrounds in dancing, there was no need for the music to conform to every choreographic detail.[84]

Danserye provides a panorama of dances of the sixteenth century. Although a few miscellaneous pieces appear throughout, the main organization of the print is cast in five main sections each devoted to a particular dance type: *Bergerettes* (discussed above); *Rondes* (nine), *Allemaignes* (eight), *Pavanes* (five), and *Gaillardes* (fifteen). Judging from concordances with French music, Susato considered the *Ronde* the Low Countries' equivalent of the *branle double* (i.e., a duple meter dance based on a form of two four-bar phrases). The Allemande, a descendant of the duple meter *Deutscher Tanz*, was relatively new in 1550. The Pavane, for Susato's clients, was a stately dance, also in duple meter; in practice it was often paired with a faster triple-time Gaillarde, sometimes using the same melodic stamp. All five of these dance types were presented with a variable number of repeated strains, usually either two or three. A few, such as the "Pavane La Bataille," have four. Susato provided one each of the Moresca ("La morisque"), Saltarello ("Salterelle"), and Passamezzo antico ("Passe e medio"). The Moresca featured grotesque and exaggerated gestures, sometimes with swords, and was evidently not a standardized dance. The Saltarello was a popular dance in the Renaissance and by the mid-sixteenth century was in a broad triple meter (i.e., 6/4, which could often shift between combining two groups of three with three groups of two). It often functioned as an after-dance, sometimes related melodically or harmonically with the preceding piece, such as a Pavan, and of which examples are contained in *Casteliono*. In Susato's example, it serves as a complement to "Ronde VI." The *Passamezzo antico* was a bass pattern

---

[83] In fact a majority of the dances between numbers 1 and 13, with varied titles, are in triple time (6/4 when transcribed into modern notation) suggestive of the basse dance, though again, they do not conform to the formal pattern demanded by that dance.

[84] On this point see Daniel Heartz, "Sources and Forms of the French Instrumental Dance in the Sixteenth Century," PhD diss., Harvard University (1957), 115–16.

laid out in two phrases often of four bars each, over the chordal ("Greensleeves") scheme I-VII-I-V | I-VII-I-V-I. The pattern (and its associated harmonies) provided a framework throughout the Renaissance for improvisation, and sixteenth-century lute books are overrun with often interminable variation settings of the Passamezzo, especially the Passamezzo moderno, with a chordal scheme of I-IV-I-V | I-IV-I-V-I. Susato's version (in the usual duple meter) actually adheres only casually to the conventional scheme. In addition to these more-or-less standard dance types, Susato inserted several pieces identified only by title. Examples include Number 24, "Fagot," and Number 25, "Den Hoboecken Dans"; both are in modern 6/4 (i.e., in duple meter with triple division of the beat) and cast in three-measure units.

Susato's print reveals a repertory in transition. The basse dance was fast declining, while the pavanes and gaillardes, known for decades, were still going strong. New on the scene were the branles (here called *Rondes*) and allemandes. Fashions in dancing changed rapidly, and the prospective buyers for the volume probably wanted only what was current. Susato was himself a fine instrumentalist and had played innumerable dance jobs. Into the bargain he was also an outstanding composer. He was superbly equipped to meet the demand. The *Danserye* was not only up-to-date, it was of very fine quality.

12) Practice meets theory: Vincenzo Galilei's *Intavolature de lauto* (Rome, 1563_7) and *Fronimo Dialogo* (Venice, $1568_2/1584_5$)

The father of Galileo Galilei, a prolific and virtuoso composer of lute music, a music theorist, a teacher, and a crucial figure in the late sixteenth-century Florentine debates about modern and ancient music that led to the creation of opera, Vincenzo Galilei (*c.* 1520–91) was devoted to research, experimentation, and discovery, with much of his large body of music and writings applied to pedagogical ends.[85] Vincenzo anticipated the New

---

[85] Among the central studies about Vincenzo Galilei and his contributions are the following: Philippe Canguilhem, Fronimo de Vincenzo Galilei (Paris, 2001); Howard Mayer Brown, "Vincenzo Galilei in Rome: His First Book of Lute Music (1563) and Its Cultural Context." In *Music and Science in the Age of Galileo*, ed. Victor Coelho (Dordrecht, 1992), 153–84; Claude V. Palisca, *Girolamo Mei: Letters on Ancient and Modern Music to Vincenzo Galilei and Giovanni Bardi*, 2nd ed. (American Institute of Musicology, 1977); Claude V. Palisca, "Vincenzo Galilei and Some Links Between Pseudo-Monody and Monody," *MQ* 46 (1960), 344–60; Claude V. Palisca, "Vincenzo Galilei's Arrangements for Voice and Lute." In *Essays in*

Science by arriving at solutions through careful observation, and he relied on his practical training as a lutenist to carry out experiments and, ultimately, rectify what he believed were musicians' uncritical acceptance of inherited music theory.[86] An early champion of the empirical method, which the younger Galileo would employ as a cornerstone in his own work, Vincenzo wrote that he was "Moved by the truth, based on the experience of things and through different demonstrations."[87] He compared the density and tensions of lute strings made from different materials and wrote up their acoustical and physical properties; he examined the acoustical qualities of the materials from which instruments were made; and as a practicing musician, as well as a teacher of lute and voice, he advocated for equal temperament, marshaling experience and observation against the accepted mathematical foundations of tuning and intonation. Practicing what he preached, he included in his large manuscript lute anthology, *Galilei 1584*, two complete cycles, one in major, the other in minor, of Passamezzo – Romanesca – Saltarello settings on all twelve degrees of the scale.[88] A similar cycle was organized with the ricercars included in *Fronimo*. Vincenzo represents a unique example of a Renaissance instrumentalist/theorist: he was a virtuoso player, knowledgeable about ancient and modern music, conscious about his own historical position during a period of paradigmatic shifts in styles and compositional practice, and most of all was dedicated to ascertaining verifiable truths. History has assessed Vincenzo's major contributions mostly within the context of his polemic with his once revered teacher Gioseffo Zarlino, leading to his rejection of counterpoint and the publication of his "manifesto," the

---

Musicology in Honor of Dragan Plamenac, ed. Gustave Reese and Robert J. Snow (Pittsburgh, 1969), 207–32; and Claude V. Palisca, *Humanism in Italian Renaissance Musical Thought* (New Haven and London, 1985), 392–6.

[86] For a reconstruction of some of the experiments carried out by Vincenzo Galilei, see Claude V. Palisca, "Was Galileo's Father an Experimental Scientist?" In *Music and Science in the Age of Galileo*, ed. Victor Coelho, 143–51; for a more general but classic study by one of the great Galileo historians, see Stillman Drake, "Vincenzio Galilei and Galileo." In *Galileo Studies: Personality, Tradition, and Revolution* (Ann Arbor, 1970), 43–62.

[87] V. Galilei, *Discorso intorno all'opere de M. Gioseffo Zarlino* (Venice, 1589), 120. A detailed study and translation of Galilei's *Discorso* is in Randall E. Goldberg, "Where Nature and Art Adjoin: Investigations into The Zarlino-Galilei Dispute, Including an Annotated Translation of Vincenzo Galilei's *Discorso intorno all'opere de Messer Gioseffo Zarlino*" (PhD diss., Indiana University, 2011).

[88] For a facsimile edition, see *Vincenzo Galilei: Libro d'intavolatura di liuto*, introduction by Orlando Cristoforetti (Florence, 1992). A useful study is in Luis Gasser, "Vincenzo Galilei's Manuscript 'Libro d'intavolatura di liuto' (1584): An Introductory Study," DMA, Stanford University (1991).

Dialogo della musica antica et della moderna (1581). Yet, it was through his experience as a practicing musician that he formed his empirical methods of investigation, and it was moreover through his training as a lutenist that he was able to rationalize the co-existence of Renaissance counterpoint and the "new" music at the dawn of opera.

His claims of composing or arranging thousands of pieces notwithstanding, Vincenzo's surviving lute music still amounts to a considerable output of around 500 works, comprising some 200 intabulations, fantasias, and ricercars in addition to nearly 300 dance and variation settings.[89] The choice and compositional style of these works underscore many of the ideas that characterize Vincenzo's complex and sometimes polarized musical constitution, while demonstrating his vast historical knowledge of sixteenth-century vocal and instrumental music. His first book of lute music, the *Intavolature de lauto... libro primo* (Rome, 1563_7), appeared at the height of the instrument's popularity in sixteenth-century Italy. More lute tablatures were published during the 1560s than in any other decade, with Italian printers bringing out new repertory by composers such as Abondante and Gorzanis while drawing on the enduring posthumous reputation of the most famous lutenist of the Italian Renaissance, Francesco da Milano, by issuing six reprints of his music during this decade. But despite what would seem to be an advantageous time to publish his first book, Vincenzo did not seem overly concerned about its commercial appeal. The contents consist almost entirely of intabulations of madrigals or strophic arias on mainly unknown models; some of them are by Galilei himself, with others by relatively obscure composers, like the Roman singer Alessandro Merlo. There are no dance or variation settings in the volume, genres that dominate the work of Gorzanis, for example, as well as Vincenzo's own 1584 manuscript collection. At the end of the book appear six ricercars he attributes (in the dedication to the volume) to Francesco da Milano. On stylistic grounds, however, these cannot be accepted as authentic works by Francesco and must be discredited. They are, at best, pastiches largely written and assembled by Vincenzo, either to

---

[89] Unquestionably prolific, but equally prone to hyperbole, Vincenzo boasts in the revised 1584 edition of *Il Fronimo* that he had written "around two-hundred *Ricerche & fantasie* on various [melodic] subjects... more than five hundred *Romanesche*, three hundred *Pass'emezzi* [and] one hundred *Gagliarde*..." (104). Later, in his unpublished counterpoint treatise of 1588, he augments this number to an alarming 14,000 intabulations, an output that, as Canguilhem (Fronimo *de Vincenzo Galilei*, 42–4) notes, could have been achieved only if Vincenzo had intabulated the equivalent of at least one work daily for thirty-eight years.

flatter the dedicatee of the volume, Alessandro de' Medici, or to capitalize on Francesco's continuing popularity in the 1560s.[90]

As Howard Brown has shown, the importance of the 1563 volume lies not in any commercial or innovative appeal, but rather in what it reveals about Vincenzo's evolving aesthetic just prior to his period of tutelage under Zarlino, a time that is otherwise mostly undocumented. Through his choice of vocal models and styles of arrangements, Vincenzo clearly eschews the ornate and virtuosic courtly madrigal of the mid- to late-sixteenth century in favor of the venerable declamatory style of singing poetry to improvised chordal formulas that was native to Italian courts and nobility during the fifteenth and sixteenth centuries.[91] This is what Castiglione was referring to in the passage from *Il Cortegiano* as to what constitutes the best music among vocal and instrumental styles: "fine singing, in reading accurately from the score and in attractive personal style, and still more in singing to the accompaniment of the *viola*."[92]

Even though we possess the original vocal models for only a third of the twenty-four arrangements in this book, Vincenzo's intabulations reveal this *aria da cantare* style with precision: they are arrangements of declamatory, repeated-note vocal models whose chordal harmonies outline the traditional accompaniment schemes of the Romanesca, Folia, and Passamezzo that had been used by singers and poets to accompany their verses for a century. Vincenzo's seemingly odd (or, at least, obscure) choices as vocal models thus become clear. Although he had not yet begun his important research into Ancient music that would lead him to repudiate Zarlino's teachings, Vincenzo's 1563 collection of lute intabulations reveals that he already endorsed the important Italian tradition of the *aria da cantare*, featuring the clear declamation of poetry set to a chordal accompaniment.[93] As a practice that Humanists connected to Orphic song, it would become crucial in the new vocal music of the late sixteenth century as one of the main stylistic conduits to monody.

---

[90] On these ricercars and their dubious authorship, see Victor Coelho, "The Reputation of Francesco da Milano (1497–1543) and the Ricercars in the Cavalcanti Lute Book," *Revue Belge de Musicologie* 50 (1996), 49–72.

[91] See Brown, "Vincenzo Galilei in Rome." In *Music and Science in the Age of Galileo*, ed. Victor Coelho.

[92] Baldesar Castiglione, *The Book of the Courtier*, trans. George Bull (New York, 1976), 120.

[93] On the *aria da cantare*, see James Haar, "Arie per cantar stanze ariostesche." In *L'Ariosto: La musica, i musicisti*, ed. Maria Antonella Balsano (Florence, 1981), 31–46, and Victor Coelho, "Raffaello Cavalcanti's Lute Book (1590) and the Ideal of Singing and Playing." In *Le Concert des voix et des instruments*, ed. Jean-Michel Vaccaro, 423–42.

Vincenzo's most important work for the lute is his treatise entitled *Fronimo*. Long known as a teaching manual for arranging polyphonic vocal music for lute, it is more precisely a curriculum for learning counterpoint through the art of intabulation.[94] Written in the classic (indeed, Classical) format of a dialogue between teacher and student, it contains more than 100 intabulations of mostly madrigals and motets that Vincenzo uses not only as a systematic process by which to learn counterpoint and voice leading, but as a necessary intermediate step to the making of fantasias. Significantly, the genesis and publication history of the work span the most important period of Vincenzo's life. First published in 1568, the book was revised significantly when it was reissued in 1584, a period that witnessed a dramatic evolution in Vincenzo's fundamental musical orientation. Radicalized by his discoveries about Ancient Greek music, Vincenzo dramatically shifted his position from a devoted advocate of the writings of his former teacher, Zarlino, to that of a combative adversary. He repudiated the orthodoxy of Zarlino's rigid rules governing counterpoint, and criticized contrapuntal music itself for the failure of its imitative textures to deliver the moral effects ascribed to the solo singing of the Ancient Greeks, the styles and aesthetics of which Galilei was now in the throes of actively recovering through his correspondence with Girolamo Mei. Further, by regarding instruments as products of nature, the proud lutenist opposed Zarlino's Boethian taxonomy in which vocal music was "natural," with instrumental music being "artificial," arguing that "the consonances that are born from the voices are not born from nature more than are born those that the strings give us...."[95]

Within this dialectic, Vincenzo's approach to instrumental music reveals a resolute but somewhat conflicted personality. Even as he finds counterpoint inadequate to the task of expressing emotions in vocal music, Galilei's relationship to the lute leads him to uphold both the "Orphic" attributes of the instrument – that is, as accompaniment to the singing of airs – as well as its role as a translator of vocal polyphony into contrapuntal instrumental fantasies and intabulations. Similarly, as he rails against the speculative branch of music theory that endured in the sixteenth century even in the face of verifiable tests, he eventually finds his mission in trying to revive the (hardly quantifiable) affective powers attributed to music by the Ancient Greeks. Vincenzo thus comes across as both a Humanist

---

[94] For a detailed study of *Fronimo*, including its publication history, revisions, and its place within the context of Vincenzo's other didactic works, see Canguilhem, Fronimo *de Vincenzo Galilei*.

[95] Galilei, *Discorso*, 81, translation by Goldberg, "Where Nature and Art Adjoin," 350.

reviving Antiquity and a consummate modern polyphonist, dedicated, like Bermudo before him, to the careful art of arranging – and, therefore, *validating* – polyphonic vocal music. Even his dance and variation settings contained in the 1584 manuscript collection are guided as much by contrapuntal textures as by inventive and virtuosic diminutions. In the end, Vincenzo's musical life was a balancing act: an advocate of counterpoint, a critic of counterpoint; dedicated to the ideal of accompanied solo song, and as well to propagating the species of arranged vocal polyphony for the lute. He knew – probably all contemporary lutenists knew – that the rise of accompanied solo song, in which the lute is an accompaniment, meant the decline of the intabulation, which is based on polyphonic models, and thus the end of the most abundant genre of Renaissance lute music: the arrangement of polyphonic vocal music into tablature. It is no surprise that in the seventeenth century, only a tiny portion of the almost 2,500 extant Italian lute pieces are intabulations, or the pieces they spawned, fantasias.

13) Keyboard music in Venice: Claudio Merulo, *Ricercari d'intavolatura d'organo* (Venice, 1567$_2$) – *Ricercari*

In total numbers, lute music dominated the printing of instrumental music between 1500 and 1600, but in Italy keyboard music began to challenge that stature in the last quarter of the century. By the early seventeenth century the balance was reversed as keyboard music, particularly with the cultivation of the ricercar and toccata, became preeminent. That shift is signaled by Merulo's *Ricercari* of 1567.

Much of our attention on Renaissance keyboard music has rightly focused on Venice, given its position as the publishing and commercial capital for music, and because of the long line of extraordinary organists associated with the Basilica San Marco, including Annibale Padovano (1527–75), Claudio Merulo (1533–1604), and Andrea Gabrieli (1532/33–85). In addition to the Venetian school, keyboard composers working in Naples and Ferrara also played an important role in the development of the sixteenth-century keyboard ricercar, canzona, and the toccata. Thus, it is in the keyboard repertory where the most significant compositional activity in late sixteenth-century solo instrumental music can be found. The *Ricercari* provides insight into the contextual setting of late Renaissance keyboard music and underlines Merulo's importance in the cultivation of the keyboard ricercar, contributing significantly to a long line of development that culminates in the toccata and fugue works of Johann Sebastian Bach. Merulo is also representative of a new type of instrumental musician of the late Renaissance, one whose training underscores the equal commitment to voices and instruments. Like his fellow organists at San Marco, Girolamo Parabosco, Claudio Reggio, and Andrea and Giovanni Gabrieli, as well as his contemporaries Dowland, Byrd, Luzzaschi, and the young Frescobaldi, Merulo was a prolific composer of both instrumental *and* vocal music, and in both secular and sacred styles. In addition, he was active in the entrepreneurial side of music, and from 1566–71 operated his own printing operation through which he published some thirty-five books, including the 1567 *Ricercari*.[96]

Born in the town of Correggio, near Parma, in 1533, "Claudio da Correggio" arrived in Venice in 1556 to succeed Giovanni Parabosco as second organist to Annibale Padovano, winning the position over Andrea Gabrieli (who nevertheless became second organist to Merulo in 1565). His Venetian years reveal a musician closely connected on the one side with nobility and patrons, and on the other with the artisanal and crafts culture of the book trade and organ builders. This wide circle of relationships with individuals of various strata is matched by the astonishing range of his musical output, spanning sacred and secular vocal works, keyboard music, and occasional music commissioned for courtly weddings, important Venetian celebrations, and political events.[97] During their eighteen years as first and second organists at San Marco, Merulo and Gabrieli were known for their extraordinary skill at improvising, and their published keyboard works inventively blend this art within a contrasting and contrapuntal texture. These qualities can be seen in particular in Merulo's toccatas, the genre that he brought to a high stage of development with the nineteen toccatas he published in two copper-engraved volumes in 1598_9 and 1604. Merulo remained in Venice until 1584, leaving finally to accept a lucrative position at the Farnese Court in Parma, where he remained until his death in 1604.

---

[96] For an extensive study of Merulo with much detail on his printing activities, see Rebecca Edwards, "Claudio Merulo: Servant of the State and Musical Entrepreneur in Late Sixteenth-Century Venice," PhD diss., Princeton University (1990). A modern edition of the *Ricercari* is in John Morehen, ed., *Claudio Merulo: Ricercari d'intavolatura d'organo* (Madison, 2000).

[97] For a study of one of these, Henry III's visit to Venice in 1574 for which Merulo was commissioned to write the music for a *Tragedia*, see Iain Fenlon, "Merulo and State Ceremonial: The Visit to Venice of Henry III." In *A Messer Claudio, Musico: Le arti molteplici di Claudio Merulo da Correggio (1533–1604) tra Venezia e Parma*, ed. Marco Capra (Venice, 2006), 261–75.

In tracing the imitative ricercar prior to its cultivation by Merulo, historians of keyboard music have generally looked to the works of Girolamo Cavazzoni, Annibale Padovano, and, more recently, the works contained in the Bourdeney Codex, written most probably by Giaches Brumel, who worked in Ferrara.[98] This chronology ignores, however, the history of the imitative ricercar for lute. Musically, the lute ricercar can be traced through three evolutionary, though overlapping, stages that developed rapidly from the beginning of the sixteenth century to around 1546: 1) the early non-imitative ricercars by Spinacino and others published in the Petrucci lute books during the first decade of the sixteenth century;[99] 2) the more fluid and texturally diverse works copied in *Capirola* from around 1517, which also contain some of the first intabulations of vocal works clearly written after 1500; and 3) the refined, imitative, and formally organized works of Francesco da Milano, Marco dall' Aquila, and Albert de Rippe, published first in 1536, but having developed for more than a decade earlier during the period of Francesco's appointment at the papal court under Leo X and Clement VII Medici.[100] While it is, of course, to be expected that Merulo was more familiar with the early keyboard models of the genre than those for lute, we must acknowledge as well the debt owed to the fully developed imitative style already present in the lute ricercar of the 1520s.[101]

---

[98] The works in this very large collection represent an important development in the imitative keyboard ricercar around 1550, splintering from its Venetian models and comprising a new Ferrarese style that formed the crucial background to the works of Luzzasco Luzzaschi and, eventually, Frescobaldi. On the musical style of the Bourdeney ricercars, see Anthony Newcomb, ed., *The Ricercars of the Bourdeney Codex* (Madison, 1991), xiv–xvii.

[99] The non-imitative ricercar did not completely "evolve" into the imitative kind, and several of the former appear as examples in the mid-century viol treatises by Ganassi (1542_2) and Ortiz (1553_5).

[100] On instrumental music under Leo X, see Cummings, *The Lion's Ear*, 144–57. Pushing the development of the imitative ricercar even earlier, Cummings suggests (153) that the lutenist Gian Maria Giudeo's performance with his group of *violini* for Leo X at the Villa Belvedere in 1513 may have consisted of ricercars. On the contextual relationship of Francesco's ricercars during the papacy of Leo X's successor (and cousin) Clement VII, see Coelho, "Papal Tastes," 277–92.

[101] The entry on the ricercar in *New Grove* (vol. 21, 306) is characteristic in placing the earliest examples in the 1540s, citing the *Musica nova* anthology (1540_3), and for keyboard, Girolamo Cavazzoni's *Intavolature...* (1543_1). Similarly, in the introduction to his edition of Merulo's 1567 *Ricercari*, Morehen, while acknowledging the lute ricercar, follows *Grove* by locating its transition to the fully imitative form only with the 1547 and 1552 collections of Simon Gintzler and Bálint Bakfark, respectively; see Morehen, ed., *Claudio Merulo*, ix. In his introduction to *The Ricercars of the Bourdeney Codex*, Anthony Newcomb does not consider any lute tablatures in his account of the development of the imitative ricercar, writing that "All of the composers of imitative ricercars between Girolamo Cavazzoni [1543_1] and Frescobaldi [1615] were organists" (xvii).

Ricercari was among the books Merulo published as part of his printing business. It inaugurated a projected, but unrealized, twelve-volume series of keyboard music featuring his own works and those by other composers, including Giaches [Brumel?] of Ferrara and Andrea Gabrieli, providing some clues to Merulo's world of influences.[102] Each of the eight ricercari in the print corresponds to one of the church modes, an organization that can be found in some keyboard, vihuela, and ensemble publications, but in this case betraying a practical organization for use in the liturgy, perhaps as preludes to prescribed vocal pieces in the same mode. Merulo's ricercars are consistently long and expansive, beginning broadly with subjects that are usually decorated – somewhat formulaically, it has been said[103] – with recurring units of faster notes in both hands. Most of Merulo's ricercars are polythematic, some with as many as seven or eight subjects, but the ricercar on the second tone is monothematic, consisting of the contrapuntal elaboration of a single subject. This focus on a single melodic idea is a progressive tendency of the sixteenth-century ricercar, one that directly anticipates the fugue of Bach's time, though similar pieces are already present in lute ricercars of Francesco da Milano printed in 1536.[104]

Formally, the ricercars normally unfold in a series of small episodes. In the *Ricercar del primo tuono*, for example, a highly embellished first section in which the subject appears together with its inversion, gives way in m. 10 to a short, undecorated chordal section in long notes with the subject still prominent in the highest voice. The rest of the piece plays off these two contrasting treatments – decorated vs. undecorated – while introducing new subjects. Combining virtuosity and skill at embellishment with a rich and varied contrapuntal framework, Merulo made an enormous contribution to the imitative genre. Through his finesse in combining learned counterpoint, improvisation, and idiomatic keyboard passagework, along with his own entrepreneurial efforts, Merulo did more than anyone to popularize the ricercar genre.

Who were his audiences for these pieces? Merulo's close relationship to Venetian society provided many opportunities for his music to be heard, particularly at the musical soirées at which he is documented as

---

[102] For a summary of this series, see Morehen, ed., *Claudio Merulo*, x–xi. On the possible identity of "Giaches," see ibid. x, n. 16.

[103] Ibid., ix.

[104] Ricercars 30 and 33, for example, using the numbering in Ness, *The Lute Music of Francesco Canova da Milano*.

attending.[105] Like dances and intabulations, the ricercar was consumed and played by amateurs, particularly, it would seem, in an ensemble setting. One of the main collections of four-part ricercars of the period, in fact, is titled *Musicque de joye* (154?$_6$), a print by the Lyons publisher Jacques Moderne that includes twenty-four ricercars (many of them originally published in the Venetian *Musica nova* print of 1540$_3$) and clearly intended for domestic and amateur enjoyment. Merulo remained influential throughout the second half of the sixteenth century, not just as composer and performer but as a teacher as well, as his student Girolamo Diruta acknowledged in his important keyboard treatise, *Il Transilvano* (which contains a dedicatory letter to Merulo), first published in 1593$_3$: "Of special interest are the tablatures of Claudio Merulo who, more than any other man, has outdone himself in this fine art of figured intabulation as you can see in his various printed work – Masses, ricercars, canzonas, and toccatas."[106]

14) International repertory on the periphery: Lerma, Archivo de San Pedro, MS. Mus. 1 (*c.* 1590) – *Lerma 1*

The prominence of sacred pieces in *Copenhagen* may testify to instrumental participation in church services, but actually provides no evidence of how or where within a service the players might have inserted their contributions. For detailed information in this regard we can turn to Spain. Churches in Spain's larger cities engaged professional wind bands as part of their permanent staff beginning in the 1530s, and by 1550 such ensembles were a prominent feature of Spanish musical culture. Documents related to the hiring of the musicians provided detailed information of what their participation in services was to be. Most importantly, they assisted in performances of psalms at Vespers, and played motets at specified points in Mass celebrations (at the Elevation of the Host, for example). Fortunately several musical manuscripts survive conveying

---

[105] See Rebecca Edwards, "Claudio Merulo, l'altro gioiello nella corona di Correggio." In *A Messer Claudio, Musico*, ed. Marco Capra, 17.

[106] Girolamo Diruta, *Il Transilvano* (pt. 2, 1609), in Edward J. Soehnlein, "Diruta on the Art of Keyboard-Playing: An Annotated Translation and Transcription of *Il Transilvano*, pts. I (1593) and II (1609)," PhD diss., University of Michigan (1975), 248. For a published translation and commentary, see Girolamo Diruta, *The Transylvanian*: Il Transilvano, ed. Murray C. Bradshaw and Edward J. Soehnlein (Henryville, PA, 1984).

repertories prepared for these ensembles as they performed their duties; of these, the two so-called Lerma codices are particularly intriguing.[107]

We can only marvel that these two collections survived at all. Kept in the small church of San Pedro in Lerma from the early 1600s, they managed somehow for centuries to evade being tossed into a rubbish bin. One was stolen in the late nineteenth century, but ultimately ended up in the safe haven of the University Library in Utrecht (*Lerma 2*). The other was at some point haphazardly tucked away in the organ case in the San Pedro church, and lay there forgotten until rediscovered in 1979 (*Lerma 1*).[108]

The background story of the manuscripts is unsavory. The Duke of Lerma in the late sixteenth century was the most powerful confidant of the Spanish king, and used his position to twist the court machinery to his own ends. He accumulated vast wealth in a classic case of corruption run wild. Some of that wealth was used in an attempt to make something grand of the inauspicious small town of Lerma, the family seat. Included in that program was an expansion of the church of San Pedro, with provision for, among other features, a wind ensemble (hired in 1607) to add grandeur to the services there. At about the same time *Lerma 1* and *2* were acquired to provide repertory for that ensemble.

Lerma 1 was actually assembled in the 1590s, clearly by a professional Spanish church musician. Its contents were thus perfectly suited for the demands in the city. It begins with seven pieces, each titled "Tono," all organized by mode. The first, for example, is indicated as being in the first mode, the Dorian (here transposed to G). It consists of six verses, and in performance these verses served during Vespers in psalm performances,

---

[107] Concerning the items played by Spanish church musicians, see Kenneth Kreitner, "The Cathedral Band of León in 1548, and What it Played," *EM* 30 (2003), 41–62. Kreitner has also provided a concise description of the primary manuscripts in "The Repertory of the Spanish Cathedral Bands," *EM* 37 (2009), 267–86. An earlier Spanish source of music for ensembles is Granada, Biblioteca de Manuel de Falla, Ms. 975; on this source, see Juan Ruiz Jiménez, "The Mid-Sixteenth-Century Franco-Flemish Chanson in Spain; The Evidence of Ms. 975 of the Manuel de Falla Library," *TVNM* 51 (2001), 25–41. The two manuscripts in Coimbra, Biblioteca Geral da Universidade, MS M. 48 and MS M. 242, contain related repertory – see Bernadette Nelson,. "The Chansons of Thomas Crecquillon and Clemens non Papa in Sources of Instrumental Music in Spain and Portugal, and Sixteenth-Century Keyboard Traditions." In *Beyond Contemporary Fame: Reassessing the Art of Clemens non Papa and Thomas Crecquillon*, ed. Eric Jas (Turnhout, 2005), 177–85.

[108] A detailed account of the survival of the manuscripts is given in Douglas K. Kirk, "Churching the Shawms in Renaissance Spain: Lerma, Archivo de San Pedro Ms. Mus. 1," PhD diss., McGill University (1993). Kirk provided a more concise discussion in the prefatory material in his edition, *Music for the Duke of Lerma; Canciones and Motets of Four, Five, and Six Voices: The Music of Archivo de San Pedro de Lerma ms. Mus. 1* (Watertown, MA, 2003).

with alternate verses being sung monophonically by the choir. The first section of *Lerma 1* (which consists of eleven numbered items) ends with a series of "Fabordones," indicated as "para chirimías", that is, "for shawms," which are also organized by mode. These were probably also to be performed *alternatim* for the performance of psalms. The remaining contents, some eighty-one items, are more substantial pieces, the function of which was primarily for insertion in the Mass at moments when an instrumental interlude would have been appropriate. A few of these are given titles, designating them as motets; number 19, for example, is a setting of *Per signum crucis* by Guerrero. Most of the pieces, however, are given neither title nor composer attribution, perhaps to disguise the fact that included are chansons by such composers as Clemens, Crecquillon, and Lasso, and madrigals by Striggio, Verdelot, and, again, by Lasso. Spanish composers are included, especially Guerrero, Morales, and Alonso Lobo, but Franco/Flemish influence is heavy, including both the older generation (Crecquillon and Clemens) and the somewhat more contemporary Lasso. In spite of the inclusion of pieces by Philippe Rogier, a Franco/Flemish composer active at the Spanish court in the 1580s and 1590s, the selection is distinctly conservative. No dance pieces are included, underlining the point that the entire repertory for *Lerma 1* was intended for use in sacred services. The lack of titles for most of the motets and, of course, for the chansons and madrigals, led Kirk to the reasonable conclusion that when wind players performed from *Lerma 1* "they chose what they liked best when they needed to perform at free spots in the liturgy."[109]

The inclusion of Italian pieces by Lasso and Striggio in *Lerma 1* marks the major shift of the musical center of gravity that occurs markedly after about 1550. This was hinted at also in *Copenhagen*, but is demonstrated quite clearly in a group of sources now in Regensburg. In the manuscript assembled by Wolfgang Küffer in the late 1550s while he was a university student in Wittenberg, about half of the contents are sacred music (mostly motets, but with a handful of Mass settings as well).[110] The rest of the pieces are secular, rather dominated by French chansons, but with the inclusion of numerous German songs as well. The striking new feature is

---

[109] Kirk, *Music for the Duke of Lerma*, xxi.
[110] Regensburg, Bischöfliche Zentralbibliothek (Proskesche Musikbibliothek), Ms. A.R.940/41. On this manuscript, see Wilfried Brennecke, *Die Handschrift A. R. 940/41 der Proske-Bibliothek zu Regensburg. Ein Beitrag zur Musikgeschichte im zweiten Drittel des 16. Jahrhunderts*. (Kassel, 1953). Brennecke edited a selection of the pieces in *Carmina Germanica et Gallica*, Hortus Musicus, vols. 137–8 (Kassel, 1965).

that Küffer also included over forty Italian madrigals. Significant, too, is the presence of one piece by Lasso, who was just beginning to make a name for himself. This shift in the direction of the madrigal is also seen in the manuscript Regensburg, Thurn und Taxissche Hofbibliothek, Ms. F.K. Mus. 3/I, from about the same time, which is entirely secular containing a mix of chansons and madrigals, and, oddly, only one German song.[111] The full impact of the late sixteenth-century vogue for Italian music, though, is seen in the later source, Regensburg A.R. 775–777, comprising six part books assembled about 1590.[112] The appeal of the earlier generation of northerners is hanging on, but just barely: only two motets by Josquin, two by Clemens, and one chanson by Crecquillon appear. The rest of the contents are completely dominated by Italians, with Lasso as the featured composer. (With his avid promotion at the Bavarian court of Italian music and musicians, by this time he is best considered a part of the Italian scene.) Significantly, three motets by Andrea Gabrieli are tucked in toward the end of the collection.

In sum, *Copenhagen* and the *Lerma* collections reflect the demands on professional players, and are geared for performance in sacred settings. In contrast, the Regensburg manuscripts, assembled for the use and enjoyment by amateurs, lean toward a secular repertory. Nonetheless they all share one feature: none contain any music that can be termed idiomatic for instruments. With the exception of the dance pieces, almost all the repertories were drawn from vocal sources, and in fact, everything in them could easily have been sung.

15) *Per sonare, non cantare*: Giovanni Gabrieli, *Sacrae symphoniae* (Venice, 1597$_5$)

With its dominant position in the trade between East and West, Venice had become the richest and most powerful city in Europe by the early Renaissance. This domination, however, was then challenged from two directions. The Ottomans began a successful campaign to capture Venetian outposts in the East. More seriously, the Spanish and Portuguese, followed by the Dutch and English, explored and exploited new trade routes that utterly transformed international commerce. Although the Venetians

---

[111] For an extensive discussion of this manuscript with an inventory, see Brinzing, *Studien*, 91–109.

[112] The full entry is Regensburg, Bischöfliche Zentralbibliothek (Proskesche Musikbibliothek), Ms. A.R. 775–777; for a discussion and inventory, see Brinzing, *Studien*, 110–28.

defeated the Ottomans at the famous battle at Lepanto in 1571, a victory that resonated symbolically in both art and music, by the middle of the sixteenth century inexorable decline had set in and Venice was no longer a major player in international politics.[113] In one of the ironies of cultural history, it was at precisely at this time that *La Serenissima* entered an era where it reigned supreme in music. The beginning of this dominion is symbolized by the publication in 1597 of the *Sacrae symphoniae* of Giovanni Gabrieli (c.1555–1612).

The *Sacrae symphoniae* contains, along with a large selection of motets, sixteen instrumental pieces comprising fourteen *Canzoni* and two *Sonate*. With these pieces ensemble instrumental music finally achieves its own idiomatic character. While the lute fantasia and keyboard ricercar began blossoming in the 1520s, the ensemble equivalent, which had a promising start about 1490 with pieces by Isaac, such as "La morra," and Josquin, with "La Bernardina," seemed to have faded away. At first glance this seems puzzling, for there was an increasing demand for instrumental ensemble music by both amateurs, as viol consorts became the rage, and professionals, with court and civic bands in all regions entering a period of vigorous expansion. Potential interest in the ensemble fantasia, however, was diverted. Dance music became a great favorite for amateurs, as shown by numerous publications by Attaingnant, Moderne, and Susato. Just as important, for professionals the chansons of such composers as Sermisy and Crecquillon on the one hand, and motets by Gombert and Clemens non Papa, on the other, all provided ready-made counterparts of the lute fantasia or keyboard ricercar. In fact, the chanson, motet, and even the early madrigal continued to provide the basic repertory for professionals until well after 1550. Professionals, at any rate seem to have ignored the few publications of ensemble ricercars or fantasias that began to appear in the 1540s. The ricercars contained in *Musica nova* of 1540_3, for example, even those by Willaert, are completely absent from the important Copenhagen and Lerma manuscripts that reflect the repertories of professionals.[114]

By the 1570s and 1580s, publications of instrumental music, particularly those of Merulo (1574_3), Maschera (1584_{10}), and Andrea Gabrieli (1589_3), reveal that the character of ensemble music was changing.

---

[113] On the artistic, mainly Roman, response to the victory at Lepanto, see Iain Fenlon, *Music and Culture in Late Renaissance Italy* (Oxford, 2002), 139–61.

[114] The conservative and densely contrapuntal style of the *Musica nova* print was continued in Jacques Buus's *Recercari* (1547_1) and Annibale Padovano's *Il Primo Libro de Ricercari* (1556_9).

The four-part ricercars of Andrea Gabrieli (c.1532–85) exploit devices that would have been effective in performance by cornetts and sackbuts. The repeated notes that are shot throughout his *Ricercar del Sesto Tuono* seem designed for performance by wind instruments, as do the contrasting blocks of high and low parts in the *Ricercar del Duodecimo Tuono*. The clear formal structures of both ricercars also work especially well for instruments. Still, Andrea Gabrieli did not consistently push stylistic boundaries in this regard. His one preserved eight-part ricercar that is contained in the *Concerti* print of 1587_3 is distinctly conservative – at least in contrast to those by his nephew Giovanni.[115] The instrumental pieces in the *Sacrae symphoniae* call for large ensembles (six for eight parts, five for ten, two for twelve, and one piece is for fifteen), divided into contrasting choirs. These numbers themselves signal a change. The four-part ricercars of Andrea Gabrieli appealed to a range of amateur and professional performers, giving his 1589 print a reasonably broad market. The large-scale pieces by Giovanni, on the other hand, were far more restricted in potential use. These were performed not only by professionals, but indeed by those attached to the very largest institutions.

One such institution was, of course, St. Mark's in Venice, where Gabrieli was appointed organist in 1585, following Claudio Merulo's departure, a post he retained until his death. In contrast, Antwerp and Augsburg at this time were only supporting five or six players and definitely could not have performed the larger pieces without considerable extra effort and expense. The *canzoni* are usually, but not always, polychoral, written to emphasize contrasting blocks of sound. The *Canzon Septimi Toni a 8* (p. 32), justifiably a great favorite of modern brass players, opens with one choir sounding a typical chanson dactylic opening, which is immediately repeated by the contrasting ensemble; a dotted-rhythm figure follows, again echoed by the second group, and this is followed by an astonishing repeated, machine-gun like effect, yet again bouncing between both choirs. This opening segment is repeated at the end of the piece, yielding an effective large-scale ABA structure. Some critics have observed that Gabrieli favored antiphonal repetition over pure counterpoint, but this was in fact a function of writing for eight or more independent parts. When he composed for four, as in the spectacular *Canzona III* from the *Canzoni per Sonare* of

---

[115] Both the 1587_3 and 1589_3 publications appeared after Andrea's death in 1585, and the pieces probably date from earlier, perhaps by as much as fifteen years.

1608, Gabrieli produced brilliant counterpoint that was at the same time highly idiomatic for cornetts and trombones.[116]

Only five of the pieces in the *Sacrae symphoniae* are provided with specific instrumentation, but it is clear from these that cornetts and trombones were a basic part of the plan. The violin could be called upon for very high parts (one exception being in the *Sonata pian' e forte*, where the "violino" is quite low and would have required an instrument of the size of a viola). Only one piece calls for the organ, but all the pieces were probably accompanied, at least on some occasions by organ.[117] As Charteris has observed, some passages, such as the two highest parts in the closing section of the ninth canzona, are highly idiomatic and were almost certainly written for the two virtuoso cornett players in the wind band at St. Mark's.[118] But little decorative roulades run throughout the volume, as, for example in the *Canzon in echo*. This is unquestionably idiomatic instrumental music.

The famous and frequently anthologized *Sonata pian' e forte* is remarkable in several respects. It is one of the first pieces to specify contrasting dynamics. Charteris has remarked that a piece by Banchieri published a year earlier had also indicated dynamic contrasts. Still, Gabrieli's *Sonata* certainly existed in manuscript before the publication date, and may have been composed well in advance of Banchieri's piece.[119] Gabrieli's piece was also one of the first to use the title "sonata." The title clearly had meaning for Gabrieli as this piece is quite different in effect than the canzonas. It avoids the repeated patterns so effectively used in the *Canzon Septimi Toni*, favoring instead a more restrained rhythmic motion. It is also a more intense and emotionally dark piece. The other sonata (number fifteen in the collection) is similarly more expressive than is the case with the canzonas.

Brilliant though Gabrieli's achievements were, his influence in Italy was blunted with the arrival of Monteverdi in Venice in 1613, which brought a different set of compositional priorities to bear. His impact north of the Alps, on the other hand, was immense, as Schütz in particular found ways to incorporate the massed choirs of wind instruments and strings into textures that also included solo voices supported by basso continuo. However mixed his influence, the expressive range, the quality, and the innovative approaches represented in the *Sacrae symphoniae* represent an

---

[116] *Canzoni per sonare con ogni sorti di stromenti* (Venice, 1608); see Richard Charteris, ed. *Giovanni Gabrieli, Opera Omnia*, Corpus Mensurabilis Musicae, vol. 12 (Neuhausen, 1998), LIV.

[117] See ibid., XVI–XVII. [118] Ibid., XIII. [119] Ibid.

extraordinary advance, and with this publication idiomatic instrumental music had truly come of age.

16) Viols, voices, and instrumental music in Elizabethan England: William Byrd, *Psalmes, Sonets, & songs... made into Musicke of five parts* (London, 1588$_2$)

The development of a distinctly English viol repertory seemed unlikely toward the mid-sixteenth century given the strong foreign influences at work. This history can be traced most distinctly from the records of the English royal court. Early in the sixteenth century a small ensemble of foreigners, playing bowed stringed instruments (called variously "vialles", "vyolles", or "viols"), were present among Henry VIII's instrumentalists. From their names it appears likely that they were Flemish. In the 1540s, however, an entirely new wave of influence arrived in the form of a complete ensemble of six musicians hired out of Italy.[120] These players were first noted as playing viols, though as Holman has noted, they were undoubtedly also able to provide music on violins when appropriate (as in, for dancing).[121] The viol playing of the Italian group seemed to have made an enormous impression. By mid-century, records begin first to show hints of local activity; this becomes a flood, and by the final decade of the century the viol became a central and essential ingredient in English amateur music making.

Despite the foreign dominance at the royal court, a distinctly English repertory developed soon after about 1550 along three fairly diverse, though overlapping, lines. The first was the consort song, the origins of which came from an unexpected quarter. At some point in the 1540s children in the Chapel Royal began to take up the viol. Soon after, this became a pattern with choir schools at other London institutions, such as St. Paul's and Westminster, as training on the viol came to be considered a valuable part of a child's education. By the 1550s, performances by these children with viols accompanying a solo vocal line became extraordinarily popular, and an entirely new genre, one unique to England, was born.[122] Chapel Royal composers such as Robert Parsons and Richard Farrant

---

[120] Ian Woodfield, *The Early History of the Viol* (Cambridge, 1984), 206–8. For further detail on both the Flemish and Italian players, see Holman, *Four and Twenty Fiddlers*, 71–80.
[121] Ibid., 87–8; Holman also notes (89) that after 1558 these musicians were consistently identified as "violins."
[122] Woodfield, *The Early History*, 212–15.

produced appropriate repertory, but the consort song surely would have been swamped by the overwhelming vogue for the Italian madrigal had it not been for the single-handed efforts of William Byrd, who found here a congenial medium.[123]

Byrd produced his first printed set of consort songs in his *Psalmes, Songs and Sonnets* of 1588 – ironically, in the same year in which the publication of *Musica Transalpina* signaled the arrival of Italian fashion at the center of English musical life in the form of the madrigal.[124] The songs were originally composed for a solo voice and four viols, though in order to appeal to a broader audience, all parts in this print were fitted with words. Many of the secular pieces in this print follow a pattern of a six-line verse with a repeat of the final two lines, set strophically for subsequent verses. Byrd's textures are uncompromisingly and elegantly imitative and contrapuntal – even the grieving outcries of "O Sidney, prince of fame" in the lament on the death of Sir Philip Sydney are cloaked in garlands of counterpoint. In the four-part viol consort the voicings shift occasionally; at times the singing part is in the medius (as in "Why do I use"), with a viol then assigned to the superius; in this case, in fact, a real treble viol would be the most comfortable choice (otherwise, the highest part often could be managed on a tenor instrument). The quality of the songs throughout the range of expression from solemn to light-hearted is of the first order. Here we see the results of genius; Byrd breathed life into the consort song as a genre, and his emotional and technical efforts were brilliantly extended in the songs and verse anthems by the subsequent generation of composers such as Orlando Gibbons and Thomas Weelkes.

In the second repertory, English composers produced pieces appropriate for ensembles of viols, consisting of many elegiac settings of the *In nomine* (and a few other cantus firmus pieces), fantasias, and dances. The densely imitative *In nomine* was unique to Britain, and all seem to trace back to the *Benedictus* section of John Taverner's *Gloria tibi*

---

[123] For a concise survey of the consort song, see Philip Brett, "The English Consort Song, 1570–1625," *PRMA* 88 (1961–2), 73–88. See also Brett's preface to *The Consort Songs for Voice & Viols*, The Collected Works of William Byrd, volume 15 (London, 1970), v–vii. For the repertory of other composers, see Philip Brett, ed., *Consort Songs*, Musica Britannica, volume XXII (London, 1967). For an extensive survey of the consort song and its sources, see Craig Monson, *Voices and Viols in England 1600–1650: The Sources and the Music* (Ann Arbor, 1982).

[124] William Byrd, *Psalmes, Sonets and Songs (1588)*, ed. Jeremy Smith, *The Byrd Edition* 12 (London, 2004).

Trinitas Mass (*c*.1530).¹²⁵ The fantasias are written in imitative style similar to the Continental ricercar, but with more sections. Byrd produced outstanding examples of both types of works.¹²⁶ On the basis of what he saw as scant evidence for use of the viol in amateur circles in the second half of the sixteenth century, Paul Doe has suggested that this repertory was more likely to have been played by professional ensembles of wind players.¹²⁷ Woodfield and Holman, however, have produced ample evidence for ownership of viols by wealthy non-professionals.¹²⁸ Moreover, the pieces are contained in manuscripts, which seem largely compiled for and played by amateurs. In short, these pieces were most likely common fare in the late sixteenth century for English amateurs playing viols. Dances, on the other hand, certainly could have been tied to performance by both professionals and amateurs, and probably involved winds and violins as often as viols.

The third English repertory involving the viol is for mixed consorts, as called for in Thomas Morley's 1599_8 publication, *The First Booke of Consort Lessons*, which specifies on its title page "Treble Lute, the Pandora, the Cittern, the Base-Violl, the Flute & the Treble-Violl."¹²⁹ What is striking here is the precision with which the ensemble is named, this in a time when mixed ensembles in most instances were quite variable in their makeup. But this exact grouping was also called for in Philip Rosseter's *Lessons for Consort* published in 1609, and is noted in descriptions of a number of contemporary performances as well.¹³⁰ However specific Morley was concerning the ensemble, his publication consists almost entirely of dance pieces. In other words, while the ensemble mixture is unusual, the repertory itself is more-or-less standard ensemble fare. Still, the dances published by Morley stand apart in that they are for six parts, where dances were more often for four or perhaps five parts in other English sources.

---

[125] Oliver Neighbour, *The Consort and Keyboard Music of William Byrd* (Berkeley and Los Angeles, 1978), 26–50.

[126] The fantasies, *In Nomine* settings, as well as a dozen Hymn-Settings and Misereres (all based on a cantus firmus), are available in Kenneth Elliott, ed., *Consort Music*. In *The Collected Works of William Byrd* 17 (London, 1971).

[127] Paul Doe, ed., *Elizabethan Consort Music*, Musica Britannica 44 (London, 1979), xviii.

[128] Woodfield, *The Early History*, 211–12; Holman, *Four and Twenty Fiddlers*, 123–4.

[129] See [Sidney Beck], *The First Book of Consort Lessons for Treble and Bass Viols, Flute, Lute, Cittern and Pandora Collected by Thomas Morley, 1559–1661, reconstructed and edited by Sidney Beck* (New York, 1954).

[130] Holman, *Four and Twenty Fiddlers*, 131–40.

17) Insular genius at work: Fitzwilliam Virginal Book, Cambridge, Fitzwilliam Museum, Music MS 168 (c.1615-20) – *Fitzwilliam*

More than a hint of mystery lurks in the origins of the Fitzwilliam Virginal Book, long believed to have been compiled by Francis Tregian the Younger while in prison for his Catholic beliefs. That view now seems highly unlikely. Recent research has shown that several professional hands were involved in the copying, and the papers in the volume are both of a high quality and a type that suggests a connection to the royal court.[131] While the arguments are convincing in their own terms, what remains unexplained are the shadowed but nonetheless undeniable traces of Catholic connections. Tregian is mentioned several times, as are other prominent Catholics, such as Lord Lumley; in addition, at least three of the primary composers (Byrd, Peter Philips, and John Bull) were professed Catholics (though Bull's links are perhaps less than convincing as he fled to Antwerp to avoid prosecution for adultery and fornication, not religious persecution).

Containing almost 300 pieces, *Fitzwilliam* is by far the most extensive collection of its kind. It can be dated between 1615 and 1620, and contains a repertory that was probably composed between 1560 and 1615.[132] We are fortunate that it survives, for it gives a broad picture of the English harpsichord repertory at the end of the sixteenth century. In fact, no published sources of keyboard music are known in England until after the turn of the century. For that matter, no keyboard manuscripts have survived before about 1560, though their numbers increase considerably toward the end of the century. *My Ladye Nevells Booke* of 1591 is an example, though while carefully and elegantly prepared it consists exclusively of works of William Byrd.[133] In contrast, *Fitzwilliam* is unmatched in the range of composers it includes.

---

[131] Ruby Reid Thompson, "Francis Tregian the Younger as Music Copyist: A Legend and an Alternative View," *ML* 82 (2001), 1-31.

[132] For a convenient edition, see J. A. [John Alexander] Fuller Maitland and W. [William] Barclay Squire, ed., *The Fitzwilliam Virginal Book* (Leipzig, 1899; reprint, New York, 1979), 2 vols. For more recent editions, see John Bull, *Keyboard Music*, ed. John Steele and Francis Cameron, Musica Britannica 14 [henceforth MB] (London, 1960; revised edition, 1967); William Byrd, *Keyboard Music*, ed. Alan Brown MB 27 and 28 (3rd rev. ed. London, 1999 and 2004); Giles and Richard Farnaby, *Keyboard Music*, ed. Richard Marlow, MB 24 (London, 1965).

[133] For a discussion of this and other sources of English keyboard music, see Alan Brown, "England." In *Keyboard Music Before 1700*, ed. Alexander Silbiger (New York, 1995), 23-89.

Much has been made of both French and Italian influences on English music in the late sixteenth century, but the repertory in *Fitzwilliam* is English to the core: less than ten are by foreign composers. In all, some twenty-three named composers of the keyboard pieces are English as against four who are clearly foreign.[134] The repertory in the manuscript is diverse and sprawling, and its formal types are blurred in that pieces in almost every category involve variation in some fashion. A brief summary can be offered only in very broad strokes. First of all, *Fitzwilliam* is a secular collection, with less than a dozen pieces having sacred titles. Most of those are straightforward cantus firmus settings (such as the *Miserere*, no. 176, of William Byrd); a few, however, are elaborate sets of variations (an example is the Psalm 140, no. 144, by Sweelinck). In the secular pieces, cantus firmus settings also figure prominently, many of them employing variation technique. The pattern *Ut, re, mi, fa, sol, la*, for example, provides the basis for seventeen variations by John Bull (no. 51).[135] Closely related in principle to the pieces based on a cantus firmus are those that incorporate varied approaches to "grounds," i.e. repeated patterns, often, but not always in the bass. *Fitzwilliam* includes versions of both the *passamezzo antico* and *passamezzo moderno* basses (Byrd's "Quadran Paven" with its "Galiard," nos. 133–4 are remarkable examples of the latter). Some patterns for grounds are quite short (Byrd's "The Bells," no. 59, consists essentially of an alternation between just two notes, *ut* and *re*), while others, like Byrd's "Tregian's Ground" (no. 50), comprise twelve versions of an eight-measure pattern. Also related in approach are the many variation sets on popular or ballad English tunes; Byrd's setting of "Carmens Whistle" (no. 58) provides an example of these charming and appealing pieces.

If any genre provides the foundation for the repertory in *Fitzwilliam* it is the dance, and it appears in great variety. The traditional pavans and galliards, ubiquitous in English keyboard and lute music, are prominent, but there are numerous almands, courants, and jigs as well, the latter being conspicuously short with often only two strains and no variations.[136] They represent, in essence, keyboard versions of the dances in Susato's *Danserye*.

---

[134] This total does not include a few pieces by such composers as Marenzio, Lasso, and Striggio intabulated by Peter Philips. A Catholic, Philips fled England in 1582 when he was about twenty-two and settled eventually in Antwerp. While he evidently never returned to England, eighteen pieces are ascribed to him in *Fitzwilliam*.

[135] Neighbour, *The Consort and Keyboard Music of William Byrd*, 228–9, considers Byrd's two settings of this pattern as fantasias.

[136] There are examples of a few other kinds of dances, these include no. 373 (a "Morisco" [Moresca]), no. 207 (titled "Worcester Braules"), and no. 68 ("A Toye").

Some almands and most pavans and galliards are more complex, usually with each strain repeated with variations. But it was the pavan that stimulated particular interest for both *Fitzwilliam* and English lute composers. John Dowland's "Lachrymae" pavan was set three times, by Byrd, Morley, and Farnaby, and while pavans are often paired with galliards, these three are stand-alone settings. The structure of pavans varied. The usual formal pattern for pavans and galliards in *Fitzwilliam* was for three strains, each followed by a variation, as in Byrd's "Pavana," no. 252, followed by the "Galiarda," no. 253. But occasionally the schemes could be complex. In Bull's "Quadran Pavan" (no. 31), the first strain is based on the *pazzamezzo moderno* pattern. The second is a variation on the first that is followed by a third strain in a contrasting tonal area. After that come five more strains, some with variations based on the bass pattern, others being varied statements referring to the third strain. Added onto this pavan is a "Variation of the Quadran Pavan" (no. 32) that adds eight more variations, followed by the "Galiard to the Quadran Paven" (no. 33), which continues the same scheme with twelve variation strains. Settings of this sort may well provide an important insight into the performance practices of professional musicians who provided music for dancing. One of the puzzling aspects of the dances in such collections as Susato's *Danserye* is that they are clearly far too short to have actually been satisfactory for dancing. But if musicians added improvised variations, following the model of Bull's "Quadran Paven," they could provide for as much time as needed on the dance floor.

Another characteristic type in *Fitzwilliam* is the fantasia, and most of the prominent composers, with the exception of Gibbons, contributed examples (though Gibbons's fantasias are preserved in other sources). These pieces are highly imitative, usually in four parts, and, in contrast to many of the other types in *Fitzwilliam*, are through composed. Similarly, the almost twenty pieces entitled *Praeludium*, shorter and freer in structure than the fantasias, are also free of any variation technique. Finally, scattered here and there are a few whimsically titled pieces, usually quite short, such as "Farnaby's Conceit" (no. 273) and "Giles Farnaby's Dreame" (no. 194).

Fitzwilliam was most likely assembled by an amateur. Telling in this regard, given the link of paper types to those in use in royal court circles, John Bull, with forty-four ascribed pieces in the manuscript, was appointed the teacher of Princess Elizabeth in 1612. Whether or not any specific connection can be established with the princess, the technical demands of *Fitzwilliam* are formidable, and several other keyboard manuscripts from roughly the same time, also apparently intended for amateurs and similarly containing demanding repertory, reveal an extended network of interested and capable non-professional performers. This circle of amateurs evidently acted as a powerful stimulus on a remarkably talented group of native composers.

18) The magnificent close: Robert Dowland, *A Varietie of Lute Lessons* (London, 1610) – *Varietie*

The notion of an English "Golden Age" that has been applied to the late Elizabethan and early Jacobean periods ($c.$1580–1625) is nowhere more applicable than to the large and brilliant repertory cultivated by English lutenists, resulting in the last great flowering of the Renaissance lute. As with the parallel, but considerably smaller, keyboard repertory, English lute music is preserved almost entirely in manuscript, comprising just over 2,000 pieces distributed among some eighty-five sources.[137] The owners of these tablatures were typically upper class, giving them access to the music cultivated at the royal court and in noble households. They were wealthy and noble amateurs, university students, courtiers, and members of the Inns of Court.[138] At the professional level, lutenists were regularly employed in royal service during the reign of Elizabeth, with an augmentation in their numbers after 1577, coinciding with the appointment of the lutenist John Johnson. Most of the other eminent English lutenists were similarly attached to the court: Robert Johnson (the son of John Johnson), and the most famous English lutenist and songwriter of the period, John Dowland, both served under James I, and Daniel Bacheler – next to Dowland, the most skilled of the English lutenists – served as "groom" to Queen Anne. Outside of a direct royal appointment, many professional lutenists served courtier-patrons or in noble households.

English lute sources from this period are decidedly insular, containing relatively little foreign music. The Marsh Lutebook (Dublin, Archbishop Marsh's Library, Ms Z3.2.25 [$c.$1595]), however, transmits some international repertory, including sixteenth-century works by Francesco da Milano and Albert de Rippe, and among the over 400 intabulated

---

[137] See Julia Craig-McFeely, "English Lute Manuscripts and Scribes, 1530–1630," PhD diss., University of Oxford (1994), 36.

[138] See Matthew Spring, *The Lute in Britain: A History of the Instrument and Its Music* (Oxford and New York, 2001), 102.

accompaniments (that is, arrangements of vocal works minus the top voice) contained in the so-called Paston lute books are many Continental works.[139] Most English lute sources are unified by their choice of a core selection of dances favored in England, fantasias, and ballad tunes, often with variations. Dominating this corpus are settings of the pavan and the galliard, which together amount to over half of the entire repertory. Unlike lutenists on the continent, English players only rarely made solo intabulations (only 53 out of the 2,000 or so total pieces), though many dances have parallel versions as lute songs, the most famous being Dowland's "Flow my tears," known in countless instrumental versions as "Lachrimae Pavan." Dowland's solo lute version of this piece appears in manuscripts from the early to mid-1590s and was even published by Barley in 1596_4, predating the published lute-song version in 1600 and the arrangement for viols in 1604. Nevertheless, for pieces that come down to us in both instrumental and vocal versions, it remains difficult to know for sure – perhaps less so in this case than in others – which came first, the lute solo or the song.[140]

Varietie is one of the very few publications of English lute music from this period. Sensing the demand for, and absence of, printed lute music, the bookseller William Barley published the first dedicated book of English lute music, *A New Booke of Tabliture*, in 1596_4. This followed by almost thirty years an English translation of a lute tutor by the French lutenist and publisher Adrian Le Roy, which was published in 1568_3 as the *Briefe and easye instruction*. Barley's short anthology contains pieces by Dowland and Francis Cutting, though in corrupt and often unplayable versions. Restricted in his efforts to publish music by an exclusive privilege previously granted to Thomas Tallis and William Byrd, Barley was forced to use crude woodblocks to print tablature instead of moveable type – a complicated venture in the best of conditions, especially for works of the complexity of Dowland. The many errors that inevitably resulted soon drove Dowland to complain in the preface to his *First Booke of Songes* of 1597_4 that "There have bin divers Lute lessons of mine lately printed without my knowledge, falce and unperfect..." and promising "to set

---

[139] The Paston lute books have been described by Stewart McCoy, "Edward Paston and the Textless Lute-Song," *EM* 15 (1987), 221–7; see also Spring, *The Lute in Britain*, 259–62.

[140] For a short but persuasive argument favoring the primacy of the solo lute versions, see Robert Spencer, "Dowland's Dance Songs: Those of His Compositions Which Exist in Two Versions, Songs and Instrumental Dances." In *Le Concert des voix et des instruments*, ed. Vaccaro, 587–99.

forth the choicest of all my Lessons in print...,"[141] a goal fulfilled to some extent, and only, by the *Varietie*. In his book, Barley also reproduced Le Roy's "sundrie easye and familiar instructions" for playing the lute, but in an abridged and truncated form, which compromised their usefulness as well. Clearly, with the lute at the height of its popularity in England, there was a need for reliably printed and commercially available lute music with pedagogical support. This vacuum was partially filled by Thomas Robinson's *Schoole of Musicke* of 1603, which contains thirty-four delightful lute solos and duets along with a well-organized and informative treatise on playing the lute.[142]

It was thus a cumulative set of factors, 1) the pressing demand in England for available lute music to satisfy a growing public of amateur lute players, 2) the consequential need for an ancillary and integrated tutor for playing this music, and 3) the lack of an authorized codification of John Dowland's musical legacy at a time when the composer was actively seeking a courtly appointment, that forms the backdrop to the 1610 *Varietie*. Assembled by Dowland's nineteen-year-old son, Robert, *Varietie* adopts the successful format of foreign lute collections in which the pieces are organized by genre. His model was clearly Jean-Baptiste Besard's widely circulated lute anthology, *Thesaurus Harmonicus* of 1603; Dowland even translated into English the Latin instructions for playing the lute that appeared in the *Thesaurus*, to which he appended some "Other Necessary Observations" about lute stringing, tuning, and fret placement "by John Douland, Batcheler of Musicke." As claimed on the title page, the *Varietie* contains an international repertory of lute works "Selected out of the best approved AUTHORS, as well as beyond the Seas as of our own Country." Naturally, the music of Robert Dowland's father achieves a place of prominence: nine pieces by John Dowland (more than any other single composer) are included among the total inventory of forty-two compositions, which are divided into seven pieces each of *Fantasies, Pavins, Galliards, Almaines, Corantoes*, and *Voltes*.

Varietie offers a pivotal look at lute music in late-Renaissance England from three different vantage points – the past, the present, and the future. The first third of the book is distinctly retrospective, comprising the *Fantasies, Pavins*, and *Galliards*, and including eight of the nine compositions in the book by John Dowland. Given the accepted dating of the

---

[141] The preface is transcribed in Diana Poulton, *John Dowland* (Berkeley and Los Angeles, 1972; revised edition, 1982), 219–20.

[142] For an edition of the book, see Thomas Robinson, *The Schoole of Musicke (1603)*, edited and transcribed by David Lumsden (Paris, 1971/rpt. 1990).

central manuscript sources of Dowland's music, we can be certain that most of his work was composed in the 1590s, with little to be added to his corpus after 1604.[143] Similarly, the other English composers represented in these first three sections, Anthony Holborne, Alfonso Ferrabosco, and Thomas Morley, were, like Dowland, active mainly in the late Elizabethan period. Among the English composers in the *Varietie*, only Daniel Bacheler, a virtuoso lutenist on par with Dowland, remained prolific during the Jacobean era. His "Mounsieurs Almaine," which opens the section of almains, is one of the most impressive pieces of the lute literature: a series of brilliant variations using the full range of the instrument – some canonic and contrapuntal, others of dazzling scales, syncopations, and arpeggios – that call up the player's entire technical vocabulary. The fantasias that open the book are drawn from an international selection of lutenists of whose music John Dowland must have become familiar through his many travels in France, Italy, Germany, and Denmark between 1594 and 1606. Typical of the late sixteenth-century fantasia, these are long, arching works. Some are built on chromatic subjects that unfold slowly in imitation and open out sonorously into broad sections of scales and free counterpoint, often pushing the harmonic capacity of the lute (which has implications on fingering) to the extreme. The seven highly ornamented pavans, like the keyboard examples described above in *Fitzwilliam*, are in three sections, usually provided with a decorated reprise. The section of galliards is devoted almost entirely to the works of John Dowland. It contains many of his most popular settings, including the "ceremonial" galliard dedicated to his former patron, the King of Denmark, with its percussive rhythms and faux trumpet calls over long pedal points, a galliard dedicated to the (by then) disgraced Earl of Essex, based cheekily on Dowland's own song "Can She Excuse My Wrongs" from 1597_4, and the regal "Most Sacred Queen Elizabeth, her Galliard," which honors the queen with a setting of her favorite dance type appended with a sprightly *volta*.

A more contemporary group of works in *Varietie* appears in the section of almains, consisting of four anonymous dances arranged for lute from Ben Jonson's *Masque of Queens* of 1609.[144] Incidental music like this – shorter, and far less intricate than both Bacheler's and the other two almains in the section – appears with increasing frequency in English

---

[143] Spring, *The Lute in Britain*, 207.
[144] For the identification of the source of the masque dances, see Spring, *The Lute in Britain*, 222–4.

sources of the Stuart period. Similarly, the final two sections of *Corantoes* and *Voltes* betray the most contemporary continental influences in the print. These works, all of them by French composers, require a larger lute – one with a 9th course – than the earlier compositions, a detail of only an extra bass note but that nevertheless constitutes an important "tipping point" away from the "Renaissance" lute. Indeed, these pieces are more similar to those found in the Parisian lute books of Antoine Francisque (1600), Robert Ballard (1611/1614), and the French works contained in the manuscript of Lord Herbert of Cherbury (c.1624–40) than to the English tradition.[145] They look decisively towards the new tunings, larger instruments, and *stile brisé* textures that would soon dominate lute music, and their presence testifies to the imminent shuttering of the Renaissance lute tradition.[146]

---

[145] The Cherbury manuscript is Cambridge, Fitzwilliam Museum, Ms. Mus. 689.
See Craig-McFeely, "English Lute Manuscripts," 182–7, and Spring, *The Lute in Britain*, 232–4 (referenced as *Herbert*).

[146] In her discussion of *Varietie*, Craig-McFeely concludes that "the appearance of the French dances (volt and courant) in Dowland 1610B marked the beginning of an influx of these forms into English manuscript sources rather than following existing trends. [...] after 1615 [the English repertory] is principally French." Craig-McFeely, "English Lute Manuscripts," 67.

3 | The players

As we have emphasized, instrumental music of the Renaissance is a shared history between professional and amateur players, and for both groups of musicians the years between 1400 and 1600 were a time of profound change. This remarkable period of experimentation and exploration brought new approaches to performance as well as completely new instruments – and fundamental alterations to traditional ones – that swept away many established practices. For professional players, the way in which they were newly categorized in the social and courtly hierarchy serves as a symbol for the extent of the altered landscape. In the fifteenth century instrumentalists were routinely classified as "minstrels" and considered to occupy a lower order than composers and music theorists. By about 1550, however, this title had been cast off, and they began to be indexed under the rubric of "musicians" – a clear signal that instrumentalists were then completely integrated into the mainstream of musical culture.

The rise of the amateur class of musicians is directly related to the advent of printing, one of the most extraordinary inventions of the Renaissance. Music printing arrived only in 1500, but its appearance fundamentally altered how a non-professional attained musical competence. In the fifteenth century, if amateurs wished to learn music they worked with a professional who taught by rote. The process would be slow and time-consuming – even a skilled amateur could take weeks to learn two or three pieces, with constant supervision usually necessary. Since music manuscripts were largely copied, circulated, and preserved within the walls of court and church, or inside the chambers of urban elites, the production of written music prior to the age of printing was primarily focused on these contexts. The vast majority of surviving manuscripts were prepared with singers in mind, with only a tiny portion written for the exclusive use by instrumentalists. In contrast, among the earliest examples of music printing were books for amateur lutenists and keyboard players, containing not only music, but instructional prefaces as well, covering rudimentary aspects of notation, fingering, and elementary music theory. These prefaces were often reprinted for many years in subsequent books, resulting in a standardization of technique by around the 1540s. All of this did not eliminate the need for a competent teacher, but it certainly revolutionized the method by which non-professionals could learn music while also creating a large and growing class of amateur musicians, providing the stimulus for the growth of many related industries like printing, instrument and string making, and teaching.

The daily life of an instrumentalist: conditions of work

On the economic scale, professionals can be categorized in a number of ways. Chamber musicians (players of soft instruments) worked differently from loud instrumentalists, and within the loud category, trumpeters were not at all the same as professional wind players. For the professionals, however, the most critical pragmatic distinction was between those who had long-term contracts and constituted the heart of the permanent musical retinue, and the mostly freelance players, who were casual employees.

Contracted employment offered numerous advantages. One was an understanding that employment offered something equal to tenure at a modern university. At court this tenure would be for life – but "life," of course, referred to the lifespan of the noble, not the musician, though in most cases employment did continue through the sequence of death and succession. In cities, employment, once settled, was often for life – or, more realistically, would continue until old age; ill health meant that a musician could no longer function effectively.[1] Economic crises, if severe, could on rare occasions interfere. The cities in the Low Countries suffered setbacks in the turbulent years following the death of Charles the Bold in 1477, and several small towns in Flanders were constrained to dismiss their ensembles. The larger cities, however, managed to keep their musicians on their payrolls despite bleak conditions. Still, having a contract and a reasonably secure income was an enormous advantage in contrast to the conditions of freelance players.

Fringe benefits came with these employment contracts. Both court and civic musicians were provided with livery, a perk that should not be underestimated as this served as their basic daily clothing as well as a uniform. Payment records reveal that these outfits were characteristically

---

[1] In 1514, Giovanni Cellini (father of Benvenuto) lost his place in the civic ensemble in Florence apparently because he "did not play very well any more and was considered to be too old..."; see McGee, *Ceremonial Musicians*, 193.

made of fine wool patterned with the heraldic colors appropriate to the court or city. Musicians at courts could also be issued clothing for extraordinary events, such as weddings, coronations, or important funerals. Performers at the English court, for example, were provided with special livery for the coronation of Henry VIII and with "mourning liveries" for the funeral of Henry VII, both events occurring in 1509, as well as yet another set of "mourning liveries for the funeral of Prince Arthur" in February of 1511.[2]

Patrons often provided housing or subsidies for the same. In the ordinances of Edward IV, it is stated that for the court minstrels there should be given "sufficeaunt logging by the herbiger for them and theyre horsez nygh the court."[3] Still, the incomes of court musicians were usually enough to be able to purchase property, and most were able to establish themselves in permanent housing. Civic musicians, at least those in the large towns, also apparently commanded the resources necessary to own property once they became established. This was the case with musicians of Augsburg in the late fifteenth century, and the same was true in mid-sixteenth-century Bruges.[4] Sculptor, goldsmith, and musician Benvenuto Cellini informs us in his autobiography that his father, a civic musician in Florence, had one colleague (also a civic musician) who owned several properties in the city. The casual manner in which this information was given indicates that such holdings were not unexpected for musicians of their stature.[5] Because smaller towns offered fewer opportunities for freelance work, which was a significant source of income in larger cities, they did sometimes provide housing. This was particularly true in German towns, with "Stadtpfeifer"

---

[2] For livery provided at the court of Burgundy around 1400, see Wright, *Music at the Court of Burgundy*, 47; for Siena (in 1446), see D'Accone, *The Civic Muse*, 522. The household ordinances of Edward IV specify that the court minstrels were to receive "clothing with the household winter and somer"; see Conklin, "Medieval English Minstrels," 119. The English records of 1509 and 1511 are in Ashbee, *Records*, 15–19 and 33–4. For a wide-ranging assessment of livery of English waits, see Conklin, "Medieval English Minstrels," 209–13. Conklin (211–12) points out that while in several cities livery was provided twice a year, in London, in 1442, clothing was provided "yerely onys." She also records payments (114) twice a year for livery at the English court.

[3] Ibid., 119.

[4] For information on the Burgundian court, see Wright, *Music at the Court of Burgundy*, 36–7; concerning the Schubingers and Augsburg, see Polk, *German Instrumental Music*, 127–9, and for Bruges, see Louis Gilliodts-Van Severen, *Les Ménestrels de Bruges*. Essais d'archéologie brugeoise, vol. 2 (Bruges, 1912), 75 and 89–90. Tielman Susato was perhaps an exception, or in any case, the city of Antwerp granted him a subsidy to cover the cost of housing (*tot . . . huyshueren*), as, for example, in 1542; see Spiessens, "De Antwerpse stadsspeellieden," 50.

[5] Benvenuto Cellini, *The Autobiography of Benvenuto Cellini*, translated by George Bull (Hammondsworth, Middlesex, 1956), 26–7.

houses, a single dwelling where all the musicians were lodged at the city's expense, established in such towns as Nördlingen, Windsheim, and Leipzig (the building in Nördlingen survived until 1967).

Travel expenses were also normally covered for official musicians. Travel as an obligation fell far heavier on court musicians, for the higher nobility was often on the move, not only between summer and winter residences, but for diplomatic reasons and surveying territories. Because of their functions as both visible and aural status symbols, musicians traveled in the high style of the court, with fresh horses and livery. The standard grant of the court of Burgundy, for instance, included funds provided to each instrumentalist for a valet and two horses.[6] Even when traveling on more private business, court musicians were furnished with horses, as shown by several grants to the Bassano family in the mid-sixteenth century.[7] Travel by town musicians was a very different matter.[8] Civic ensembles called for heavy investment of municipal funds, and in return cities demanded a high level of service. Musicians in Florence, as shown above, were expected to play daily in the Signoria, while those in England had regular obligations to doing their rounds as waits. In the Low Countries, the musicians provided daily performances, at least when the weather was reasonable, from the balconies of city halls or from church towers. The sense of "obligation" was so strong that in Florence the town *pifferi* were not allowed to accept engagements outside the city without express permission from the city council. Of course, all of these performers did from time to time travel – the resolution by the city council in Florence that limited such jaunts undoubtedly arose because the *pifferi* had been absent more frequently than was acceptable.[9] In the exceptional situations where they might be sent out as part of an official delegation, they, like the court players, would be sent out in fine livery and on horseback.

Income and benefits

The primary advantage of a permanent position was the steady and predictable base income. Thousands of salary payments are extant from

---

[6] Wright, *Music at the Court of Burgundy*, 36.
[7] Ashbee, *Records*, 86 (in 1542); 97 (in 1545) and 120 (in 1552).
[8] Walter Salmen, *Der Spielmann im Mittelalter* (Innsbruck, 1983), 95–104, provides an extensive discussion of a minstrel's travels (as well as a survey of previous writing on the subject), with striking graphs showing travel networks to and from various locations.
[9] McGee, *Ceremonial Musicians*, 167–9.

throughout Europe for the Renaissance, but translating such records into an estimate of the actual standard of living remains conjectural. We lack information on such matters as the real costs of housing, food, clothing, and the value of gifts, sometimes including real estate. We also lack hard information on what the complete income of a musician might be. While we might know the base salary, detailed information on other sources of income is scarce. These sources could be compensation for extra freelance work within a city, performance fees for services at other locations, or income from apprentices. Nothing reveals the advantage of contracted status more than the case of Antwerp, where in 1431 the city authorities granted the civic musicians a complete monopoly in the hiring of performers for special events.[10] Such monopolies were offered more by middle-sized and smaller cities as a means of providing for adequate total income in order to attract and retain qualified musicians. In larger cities such as Ghent and Bruges, there was evidently so much work available that specifying a monopoly was unnecessary. Evidently most employers preferred to engage the most prestigious group available, which would be the official civic ensemble, and there was probably enough work to go around.

We can speculate that contracted civic musicians usually had a lock on the best of such potential sources of income, but if any musician kept track of that income, no trace of that remains. Both negative and positive indirect information confirms that such outside sources were profitable. From the negative side is the highly unusual decision taken by the town authorities in Bruges in 1481–2 to confer on the four members of the city's wind band a special subsidy. The city was suffering a severe economic crisis due to its attempt to resist the authority of Maximilian I. The wording reads that the subsidy was granted because the band "had little or nothing to do because of the sober times that now reign."[11] They had received their salary as usual, but without the support of extra income, that salary was insufficient.

A more positive outcome is chronicled in the tax records of Augsburg, which offer the most explicit estimates of potential total income available for musicians anywhere, for the city maintained detailed records throughout the Renaissance. The figures are startling. At the end of the fifteenth century the musicians who had been in service for a decade or more were in

---

[10] Spiessens, "De Antwerpse stadsspeellieden," 18.
[11] Gilliodts-Van Severen, *Les ménestrels*, 50, "dat zy lettel of niet te doene en hadden mids den sobren tyd die jeghenwoordelike regneert."

the top 15% of the income levels of the city. This picture of comfortable prosperity is not accurate for all cities at all times. Augsburg in the last decades of the fifteenth century experienced a generally upward movement in terms of its economic development, and it was a fairly large city. This probably meant that not only did the city offer a secure base salary for the city musicians, but also an ample opportunity for extra income from freelance activity, such as playing for dances and banquets. Meanwhile in Bruges, the city musicians were facing very difficult times, as shown above.

When several key elements were in place, a contracted urban musician could have a prosperous career. These elements were 1) being an official musician of the city, which gave not only a solid base salary, but opportunities to augment that salary significantly with extra work – for which the civic ensemble had priority; 2) that they remained in the city long enough to establish themselves firmly; and 3) that the city itself would continue to maintain a prosperous environment. An inescapable and harsh reality, however, was that even the most accomplished musicians could maintain the income stream only as long as they could perform. When old age arrived or illness struck, players who had been successful for years might sink into poverty. The stature of Florence and its commitment to the arts is reflected in the city's commitment to providing small pensions to retired musicians, but this was not at all a standard practice. Many cities granted old and impoverished players small individual grants, but when this occurred it resembled more a charitable donation rather than as a formal pension scheme related to years of service.

Our discussion of income to this point has emphasized the remuneration of civic musicians whose regular and functional duties were recorded with perfunctory administrative bookkeeping. Even when we consider the musicians of the court, here, too, practical detail is absent. We have available extensive payment records from such widely separated locations as the courts of Burgundy, Ferrara, and the royal court in England. Records from Ferrara are quite clear; the highest paid musician at the court in 1456, for example, was Corrado d'Alemagna, a wind player, who at thirty *lire* per month was earning more than three times the allowance for the lutenist Pietrobono, and was, in fact, the best-paid musician at the court. He was obviously well compensated, but any more detailed assessment of his total worth is impossible to assess: we know nothing of his property, of his routine expenses, or the total amount of his assets at any point in his life.[12]

---

[12] On relative compensations in Ferrara, see Lockwood, *Music in Renaissance Ferrara*, 177–84.

One useful and relative comparison of courtly salaries has been assembled by Craig Wright with reference to Burgundian musicians around 1400. He noted that by adding together the base salary of the Burgundian minstrels, along with frequent extra grants for "bons et agreables services," the incomes totaled around 400 francs per year. This was, as he notes, "almost ten times [the income] earned by a typical carpenter, mason, or town minstrel of this period."[13] Even this striking figure is understated, since Wright included only compensation from the court treasury, while ducal musicians had ample opportunity for outside income as well. As one example, the Duke of Burgundy made a regular round of visits to the wealthier cities in his domain, including Bruges and Ghent. When his minstrels performed in these cities, they were paid for their services from civic funds. A factor that clouds our judgment was that most of the high nobility were chronically in debt, as tax systems and accounts payable operations were generally inefficient. Maximilian I, because of his constant military campaigns, provides a prime example; it remains unclear how often he actually paid those who held the title of "Imperial Musician." Still, the attraction of court appointments was evidently irresistible.

In Augsburg, a city for which we have reasonably explicit information concerning the status of civic musicians, the contracted musicians were well paid, and yet consistently they would leave the city to serve in court ensembles in Germany and Italy. The Schubinger brothers (Michel, Augustine, and Ulrich the Younger) all began their careers as members of the Augsburg city ensemble, and all went on to distinguished service elsewhere (respectively in Ferrara, with Maximilian I, and in Mantua). We can assume that such moves carried the promise of even higher income potential for musicians than available in their home city. Court service offered pensions to instrumentalists more consistently at the end of their careers than was the case in cities, but as with civic musicians, the difference between their standard of living and their ability to sustain their career with full vigor and quality could be dramatic. Two of the preeminent players of the Burgundian court at the end of the fourteenth century, Jean de Dinant and Nicolas Alfons, were granted special pensions in 1409. This was not out of the ordinary, but the distressing reason given in the accounts for these grants was because of "their great age, poverty, and weakness."[14]

[13] Wright, *Music at the Court of Burgundy*, 43.   [14] Ibid.

While a firm correlation between financial compensation and social realities of civic and court musicians is difficult to extract, we possess many sources that at least suggest the basic outlines of their careers. For freelance musicians the documentation is largely blank. Their careers were urban, but for many cities – if we trusted the surviving sources – we would have to assume that they never existed, for little trace of their activity remains. Many of their contracts were evidently handshake agreements, or else their presence was so regular and functional that logging their daily activities would be as absurd as accounting for every horse and mule that trotted through town on any given day. Besides, many of these musicians may have been illiterate, thus the absence of documentation such as receipts, letters, and the like is hardly surprising.

Jobs for freelancers came from the same sources that supported contracted musicians, cities, urban confraternities, and occasionally the church, and for the same kinds of events, weddings, dances, and festival occasions. Paradoxically, opportunities seem to have been less (or at least less documented) in cities that had the strongest support of contracted performers. Confraternities in these cities hosted a regular round of occasions for which instrumental music might be considered desirable, but when this was the case, as for example at the Confraternity of Our Lady of the Snow in Bruges, the performers hired were almost exclusively the town civic ensemble.[15] This bias against freelancers is very clear in the extensive accounts recording payments to "traveling players" in Augsburg. During the fifteenth century, hundreds of instrumentalists are listed as receiving stipends, which were almost invariably awarded to either court musicians or performers attached to contracted civic bands. Gretchen Peters documents a range of potential income sources from processions, dances, weddings, and teaching, but even here the information is so scattered that we can get little sense of how musicians made a living without the steady support of contracted salaries.[16]

From the few tax records that have survived, we can occasionally reconstruct the situation with more certainty. In Augsburg, a few independent musicians were listed, mostly in two groups: one consisted of the non-contract wind players (the *Pfeifer*, as opposed to the *Stadtpfeifer*); the other was composed of players of soft instruments like the lute, harp, and fiddle. Judging from the taxes that they paid, their incomes were significantly lower than those of the most prosperous civic musicians. In cities where music guilds were established, it was the freelance players who formed the

---

[15] Strohm, *Music in Late Medieval Bruges*, 47–8. [16] Peters, *The Musical Sounds*, 165–89.

membership, and while the guilds may have been effective in achieving some of their goals, there is little evidence that their presence made any measurable difference in the gap between the incomes of contracted and freelance musicians. The wording of the 1481–2 decision by the Bruges city council tolls out what must have been a dreadful situation. The civic musicians had "little or nothing" to do beyond their contracted duties, though they retained their base pay and could petition the city for relief. Independent musicians had even less, and in most cases the city ensemble had first call on any work that was available. Their incomes in the best of times were probably marginal, and in the serious downturn in Flanders during those years, their existence must have been truly appalling. Just as in modern times, contracted employment was more secure and distinctly better rewarded than piecemeal work.

Guilds and education

Renaissance cities seethed with internal tensions. Political control was almost universally in the hands of a very small group of patrician families with the great majority of the urban population of journeymen, apprentices, and various day labors completely excluded from any direct influence on civic affairs. In such an atmosphere the trade guilds offered distinct advantages. For those within a trade, even a less prominent one, a guild offered protection, organizational by-laws, and some access to the power elite. Most importantly, the guild regulated conditions within a particular trade through limiting competition, establishing professional standards, settling disputes between members, and setting up the conditions for training.[17] Many instrument makers operated within the guild system, the lute and violin guilds at Füssen being among the most famous.[18] A fascinating document from the Füssen Lute Makers Guild in 1562 indeed reveals a highly regulated culture in which the Guild's techniques and monopoly are fiercely protected. Their charter describes an apprenticeship period of five years for aspiring makers with a further three-year embargo to imparting the acquired knowledge to others. Following this period, the apprentice can graduate to the level of master only through presenting his first lute to the guild for acceptance, after which he may not take an

---

[17] For an extensive discussion of guilds, see ibid., 192–211.
[18] See Douglas Alton Smith, *A History of the Lute from Antiquity to the Renaissance* (n.p., 2002), 63.

apprentice for another three years. Finally, in order to protect its monopoly on lute making, the Guild decreed that any other lute maker that learned the trade outside the Guild "be put out of business by the guild and also punished...."[19]

For musicians, however, the guild structure offered problems as well as advantages. To begin with, many cities did not have guilds at all, opposition to them being somewhat like contemporary attitudes in certain areas towards organized labor unions. In Nuremberg, guilds were forbidden since they had been at the root of violent, but suppressed, revolts, and trade was regulated by the city council. Even where guilds were active, often the cities were too small to have a large enough population of musicians to make a musician's guild worthwhile. Moreover, though it might be present, a musician's guild had no jurisdiction over court musicians who might perform within the city walls, and in many cities, like Bruges, the civic ensemble itself was immune from guild regulation by virtue of its contract with the city. In short, two of the most visible and prominent strata of musicians were beyond reach.

Membership in a guild nonetheless afforded a means for cohesion within an urban environment. Similar to the ancillary services provided by the American Federation of Musicians (pension plans, collective bargaining, legal counsel), Renaissance guilds were also involved in charitable donations and assisted musicians and their families in need. A regular round of banquets and church services provided a framework for involvement in both social and religious life. In addition, and of direct concern for this discussion, the medieval guild structure supplied the model for the training of young musicians.

The age at which musical instruction began is difficult to establish, as very little documentation is available. This probably followed the pattern of other guilds and would usually begin at the age of eleven or twelve and finish at about eighteen. One significant exception was in the case of the offspring of master musicians. If these youngsters showed talent, their training began much earlier. This gave them a significant advantage to face the competition of the marketplace as they matured. A verification of such early training comes again from Cellini (see CS 6). He recounts in his autobiography that when he was very small, he was carried on the back of one of the other players of the civic ensemble of Florence and performed with the group in front of the Signoria. He did not give his exact age, but he

---

[19] Ibid., 322–4.

must have been about six years old to be carried comfortably.[20] For all his protestations that he detested playing, Cellini must have been very capable, for he was briefly made a member of the wind ensemble supported by the Pope when he was about seventeen.[21]

Case study 6

An artist in his own words: Benvenuto Cellini on the training and early career of an instrumentalist

1. "When I was still very young ... my father had me carried to the Signoria and made me play the [recorder] as a soprano accompaniment to the palace musicians" [relevant date, c.1507].

Benvenuto Cellini [1500–71] must have been about age six or seven on this occasion, and he was obviously already capable of at least an adequate professional performance. By his own testimony he had been trained by his father, Giovanni Cellini, a member of the civic ensemble in Florence from 1480 to 1514.

2. "When my father began teaching me to play the [recorder] and to sing... I was at a tender age... I hated every moment of it..." [relevant date, c.1504].

Given Benvenuto's age when he appeared before the Signoria, this teaching must have started by age four or five. One important aspect of this comment is that it helps explain the frequency of highly successful players within families. Normally musicians began serious study of a profession (instrumental music included) within the traditional guild system of apprenticeship, which normally began around age eleven. When musical training took place within the family, the musician gained a double advantage, for not only did the son have an early start, but often the father had political capital to influence a hire.

3. "When I reached the age of fifteen, against my father's will I placed myself in a goldsmith's shop with a man called Antonio de Sandro.... For all this, I remembered to cheer up my lovable old father now and then by playing the recorder or the cornetto" [relevant date, 1515].

At this point Benvenuto set off firmly in what was to be his chosen field, a goldsmith, at which he became perhaps the finest exponent of

---

[20] In any case, this occurred, as Cellini states, soon after Piero Soderini was elected as Gonfaloniere of Florence in 1502, at which time Cellini was two.
[21] Cellini, *The Autobiography*, 23 and 45–6.

the time, producing splendid decorative objects. Note, however, that his musical range had expanded, for he was now also a capable performer on the cornett, an instrument that was just coming into vogue, but difficult to master. But within the next year he and his younger brother became involved in a violent dispute with another group of young men, which led to a brief period of exile. After a time their father appealed to Cardinal Giulio de'Medici (later Pope Clement VII), and they were allowed to return. Shortly thereafter, however, came the following development.

4. "Then one of my father's pupils... suggested to the Cardinal that I should be sent to Bologna so that I could learn how to play really well from a famous professor there called Antonio.... the Cardinal informed my father that if he sent me to Bologna he himself would provide me with useful letters of introduction. My father, who nearly died of joy at such a prospect, had no hesitation, and at the same time as I wanted to see the world I was only too willing to go. At Bologna... I used to go along every day for my music lessons, and within a few weeks I had made very good progress in that cursed art" [relevant date, sometime later than the previous, late in 1515 or in 1516].

This is an intriguing entry from a variety of perspectives. Most apprenticeship training for musicians was distinctly local and insular. For most young players their greatest opportunities lay within their own community where they developed close working relationships with established players. But in some instances, probably only for those with outstanding talent, travel to other centers was possible. Bologna was not only some distance away (just over 100 kilometers), but was also a city with few close ties to Florence. One might have anticipated finding a master in Rome, Milan, or Venice. Members of the Ganassi family were active in Bologna during this period, but the reason for the choice was because of this Antonio, who appears to have had a formidable reputation. This was certainly the Antonio mentioned in a 1523 letter from the Spataro/Aaron correspondence, and bolsters suggestions that Bologna was a city in which there was a long tradition of nurturing young Italian musicians.[1] Significantly, the lessons were daily, which seems to have been typical of how Renaissance instrumental teachers operated, and we note also the personal involvement of the Medici cardinal; Medici connections clearly played a large role in the careers of both Cellinis.

Benvenuto's stay in Bologna was for a term of six months, after which he returned to Florence. For the next several years he moved between Siena, Pisa, and Florence, and, finally remained for a relatively long stay in Rome, with most of his professional energies focused on his trade as a goldsmith. During this span there are only occasional references to music. But in about 1525 we read of one final important musical episode.

5. "A man called Gianiacomo, who was a shawmist from Cesena in the services of the Pope... got in touch with me. He sent a message through Lorenzo, the trumpeter from Lucca, asking me if I would help them at the Pope's August festival in some very beautiful motets they had chosen, by playing the soprano part on my cornetto... as music is a marvelous business ... I was quite ready to join them. We spent a week before the festival practicing together two hours a day... while Pope Clement was having dinner we played the motets ... so well that he had to admit he had never heard music played more exquisitely or more harmoniously... he called Gianiacomo over and asked him how... he had put his hands on such a fine cornetto player... 'So he is Giovanni's son' said the Pope ...and then the Pope said he would like me to enter his service along with the other musicians." [relevant date probably about 1525].

The musicians engaged in daily rehearsals of two hours each in order to present a repertory of motets (with no chansons in the mix), amounting to perhaps a half dozen pieces in all. One wonders how the musicians spent that rehearsal time. They may have committed the pieces to memory, and some element of improvisation might also have been involved. Other possibilities are that the context of Clement's request demanded the more involved, contrapuntal idiom of the motet, which would demonstrate the musical training of the musicians, or that he had specific pieces in mind. Another important detail in this passage is that a player from Cesena, active in Rome, somehow knew that Benvenuto was a competent cornett player, but also knew that the mutual link would be Lorenzo, the trumpet player from Lucca. This suggests the existence of a tight-knit community or pool of Italian instrumentalists, about which we know almost nothing today. There must have been a similar network within the community of German musicians, given how many were active in Italy. Benvenuto boasts of his relationship with the Medici Pope, but we should note a bit of an anomaly here: at this point the Pope was evidently unfamiliar with him, yet this is the same man who Cellini had said was willing to write letters of introduction for him less than ten years earlier.

In sum, *The Autobiography* introduces all of the problems of a memoir, in this case one written in 1558–66, long after the events described above. The passage of time involved calls to question the accuracy of Benvenuto's comments even if he were considered to be a generally reliable witness to events, and a reading of the entire text makes it clear that he was notoriously unreliable and self-serving in his writing. Nonetheless, many of his mundane, temporal entries about his musical background – ones that are perfunctory enough to pass the test of veracity – are invaluable in that they are the only document of this sort that we have, conveying information about such matters as the dates when a master might begin teaching a member of his own family, the daily nature of instruction, and that singing might be included in an instrumentalist's training. Benvenuto certainly exaggerated his (and his father's) connections with the Medici family, but it is clear that this relationship was extremely important at several points in the careers of both men, and serves as a reminder that all instrumentalists then were part of a system in which musicians had direct links with their patrons.[2]

Notes

1 Susan Forscher Weiss, "Bologna Q18: Some Reflections on Content and Context," *JAMS* 41 (1988), 88; see also Keith Polk, "Foreign and Domestic in Italian Instrumental Music of the Fifteenth Century." In *Musica Franca; Essays in Honor of Frank A. D'Accone*, ed. Irene Alm, Alyson McLamore, and Colleen Reardon (Stuyvesant, NY, 1996), 329–30.
2 The quotes are drawn from Benvenuto Cellini, *The Autobiography*. For quote 1, see 21–2; quote 2, 20; quote 3, 23; quote 4, 25; and quote 5, 45. For the reference to Antonio in Bologna, see Weiss, "Bologna Q18," 88–9. For a discussion of civic music in Florence including a treatment of Giovanni and Benvenuto Cellini, see McGee, *Ceremonial Musicians*, 204–6; for further on Giovanni Cellini, see also McGee's "Giovanni Cellini, Piffero of Florence," *HBSJ* 12 (2000), 210–25 (an English translation of his "Giovanni Cellini, piffero di Firenze," *RiM* 32 [1997], 201–21).

At the end of the guild training period an examination was scheduled in order to judge if the standards of the profession had been met. These were probably held for apprentice musicians, but unfortunately no records of any such assessments have survived. Once a performer had passed beyond apprenticeship, his career resembled that of most other medieval and Renaissance trades. In most professions a master maintained a workshop, a bustling enterprise that comprised two or three masters, several journeymen, a few apprentices, and also a further group that included one or two others functioning as servants or as day laborers to take care of day-to-day manual tasks for which professional skill was unnecessary. Attaining the status of master was a crucial step and was out of reach of many journeymen. Each shop had a limited number of slots for masters, and most masters would reserve such a position for one of their own sons. The case of lutemakers in Venice helps to delineate the formative stages of guild members. Their apprenticeship (*lavoranza*) began as *garzone* at around the age of twelve, with a number of simple duties. After around four or five years at this stage, they served three more years as *giovane*, so that by the age of eighteen or twenty they were sufficiently trained as *maestri* to open their own *bottega* or to work in the *bottega* of others as an *agente*.[22]

While efficient for the bulk of trades, this layered professional framework was ineffective for music. Any attempt by a guild to distinguish instrumentalists between journeyman and master broke down because of the realities of musical performance. In music, a very fine player would be in demand over a mediocre one, regardless of one's age, title, or affiliation. In any case there does not seem to have been a large pool of middle-grade instrumental performers anywhere distinguished as "journeymen." Moreover, the title of "master" was rarely encountered in connection with musicians. When used, it seems to have been an indication of high ability and did not have any particular tie with status within a guild.

A major thrust of guild regulation was controlling competition. In the major trades with larger guild membership, masters generally took two or perhaps three apprentices.[23] In music the limitation – perhaps connected to the positions available in the market – was often to accept just one, but again the guilds had difficulty in enforcing their regulations on either civic or court musicians. In the Ghent contract of 1493, Jooris Zoetink, a member of the civic ensemble, clearly accepted two young students.[24] Another aspect peculiar to the music profession was that potential teachers were often unavailable. Young musicians of outstanding talent would have been attracted to the centers where fine performers were established and active, yet the most visible of such musicians were those attached to the prominent courts, such as Burgundy in the fifteenth century, and several decades later those of Henry VIII and Francis I. But courts were constantly on the road and the pragmatic considerations were relentless. When the court traveled, the musicians accompanied. Travel involved a very large expense: horses had to be provided, as well as housing, meals, and

---

[22] Pio, *Viol and Lute Makers of Venice*, 16.
[23] On this point, see N. J. G. Pounds, *An Economic History of Europe* (Harlow, Essex, 1974), 297. On the general status of apprentices in the guild system, see Steven A. Epstein, *Wage, Labor & Guilds in Medieval Europe* (Chapel Hill, NC and London, 1991), 103–12.
[24] Concerning the efforts of guilds to limit the number of apprentices, see Woodfill, *Musicians in English Society*, 22–3, and Conklin, "Medieval English Minstrels," 235.

sometimes a stipend. The patron would not pay for the expenses of a student musician, so for long periods, apprentices attached to a court master did not have available the daily instruction that was considered the standard of the time.

Recruiting professionals

The need for new talent to replace contracted performers was inevitable in both courts and in cities. Despite the fact that personnel could be stable for decades, at some point old age, illness, or death intervened. Other factors entered in as well, such as the constant press of innovation. In modern times we tend to think of the pace of change in that distant past as being leisurely. This was not the way it was viewed at the time, as revealed by this remarkable comment in the Limburg Chronik:

> The manner of shawm playing, which was previously not so good, has been changed and improved. Thus, one who was considered a good player in this area just five or six years ago doesn't amount to a hill of beans now.[25]

Documents throughout the Renaissance frequently mention the arrival of new music or instruments on the scene, and it was imperative, though difficult, for players to keep up with innovations. When they didn't, they could be replaced, as we know from the dismissal of the Florentine *pifferi*.

The process of recruiting aroused conflicting, sometimes deeply contentious forces that could undermine the selection of new performers. From one direction came the desire to find the best talent available and to conform to new fashions as they swept through the cultural scene. Resistance to this was rooted in the nature of patronage, especially as it functioned within cities. Too often our view of patronage is simplistic, our attention focused on a particular individual with vast wealth available to dispense for cultural ends – Lorenzo the Magnificent, for example, Maximilian I of Habsburg, or the Mantuan and Ferrarese courts. But, of course, the machinery of patronage was much more complex. "The world was divided into two camps... friends and strangers," Ronald Weissman wrote about the context of Italian cities during the fifteenth century: "In this world one promoted the interests of family, friends and patrons,

---

[25] The translation was suggested by Edmond Bowles; for the German text, see Keith Polk, "Instrumental Music in the Urban Centres of Renaissance Germany," *EMH* 7 (1987), 164.

for one assumed that everyone else did likewise... one did not seek to treat all citizens with bureaucratic impartiality."[26] Accordingly, whenever a vacancy occurred in an ensemble, almost invariably there were local musicians available who aggressively sought to fill the position and set in motion as much of the patronage apparatus as was available to them.

Given the deeply rooted linkages of local patronage, such as family kinships and local networks, it is remarkable how often cities authorized wide-ranging searches to fill vacancies in the ranks of their performers. In 1479, the town council in Bruges dispatched one of their musicians to "Namur, Maastricht, Cologne, and to other places" to audition prospective players to fill a vacancy in their ensemble.[27] And, as already mentioned above, when Bruges engaged a completely new ensemble in 1456, the group was not only from outside, they were all French-speaking. One overriding reason that a city wanted accomplished performers was that the strength of the ensemble promoted a favorable impression of the town, a situation not unlike the relationship today between the quality of the university symphony orchestra or choir (or, in many places, the marching band) and the reputation of the institution itself.

A potent force from a different direction came from the strength of family dynasties and tradition. In essence, with the right contacts, pursuing music as a profession was a good career move. Sons would follow fathers in trades, a succession that is very pronounced in lute music and with ensemble musicians.[28] In contracted ensembles, fathers would exert considerable influence to assure that their sons were granted positions when vacancies occurred. In Augsburg, Ulrich Schubinger the Elder was appointed to the civic ensemble in 1457. Subsequently, three of his sons found places in the ensemble, and they soon become among the preeminent players of the day. Besides the Schubingers, the Hurlachers, Rauchs, and Schnitzers were others that were active in southern Germany, the latter two families also being instrument builders. The Low Countries, too, provide examples, especially with the van Winckel family of Ghent, the Fausets (active in Leuven and Bruges), and the Conijns (in Mechelen and Antwerp).

[26] Ronald Weissman, "Taking Patronage Seriously: Mediterranean Values and Renaissance Society." In *Patronage, Art, and Society in Renaissance Italy*, ed. F. W. Kent and Patricia Simons (Oxford, 1987), 43–4.
[27] Gilliodts-Van Severen, *Les Ménestrels*, 49.
[28] See Victor Coelho, *The Manuscript Sources of Seventeenth-Century Italian Lute Music* (New York, 1995), 21. Some Renaissance lute families include the Garsi (Santino and Donino), Piccinini (Leonardo, Alessandro and Filippo), Dowland (John and Robert), and Johnson (John and Robert) families.

Direct intervention by a powerful patron was common and, of course, trumped all other recruiting considerations. Lorenzo the Magnificent took a personal interest when a sudden vacancy had occurred in the civic wind ensemble in Florence in 1489. His concern led to the hiring of Augustine Schubinger, and while the appointment was certainly approved by the Signoria of Florence, there seems little question that the final authority in the matter lay with Lorenzo.[29] Sometimes the ultimate power over decisions was delegated. The importation of Italian string and wind players at the Munich court in the 1560s and 1570s (which abruptly erased the tradition of hiring German players for the court) was probably due to the dominance of Orlando di Lasso as chapel master, acting under the authority of Duke Albert V.

Professional players and their origins

For ordinary individuals, systematic record-keeping concerning primary events in one's life, birth, death, and marriage was essentially non-existent in the fifteenth and through most of the sixteenth century. The lack of information constantly frustrates attempts to establish some idea of the origins of musicians, and this is often the case for the most famous figures. Heinrich Isaac, for example, is known to be from Flanders, and that his father's name was Hugo. We do not know where in Flanders he was from, nor do we have more than a guess as to approximately when he might have been born. Needless to say, the situation is even starker when we consider the lives of the stratum that included professional instrumentalists, even with some of the most prominent performers. Of the renowned chamber duo at the Burgundian court, for example, we know little of them before their arrival in the north in the early 1430s. They were evidently from Spain, but specifically where is unknown. After they left the court in the late 1450s there are but a few scattered references to them, and then they vanish from our view.

Contemporary records provide some information concerning the place of origin for many musicians and give some idea of the social rank to which they belonged. It is clear that many musicians, as we have mentioned, followed their fathers into the trade, and that clans of musicians were a common feature. An intriguing aspect of these clans was their expanding networks of influence. In Bavaria, at various times one or another of the

---

[29] McGee, *Ceremonial Musicians*, 185–6.

Schnitzers were town musicians in Munich, Nuremberg, Nördlingen, and Schwabish-Hall, as well as at the court of the Duke of Bavaria and the Imperial court of Maximilian I. The reach could even extend internationally. The sons of Ulrich Schubinger the Elder, as noted above, went on to careers in Florence, and at the courts of Brandenburg, Ferrara, Mantua, with Maximilian I, and Philip the Fair. The van Winkels of Ghent were also internationally active, with some of the family finding service in other cities in Flanders and at the English court. An underlying point is that for a young musician at that time, being from a major center (Ghent or Bruges in Flanders, for example, or Augsburg or Nuremberg in Bavaria and Venice or Florence in Italy) and from a musical family offered enormous advantage.

Talent, however, was still a determining element especially since significant numbers of musicians were not from musical families. Indeed, some came from very small villages. The records of Augsburg between 1450 and 1500 indicate that several musicians engaged by the city in that span were from places that must have had tiny populations – 200 or less in several cases. The obstacles for young boys from such villages must have been substantial and one wonders how they gained access to instruments and to instruction; the sources provide no information on such matters.

A remarkable case is that of the minuscule Bavarian town of Schrattenbach, which has a *modern* population of just over 300, and was probably distinctly smaller in the fifteenth century. This was the home of the Rauch family of musicians and instrument makers. In 1473, Claus Rauch provided the city of Augsburg with three "pfeiffen" (at this date these were probably shawms). Schrattenbach was such an obscure place that the Augsburg accountants and scribes felt it necessary to take the extremely unusual step of describing the location in relation to its neighboring city when they listed the payment: "paid, four gulden to Claussen Rauchen van Schrattenbach, [which is] two miles from Kempten" – and Kempten itself was one of the smallest of the Imperial cities.[30] A David Rauch was engaged as a civic musician in Augsburg in 1495. Subsequently, members of the Rauch clan then became some of the most preeminent makers of wind instruments in the sixteenth century.

A small but important category of musician that probably did not conform to the usual social norms comprised those who were blind,

---

[30] Augsburg, Stadtarchiv, Baumeisterbücher, 1473–4, fol. 35. The relevant portion of the document reads, "[paid to] Claussen Rauchen von Schraittenbach, ij meyl von këmpten…"

which included the Burgundian viol duo, a Bruges viol duo documented by Tinctoris, as well as Conrad Paumann.[31] Indeed, for someone who was blind in the fifteenth century, options were drastically limited. If a youngster who was sightless showed any talent, music offered at least some possibility of a successful career. This may well have been the case with Conrad Paumann, who was born blind into a craftsman family but as a result of extraordinary talent, was sponsored in his early years by a prominent patrician in Nuremberg. Even with music, though, the choices were severely limited, and most blind performers were in the category of chamber musicians. All of the professional wind players were called upon to move or stroll for performances, and they often took part in processions – a function that would have engendered nearly impossible practical conditions for someone who was blind.

Case study 7

The *cieco miracoloso*: Conrad Paumann

From the perspective of surviving sources, music in the mid- to late fifteenth century was dominated by Franco-Flemish composers active in a cultural channel that flowed from the Low Countries, through France, and into Italy. From this point of view Germany was clearly an artistic backwater. Even German manuscripts, which exist in ample quantity, appear to support this model, for the products of German composers were clearly inferior in sophistication and elegance to those by such Franco-Flemings as Dufay, Ockeghem, and Busnoys. We must recognize, however, that this perspective represents a serious distortion of the views held at the time. If one asked a member of the court of Mantua around 1470, for example, to name the five most famous contemporary musicians, the list would certainly have included Pietrobono of Ferrara, but also Conrad Paumann, then working at the court of Bavaria. In fact, Lewis Lockwood has argued that Pietrobono was "beyond doubt one of the most important figures in all of fifteenth-century music, certainly in Italy," but the same can be said of Paumann in Germany.[1] Of course, both were primarily performers – and as was the case of all performers before the age

---

[31] On the Bruges and Burgundian viol duos, see Rob Wegman, "From Maker to Composer: Improvisation and Musical Authorship in the Low Countries, 1450–1500," *JAMS* 49 (1996), 422.

of film and recording, their efforts existed only in the moment and have thus been lost into the proverbial sands of time.

Conrad Paumann presents an especially intriguing case, as he was evidently blind from birth, the precise date of which is unknown, but probably between about 1410 and 1420. Nothing specific is known of his immediate family, but he was evidently a native of Nuremberg, and it is likely that his class was somewhere toward the upper echelons of society in the city, as he was sponsored early on by Ulrich and Paul Grundherr, prominent Nuremberg patricians. Nuremberg was an ideal location for young Conrad at just the time he would have begun his training. By 1420 the city had several organs available among its main churches, and there were even organ builders in residence there. More important, in 1425 the city council authorized the establishment of a chamber duo of organ and lute on the civic payrolls. This was highly unusual, since in most German cities – Augsburg is a good example – such subsidies were directed exclusively to wind bands. Because he was blind, in order to develop his musical skills he gravitated to the lute and organ, the unrestricted physical mobility required of a professional wind player ruling out any of the loud instruments. Thus, Conrad could look to established professionals on both of these instruments for instruction. His career unfolded quickly, and by about 1445 he was named organist in the St. Sebald church in Nuremberg. When a position opened in the civic organ/lute duo in 1447, he was named to the post, swearing on oath to serve the city faithfully and not to leave his duties without the permission of the city council. Neither the position nor the vow held him long, however, and in 1450 he was enticed into the services of Albert IV, Duke of Bavaria, in Munich, in whose service he remained until his death in 1473.[2]

Association with the Bavarian court quickly projected Paumann onto a much wider stage than would have been possible had he remained in Nuremberg. He had already established himself as the outstanding organist in the region, but it was as a representative of the Bavarian duke that his astonishing versatility was demonstrated. Within two or three years he was sent to several of the most prominent cities in the region, especially Augsburg and Regensburg – not, at least for a number of years, to Nuremberg, where his relationship understandably remained tense – and in these cites he was usually noted as being a master lutenist, not an organist.[3] In Landshut in 1454 he was heard by the Duke of Burgundy, Philip the Good, who was in the region on a diplomatic mission. That was undoubtedly a fascinating encounter, for probably included in Philip's entourage was the chamber duo of Fernandez and Cordeval, whose fame and abilities certainly matched Paumann's. Over the years his reputation became such that at the Reichstag called by Emperor Frederick III in Regensburg in 1471, it was Paumann who was selected to play, this time as an organist, in front of the emperor and the assembled nobility. His international fame reached a pinnacle with a series of performances in Mantua in 1470. Here, Paumann was described as "marvelous on any instrument." His abilities were such that he was termed the "cieco miracoloso."[32] In Mantua it was not only Paumann's virtuosity that was praised but also his almost inconceivable versatility, for he seemed equally capable on organ, lute, fiddle, and recorder. The honors paid to him there were astonishing. He was knighted by the Mantuan duke, and was showered with gifts from the dukes of Ferrara and Milan, as well the King of Naples. The fact that the Duke of Ferrara heard Paumann is telling, as this encounter would have brought him into contact with Pietrobono, the brilliant lutenist at the Ferrarese court. It was also at this time that Paumann's abilities came to the attention of the composer and theorist Johannes Tinctoris, who was then serving at the court in Naples.

Shortly after the Mantuan visit, Tinctoris described the formidable abilities of both Pietrobono and Paumann as lutenists. Pietrobono was praised for his unparalleled skill at elegant embellishment of a monophonic line. But concerning Paumann, he wrote that "Others do what is much more difficult [than play a single line], namely to play a composition alone, and most skillfully, in not only two parts, but even three or four . . . Orbus the German [i.e. Paumann] . . .was supereminent in playing this way."[4]

The narrative poet Hans Rosenplüt had provided a more detailed and lavish commentary some two decades earlier, in 1447. He named Paumann "master of all masters," and emphasized Paumann's ability to control all of the parts within a contrapuntal texture (i.e. discant, tenor, and contratenor), as well as being able to improvise (in various manners, including in Faburden), and to compose. He stated that Paumann was equally comfortable with sacred and secular repertories, and also praised his prodigious memory:

respons, Antiffen und Introitus,
Impni, Sequenzen un Responsoria,
Das trägt er alles in seiner Memoria.[5]

---

[32] Paumann's visit is discussed by William Prizer, "The Frottola and the Unwritten Tradition," *Studi Musicali* 15 (1986), 12–14.

Alone among the other leading instrumental masters of the era, Fernandez, Cordoval, and Pietrobono, Paumann left some written records of his efforts. In most instances, these sources were probably transcribed by his students, for Paumann was the leading teacher in the region. In fact, the bulk of what survives by Paumann is embodied in his instruction manuals, termed *fundamenta*, and several of them allow us a close look at Paumann's teaching methods. Most of the material is firmly didactic, which, reflecting the traditional aural nature of most contemporary instrumental training, is unflinchingly repetitive. The examples in the *fundamenta*, however, do reveal how a young player can learn to provide graceful decoration to a soprano line, and support that line with well-wrought, though relatively simple, accompaniment in the lower parts. Interspersed here and there are a precious few more ambitious efforts, and we even have one highly polished secular piece, *Wiplich figur*, which has survived in both a keyboard version and as a three-part German song.[6] A regular feature of the performance of chamber instrumentalists was to produce, on the spot, elegant improvised pieces. One contemporary observer heaped generous praise on Fernandez and Cordoval, noting that even Binchois and Dufay, who were present at one of their performances, were jealous of the manner in which these two players invented turns of phrase that were superior to what they, though famous composers, were capable of producing. Still, not one single note seems to have survived from Fernandez, Cordoval, Pietrobono, or a host of other fine chamber players of the day. *Wiplich figur* may be a unique example, but it provides an invaluable insight into what the leading instrumentalists of the age were probably producing on a day-to-day basis in their spontaneous performances.

Notes

1 Lockwood, *Music in Renaissance Ferrara*, 98.
2 The most extensive and reliable source for the career of Conrad Paumann is Franz Krautwurst, "Konrad Pauman." In *Fränkische Lebensbilder*, ed. G. Pfeiffer and A. Wendenburg, Veröffentlichen der Gesellschaft für fränkische Geschichte, Series VII A, 7 (1977), 33–48. Krautwurst suggested the birth date of 1410. For the establishment of the organ/lute duo in Nuremberg, see Nuremberg, Bavarian State Archive, Repertorium 54/79; 1425, folio 228v; the organist was Hans Kratzer, the lutenist Herman Kirschbaum.
3 See Polk, *German Instrumental Music*, 121.
4 Concerning Tinctoris and his evaluations of Pietrobono and Paumann, see William Prizer, "The Frottola and the Unwritten Tradition," 3–37. The translation of Tinctoris's comment is by Prizer.
5 "Responds, Antiphons, and Introits; Hymns, Sequences, and Responds; he carried all these in his memory." Hans Rosenplüt's description of Paumann is

available in the Krautwurst article, cited *supra*; a more readily available source is Polk, *German Instrumental Music*, 19–20.

6 For sources and editions of *Wiplich figur*, see Fallows, *A Catalogue*, 493.

Female instrumentalists

For instrumentalists, the professional arena remained the domain of men. The almost complete accounts of Augsburg in the fifteenth century convey hundreds of payments to players of a great variety of instruments; none were to women. One small qualification, however, was that occasionally a female singer would be noted in the records in relation to music at court. Maximilian I, for example, maintained a small ensemble of singers in the early 1490s that included a woman. Another significant occasion was a performance of a female singer accompanied by the duo of Fernandez and Cordoval at the celebrated Feast of the Pheasant in Lille in 1454. In fact, in a majority of the cases in which the presence of a woman is indicated in the accounts, the performance includes a vocal element with an accompaniment of one or more soft instruments. In one instance the female singer also provided her own accompaniment: in the festivities in Frankfurt in 1486 surrounding the election of Maximilian as King of the Romans, "the best singer and instrumental performer... anyone had yet heard... performed alone chansons and motets, singing and playing on the lute, harp, rebec, and clavicembalo."[33] Young girls did have instruction available. In Florence in 1432 a lutenist, a harpist, and a singer signed a contract to establish a music school to teach young boys and girls the elements of music.[34] Basic instruction in instruments, almost exclusively those in the soft category, was undoubtedly part of the offering, and two of the central sources of English lute music were compiled and owned by women, the lute books of Jane Pickering and Margaret Board.[35] For women from noble families, instruction in playing was certainly not unusual. Margaret of Austria received instruction on keyboard instruments, and Isabella d'Este was an enthusiastic player and collector of lutes and viols. But the young girls in Florence, as well as those from noble families, were not being prepared for professional careers. The economic reality was that while there were many well-trained female

[33] Louise Cuyler, *The Emperor Maximilian I and Music* (Oxford, 1973), 35.
[34] The contract is in Florence, Archivio di Stato, Archivio Notarile Antecosimiano, G 24 (1423–33), fol. 178r-v.
[35] See Spring, *The Lute in Britain*, 115.

performers in the fifteenth and sixteenth centuries, and there is ample iconographic evidence that they were significant practitioners of the guitar, lute, viol, flute, and keyboard (see, for example, Chapter 6, Figure 25), the conditions relating to the trade of music placed huge barriers in front of a woman desiring a career as an instrumentalist. An important avenue to pursue would be the relationships during the Renaissance between genre, instrument, and gender, particularly since the notion of musical genre is the product of many levels of systematic compositional training and, therefore, access to privileged information, with instruments, both in the Western and non-Western worlds, having their own symbolic and gendered associations.

During the sixteenth and especially seventeenth centuries, a great deal of musical instruction, composition, and production took place in convents, mostly in the realm of vocal polyphony. But nuns also learned to play the organ and the viol in order to account for the lower voices needed for this music, and documents show regular string purchases and string teachers for these institutions.[36] At the same time, some instruments were occasionally prohibited; the violin's associations with dancing and secular society led to it being banished in some Milanese convents, and when a convent was ordered to stop using viols, which they required to play the lower voices, the nuns were forced to file a petition to have them restored, rather than abandon polyphonic music altogether.[37] The keyboard manuscript of Elena Malvezzi, a descendant of one of Bologna's most noble families and a member of the Convent of Sant' Agnese, offers further information about both instrumental training for cloistered women and their choice of repertory.[38] Dated to the late 1550s, the manuscript contains eighty-two arrangements of, in order of quantity, Italian madrigals, Latin motets, and French chansons, with a clear preference for the madrigals of Cipriano de Rore, who often set the spiritual *Vergine* texts of Petrarch. According to Monson, it is the largest keyboard manuscript of intabulations of the Renaissance, and the repertory it contains shows that not all of the pieces were copied from printed sources; Suor Malvezzi and her sisters clearly had access to an important internal circulation of music in manuscript.[39] Towards the end of the century, the professional avenue

---

[36] See Robert Kendrick, *Celestial Sirens: Nuns and Their Music in Early Modern Milan* (Oxford, 1996), 196–8.
[37] Ibid., 196.
[38] This discussion is indebted to the excellent study by Craig Monson, "Elena Malvezzi's Keyboard Manuscript: A New Sixteenth-Century Source," *EMH* 9 (1990), 73–128.
[39] Ibid., 87.

was finally being paved for female singers in courtly ensembles, such as those in Mantua and Ferrara, and on the stage in Florence, all of which have been well documented. But many of these women were also expert instrumentalists, like the Florentine singer Vittoria Archilei and the great *Commedia dell'arte* actor and member of the Gelosi troupe, Vincenza Armani.[40] In the oration given on her death, her fellow actor, Adriano Valerini, wrote in 1570 that "She played a variety of musical instruments with such grace that it seemed that an angelic hand touched their concordant wood, and it appeared almost as if she spoke with her fingers."[41]

Amateurs

Today we tend to group all amateur musicians into one general category, even though they are drawn from many social levels; in a non-professional civic orchestra, a wealthy lawyer might sit on the same stand as a student or a schoolteacher. This was unlikely to occur in the Renaissance, when amateurs divided into two distinct categories: one consisted of those from the nobility, the other of commoners – but within the latter by far the most important group consisted of those that we may generally classify as "elites." Nobles and commoners rarely mixed in musical recreation. When the young Henry VIII gathered with "hail fellows well met" to play at recorders or viols, all those "fellows" were undoubtedly titled members of the aristocracy. The commoners could be exclusive in their own way in that the elites, drawn from the higher echelons of urban society, would seldom have joined forces with anyone from the lower social orders.

Nothing was more decisive in the development of instrumental music in the Renaissance than the perceived importance of musical training in the education of a young noble. The ability to perform on the lute or viol was prized among the activities appropriate to young members of that social class, and the necessity of this training is codified in Castiglione's *Il Cortegiano*, which through the sixteenth century

---

[40] Archilei played a "leuto grosso" (chitarrone?) while descending from a cloud while singing the opening piece "Dalle più alte sfere," of the *Primo intermedio* for the play *La Pellegrina*, staged for the Medici wedding of 1589. For an argument that Archilei was likely the *composer* as well of this piece (for which Cristofano Malvezzi is listed), see Nina Treadwell, "She Descended on a Cloud 'From the Highest Spheres': Florentine Monody 'alla Romanina'," *Cambridge Opera Journal* 16 (2004), 1–22.

[41] Quoted in Anne MacNeil, *Music and Women of the Commedia dell'Arte in the Late Sixteenth Century* (Oxford, 2003), 36.

provided a self-fashioning guide for young nobles. Philip the Good was provided with instruction in the harp in 1410 and his son Charles was reported to play the same instrument at the early age of seven. Maximilian's background is unclear, but his children Philip (later Philip the Fair) and Margaret (Margaret of Austria) were given instruction by the superb organist Govard Nepotis. The fashion continued into the sixteenth century. Maximilian's grandson Charles (Charles V) and granddaughter Eleanor (of Austria) received lessons from the organist Bredemers, and the Tudors carried on the tradition in England. According to Holman "all the Tudors were lutenists, while Henry himself, his sister Mary, and his daughters Mary and Elizabeth played the keyboard as well." And it goes without saying that the fashion among the very highest nobility provided the template for those of lower ranks. If the children of the dukes of Burgundy, of Maximilian I, or of the king of England were provided with instruction in musical instruments, that would have been the pattern among the nobility in general. Indeed, courts had an obligation to provide models for behavior and manners, what we might call "aspirational culture." It is no wonder that the contents of amateur Florentine lute books of the late sixteenth century, such as *Cavalcanti*, owned by a young member of a noble Florentine family (see *CS* 8), resound with many echoes of the dance and vocal music heard at the Medici Court, including even some the "new" music composed around the birth of opera in the manner of lute-accompanied song.

When noble instrumentalists also occupied the role of patron, they were able to provide direction in the development of new genres and new concepts for instruments and ensembles. Isabella d'Este played a central role in stimulating interest in the native Italian genre of the frottola, a strophic form of song accompanied either by an instrumental group or by a lutenist playing a reduced arrangement (*tenore e contrabasso*) of these parts. In England, the development of the English viol repertory of the late Renaissance was built on the enthusiasm of Henry VIII for the novel sounds of bowed strings in the early decades of his reign. Similarly, Margaret of Austria appears to have played a key role in the introduction of bowed-string ensembles into the Low Countries, and in Rome, Pope Leo X, an expert lutenist and composer, supported both the lutenists Francesco da Milano and Gian Maria Ebreo, as well as the keyboard composer Marc Antonio Cavazzoni.[42]

---

[42] See Cummings, *The Lion's Ear*, 144–57.

Crucial support of instrumental music also came from "elites" – but it is important to define more accurately to whom this designation might apply. In general during the Renaissance, populations considered themselves as belonging to one of three classes, clergy, nobility, or commoners. In many ways this facilitated administration (concerning legal systems, for example) and the notion of privilege, but for our discussion the categories are far too general. As a demographic, "commoner," for example, could include everyone from the most fabulously wealthy to the poorest beggar in the square.

Thus, "elites," for the purposes here, were almost exclusively urban, and mostly drawn from the very top economic levels of their respective communities. It should be remembered that in a Renaissance city all but a tiny minority of the population had to work, a day of labor being from sunrise to sundown over the course of a six-day work week. Moreover, boys joined the labor force as early as was practical and except for noble males, there were no teenage years of ease during which achieving competence on an instrument or in other arts was possible. That said, wealthy urbanites, almost certainly in imitation of the aristocracy, paid to have their children trained in music. And while these individuals couldn't match the influence of the highest nobility (especially as the power of centralized states developed from the late fifteenth century onward) their contribution was vast. They constituted the market for the outpouring of printed music for instruments in the sixteenth century, they were the main buyers of instruments, and the tastes of the elites shaped the nature of the repertories that were made available. Sixteenth-century printed collections like *Casteliono* and *Susato*, described in Chapter 2, are perfect examples of books intended for this demographic. Elite amateurs left reasonably ample evidence of their enthusiasm for instrumental music, with, for example, inventories of instruments, indication of ownership of manuscript and printed music, and commissioned portraits. For amateurs from lower strata of society, such as artisans and lesser merchants, remnants are more modest. Still, as a study of wills and notarial documents in sixteenth-century Venice reveals (see Chapter 6, 231–2), in a large city there was indeed a widespread interest in instrumental music that crosses several demographic lines.

Amateur participation in instrumental music took place within distinct limits. The choice of instruments was almost entirely within the soft category, most prominently lute, viol, and keyboard. Trumpets, shawms, cornets, and the like were utilitarian instruments of the "vulgar" professionals and were not considered suitable for those of higher social status – less than 1% of the almost 300 instruments listed in the Venetian notarial documents are from the loud category. Professional trumpeters, in fact, were usually not even acknowledged in payment records within the rolls of "musicians." But these preferences were not static. At the beginning of the fifteenth century the harp was favored, particularly among young members of the nobility. The lute began to take over the privileged role from about 1430, with the options of the clavichord and harpsichord added shortly thereafter. By the end of the fifteenth century, evidently stimulated by a growing fascination with three- and four-part contrapuntal textures, ensemble instruments, especially the viol and recorder, were added to the preferred category. What is striking about the instrumentarium of amateurs in the sixteenth century is its rich variety, for judging from the publications churned out by the presses of the time, all of these instruments – not just lutes, but clavichords, harpsichords, viols, and recorders – had eager and devoted practitioners.

While an entire class of instruments was off-limits for them, amateurs as a group cultivated their own repertory that largely ran in tandem with that of the professionals. For both, a set of dance music, international hits (usually arrangements of chansons or well-known dances), some regional favorites (frottola arrangements in Italian sources, Tenorlied in German ones), and a selection of sacred items formed the basis of what they played. The specific makeup changed over time and often quickly, but the general outline remained. The French chanson provided the model for arrangements throughout the Renaissance – those of Dufay and Binchois in the 1450s, and works by Crequillon, Clemens, and Lasso all the way through the 1590s, being popular among players.

Case study 8

Two Renaissance playlists: the lutebooks of Raffaello Cavalcanti (*Cavalcanti*) and Emanuel Wurstisen (*Wurstisen*)

A good example of the extent to which amateurs collected and consumed music at the end of the sixteenth century is revealed by two manuscript lute anthologies: one owned by Raffaello Cavalcanti (*c*.1575–1649), a young Florentine noble, the other copied by Emanuel Wurstisen (*c*.1572–1635), a nineteen-year-old student at the University of Basel. Both manuscripts are dated to 1591.[1] What is immediately striking is the size and diversity of both collections: *Cavalcanti*, written in sometimes cluttered Italian lute tablature with many ambiguous rhythmic indications, contains around 250 dances, settings of the passamezzo, fantasias, intabulations, local favorites, and a large and important collection of songs with lute accompaniment. Wurstisen's even larger book, copied meticulously in neat German tablature, contains over 300 pieces that are much more international in scope and, like the large printed anthologies of this period by Besard (1603) and Robert Dowland (1610), arranged diligently by genre into eight books, comprising (1) preludes; (2) motets; (3) fantasias; (4) madrigals and chansons, some by Lasso and Clemens non Papa; (5) over 100 settings of the passamezzo, some paired with a saltarello; (6) over 170 German dances (one with the somewhat ironic title "Der Calvinisten dantz"!); (7) unpaired settings of the pavan and galliard; and, (8) sacred songs in German along with some dances.[2] Both compilers provided some attributions to the pieces, though there are fewer given by Wurstisen. The beginnings of both manuscripts also contain a few pages of elementary music theory, and in the case of *Wurstisen*, a dedicated section on lute tablature.

 As personal anthologies assembled over time, *Cavalcanti* and *Wurstisen* reveal not only the musical tastes of their owners, but also their technical ability, the range of musical sources, oral and written, at their disposal, and the context of the repertory. As a member of a centuries-old Florentine family, the seventeen-year-old Cavalcanti reveals in his choices a strong historical, even courtly, temperament, resulting in a selection that is far more retrospective and insular in scope than Wurstisen's. Containing pieces from the first half of the sixteenth century by Francesco da Milano, who by the end of the century had achieved a "classic" status, as well as dances and passamezzo settings concordant with mid-century lute books, the manuscript was infused with a particular Florentine flavor, and some of the repertory was surely made available to him through internal Florentine connections, local patronage, and family networks.[3] More defining in this regard is the large selection of vocal music in the manuscript, particularly his inclusion of written-out formulas (*arie da cantare*, or *arie per cantar stanze*) that originated in the Italian courts with singer/improvisers more than a century earlier for singing poetry accompanied by lute. This repertory, deeply valued by humanists and endorsed by Vincenzo Galilei (see *SBS* 12), reveals the continuing importance of the long tradition, particularly in Florence, of singing Italian poetry accompanied by lute. It further testifies to the pedagogy of the late sixteenth century that taught competence in singing, in playing an instrument, and, indeed, singing to the lute, bringing us to the doorstep of monody. Cavalcanti's is an individual repertory, made even more personal, like a journal, by the idiosyncratic manner in which the tablature is notated, one that binds the relationship, in this case, between a single player and his music.

If *Cavalcanti* represents the private repertory of the educated nobleman – one of those young cultured Florentines we see in the elegant Bronzino portraits of the early sixteenth century[4] – *Wurstisen* reveals the diverse, shared, and more public music known and played by students at the University of Basel.[5] Copied entirely by Wurstisen between 1591 and around 1594, the manuscript contains French, German, Italian, and even English music, including local popular dances and German songs. It is clear that Emanuel had access to foreign sources, in which case he had to re-intabulate the pieces from French and Italian tablature into German tablature. Much of the repertory, however, was probably gathered from more local sources, or else composed, arranged, or notated from memory.

As for the manuscript's owner, he was the son of the well-known Basel chronicler, doctor, and professor of mathematics and theology, Christian Wurstisen (1544–88). Emanuel matriculated at the University of Basel in 1586 and remained at the university until 1594, becoming a physician, practicing first at Orléans and then at Biel. His passion for music, however, seems as strong as his interests in medical science. Indeed, the two fields join briefly in the telling inscription he wrote on the title page, *Musica laetitiae comes & Medicina dolorum*, the well-known motto we find later inscribed on the virginals in Vermeer's *Music Lesson* of 1662–4.[6]

In sum, not just the sheer amount, but the various sources of music to which these two amateurs had access is remarkable. It is not an exaggeration to compare the inventory in these lute books to our modern conception of the "playlist" – a personal input of hand-picked selections from a variety of sources and styles, unregulated (in contrast to printed anthologies) by market considerations, compiled by personal choice and over time, regional, often multi-curated or including a repertory shared by others, and freely mixing past and contemporary styles.

Notes

1 The Cavalcanti lute book (*Cavalcanti*) is located in Brussels, Bibliothèque Royale de Belgique, MS II 275. Wurstisen's book (*Wurstisen*) is in Basel, Universitätsbibliothek, F IX 70. For a general study of the Cavalcanti manuscript with a specific focus on the formulas it contains for singing

poetry, see Coelho, "Raffaello Cavalcanti's Lute Book." Biographical information about Raffaello and related archival information about the Cavalcanti family appears in Coelho, "The Players of Florentine Monody." For an inventory of the manuscript, see Leslie Chapman Hubbell, "Sixteenth-Century Italian Songs for Solo Voice and Lute," 2 vols., PhD diss., Northwestern University (1982), 461–95. For a description and inventory of *Wurstisen*, see John Kmetz, *Die Handschriften der Universitätsbibliothek Basel: Katalog der Musikhandschriften des 16. Jahrhunderts. Quellenkritische und historische Untersuchung* (Basel, 1988), 206–29.

2 For a useful checklist of Dutch and German lute anthologies printed between 1584 and 1625, see Spring, *The Lute in Britain*, 223.

3 As the lutenist to two successive Medici popes, Leo X and Clement VII, Francesco maintained a strong Florentine connection that was strengthened, posthumously, in the last half of the sixteenth century. On these connections, see Coelho, "Papal Tastes and Musical Genres," 290–2.

4 On the larger musical context of these paintings, see Coelho, "Bronzino's *Lute Player*."

5 For information on two other lute manuscripts in the University of Basel collection giving evidence of the student repertory of a previous generation, see the descriptions in Kmetz, *Die Handschriften*, of F IX 23 (84–8) and F X 11 (272–6).

6 "Music: Pleasure's companion, remedy of sorrow." On the history of this motto, see Roger Harmon, "'Musica laetitiae comes' and Vermeer's *Music Lesson*," *Oud Holland* 113 (1999), 161–6.

The deepest divide between amateurs and professionals in the fifteenth century concerned performance practice. Prior to the age of printing, written musical collections were very expensive to assemble and not widely available. Much of what professionals then produced was based on memory or on a variety of improvisational techniques learned through long hours of tedious repetitions that most amateurs did not have the time or ability to acquire. An exception is Vincenzo Capirola, a lutenist active in northern Italy at the beginning of the sixteenth century. His manuscript tablature *Capirola* (see SBS 8) compiled around 1517 is one of the central sources of lute music of that period, containing a diverse, contemporary (even anticipatory), and technically challenging repertory, with some of the pieces titled according to difficulty. His upper-class status placed him within important networks of kinship and alliance that were crucial in musical transmission and circulation. His intabulation of excerpts from Josquin's *Missa Pange Lingua*, for example, predate the publication of this Mass by almost twenty years, showing that Capirola had internal access to this work and was within the loop of manuscript circulation of this, one of

Josquin's crowning achievements. But nothing was more fundamental than the change wrought by the availability of printed music. By about 1550, a small group of amateurs equipped with a chanson volume or two published by Attaingnant, a dance volume published by Susato, and perhaps with the recorder treatise of Ganassi, could, with a few evenings of rehearsals, have given a credible imitation of a performance of a professional ensemble – something that was quite impossible a few decades earlier.

4 | Instrumental music for celebration and ceremony

Instrumental music formed an integral part of Renaissance celebrations, and when designed for the Renaissance courtier or urbanite these events typically bundled an expansive, opulent series of events together, sometimes lasting over several days or even weeks. When the Duke of Burgundy made an entry into Bruges or the Medici programmed an important wedding, the festive template included a reception ceremony, a procession (with music and the presentation of small dramas), a religious service, and banquets invariably followed by dances. For religious ceremonies an almost analogous series would take place, sometimes, if in Florence or Siena, with a *palio* thrown in for even more intense entertainment. For an entry, troupes of artists, including the most prominent available, created vast quantities of painted banners and other ephemera to be suspended from windows and to serve as backdrops along the route, actors presented short dramatic presentations in stage settings on platforms above street corners, and small ensembles of chamber players would often perform in front of the image of the Virgin as it was carried along the procession route. The musicians who participated in these ceremonies were capable of high art, which was usually realized in the more highly choreographed or intimate settings. But one can only wonder how much quality music was really produced in the three hours or more of a long procession, especially when the conditions included cold, blustery weather, noisy crowds, musicians having to play outside their normal posture, cannons firing from the town's fortresses, and trumpets blaring from rooftops.

Given that so little actual music survives for these events, it may be useful to begin by considering the typology used by Anthony Cummings in his study of Medici festivals of the first half of the sixteenth century, which places the different types of instrumental music used in Renaissance celebrations into broad categories. Occupying the "low end" of his classification is "spontaneous instrumental playing," a more or less unregulated public activity at civic events likened to New Year's revelers in Times Square; a second category includes instrumental fanfares, probably improvised or memorized that highlighted important moments of arrival and presence, and served as well as a means for communication; a third category involved music for processions and entries, one example being the works played by the instrumentalists of the Signoria in 1515 as the papal procession passed in front of the Palazzo Vecchio. At a more sophisticated level is the music played on the famous adorned carts as they rode through the streets during Carnival or as part of the festivities for a Medici wedding. A final, elevated, category for instrumentalists is "convivial" playing – essentially the music, mostly private, provided at noble entertainments, whether for a banquet, dancing, or wedding feast.[1] As a final preliminary, it is useful to compare the place of instrumental music in Renaissance celebrations with a present-day perspective. When we venture out to listen to a musical performance we assume that the normal venue will be a "concert." This was not the case in the Renaissance, when the idea of a musical performance being the primary objective was still in its early development. Far more often music served a broader context, which we will explore in this chapter through three events, political, matrimonial, and liturgical, in which music was woven into their basic social and cultural fabric.

Festivals

The great celebrations of the Renaissance can be broadly described as "festivals," and these were produced in great variety. One that was celebrated everywhere well into the sixteenth century, even in Protestant regions, was Carnival, occurring immediately before Lent, which is itself calculated as the forty days preceding Easter. Other important festivals featuring instrumental music were the civic observances connected to deeply rooted local devotion, such as Feast of San Giovanni in Florence, the Feast of the Assumption in Siena, or the veneration of the relic of the Holy Blood in Bruges; in the same vein were the celebrations of Corpus Christi in many cities, especially those in the north. While the focus here is essentially on sacred celebrations, the accompanying events everywhere could be distinctly secular. This worldly aspect was in play especially north of the Alps in what may be termed "market festivals," whose underlying motive was often economic in that they were timed to coincide with important "markets" – short periods when a city was granted special privileges to display and sell goods. Even the religious aspect could be

---

[1] Anthony Cummings, *The Politicized Muse: Music for Medici Festivals, 1512–1537* (Princeton, 1992), 164–8.

bent to conform to this priority. In Bruges "the city government... agreed that the Holy Blood procession... should always be held on the feast of the Invention of the Holy Cross, and that the two-week-long celebrations associated with it should correspond to the yearly May market."[2] Clearly the market festival wove together many religious, cultural, and economic interests. Finally, some festive occasions were associated with the nobility, such as weddings of heirs apparent, or the "joyous entry" of a lord into one of his cities. In the following account, we will first describe some of the more important festivals. This will be followed by a consideration of individual activities, like dancing, to examine their characteristics and how they were adapted over the course of the fifteenth and sixteenth centuries. Finally, we will examine the role of instrumental music in the theater and in religious celebrations, events in which instruments have both a musical and non-musical importance.

Case study 9

Music and political ceremony: the ritual granting of privileges and forgiveness, Bruges, 16 May 1488

When Charles the Bold of Burgundy died on the battlefield of Nancy in 1477, the Burgundian territories in the Low Countries came under immediate threat from the forces of Louis XI of France. Desperate to maintain their independence from the French crown, the Flemish burgers hurried the arrangements for a marriage of Charles's daughter, Mary, with Maximilian of Habsburg, the son of Frederick III, the Holy Roman Emperor. At first all went well, as the young Maximilian led a combined army that defeated the French at Guinegatte in 1479, but relations between Maximilian and his Flemish subject soon soured as Maximilian tried to expand his control of the region. Conditions grew ever more tense after the death of Mary in 1482, when his claim to authority as regent for his son Philip was widely resisted. He seemed to be gaining the upper hand in 1485, and his authority was bolstered in 1486 when he was crowned King of the Germans in Aachen. On his entry into Bruges in 1488, however, conditions had again deteriorated and the town officials there took him prisoner in an attempt to compel Maximilian to guarantee their traditional rights and privileges.

---

[2] Barbara Haggh, "The Beguines of Bruges and the Procession of the Holy Blood." In *Uno gentile et subtile ingenio*, ed. Jennifer Bloxam, Gioia Filocamo, and Leofranc Holford-Strevens, 82.

After three months of negotiations a resolution seemed at hand, and an imposing ceremony was organized at which Maximilian spelled out the freedoms he was willing to grant his subjects.

We are fortunate that an anonymous citizen of Bruges provided an eyewitness account of what transpired.[1] He noted that this event was held "on the 16th day in May, in the year 1488" and it began with a solemn procession. The line of the march was headed by an assembly of the most imposing sacred objects housed in the city – the relics of St. Donatian (belonging to the church of St. Donatian), the Holy Cross (belonging to church of Our Lady), and the Holy Sacrament (also held in the church of St. Donatian) – underlining the gravity of the occasion. Present were officials of the "Four Members" (the traditional leaders of the region, Bruges, Ghent, Ypres, and the Franc of Bruges) as well as representatives from "Flanders, Brabant, Holland and Zeeland." All made their way to the residence of one Jan de Groos, where Maximilian had been confined for "11 weeks and one day." From there, with Maximilian now in tow, all processed "on foot" to the Grand Place of Bruges, stopping there first in front of the house "called *in Cranenburch*" where a "park" had been prepared. At this point Maximilian took an oath that forgave all those who had been involved in the insurrections that had let to his being taken captive in Bruges. The official party then ascended a large platform on the Grand Place where Maximilian further put his hand in turn on the relics of St. Donatian, the Holy Cross, and the Holy Sacrament, and swore that he would respect the privileges of his subjects and be a good and true ruler. At this point the *Te Deum laudamus* was sung. This was followed by a short performance by the city minstrels of the *Ave regina c[a]elorum* and then "other pieces of music." This marked the end of the ceremony, and the party left the stage for a banquet in a nearby mansion.

This event was carefully calibrated to demonstrate the stature of the Flemings in relation to Maximilian, as well as the gravity of the day. Everyone processed on foot. On normal festive occasions Maximilian rode on horseback, while the civic officials, as commoners, were on foot. For this event Maximilian was denied his usual privilege and all processed together. The conspicuous lack of ceremonial trumpets also underlined Maximilian's constrained state; there were no fanfares to herald his presence. Also, in earlier festive occasions, such as the entry of Philip the Good into Bruges in 1440, musical ensembles were in position to perform at various points in the marching line. But from our perspective the most extraordinary detail is the chronicler's perspicacious observation that the ensemble performed a version of *Ave regina celorum*. Most such chronicles refer to music only in passing (if they refer to it at all), and almost never are as specific as this.

Fortunately, we also have available a great deal of supporting documentation. The Bruges account books reveal that the civic ensemble at this time consisted of four musicians, three playing various sizes of shawms and one trombonist.[2] Obviously when they performed the *Ave regina celorum* they would have played a four-part polyphonic version. We also know that at precisely this time, the tradition was developing in the Low Countries for civic ensembles to perform in special services devoted to the Virgin held in the late afternoon or early evening (*Salve* or *Lof* were the terms used in the region). Contracts for the city bands in such cities as Antwerp, Bergen op Zoom, and Utrecht specified that their ensembles were to perform motets or songs at these services, and in a few instances further stated that the musicians were to play "gezetten stukken," literally, "set pieces," implying most probably written or memorized compositions, as distinct from improvised ones, lending an air of formality and tradition to this stage of the ceremony.[3]

Our chronicler unfortunately mentions only the titles of pieces, not composers. However, Jacob Obrecht was chapel master at St. Donatian's church for a few years at around this time, and this has led Reinhard Strohm to suggest that several of the Marian motets by Obrecht (including settings of *Ave regina celorum* and *Salve regina*) were composed specifically for *Salve* performances.[4] Given the solemnity of the occasion on 16 May, we can assume that the musicians prepared a particularly ambitious version of the *Ave regina celorum*, and it is quite possible that they did, indeed, following Strohm's observation, perform the four-part version by Obrecht.

In any case, we have here a remarkably clear instance of the role that music could play in Renaissance ceremonies, both in its absence and its presence. The lack of trumpets sounding served to remind all present that Maximilian's authority was being restrained. The absence of music along the route also underlined the more solemn character of this ceremony. Finally, the decision by the city authorities that the event could conclude with the sounding of a motet by the civic ensemble speaks volumes for the central role of instrumental music in Renaissance ceremony.

Notes

1 The anonymous chronicle is available in *Het Boeck van al 't gene datter geschiet es binnen Brugge sichtent Jaer 1477, 14 Frebuarii, tot 1491*, ed. Charles Carton, Maatschappy der Vlaemsche Bibliophilen, ser. 2, no. 2 (Ghent, 1859); see 222–4 for the events of 16 May 1488, 211–12 for those of 5 April in the same year.

2 References to music from the account books of Bruges are available in Gilliodts-Van Severen, *Les Ménestrels de Bruges*; for the listing of four musicians as three shawms and a trombone, see 56.
3 Polk, "Susato and Instrumental Music." In *Tielman Susato*, ed. Keith Polk, 68–91.
4 Strohm, *Music in Late Medieval Bruges*, 87, 144–5.

The wedding as festival

The wedding of William, son of Albert V of Bavaria (and future duke as William V), and Renata of Lorraine in 1568 provided the occasion for one of the most lavish celebrations of the Renaissance. Albert V, as we have shown above, was extraordinarily enthusiastic in his artistic patronage, and music played a prominent role in the festivities associated with the wedding. Characteristic of events involving the highest nobility, ceremony was elaborate at every level, and thanks to the descriptions of Massimo Troiano, we are particularly well informed about how these ceremonies unfolded and the role music played in them. Troiano (d. after 1570) was an expert witness, for he was himself both a composer and performer. As the wedding party arrived in Bavaria, they were received by an official delegation accompanied by the ducal band of trumpets and tympani. There followed a sequence of events, consisting of masquerades, dramatic productions, banquets, dances, tournaments, and, of course, the wedding celebration itself. Troiano included information about dress and costume, the food selections served at each course of the main banquet, the mock dramas of the tournaments, and other precious details. From our perspective, the most valuable aspect of his commentary is the precise information concerning musical repertory and performance practice, of which his description of the central banquet of the wedding festival can serve as an example.[3]

Case study 10

Taste and magnificence entwined: the Bavarian wedding of 1568

[Trumpets announced each course]; with the salad, the diners were entertained with the sound of various wind instruments... trombones and cornets played an eight-part Battaglia by the organist Annibale [Padovano] from Padua, and other

---

[3] [Troiano], *Die Münchner Fürstenhochzeit*, 134–63. All English translations are by the authors.

eight-part pieces; ... [with the first course] the ducal musicians performed... various pieces, including a seven-part motet by Orlando di Lasso with five cornets and two trombones.... [with the second course] the musicians played several six-part pieces, among them a madrigal by Alessandro Striggio with 6 large trombones, of which the bass was an octave lower than the usual size; [with the third] various six-part pieces were performed, including a work by Cipriano de Rore with six violins, which continued until the arrival of the 4th course.

[Then] various lovely 12-part pieces by Annibale Padoano and others were played on 6 violins [*viole da brazzo*], 5 trombones, a cornett, and a gentle regal; with [the fifth course] sounded lovely music by six viols, tuned a fourth lower than normal, six recorders, six singers and keyboard....With [the sixth course] a cembalo, trombone, recorder, lute, crumhorn, a still cornett, a viol and a flute played beautifully [no specific piece mentioned]... [with the seventh course] the musicians performed a 12-part piece in three choirs, the first of 4 viols, the second of 4 large recorders, and the third of varied instruments, that is, a dulcian, a crumhorn, a flute, and a mute cornett and then the fruit was brought in... [with the fruit course] the assembled vocal choir sang, including a performance of a four-part piece by especially selected singers... at the end of the banquet, the hall was cleared, and twelve trumpets with tympani sounded a festive fanfare to announce the Dance.[1]

This banquet was the highlight of the entire wedding festival, and this relatively short passage contains an illuminating wealth of detail about instrumental music on several levels. One of the finest composers of the age, Orlando di Lasso, supervised every step in the program. He himself then approved of the performance of one of his vocal motets by cornetts and trombones. With his insider's eye and ear, Troiano clearly traces the outlines of the instrumental repertory: madrigals, motets, chansons, but not *ricercare* or *canzone per sonare*; in other words, the instrumental repertory was based on arrangements or faithful renderings of music originally composed for voices. Troiano also precisely described the instrumental forces, revealing clearly that the notion of complete consorts (of trombones and of violins) was still firmly in place, but that broken consorts (i.e. mixtures of instrumental colors), too, provided contrast. He keenly noticed the presence of the regal (a small organ) during the fourth course, which was probably providing chordal foundational support anticipating the figured bass of the Baroque era.

Albert V had obviously given his chapel master, Orlando, free rein to hire the best musicians in whatever extravagant quantity the composer thought appropriate. The result strained the ducal treasury to the breaking point – the close relationship of Albert V and Orlando brings to mind the musically fecund but economically ruinous relationship between King

Ludwig II and Richard Wagner three centuries later. Albert undoubtedly felt that his generosity was vindicated in that the quality as well as the quantity of music brought to bear throughout this celebration was unsurpassed. The outstanding corps of trumpets sounded constantly, strings and winds played for banquets and dances, and singers provided their contributions. All provided music supporting ceremony at the most opulent level.

Note
1 Ibid., 134–63; "cornett" here as a translation of *cornetti alti*, suggested by Herbert Myers.

Processions

In a medieval and Renaissance city hardly a day would pass without a procession somewhere. Many were religious, often within the confines of a church or cathedral, and, in fact, almost all had some sacred context, which, as shown above, could be manufactured if it didn't already exist. And we have noted earlier, processions had links to the economic infrastructure, as the major festivals were often designed to complement a city's designated market period. Some were more political, as the annual procession in London marking the inauguration of the Lord Mayor, or those associated with royal entries. In short, processions reveal a vast range of Renaissance life, for they called upon all the resources that a Renaissance city could bring to bear: dance, drama, exotic marvels brought back by returning explorers (such as elephants and camels, live when available, invented when not), ephemera, and music, affecting all social classes. To study processions is to watch the Renaissance come alive.

While the most extravagant processions took place when a ruler made an official entry into one of his or her cities, the civic processionals offered in many ways a more entertaining and vivacious presentation. They combined the comic and deadly serious, a wondrous mélange of giants and fanciful creatures, a parade of local dignitaries and tradesmen dressed in their most impressive regalia, and carts carrying *tableaux vivants*, many with actors playing out dramatic scenes. Sonically, all of this was accompanied by the constant sounds of bells ringing, trumpets blaring fanfares, the singing of choirs, children, and the best church singers of the city, and the participation of all varieties of instrumental ensembles. What shines through all the panoply is the depth of a city's pride and ambition.

In the Dutch city of Bergen op Zoom the most elaborate procession was intimately linked with the Easter Market, a six-week period during which goods could be traded in the town with special tax exemptions. Thanks to C. J. F. Slootmans, the distinguished scholar of Bergen op Zoom's history, we can reconstruct a general picture of the procession. By the early sixteenth century it opened with a phalanx of drummers who cleared the way for the militia guilds of the city. Before the first of the militia groups the civic wind band played, taking the most prominent position. Then, as in 1447–8, the shawms and trombones of Antwerp preceded the senior infantry, the wind band from Middelburg introduced the senior crossbowmen, and the Utrecht civic ensemble the junior crossbowmen.[4]

Next in the order of march would be representations drawn from the Old and New Testament. First would be figures representing the Prophets, with one of the leading images being that of Moses carrying stone tablets with the Ten Commandments. Then would come one of the more elaborate presentations, that of the Golden Calf, surrounded by dancers representing Jews – with costly clothing, arresting headdresses, and accompanied by a variety of musicians. Striking among this group were the appearances of Death and a Wagon from Hell, replete with devils. Following this grouping came the floats with presentations of the *tableaux-vivants*, in some years more than thirty in all.

The final section of the procession consisted first of the trade guilds, each with their individual colored banners, all carrying candles, and many headed by their own set of hired musicians, usually wind players. The members of the Town Council followed, but in front of them was carried the relic of the Holy Cross, the most precious object the town possessed. The relic was also accompanied by musicians, traditionally in Bergen op Zoom by a group of soft players: in the fifteenth century it would be a mixed group of lutes, harps or fiddles; in the sixteenth century it probably included players of bowed stringed instruments, either viols or, later, violins.

Processions required considerable expense, and some of the most valuable information concerning details of instrumental musical practices comes from the listings of payments for these events in city records. The diminutive city of Dendermonde in Flanders supported an astonishing number of musicians for its local festival and procession. Detailed records have survived for the city and one development revealed by these records is

---

[4] On the procession in Bergen op Zoom, see C. J. F. Slootmans, *De Heilig Kruis Ommegang van Bergen op Zoom* (Bergen op Zoom, 1946), for the reference to the Antwerp band in 1447–8, see 51.

the emerging prominence of ensembles of viols and violins in Flanders during the sixteenth century. In addition, processional records sometimes document ensembles for which no other records are available. In the Dendermonde accounts we find details of the size and personnel of the Antwerp civic band for years in which no records survive from Antwerp itself. Similarly the procession accounts for Bergen op Zoom document the existence of a town ensemble for Reimerswaal – a city that was struck by a series of floods in the 1530s and which ultimately sank beneath the waters. The payments in Bergen op Zoom are one of the few dreary reminders that the town – and its musicians – ever existed. To turn to Italian sources, the Siena accounts for the procession (and the associated *palio*) of the festival of the Assumption are frequently quite ample, providing a variety of insights into instrumental practice. In 1463 among those present were "two players of lute of the Duke of Bavaria" – this at a time when Conrad Paumann was attached to the Munich court as a lutenist and organist.[5] Tinctoris, discussing lute performance practice of exactly this period, pointed out that Paumann, and almost certainly other of his lute playing colleagues, had developed a new way of playing the lute which involved individual lutenists playing polyphonically. This was in contrast to the Italian manner, associated with the Ferrarese virtuoso Pietrobono, which emphasized elaboration of a single melodic line. The presence of Munich musicians in Siena provides evidence that the new approach was certainly being brought front and center to musical circles in Italy.

The placement of music in processions can serve as an apt metaphor for the role of instrumental music in the late Middle Ages and Renaissance. The central function of the processions in Bruges or in Bergen op Zoom was to dramatize the opening of the local market and thus to attract a broad and potentially profitable public of merchants, foreign and domestic. And as colorful as the assembled forces might be, which included giants, exotic animals, and bright uniforms, the reality was that these processions lasted for hours. For the Renaissance mind such ceremonies were inconceivable without instrumental music.

Instrumental music and banquets

For most English-speaking families, dining is an increasingly casual matter, with on a normal day expedience and convenience taking

---

[5] See D'Accone, *The Civic Muse*, 689.

precedence over ceremony. Today, banquets are experienced only occasionally (such as at the ends of conferences, institutional events, or fund-raising galas), and are usually characterized by tedious speeches and perfunctory cuisine. A noteworthy exception is "high table," a type of regular banquet that is still held at the colleges of Oxford and Cambridge. This daily event follows a firm protocol and serves as a reminder of what banquets meant to the courtiers and citizens of the Renaissance.

Banquets were not limited to occasional events; daily dining was also elaborate, involving multiple courses. Music played an integral role in the carefully orchestrated presentation of court cuisine, as performers provided a pleasing distraction during the necessary machinations of ending the serving of one course and preparing for another. Special events of course would call for greater luxury, and, at times, extravagance. A few descriptions survive offering details. The most spectacular in the fifteenth century was certainly that of the Feast of the Pheasant given by the Duke of Burgundy in 1454, which was so extravagant that it received multiple contemporary descriptions from astonished chroniclers. Among the sixteenth-century descriptions, Massimo Troiano's commentary on the Bavarian court wedding in 1568 stands out for its detail and authority in relation to music (and again, Troiano was a particularly reliable witness). These surviving descriptions are useful in providing information in three directions: first, they indicate the musical performers and performing combinations involved; second, they give a clear general picture of the repertories that were heard; and third, they provide valuable hints with regard to performance practice.

Case study 11

Pressing the boundaries of extravagance: the Feast of the Pheasant – Lille, 1454

At the Feast of the Pheasant, the primary goal was to dazzle all in attendance with the full range of performing forces available to the Burgundian court. Trumpets announced the beginning and the end point, and occasionally blew fanfares at other important moments.[1] Entertainment was offered between each course, most often by musicians, both singers and instrumentalists. At one point adult singers performed with an organ (almost certainly a motet), and at another, three choirboys with an adult singing tenor performed a chanson. At about the midpoint in the program, three singers ("trios douches voix") performed the chanson "La Saulvegard de ma vie"; shortly thereafter a young girl of twelve sang the chanson "Je ne vis onques la pareille," accompanied by an adult tenor. This was followed by the singers of the duke singing a motet, followed in turn by two singers accompanied by a lute. Later, a solo female singer performed another chanson, this time accompanied by the two blind chamber musicians of the court, at least one, and probably both, performing on lute. Instrumental performances included some by solo organ, a bagpipe, a German cornet "moult estrangement" (probably accompanied by organ), a "douchaine" accompanied by another instrument, probably another wind instrument, and an ensemble of four recorders ("fleutres" – the term in this instance not referring to transverse flutes).

The descriptions make clear that the entire court stable was on call. The Burgundian payrolls, as well as the ordinances laying out the ducal personnel, indicate that a chapel choir of about sixteen was available, and that the instrumental forces were divided into three basic groups: two or three chamber musicians, a group of trumpets, and a wind band. Clearly, from the descriptions, all of these were present in some form. An intriguing feature is that a few performers were evidently not on the regular payrolls. The presence of a female singer was remarkable, as well as a young boy twelve years of age ("ung josne filz de eage de XII ans"). Another sidelight is that even though no organist is listed either in the pay lists or in the ordinances, the organist was assigned a distinctly prominent role. One suspects that lurking among the list of singers was probably an organist. It is interesting to note also that no performance by the superb Burgundian wind ensemble on shawms and sackbut was indicated, though it was almost certainly the court shawmists who performed on recorders and probably on the bagpipe, "douchaine," and on that "strange German cornet." It is possible, though, that these last were taken care of by outside freelancers hired for the occasion.

The repertory consisted of motets and chansons, and serves as a reminder that such events called for a mixing of the sacred and profane, to the extent that singers from the chapel choir sang chansons and instrumentalists played arrangements of motets. The descriptions raise intriguing issues relating to fifteenth-century performance practice. The performance of "Je ne vis onques" was indicated as performed by two singers, one young the other an adult, but the piece (attributed both to Dufay and to Binchois) is for three parts.[2] Given the context – Binchois himself was probably present – the omission of one part (the contratenor) was perfectly acceptable. Two of the performances combined voices and singers (one with two voices and lute, the other with female and the two blind chamber musicians). No pieces are named, but again, given the context (with the probable presence of Binchois), combinations of voices and instruments, especially those played by chamber players, were part of the calculation by the composers. The notion that the compositional "ideal" of the era was for all-vocal, or *a cappella*, performance – which prevailed in many circles of Renaissance musicology – is clearly at odds with the evidence of the 1454 witnesses. All-vocal performance was certainly one option, maybe even a preferred one, but it was neither the only option nor the only solution. The performance by four "flutes," surely by the court shawm ensemble, raises a number of questions. The court band was described as a "loud" ensemble, but the recorder was, of course, a member of the "soft" cohort. The indication underlines not only that the players, as professionals, were expected to play more than one instrument, but further, in doing so they would play whatever was appropriate for the occasion. In short, the distinction between "loud" and "soft" was highly flexible. Yet another issue with this particular group was its specific description as being an ensemble of four, while the normal texture in compositions at the time was for three parts. One possibility is that the players simply memorized one of the exceptional contemporary four-part pieces. Three players could also have played a three-part piece from memory while the fourth improvised a free counterpoint. Unfortunately, with so little information such suggestions remain as speculation.

Notes

1 All of the following quotations relating to the banquet of 1454 are from Marix, *Histoire*, 37–43. See also David Fallows, "Specific Information on the Ensembles for Composed Polyphony, 1400–1475." In *Studies in the Performance of Late Medieval Music*, ed. Stanley Boorman (Cambridge, 1983), 109–59, also available in Fallows, *Songs and Musicians*, Essay XI.
2 The piece was widely circulated, appearing in French, Italian, and German manuscripts; see Fallows, *Catalogue*, 215–16.

To return to the 1568 Munich wedding banquet, Troiano prefaced his commentary with an overview of how music at table in the ducal household was offered as a daily dining routine:

After the first course... and the first call has sounded, the winds perform with crumhorns [*cornamusa* in the original, hereinafter given as "crumhorns"], or flutes, or trombones and cornets until the second course. They play French chansons and other cheerful pieces. After that Antonio Morari and his fellow violinists (or violists and other stringed instruments) play chansons in heavenly fashion, or lovely motets, or light-hearted madrigals up until the last course. When the fruit is served Orlando di Lasso appears with his singers – with sweet, full voices they bring new pieces every day, some in four and others in three parts.[6]

Troiano makes clear that this *Tafelmusik* was a regular feature of courtly life, and while the quality was extraordinary in Munich, the general framework was probably observed at courts throughout Europe at the time. One crucial point that can be gleaned from Troiano's description is that those in attendance were actually focused on listening to the music being performed; the *Tafelmusik* was not intended as ambient sound.[7] When the eminent Lasso appeared with his singers we can assume that something of a hush would have fallen over the hall, and those in attendance became, at least for a short while, a devoted and attentive "audience." At the same time we must recognize that here, too, a tension was at play. Courtiers had other things on their mind than paying attention to music, no matter how artistic. Moreover, the serving staff constantly had to deal with the realities of presenting and clearing the tables, and paintings of meals and banquets from this period often show dogs or cats wandering around, looking for scraps. In short, the Renaissance banquet was perhaps the primary context for the performance of instrumental music representing high culture – but it was an imperfect venue.

Dance and its context

Dancing reigned as the supreme social recreation of the time, its mastery fundamental to noble education, its use essential for social events, and its influence extending even into architecture and politics. Concerning architecture, the popularity of dance was so overpowering that courts and cities were obliged to ensure that adequate spaces were available for dancing. In many cases, the rooms were polyvalent; halls used for official meetings

---

[6] Troiano, *Dialoge*, 104.
[7] On music at the Bavarian court in the later sixteenth century, see Nösselt, *Ein ältest Orchester 1530–1980*; Sandberger, *Beiträge zur Geschichte der bayerischen Hofkapelle unter Orlando di Lasso*; and Nicole Schwindt, "Hans Mielichs bildliche Darstellung der Münchner Hofkapelle von 1570," AcM 68 (1996), 48–85. In addition, Ruhnke, *Beiträge zu einer Geschichte der deutschen Hofmusikkollegien im 16. Jahrhundert* includes useful information on the forces at the Munich court.

or banqueting were frequently cleared for dancing, which took place in the middle of the room. The evidence for this can still be seen in countless large rooms where a minstrel's balcony still overlooks the floor below – as in, for example, the old city hall in Leipzig or the Salone dei Cinquecento of the Palazzo Vecchio in Florence.[8] But in some cases, especially in German cities, this was not enough,. In the small city of Nördlingen (about 100 km southwest of Nuremberg), the city fathers in the early fifteenth century determined that their dance house was too small, and they set about building a new one. This structure still survives, and its size is imposing. It consists of three floors up to the broad roof, which itself contains three more floors. It is in fact far larger than the Gothic city hall, which also survives, directly across the street. Other cities such as Cologne, Coburg, and Passau also erected separate buildings designated as dance houses.

Dance's reach into politics extends in two directions. The first is how dance reflects nobility, courtly (and courtship) ritual, and dynastic legacy through its narration of mythology, metaphor, and allegory. This is particularly evident in dances that were choreographed as part of courtly theatrical productions. The second direction leads to a consideration of how dance is used as a social and class marker. In Nuremberg in 1521, for example, the patrician element in control of the city decided to impose restrictions on those who had access to the inner workings of civic power. To do this they needed a way to define their own faction; they did this with the provision that only "those families who used to dance in the *Rathaus* in the olden days, and who still dance there" had the privilege of voting.[9] Nevile has discussed how dance at courtly spectacles unleashed intense interest and enthusiasm that permeated all areas of Europe and all classes – nobles, city dwellers, and peasants.[10]

Throughout the Renaissance, familiarity with dance was achieved in much the same way as with music: in an oral fashion through a master-student relationship, and from a texted tradition through treatises, written instructions, and figured choreographies. The learning of dances included knowing their associated melodies, many of which were internationally famous and became standard repertory for instrumentalists of all types. "La Spagna," the "Spagnoletta," "La Cara Cosa," "La Traditora," "La Barriera" the "Pavana alla Ferrarese" (or "alla Venetiana"), and the Passamezzo,

---

[8] Jennifer Nevile, "Dance in Europe 1250–1750." In *Dance, Spectacle*, ed. Jennifer Nevile, 40.
[9] Gerald Strauss, *Nuremberg in the Sixteenth Century* (Bloomington, 1976), 79.
[10] Nevile, *The Eloquent Body*, 44–7.

among many others, are all famous dances associated with well-known melodies or chordal schemes, and they appear throughout lute and keyboard collections of the late fifteenth and sixteenth centuries. The close familiarity with these models provided a template onto which instrumentalists could build their structures. It is no overstatement to say that in the Renaissance everyone danced, young more than the old, but youth was not a prerequisite. All classes joined in – the nobility, the urban elites, urban workers, and peasants – and we know from a variety of sources that every one of these groups enthusiastically participated. Detail concerning the lower social orders is, as usual, completely lacking. Still, the fabulous Brueghel paintings of village weddings and dances, with hefty peasants stomping away to the blaring of round-cheeked bagpipers, provide vivid testimony to the ubiquitous appeal of dancing.[11] In short, dancing was responsible for introducing an enormous repertory of melodies across a very wide geographical and social spectrum, ones that would be further arranged, expanded, and disseminated by instrumentalists.

Given the presence of dance at every level of society, providing music for dancing was for most Renaissance musicians their most reliable source of income, and well-known dances were common fare in music publications, not least for their appeal to popular taste. When large groups were involved, from about 1400 to 1550, the standard ensemble for dancing was the wind band. By the early sixteenth century, the lute (or groups of lutes) could also provide the accompaniment for both small and large gatherings, with lute ensembles common at courtly events; this is clearly seen in the painting of the wedding of Anne Duc de Joyeuse and Marguerite de Vaudémont in 1581 (Paris, Louvre, Inv. 8731), which shows four identically costumed lutenists playing during what appears to be a nuptial dance, as well as in the festivities for the Florentine wedding of Cosimo II Medici and Maria Magdalena of Austria in 1608, which we will return to below.[12] By the mid-sixteenth century, the violin becomes increasingly used, and though it did not replace the winds completely until many decades later, it was used by dancing masters, such as Cesare Negri, who was the author of the important dance treatise *Il gratie d'amore* (Milan 1602) as well as a *violon du roi* in the court of King Henri III.[13]

---

[11] See Chapter 6, Figure 6.20.

[12] On the lutes used for the 1608 Medici wedding and related documentary evidence, see Victor Coelho, "Public Works and Private Contexts: Lorenzo Allegri and the Florentine *Intermedi* of 1608." In *Luths et luthistes en Occident*, ed. Joël Dugot (Paris, 1999), 121–32.

[13] On Negri, see Katherine Tucker McGinnis, "Your Most Humble Subject, Cesare Negri Milanese." In *Dance, Spectacle*, ed. Jenifer Nevile, 211–28.

For smaller groups of dancers the pipe and tabor or a single lutenist could be called upon, and given the presence of so many lute arrangements in the treatises of Caroso and Negri, the lute was clearly one of the main instruments for both the dance master and for everyday dancing at court and home.

For public and theatrical events, the conditions were hardly congenial. Dances often lasted for many hours, and "all night long" is a frequent comment in the chronicles. For wind players this must have been particularly exhausting. Also, the players had to be able to produce on the spot, without written texts, hour after hour of fresh music. One further inescapable element was the space in which dancing would occur. For a small group, up to about a dozen, this aspect was of no particular concern – even out of doors a lute and fiddle could have easily provided the necessary background. But indoors, when a hundred or more danced in a large hall, the din would have been fearsome. Even the loudest of the shawm ensembles must have struggled to project their sound. Again, we hear nothing of how the players coped with these challenges at the time, but in analogy to present-day performers, we can imagine that the shawmists selected reeds with maximum buzz-saw quality. The sound context also helps explain why it was the violin, not the viol, which soon became the dominant orchestral instrument. A fretted instrument, the viol, like the lute, could produce only a distinctly limited volume. With the fretless violin, the player could dig into the string with the bow producing a much more penetrating sound – and indeed the primary association of the violin in the late Renaissance was as an instrument to accompany dancing. The vast quantity of dance music preserved in sixteenth-century sources vividly demonstrates the enduring popularity of dancing and the ability of instrumentalists to vary dance melodies in an astonishing variety of ways. The appeal, in fact, is reflected in that few of the preserved settings were apparently used for actual dancing. The dance was such a universal phenomenon that its music could also provide the raw material for a great swath of activity beyond dancing itself, from simple amateur home entertainment to dazzling sets of variations for virtuosos.

Music in the theater

Only late in the Renaissance did the role of music in theater change, but change it certainly did. From 1400 to around 1550, music continued to play a supporting role as it had throughout the Middle Ages. Howard Brown observed that "music had no leading part in the dramas, but served merely as an adjunct to the often brilliant spectacle ... These were not musical plays; they were plays with incidental music." [14] Indeed, some of the most opulent music of the Renaissance, such as the famous Florentine *intermedi* of 1589, was performed *between* the acts of a play, not with it. It was not until the first operatic masterpiece, *L'Orfeo* by Monteverdi (1607), that music played an equal role with drama.

The two centuries prior to about 1575 represented something of a paradox in that cities such as Bruges, Lille, Nuremberg, or York had no theaters as distinct structures, but nonetheless witnessed a constant round of theatrical presentations of immense variety. Their sacred drama could range from play cycles that ran for forty days and requiring vast resources of time and labor, to short recreations of Biblical scenes. Secular theater, too, existed in many forms, though it was not nearly as extensive as the sacred cycles. Some genres, farces and morality plays, for example, were clearly theatrical presentations. A variety of other types falling loosely under the rubric of "theater" included the English masques and disguisings, the *tableaux vivants* considered so essential in processions and entries, and even the more elaborate Italian dances (in which the dramatic element was central). While instruments were no doubt used to provide fanfares or fill other functional roles, the subject of instrumental music for late medieval staged drama is easily dealt with – in essence there was none. Similarly, we have little specific information about instruments participating in the fifteenth-century theater. Even for a work as seminal as Poliziano's *Orfeo*, performed sometime between 1471 and 1480, Nino Pirrotta is only able to suggest the presence of a lute to play a part in a ballata, and various percussion instruments on stage, like cymbals and percussion, as representative of Bacchic dancing.[15]

Dramatic productions formed part of most important Renaissance ceremonial occasions. As such they frequently attracted comment, and a number of descriptions in letters and diplomatic reports have survived. Still, sometimes even fairly detailed information yields little firm evidence concerning actual practice. In 1519, for example, in a performance in Rome with Leo X present "there was an intermedio for every act with the music of fifes, bagpipes, two cornetti, viols and lutes, and the small organ" – which tells us nothing about which instruments might have been called upon for

---

[14] See Howard Mayer Brown, *Music in the French Secular Theater, 1400–1550* (Cambridge, MA., 1963), 42.

[15] Nino Pirrotta, *Music and Theatre from Poliziano to Monteverdi*, trans. Karen Eales (Cambridge, 1982), 21.

a particular *intermedio*, or how they might have been combined.[16] More informative are the reports in 1502 by Isabella d'Este in which a drama was presented during one of her visits to Ferrara. She indicated that in the third act came "a consort of six viols" followed in the third *intermedio* with a cart drawn by a horse on which were placed "four singers with a lute."[17]

The richest sources of information on music in Renaissance drama are several descriptions of festivals connected with the Medici family, especially those held in Florence in 1518, 1539, 1565, 1589, and 1608. A similar performance connected to the Medici family was held in Lyons in 1548.[18] In these Medici *intermedi*, instruments played both a supporting and contrasting role. When singers were present, conveying the text was the first priority. In a similar perspective, dancers, when they appeared, were highly accomplished, performing elaborately prepared choreographies, and while instrumental music provided an essential background, attention was focused on the dance – "the single most important item," as Pirrotta observed.[19] Focus of attention or no, the instruments reveal a musical craft in transition. The festival instrumentations highlight the fact that the medieval classification of instruments as loud and soft had dissolved completely, now replaced by quite different concepts of how ensembles should be assembled. There are practical notions for the choice of instrumentation, and there are allegorical ones. The aggregation of many like instruments – four or more lutes of different sizes, or groups of wind instruments – were dictated by sonic demands, such as to fill a large indoor space or to be heard at an outdoor event. But instruments were also chosen for their imagery or mythological symbolism as part of the overall spectacle of the event. At other times, as we know from the considerable visual testimony to these events, instruments were chosen for their ability to be played on elaborate carts, floating rafts, or by musicians descending from suspended clouds. The descriptions also make clear the tension between two contrary directions. On the one hand was the notion that ensembles should be made up of like instruments, such as consorts of lutes, viols, violins, or of trombones. At the same time there was an obvious delight in mixing colors, as in the "O quale, O qual risplende nube" by Cristofano

---

[16] Ibid., 48, the "fifes" in this context were most likely shawms.   [17] Ibid., 52.
[18] Other festival performances were held in 1568, 1586, and there was also an additional one in 1589. For a description of the entire series of celebrations, see Brown, *Sixteenth-Century Instrumentation*, though with some caution as to Brown's proposed instrumentation for the 1589 *intermedi*. For a detailed musical and contextual account of these events prior to the Grand Ducal period, drawing on an impressive variety of archival, visual, and musical sources, see Cummings, *The Politicized Muse*.
[19] Pirrotta, *Music and Theatre*, 50.

Malvezzi written for the 1589 celebration of the marriage of Ferdinando I Medici and Christine of Lorraine. The work, part of the sixth musical interlude between the acts of Bargagli's play *La Pellegrina*, calls for twenty-four voices and twenty-three instruments, including four lutes, four viols (two of them basses), four trombones, two cornetts, a cittern, psaltery, mandola, lirone, and a violin. Allied with the penchant for mixed colors was the obvious enjoyment of assembling a vast force of performers, especially to achieve a dramatic finish. This interest in large-scale effects was obviously intended as a *coup de théâtre*, but it would ultimately lead to the more organized and regularized ensemble of an orchestra based on a foundation of violin types – a development for which initial steps were taken within two or three decades following the 1589 festival.[20]

Thanks to an unusually rich and diverse corpus of documentation – musical, iconographical, archival, testimonial – the elaborately staged events for the 1608 Medici wedding between Cosimo II Medici and the Habsburg Archduchess Maria Magdalena of Austria provide another revealing look at the ingenious way in which instruments were employed in Florentine theatrical events of the late Renaissance.[21] Initiating a month-long celebration of the nuptials, the bride's sumptuously decorated cavalcade into Florence on 18 October was announced by trumpeters on horseback. The next day, a large banquet in the Salone dei Cinquecento of the Palazzo Vecchio featured singers of madrigals appearing in clouds, with almost 100 instrumentalists and singers arranged in tiers performing from the balcony at one end of the hall. Later, instrumentalists were also called on to provide music for an equestrian ballet in the Piazza Santa Croce, for which they were seated in carts, for an *argonautica* on the Arno for which the instrumentalists were placed in allegorical floats, and, of course, for the *intermedi*. For the evening entertainment (*veglia*) on October 22, appropriately entitled *La Notte d'Amore*, the music was composed by court lutenist Lorenzo Allegri for a six-part string band that included multiple lutes playing a full-voiced chordal realization of the bass line.[22] But the main event was the performance for 5,000 people of the

---

[20] On this development, see John Spitzer and Neal Zaslaw, *The Birth of the Orchestra: History of an Institution, 1650–1815* (Oxford and New York, 2004), 37–44.

[21] For a description of the 1608 celebrations based on contemporary documents, see the following: Alois Nagler, *Theatre Festivals of the Medici, 1539–1637* (rpt. New York, 1976), 101–15; Federico Ghisi, "Ballet Entertainments in Pitti Palace, 1608–1625," *MQ* 35 (1949), 429–32; Tim Carter, "A Florentine Wedding of 1608," *AcM* 55 (1983), 89–107, and Janie Cole, *Music, Spectacle and Cultural Brokerage in Early Modern Italy: Michelangelo Buonarroti il Giovane* (Florence, 2011), 209–62.

[22] See Coelho, "Public Works and Private Contexts," 125–6.

pastoral *Il giudizio di Paride*, written by Michelangelo Buonarroti *il giovane*, which featured flute, violin, trombones, viols, keyboard instruments, guitars, and sixteen lutenists.

Finally, concerning the Florentine *intermedi*, it should be noted that the 1589 performance included five *sinfonias* specifically written for ensemble instruments. The *sinfonias* are among the earliest examples of ensemble instrumental pieces designed to stand alone – they had no relation to texts or text styles (i.e. they were not *canzone francese per sonare*), they did not accompany voices, and they were not combined with dance.

Instrumental music in sacred celebrations

The incorporation of instruments into sacred ceremony, as with other aspects of performance practice, falls into a fairly clear chronological division. The fifteenth century was a period that can be termed conservative in the acceptance of instruments, with distinctly more adventuresome approaches arising in the sixteenth century – at least in terms of instrumental ensembles. The organ held a unique place and for the most part fell outside the general practices and taxonomies that governed other instruments, in that throughout the Renaissance it was completely integrated into liturgical practice. This was due to its ability to support voices, which was manifested particularly in the notion of *alternatim* practice, in which voices and organ would alternate, with one verse of a text taken by the choir (often in plainchant), with a following verse performed by the organ alone. This was so functional and pleasing that even in the celebration of the Mass a standard pattern or exchange evolved. In the *Sanctus*, for example, the first and third statements of *Sanctus*, the *Dominus*, and the *Benedictus* would be played while the other portions would be sung. Most often this was probably a utilitarian kind of music, but could, at times, be more elaborate. Isaac seems to have written Masses specifically with this *alternatim* approach in mind. Moreover, the presence of the organ within the liturgy had become so accepted that other contributions of the organ were also welcome. As early as *Windsheim*, dated about 1440, we find short preludes, with similar pieces appearing in later sources. As these were evidently for the large organ (always located, of course, in a church) they were designed to provide introductory music to a portion of some liturgical service. These fifteenth-century essays were forerunners of the extensive preludes that would be associated particularly with Lutheran services in the following centuries.

While ensemble instruments in the fifteenth century were seldom incorporated into the actual liturgy (they did not play, for example, in the sections of the Mass Ordinary), their contributions were embraced in several contexts. Chamber instruments were a standard accompaniment in some paraliturgical devotions, as the late medieval mindset appears to have felt a special connection between instruments such as the harp, lute, and fiddle, and sacred contexts. In Florence, the outpouring of late medieval popular piety led to the rise of confraternities with a primary objective of singing devotional songs, such as the *laude*. Originally the repertory of the *Laudesi* companies was sung, but by about 1400 they regularly hired lutenists and fiddlers to assist in their singing. To give a sampling, in 1421 a certain Pagolo was paid to "play the rebec and sing the laude" for the evening services, and in 1467 "two players of harp and lute" were called in to perform in the Lauda services during the Christmas season.[23] Confraternities (*scuole*) reflecting a similar concentration on popular piety in Venice followed an analogous path. Consisting at first of all amateur singers, the six major *scuole* initiated the hiring of professionals in the 1440s, but apparently did not begin to hire professional instrumentalists regularly until the 1480s – initially, as in Florence, consisting of exclusively soft instruments such as harp and lute. The first recorded instance of the participation of a wind band with one of the *scuole grandi* was not until 1502.[24] Oddly, the lesser *scuole* in Venice were more assertive in incorporating instrumentalists into their services than the *scuole grandi*. From early on these included wind instrumentalists, and significantly in 1506, the "trombones and shawms" of the Doge joined the Scuola di Santa Maria dei Mercanti. This is significant in that it may help to explain the extraordinary letter from one of the Doge's musicians, Giovanni Alvise, to Francesco Gonzaga in Mantua in 1494 (see Chapter 1, note 30).[25]

Confraternities in the north engendered similar involvement of instruments. The Brotherhood of Our Lady in 's-Hertogenbosch in 1406/7 engaged an organist to teach members of the group "to sing and to play" in order to contribute to the organization's devotional services. The instruments in this context were certainly of the soft variety, as loud

---

[23] Blake Wilson, *Music and Merchants: The Laudesi Companies of Republican Florence* (Oxford, 1992), 94 and 116–17.

[24] On the hiring of instrumentalists in the late fifteenth century, see Jonathan Glixon, *Honoring God and the City: Music at the Venetian Confraternities, 1260–1807* (Oxford and New York, 1993), 89–104; for the hiring of winds in 1502, ibid., 130.

[25] Concerning the hiring practices of the Venetian *scuole*, see Glixon, ibid., 198–200.

instruments, as shown above, were not played by amateurs.[26] An affirmation of these instruments as appropriate to religious circumstances can be seen in the imagined scenes in art, for the instruments placed in the hands of angels by contemporary painters were most often of the soft variety.

The intense veneration of the Virgin Mary in the Low Countries resulted in a special type of ceremony that had noteworthy impact on the evolution of instrumental music. Called the *Salve* (or *Lof* in Dutch), these were devotional services held in the late afternoon or early evening after Vespers or Compline. Originally rather limited in scope, by about 1480 they became perhaps the most prominent feature of public religious observance.[27] Cities such as Bruges took over financial backing, and extended themselves to ensure the most imposing effect possible. A whole range of performing forces was soon brought to bear, including singers, the choir, an organist, someone to ring the church bells, and civic minstrels. The importance of the service was such that when the *Lof* services in Bruges became a mismanaged shambles in 1500, the chapel master in charge, Jacob Obrecht, was ignominiously fired from his post. His international eminence was of no consequence weighed against the perceived mortification resulting from the poor quality of the *Lof* performances. The increase in the enthusiasm for the support of the *Lof* was undoubtedly gradual, but around 1480 a new phase was suddenly reached, with new wordings on contracts from one end of the Low Countries to the other – from Kampen and Utrecht in the north, to Bergen Op Zoom, Antwerp, Bruges, and Brussels in the south – specifying the participation of civic musicians. The importance of this new context was twofold. First, some of the contracts detailed that the bands should play appropriate repertory and, in fact, called specifically for the performance of motets. Second, while at the early stages the ensembles were an external decoration, playing from the church balcony before or after the service, they gradually moved inside and took a role in the services themselves (some documents indicate that the bands were to play *binder kerken*, or "inside the church"). That composed works as well as improvised pieces were part of the repertory is confirmed by references to actual titles (*Ave regina celorum*, *Salve regina*) and by the remarkable payment in 1484 in Bruges (mentioned above) to Nicasius de Brauwere, the succentor of

---

[26] Albert Smijers, *De Illustre Lieve Vrouwe Broederschap te 's-Hertogenbosch*, Uitgave der Vereeniging voor Nederlandsche Muziekgeschiedenis, I (Amsterdam, 1932), 32.

[27] For a general discussion of the *Lof* services, see Haggh, "Music, Liturgy, and Ceremony," 397–421.

St. Saviour's church in the city, for compiling a book of motets to be used by the civic band.[28]

Through the fifteenth century the steps toward acceptance of instruments in sacred celebrations had been halting and even to the end of the century very modest. Once the notion of such acceptance had taken root, however, what followed was a sudden outburst of creative energies in new directions as traditional barriers to instrumental participation within the liturgy were breached. The changes came quickly. In Mechelen in 1501, the Habsburg court cornettist Augustine Schubinger was paid by the city for performing in the Mass. Augustine had evidently been sent to Flanders by Maximilian I to bolster the prestige of his son, Philip the Fair. Shortly thereafter, Philip traveled with his musicians and his choir (which included Alexander Agricola and Pierre de La Rue). When they performed as they did in Toledo in 1503, the chronicler simply mentioned that the choir sang, then focused his comments on the contributions of Augustine on the cornett, saying that "it was marvelous to hear" such dazzling playing – this specifically within the liturgy of the Mass. In the same year, Philip visited his father in Innsbruck, and the forces of the two courts joined in for a particularly splendid Mass celebration. In the course of this the "trombones... began the Gradual and played for the *Deo gratias* and *Ita misa est*."[29] A charming verification of the integration of trombone and cornett into the sacred music at the Imperial court comes in one of the illustrations of the *Triumphal Entry of Maximilian I*, which pictures the vocal chapel in performance, including the participation of Augustine Schubinger (on cornett) and Georg Stewdlin (on trombone).[30]

The concept of combining winds (especially cornetts and trombones) with voices within sacred services was an idea whose time had come, as shown by references from widely scattered sources. Probably the most dramatic instance occurred at the meeting between Francis I and Henry VIII in June of 1520, at what came to be called the "Field of Cloth of Gold"

---

[28] Much of the information concerning Bruges was first reported by Strohm, *Music in Late Medieval Bruges*. For discussion of the *Lof* and instrumental music in the Low Countries, see Polk, *German Instrumental Music*, 121–3. On the dismissal of Obrecht from his post in Bruges, see Keith Polk, "Ensemble Instrumental Music in Flanders-1450–1550," *Journal of Band Research* 11 (1975), 20–1. A document specifying the performance of the Bruges band "inside the church" of St. Donation may be found in Bruges, Stadsarchief, Stadsrekeningen, 1484/5, fol. 53, cited in ibid.

[29] On the various performances by Augustine Schubinger, see Polk, "Augustein Schubinger," 83–92. The Mass performance in Innsbruck in 1503 is described in Cuyler, *The Emperor Maximilian I and Music*, 67.

[30] For discussion of the travels of the choir of Philip the Fair and of the illustration in the *Triumphal Entry*, see Polk, "Augustein Schubinger," 87–9.

because of the extravagance of the ceremonies. At the conclusion of the event the musical chapels of both courts celebrated Mass together. Forces from both alternated, and at the *Patrem*, the French choir performed, accompanied by sackbuts, shawms, and, probably, cornetts, since the French court wind band at this time included a pair of outstanding Italian cornettists. English descriptions of the service make it quite clear that the English singers performed unaccompanied by winds, and as Trevor Herbert has suggested, this was probably an instance when the French outmaneuvered Henry in presenting an ensemble interaction that was not yet common in England.[31] The embarrassing lag was soon corrected, of course, and the cornett and sackbut ensemble quickly became a standard unit to be drawn upon in English sacred performances. In Italy, a colorful example of cornetts and trombones playing sacred repertory is recorded in the autobiography of Benvenuto Cellini when he joined in the Papal wind ensemble as a cornettist to play motets in front of the Pope in the early 1520s.

The presence of instruments in sacred services had become common everywhere by about 1520, but then became thoroughly ensnarled by the dominant issue of the time, religious reform. The decisions made, and paths taken, determined the contexts for the participation of instruments in sacred service. In most of Italy and Spain, instruments found ready acceptance, though the Papal choir continued to perform exclusively *a cappella* throughout the Renaissance. Where Luther was the predominant force, instrumental music was generally welcomed; where Calvin and Zwingli held sway, the place of all polyphonic music was sharply limited. England, as we have seen, went its own way.

---

[31] See Herbert, *The Trombone*, 102–3.

5 | The instrumentalist's workshop
Pedagogy, intabulation, and compositional process

Regole per quelli che non sanno cantare – "Rules for those who do not know how to sing" – is how the brief but prescient performance instructions are introduced in the first printed book of lute music, Spinacino's *Intabulatura de Lauto* of 1507, and subsequently reprinted in all of Petrucci's lute publications.[1] Providing just rudimentary explanations of lute tablature notation and rhythmic values, this brief and simplistic introduction nevertheless introduces a fundamental distinction between instrumental and vocal training. It locates a pivotal moment in the transition from an improvisatory to a largely – and now unstoppable – written practice in instrumental music of the Renaissance, and allows for both rear-view and windshield views of musical pedagogies of the fifteenth and sixteenth centuries.

"To sing," in the 1400s, was understood as much more than the physical activity of making music with one's voice; it was part of a foundational pedagogy. All composers were trained and identified primarily as "singers" – Isaac is probably the first to be known as a "composer," rather than a singer – and the term usually denotes professional status.[2] It was through singing that students learned the modes, the system of solmization, the rules of consonances and dissonances, notation and rhythm, improvised and written counterpoint, and the placement of words to music.[3] The essence of this pedagogy was famously distilled by the Flemish theorist Adrianus Coclico, who, claiming first-hand experience, wrote that Josquin "... saw that his pupils were well grounded in singing,

---

[1] *Spinacino*, 2. An excellent survey of all printed lute instructions beginning with Petrucci is in Dinko Fabris, "Lute Tablature Instructions in Italy: A Survey of the *Regole* from 1507 to 1759." In *Performance*, ed. Victor Coelho (1997), 16–46.

[2] This is not to say that some singers/composers were not also capable instrumentalists. Binchois was known to have been an organist, and Hayne van Ghizeghem was credited with skills as a lutenist. One possible exception is Conrad Paumann, from whom we have one piece in *Buxheim*; Paumann was without question primarily an instrumentalist.

[3] For an accessible and clear summary of these pedagogical procedures as they related to contemporary theory, mainly in the sixteenth century, see Anne Smith, *The Performance of 16th-Century Music: Learning from the Theorists* (New York, 2011). On the evolving notion of the "composer," see Wegman, "From Maker to Composer," 409–79.

had a good enunciation and knew how to embellish melodies and fit the text to music, then he taught them the perfect and imperfect intervals and the different methods of inventing counterpoint against plainsong."[4] The same pedagogy was formalized in the training of singers at the larger cathedral schools, like Cambrai, and it was described – with some variants, to be sure, but with general consensus – by most of the major theorists of this period, including Tinctoris (*Liber de arte contrapuncti*, 1477 – about which we will say more, below), Gaffurio (*Practica musicae*, 1496), Glarean (*Dodecachordon*, 1546), and especially Zarlino (*Le istitutioni harmoniche*, 1558), with all of these writers commonly grounded in the larger Western theoretical tradition derived from Boethius and Guido d'Arezzo.

To place instrumental music in its larger theoretical context, it is important to remember that *pure* instrumental music – that is, devoid of singing – was deemed a utilitarian and competitive art, rather than a morally edifying one, by the ancient Greeks, and was marginalized in most medieval taxonomies of music, leaving instrumental music without a theoretical tradition or scholastic authority. As the primary conduit of ancient music theory to the Middle Ages, Boethius (*c*.480–524/26) consigned instrumental music to the lowest category in his widely consulted treatise, *De Institutione Musica*, which prioritized the ethereal *Musica Mundana* (the Music of the Spheres) as the highest form of music making, followed by *Musica Humana* (the relationship between the mind and the body, including the alchemical fusion of the bodily Humors). *Musica Instrumentalis*, the only category having to do with actual performance and clearly referring to both instrumental and vocal – in short, "heard" – music, was relegated to the lowest level.[5] But Boethius's disdain for instrumental music in particular is clarified in his description of "What a Musician is":

But that class which is dedicated to instruments and there consumes its entire efforts, as for example, the players of the cithara and those who show their skill on the organ and other musical instruments, are cut off from the understanding of

---

[4] Quoted in Jessie Ann Owens, *Composers at Work: The Craft of Musical Composition, 1450–1600* (Oxford, 1997), 11. Regardless of whether Coclico's claim to being Josquin's pupil is legitimate, Jeffrey Dean has shown Coclico's text to be persuasive within the context of other, similar accounts. See Jeffrey J. Dean, "Josquin's Teaching: Ignored and Lost Sources." In *Uno Gentile et Subtile Ingenio*, ed. Jennifer Bloxam, Gioia Filocamo, and Leofranc Holford-Strevens, 741–50.

[5] An excellent translation of Boethius' treatise is by Calvin M. Bower, *Fundamentals of Music [by] Anicius Manlius Boethius* (New Haven, 1989). Excerpts of the sections that are relevant to our discussion are accessible in *Strunk's Source Readings in Music History*, ed. Oliver Strunk; revised edition, ed. Leo Treitler (New York, 1998), 137–43.

musical science, since they are servants, as been said, since they do not make any use of reason, and are altogether lacking in thought.[6]

Instrumental music was similarly ignored within the curricular framework of the Medieval *quadrivium*, in which the study of music, indebted to Boethius's classification and linked by the Pythagorean tradition to mathematics, geometry, and astronomy, was devoted mainly to the study of music theory, not musical practice.[7] In short, the education of those who knew "how to sing" around 1500 was formed by an understanding of music theory, which, based on a codified set of rules, governed musical composition.[8]

By contrast, the designation of those who *do not* "know how to sing" applied to the large majority of instrumentalists around 1500: musicians working outside the written theoretical and compositional parameters of the singing tradition, and whose music was performed without a notated score. Their training was primarily oral, through a guild-like, master–apprentice relationship that varied according to the instrument.[9] Consequently, prior to the appearance in the sixteenth century of instructional prefaces, manuals, and treatises in great numbers, we have little direct evidence of an established pedagogy for instrumentalists. Young amateur lute players, for example, learned where on the instrument to put their fingers, and were taught everything else by rote. That this was the case is clearly indicated by the quick rise of tablature notation, which indicates not pitches, but on which frets and strings the fingers are to be placed. In a similar way, professional instrumentalists learned everything completely by ear and through execution, with minimal recourse to written models or theoretical rules.

Instruction, composition, and performance in the fifteenth century

A useful analogy is to place the overall compositional and performance procedures of fifteenth-century instrumentalists in a broad artisanal

---

[6] Ibid., 142.
[7] For a study of one such curriculum in the sixteenth century, see Roger Bray, "Music and the Quadrivium in Early Tudor England," *ML* 76 (1995), 1–18.
[8] It should be mentioned that it was not only professional or courtly musicians who achieved this kind of musical competence. Wegman ("From Maker to Composer," 420–6) has documented an oral, popular tradition of counterpoint in the fifteenth century through the practice of simple discant (improvising an upper voice to a preexisting one), of which there were many regional variants.
[9] On guilds and instrumental music, see Howard Mayer Brown and Keith Polk, "Instrumental Music, c.1300–c.1520." In *Music as Concept and Practice in the Late Middle Ages*, ed. Reinhard Strohm and Bonnie Blackburn (Oxford, 2001), 103–8.

context, analogous to the activities of a craftsman. In assembling materials for a performance they essentially worked in the time-honored manner of a traditional guild. They first chose their fundamental building material – a rhythmic or melodic template of a dance, song, or motet. If a dance, the player would tailor the work to the character (military, amorous), and rank (noble, aristocrat, merchant, peasant) of the client or to the conditions of the event (wedding, banquet, dance, feast). The clients would also determine the size, which would involve the choice of instruments. If a small group danced indoors, a single lute, lute duo, or perhaps a lute and a fiddle would suffice. A larger group, particularly if held in a larger hall or outside, might call for a three-part wind band. For the craftsman as well as the instrumentalist, local or national traditions determined the outlining structure (Burgundian, French, German, Spanish, Italian); in a Burgundian dance, a melody would be stretched out (in a three-part performance played by the tenor instrument) to provide the foundation, with the shape of the melody determining the overall form and cadence points. Between the cadence points the player of the uppermost part devised a counterpoint above the tenor. In many cases the performer proceeded from note to note while inserting decorative patterns that had been ingrained from hours of training and practice. The player below the tenor followed a similar procedure, though his patterns were usually less complex. The essential difference between instrumentalists and our hypothetical craftsman is that the latter would add a piece at a time; he would be able to reflect on his efforts, and there was of course a final, fixed object at the end of his labors. For musicians improvising counterpoint, everything happened at once: the tenor sounded the tune, the soprano constructed a line from melodic fragments while adhering to basic contrapuntal rules to avoid dissonant clashes with the other voices, and the bass (if present) would calculate his melodic design again, noting which intervals to use (and avoid) in order to coordinate with the other two voices. Their results were ephemeral: once sounded, they were gone forever. But improvising counterpoint, as described above, was not the only manner in which instrumentalists performed. Instrumentalists also committed written compositions to memory and performed without a written score, essentially "freezing" these works (and their performance) in time. In fact, many musical traditions are sustained and remain stylistically unvaried over generations through memorization, a cognitive activity that is duplicative rather than discursive.

Whether improvised or memorized, since instrumentalists of the fifteenth century usually performed without written music, evidence of both pedagogy and performance is scarce. In fact, no pedagogical sources at all for ensemble instruments have survived – if they ever existed – for the entire fifteenth century. Both amateurs and professional musicians would have played pieces from memory, but a major expectation of professionals was that they could improvise. At the structural, contrapuntal level in the fifteenth century, this would always be accomplished with a melody borrowed from a dance or chanson tune, for example, or perhaps a chant melody, such as *Salve regina*. The melody was usually placed in the tenor, and new melodies created on the spot; if in three parts, one part would be improvised above and the other below that tenor. In between these extremes, a continuum of options was available to players. They might take a three-part piece but add an additional – again, improvised – part, or they could delete one voice of a three-part piece, and create, again on the spot, a new third voice. At the decorative level, players normally embellished the upper voice with melodic interpolations and decorations, as we see in *Faenza* and *Pesaro*, as well as with such rhythmic variants as adding short triple-meter divisions. In both cases, all the procedures beyond performing the piece as retrieved from memory involved the performers adding compositional elements *ex tempore*.

More importantly, it is clear from documentation as well as from the extant sources of fifteenth-century instrumental music – *Faenza, Buxheim, Pesaro*, even *Casanatense* – that instrumentalists followed exactly the same contrapuntal or decorative procedures that were applied to the composition of vocal music, whether they were worked out in notation or rendered through improvisation. While our only direct testimony to the unwritten tradition is, ironically, through written sources, there is substantial agreement that they, along with the Petrucci lute tablatures of 1507/08 – represent accurate *ex post facto* reflections of the improvised tradition (see *SBS* 6). What these sources tell us is that to a Renaissance instrumentalist, improvisation was akin to *composition*.

Permanence and evanescence in fifteenth-century composition

Being an improvised, "evanescent" art that existed only in the moment, rather than a notated, "permanent" one that might still survive today, instrumental composition was excluded from discussion by all but a few music theorists. Despite what surviving sources reveal about the common procedures shared by instrumental and vocal music, modern scholars of Renaissance music, too, have drawn rigid boundaries to separate works that are notated according to contrapuntal rules from those that are conceived at the moment. The latter category includes improvised vocal polyphony (by singers who created melodic contrapuntal lines on the spot against preexisting, borrowed melodies), and almost all of the work of instrumentalists, from lute duos to wind ensembles, who worked in the unnotated and improvised musical environment – in short, essentially all fifteenth-century players.

Johannes Tinctoris has been a key informant in this debate with his distinction of *res facta* and counterpoint *super librum*. The former can be defined as a written composition, like any vocal motet, Mass, or chanson that was committed to notation. Performing *super librum*, on the other hand, denotes a process of creating counterpoint *ex tempore*, which occurred when two singers (or, indeed, instrumentalists) improvised lines above and below a borrowed melody, whether it is a centuries-old antiphon like *Salve regina* or a contemporary chanson tenor like "Le souvenir." It is important to note that Tinctoris in his more elaborate examples in the *Liber* made no distinction in terms of style between composition and improvisation. This in turn means that when young musicians were learning style they were strongly influenced by the music that they heard in their own environment, including pieces by leading composers. Time and location were potent determinants in this regard: a dominant role model in Florence in 1490 was Isaac; at the same time in Bruges, young players might have looked to Obrecht.

Modern musicological scholarship of this period has prioritized almost exclusively *res facta* (written compositions), to the exclusion of improvised counterpoint, which has prejudiced the objective evaluation of almost all instrumental and largely unwritten works before the age of printing. In short, the primacy given to *res facta* and the associated emphasis on "permanence" have resulted in an obfuscation of the contributions by fifteenth-century instrumentalists whose musical output existed only in the moment of its creation. This is a problematic and flawed accounting of music history. Indeed, the debate over the conceptual difference between written and unwritten music becomes completely irrelevant when dealing with works like the ricercars in *Spinacino*, pieces that clearly began as improvisations, but were soon "frozen" in print, thus classifying them in both the evanescent and permanent categories. At stake is the desire to arrive at a precise definition of "composition," but the debate also misrepresents or largely ignores the contributions of instrumentalists and of non-professionals in general, resulting precisely in the marginalization of this repertory that Renaissance music scholarship needs to redress.

In a larger aesthetic sense, this debate suggests a desire to assess the cultural value of artifacts. "Culture survives and develops under the aegis of permanence," writes the conservative critic Roger Kimball, expressing a traditional but also durable musicological view, in which evanescence is pejoratively equated with the transient and colloquial, but also the culturally subversive: "Instantaneity [is] the enemy of permanence...."[10] In Musicology, this conflict has had significant implications for how the "composer" has been defined across musical cultures that span written, unwritten, Western, non-Western, popular, jazz, and art music traditions.[11] Returning to the Renaissance, limiting "composition" only to works that have "permanence" fails to acknowledge the broad outputs of instrumental pedagogy and performance during the fifteenth century, and, by extension, the creative, if evanescent, works of such brilliant musicians as Pietrobono, Paumann, Fernandez, and Cordoval, all of whose music received praise by the most eminent literati of the period, but of whom we have no musical evidence. As Lewis Lockwood has written with regard to Pietrobono's reception,

> Only the tendency of modern historiography to base its views entirely on written sources, rather than on these in relation to the larger landscape from which they emerge, could prevent our seeing Pietrobono, in his domain, as a figure comparable to the greatest polyphonic masters of the period.[12]

There is no question that through improvised composition, reduction, arrangement, and extemporization, Pietrobono and other musicians

---

[10] Roger Kimball, "The Fortunes of Permanence," *The New Criterion* 20/10 (2002), 6. The idea of "permanence" as a necessary precondition for cultural status, even civilization, has a long history of support, mainly to prioritize Western culture and its texted literary traditions over orally based cultures. A blatant and widely seen example of the aesthetic primacy placed on permanence over evanescence in European history can be observed in Sir Kenneth Clark's popular 1969 series *Civilisation*. In the first segment, following a discussion of conquests by the nomadic Norsemen, Sir Kenneth marvels at their surviving art, craftsmanship, and engineering skill at building their vessels, but argues that "Civilization means something more than energy, and will, and creative power.... How can I define it? Very shortly, [came] a sense of permanence." He then turns to the Baptistery of Saint Jean at Poitiers, which having survived the barbarian invasions of Europe, is cited as the earliest stone monument in existence after the Fall of Rome. The building is "pitifully crude" he admits, "but at least this miserable construction was meant to last: it isn't just a wigwam." Kenneth Clark, *Civilisation*, Pt. 1: "The Skin of our Teeth," BBC TV (1969).

[11] For an excellent historical and cross-cultural perspective of this topic, see Stephen Blum, "Composition." In *New Grove*, vol. 6, 186–201.

[12] Lockwood, *Music in Renaissance Ferrara*, 98.

brought the same creativity and sophistication to pieces as those otherwise committed to notation or memory. Fortunately, we are afforded a close look at this unwritten repertory from two directions. First, several small manuals of instruction for keyboard players (all German) are extant, of which the four *Fundamenta* ("Basic Lessons") by Conrad Paumann from the Buxheim Organ Book are of particular importance.[13] Second, given the fact that instrumentalists adhered to the same basic musical rules as singers, several contemporary counterpoint treatises can be reliably consulted for information about instrumental training. These two groups of sources reveal that music education for instrumentalists focused on three main tasks: (1) training in the basic fundamentals of music; (2) acquiring technical skill on the instrument of choice; and (3) learning to adapt the repertory.

Case study 12

The theorist speaks: Tinctoris on counterpoint, *res facta*, and singing *super librum*

In the *Liber de arte Contrapuncti* Johannes Tinctoris (completed in 1477) described two ways of making counterpoint, one resulting in *res facta*, the other involving singing *super librum*. Since Ernst Ferand first drew attention to the importance of this description, debate has continued among musicians and scholars as to whether Tinctoris was making a distinction between written composition and improvisation.[1] The debate raises issues at the core of understanding instrumental performance practice of the Renaissance, and can be reduced to three basic questions: (1) Did Tinctoris provide instructions for improvisational counterpoint? (2) If so, what was the nature of that improvisation? (3) Was that approach to improvisation part of instrumental performances?

Musicians and theorists from early in the fifteenth century made a distinction between two phenomena; one referred to "things made" and the other to "sung counterpoint." Prosdocimus, in 1412, for example, mentioned counterpoint as being in two classes "vocalis et scriptus," and there are occasional references to pieces of music being "choses faictes" ("things made").[2] But it was Tinctoris who provided an extended

---

[13] There are two earlier versions of Paumann's *Fundamenta*. See Christoph Wolff, "Conrad Paumanns Fundamentum organisandi und seine verschiedenen Fassungen," *AMw* 25 (1968), 196–222.

discussion of *res facta* and singing *super librum* in his book on counterpoint. He distinguished between *res facta* as something that was written ("qui scriptus est") and was thus a procedure of creating counterpoint resulting in a "thing made," i.e. the written piece, and singing *super librum*, which was a procedure of creating counterpoint, but was a process *tout court*; that is, it was spontaneous, and did not produce a fixed, permanent object.[3]

The nature of singing *super librum*

The idea of singing "on the book" evokes a picture in words of what was actually taking place in the choir loft. Singers gathered around a large open book; in that book appeared a written melody, and that melody provided the foundation for spontaneous counterpoint. Producing music in this way was eminently practical, as musicians had to produce quantities of music every day of every week of the church year. Composing written scores for every voice part and then rehearsing those pieces would have been monstrously complicated and demanding, and therefore never done.

To sing *super librum*, one singer was assigned the given melody, which was normally in the tenor range. Another singer then invented a counterpoint above that tenor, while another singer provided one below. In this particular case of "singing on the book" the singers had the guiding melody in front of them. Skilled singers, however, had committed a great number and variety of tunes to memory, and they could easily have followed the same procedure with a well-known melody such as *Salve regina* or *Alma redemptoris mater*. It cannot be overemphasized that these spontaneously added counterpoints adhered to the standard rules of counterpoint, of which Tinctoris provided eight, such as beginning and ending on perfect intervals, avoiding parallel perfect intervals, and so forth. Tinctoris specified one difference between a *res facta* and singing *super librum*: with counterpoint that resulted in *res facta*, all voices had to observe the rules of consonance and dissonance not only in relation to the tenor but also to each other. In improvisation (i.e. in singing *super librum*), on the other hand, each voice had only to calculate its progress in relation to the tenor; this might result, as he admitted, in occasional dissonances between the free voices. If the tenor was on C, for example, and the top voice sang a fifth above, i.e. a G (an acceptable interval), and the bottom voice sang a fifth below, an F (also acceptable in theory), the result would be a dissonant clash between the outer voices. He did add, however, that it would be better if such dissonances could be avoided.[4]

Our interpretation of Tinctoris' discussion of *res facta* and *super librum* follows an important 1983 study by Klaus-Jürgen Sachs that places the practical execution of these principles at the forefront of the discussion. Other scholars, Margaret Bent foremost among them, have been reluctant to accept that interpretation, insisting that improvisation as it is commonly understood is "haphazard" and "undisciplined" and thus cannot be an approach that the highly rational Tinctoris could have endorsed. But, of course, fifteenth-century singers did not engage in totally "free" counterpoint in that sense. They worked from a given melody, which had built-in constraints; it determined the mode, and the points on which the singers made cadences. Moreover, Tinctoris and other theorists provided singers with a series of quite specific rules for how to proceed. Bent has also suggested that singing *super librum* required "careful, successive preparation," which is also problematic in that when two singers improvised around a tenor it was obviously a simultaneous, not a successive process.[5] This is manifest from the fact that Tinctoris granted that errors might result, ones that could only occur when the process was simultaneous. But Bent cannot be dismissed entirely; in some instances, such as for especially important performances, singers might have tried out different solutions ahead of time, and may have done this with one singer going first, then a second singer, knowing now what the first singer had done, adding his contribution. Still, that would have been exceptional.[6]

Applying the rules of improvised counterpoint to instrumental performance

In the *Liber*, Tinctoris addresses his instructions to singers, and he is silent about whether instrumentalists should be subject to his rules. The Spanish theorist Durán, however, did take up the matter, and for him singers and instrumentalists were subject to the same system of counterpoint. As he put it, the rules of counterpoint "apply to playing as much as singing. For playing is the equivalent of singing. In each case the written or improvised notes are the same, and there is no difference except that at one time the music is sung and at another time played on an instrument."[7] The instructions for young organists in the *Fundamenta* of Conrad Paumann follow quite similar approaches to the way Tinctoris taught consonances, for example, and while the music of Tinctoris and that of Paumann are different in terms of detail, they both conform to similar stylistic precepts. In addition, the pieces in *Casanatense*, which appear intended for instrumental performance, conform completely to the rules of counterpoint as specified by Tinctoris.

In short, instrumental improvisation may have occasionally fallen short of the strict rules that would be applied to counterpoint *res facta* (even considerably short as seen in the efforts of Zorzi Trombetta). Still, there is little doubt that the general rules as well as the stylistic ideals were the same for instrumentalists as they were for singers.

Notes

1 The treatise by Johannes Tinctoris is available in translation as *The Art of Counterpoint*, translated and edited by Albert Seay ([S.i.]: American Institute of Musicology, 1961). Ernst T. Ferand first explored the subject of improvisation and *Res facta* in his *Die Improvisation in der Musik* (Zurich, 1938); see also his "What is Res Facta?," *JAMS* 10 (1957), 141–50. His views were refined and updated in Klaus-Jürgen Sachs, "Arten improvisierter Mehrstimmigkeit nach Lehrtexten des 14. bis 16. Jahrhunderts," *BJhM* 7 (1983), 166–83. The topic has been explored as well by Margaret Bent, "Resfacta and Cantare Super Librum," *JAMS* 36 (1983), 371–91, available in Bent's, *Counterpoint, Composition and Musica Ficta* (New York and London, 2002), 105–14, but see the extensive updating of her position in her introduction, 46–57; see also Bonnie J. Blackburn, "On Compositional Process in the Fifteenth Century," *JAMS* 40 (1987), 210–84, and Wegman, "From Maker to Composer," 409–79.
2 See Sachs, "Arten," 182.
3 Ibid., 169; 182–3.
4 Tinctoris, *The Art of Counterpoint*, 102–5.
5 See Bent's updated views in *Counterpoint, Composition and Musica Ficta*, 46–57.
6 Blackburn, in "On Compositional Process," 246–60, is of course more correct in describing *super librum* as being simultaneous, though the intent of her discussion is to connect the subject to her notion of a very early existence of simultaneous composition, that is, when an individual composer controlled all parts of a piece at the same time rather than building a structure up one voice at a time. Such concurrent control by an individual is patently a very different phenomenon than the simultaneity resulting from several performers improvising at once.
7 Domingo Marcos Durán, *Súmula de canto de organo: contrapunto y composición vocal y instrumental: practical y speculative* (Salamanca, c.1507), fol. 5; translation taken from Robert Stevenson, *Spanish Music in the Age of Columbus* (The Hague, 1960), 69; see also Polk, *German Instrumental Music*, 167–8.

Learning the basics

For all but a few beginning amateurs, chamber musicians from at least 1400, and for the better wind minstrels probably from 1440 (if not sooner), the requirement was for a complete command of basic rules. These young musicians would learn from their teachers to read music, become acquainted with the rhythmic system, and be introduced systematically to improvising in counterpoint.

The introductory stages of reading music began with learning the various clefs, and this remained a pedagogical point of departure through the end of the sixteenth century. For some, this was facilitated in that ensemble players specialized in a particular range and thus only had to learn the clefs relevant to them. We know that this stage also included at least the elements of the hexachord system – and this was sustained for another century – in order to construct scales and subjects, as suggested by the titles of pieces played by instrumentalists that were identified by hexachord pitches (*La mi la sol* of Isaac, for example). The basics of the rhythmic system were also taught very early, as is shown not only by Petrucci in 1507_1, but by many other sixteenth-century tutors in which a table of rhythmic values is included as a preface. This information was relatively easy for instrumentalists to absorb, since by about 1450 the system had evolved to the point that it was quite similar to the one in use today. At the basic level, beats were duple (i.e. organized in units of two), as were divisions of the beat. Triple values were also possible, both at the level of the beat, and as subdivisions of the beat, but the default system was duple. Some subtleties of the system, such as instances when three beats would be called for in the space of two normal beats, would have been included at a later stage, and as needed. One distinctive feature of instrumental music was that the ability to play very rapid notes was a standard expectation for players as they moved to more advanced levels.

With the learning of counterpoint, the path for most amateurs diverged from that of the professionals. Learning to create counterpoint mandated a commitment of time and effort, not to mention ability, which was beyond what was possible for most amateurs. Judging from the available sources, counterpoint was learned in two ways. The first was a painstaking step-by-step process in which the young musician began by learning the intervals that were consonant and those that were dissonant.[14] This was done orally; for the consonant intervals, the teacher would play one pitch and have the

---

[14] On the steps taken to learn counterpoint, see Anna Maria Busse Berger, "The Problem of Diminished Counterpoint." In *Uno Gentile et Subtile Ingenio*, ed. Jennifer Bloxam, Gioia Filocamo, and Leofranc Holford-Strevens, 13–27. For a discussion relating specifically to how instrumentalists mastered counterpoint, see Polk, *German Instrumental Music*, 169–213. The basic study of counterpoint in the Renaissance is Klaus-Jürgen Sachs, *Der Contrapunctus im 14. und 15. Jahrhundert. Beihefte zum Archiv für Musikwissenschaft*, vol. 13 (Wiesbaden, 1974), see also his *De modo compenendi: Studien zu musikalischen Lehrtexten des späten 15. Jahrhunderts* (Hildesheim, 2002).

student play a third above, then a fifth above, then a sixth, then an octave, then a twelfth, and so on. Then the teacher might move up one pitch and duplicate the procedure, and so on, until the student knew without hesitation how to play the various intervals and their sound qualities. At the same time the student learned the distinction between the perfect intervals (basically the fifth and octave) and imperfect ones (thirds and sixths). It goes without saying that the young player almost certainly had to play well in tune, and instances did occur where players were fired for playing out of tune.[15]

In the next stage the student learned to apply the consonances in two-part note-against-note counterpoint. The teacher would play a short, simple melody as a tenor, and the student learned to play above (or perhaps below) this tenor with one note for each note of the melody. It is here that the apprentice learned a core group of contrapuntal rules, most importantly that (1) all counterpoint had to begin and end in a perfect consonance; (2) consonances only were allowed; and (3) consecutive parallel perfect intervals were forbidden. This approach is still the basic method with which counterpoint is taught even today – with the very important difference that players then learned this by ear, and not through written exercises.

Once the student was fluent with the note-against-note texture, the teacher introduced more active counterpoint, that is, more than one improvised note per note of the tenor. Here is where more complex rhythmic ideas were incorporated, and the treatment of dissonance was also introduced as the student learned when and where seconds, fourths, and sevenths could be added to lend counterpoint color and variety.[16]

---

[15] An example occurred in Milan in 1480, when a new member of the court ensemble was dismissed because he couldn't play in tune with the others in the band ("non se potendo intonare con loro"); see Guglielmo Barblan, "Vita musicale alla corte sforzesca," *Storia di Milano* 9 (Milan, 1961), 800. Modern equal temperament sacrifices the quality of the thirds in favor of the ability to perform music in every tonality. All tuning systems are compromises, and in the Renaissance, musicians worked within a distinctly narrower range of pitch choices than is the case in modern times. Their compromise was to sound very good in the most commonly used tonalities while rendering the lesser-used areas somewhat out of tune. Renaissance musicians developed sophisticated techniques to work around the occasional tuning glitches so that they caused little harm. For a useful and engaging survey of tuning, see Ross W. Duffin, *How Equal Temperament Ruined Harmony (And Why You Should Care)* (New York, 2007); see also David Dolata, *Meantone Temperaments on Lutes and Viols* (Bloomington, 2016).

[16] On applying dissonance in learning counterpoint, see Anna Busse Berger, "The Problem of Diminished Counterpoint," 21–22.

It is at about this point that the teacher acquainted a student with the skill of embellishing a melody. One way performers created a sense of novelty or originality was to treat an existing, often well-known, composition as a framework on which they would hang garlands of decorative figures. Students learned to do this much as they learned counterpoint. The teacher would play a two-note figure, beginning with a second (i.e., *ut* and *re*), then give several examples of how this could decorated. The teacher then showed how the third could be embellished, followed by the fourth, and so on. In the musical textures of that time the soprano part received the most decoration, with the tenor and contratenor given more restrained treatment, but having figures appropriate to their particular functions within the harmonic framework.

When a student was thoroughly grounded in all of the above, the teacher moved on to the most complex step: the application of these principles towards the creation of extemporaneous counterpoint in three (and perhaps more) parts. For professionals, most improvisation was for three parts until about 1485. It was based on a borrowed melody, and could be accomplished in two ways. The first involved what were, in effect, parallel chords, and was the most elementary of the improvisations of the Renaissance. In three parts, the upper two, soprano and tenor, proceeded in parallel fourths (based on a borrowed melody that was usually in the lower of the two parts). Below these two parts, the third (contratenor) would play fifths and thirds under the tenor (with thirds predominating). When enlivened with ornamentation in the top voice, this could be an effective technique for short pieces or brief passages in larger frameworks. The second kind of improvisational technique was distinctly more complex, and was accomplished within a layered texture. The players would again start with a borrowed melody, which was usually played by the tenor instrument, and the two other parts spun out new counterpoints, one above and one below the tenor. As indicated by Tinctoris (see *CS* 12), understandings between the two free voices had to be developed, but with proper training and experience skilled players were capable of impressive results. In fact, providing new music on the spot for whatever context they might face was a routine expectation for professional instrumentalists of the era.[17]

---

[17] For a more detailed discussion of these improvisation techniques, see Polk, *German Instrumental Music*, 169–213. For specific ways in which improvisational techniques were put into practice, see Ross W. Duffin, "*Contrapunctus Simplex et Diminutus*: Polyphonic Improvisation for Voices in the Fifteenth Century," *BJhM* (2007), 69–90; see also Adam Gilbert, "Reverse Engineering Fifteenth-Century Counterpoint: *Es solt ein man kein mole farn* and

Acquiring skill on an instrument

Each instrument presented its own individual demands for the student, and only for the keyboard do we have even rudimentary indications from the fifteenth century of the steps required for the mastery of instrumental technique.[18] What is clear is that in most cases amateurs focused on learning one instrument, while the professional apprentice was required to learn a variety of them (a feature clear from the handful of contracts that have survived).[19] Some degree of specialization, however, helped focus the efforts of even the professional apprentice. If one's special interest were the lute, for example, the player would be restricted mostly to the soft instruments, while a young wind player would focus on the loud ones. Moreover, while a student was usually required to learn several instruments, during the course of the fifteenth century an increasing level of specialization was becoming the order of the day. Conrad Paumann, trained about 1440, was known as a master of both lute and organ, while Paul Hofhaimer, three decades later, appears to have been active exclusively as an organist. In the sixteenth century, such specialization is the norm. Another conditioning feature was that players, both loud and soft, specialized in a particular register (i.e. soprano, tenor, or contratenor), and thus they needed to learn only the appropriate technique for that register.

The production of instructional manuals and their contents during the Renaissance can be seen as testimony both to changing pedagogical practices and to shifting aesthetics. The extreme rarity of these in the fifteenth century confirms that the teaching of instruments remained an oral, somewhat idiosyncratic rote practice, and that there was relative stability in matters technical and stylistic until around the last quarter of the century. Of the few instructional manuals that survive, the *Fundamenta* of Paumann reveal that learning to play an instrument then was not so different than now. It required many hours of practice, much of them devoted to repetitive exercises, until the fingers or embouchure could respond to whatever demands might be met. The equivalent today consists of major and minor scales in all keys (or scales and arpeggios in the case of

---

Cançon de pifari dco. el Ferrarese." In *Instruments, Ensembles, and Repertory*, ed. Timothy J. McGee and Stewart Carter (Turnhout, 2013), 173–94.

[18] The function of the *Fundamenta* in German keyboard sources, such as the Buxheim Organ Book, was to provide such elementary instruction; see Wolff, "Conrad Paumanns Fundamentum."

[19] One such contract states that Joos Zoetens, at the time a musician in the civic ensemble in Ghent, would provide two apprentices with instruction on "shawms, flutes, and other instruments"; see Polk, "Ensemble Instrumental Music," 18–26.

brass players). The tonal system did not exist, of course, in the fifteenth century, so their interest was to memorize a great variety of embellishment patterns, essentially mapping an almost infinite number of ways to get from one pitch to another. These were practiced over and over again until they could be applied automatically when needed, similar to the way Renaissance students collected phrases in a commonplace book and then committed to memory hundreds of classical or well-known literary quotes to be used in daily conversation, writing, and debate.[20]

Performing the repertory

While much of the instrumentalist's performance activities were attached to improvisation, it was necessary at the same time for students to memorize a large body of contemporary music. They certainly had to be familiar with all the international hit tunes of the day, as well as regional favorites and many of the common sacred melodies as well. Different instruments called for different approaches to learning repertory. Solo instrumentalists playing lute and keyboard had to learn entire pieces. A specialist in a melodic instrument (the shawm, for example) would, of course, focus on his individual part, though such players also had to learn at least the tenor parts of a very large repertory as well, for tenor parts formed the basis for their contrapuntal improvisations.

The apprentice-professional acquired skill at memorizing even fairly complex pieces by ear. The debate about whether minstrels could read music is ongoing, but we can assume that in the early fifteenth century professional musicians, too, were occasionally musically illiterate, relying completely on their ear and memory to assemble the repertory they needed. On the other hand, the notated source *Zorzi* (see *SBS* 2) provides evidence that its owner could not only read music, but by about 1440 instrumentalists were capable of writing rudimentary counterpoint. Of particular relevance in this context is that Zorzi's collection included two brief sets of pieces written in an idiosyncratic notation that seems designed for use by instrumentalists. These imply that while wind players

---

[20] For an excellent account of the role of commonplace books and the committing to memory of textual excerpts for practical use, see Anthony Grafton, "The Humanist and the Commonplace Book: Education in Practice." In *Music Education in the Middle Ages and the Renaissance*, ed. Russell Murray, Jr., Susan Forscher Weiss, and Cynthia J. Cyrus (Bloomington, 2010), 141–57; for a central study of the facets of musical memory, retrieval, and performance, based on theoretical evidence, see Anna Maria Busse Berger, *Medieval Music and the Art of Memory* (Berkeley and Los Angeles, 2005).

in the mid-fifteenth century probably learned much of their repertory by ear, there were also manuscripts copied especially for their use. *Faenza* and *Buxheim* are just such sources, which beyond transmitting the repertory played by chamber musicians, reveals that this class of minstrel could absorb repertory either by ear or from written-out musical texts.

By the second half of the fifteenth century the picture becomes clearer. After around 1475, the large corpus of French chansons copied in Italian polyphonic manuscripts, though composed by northern composers, was heavily appropriated by Italian instrumentalists. We can easily deduce that between 1450 and 1475 many young apprentices had learned to read music – not just melodies, but polyphony in notation and even in tablature – and this skill allowed them to learn the more sophisticated, mainstream art-repertory they needed to further adapt and expand their repertory. These enhanced skills, too, provided musicians with greater access to the upper ranks of the profession, leading to the new designation for the instrumentalist as a "musico" – musician – rather than a mere "piffero" (piper) or "pulsator" (player).[21] A representative example of this important change of nomenclature comes from sixteenth-century Bologna. In 1534, the civic ensemble included 5 "piffari" [sic] and one "tombone," but in 1546 the members of the ensemble (including several of the same instrumentalists) were all included under the rubric "Musici."[22] To be sure, amateurs continued to learn through rote teaching, as implied by the readership ("those who cannot sing") to which Petrucci's preface of 1507 is aimed.

Performance practice and instrumentalists, 1400–1500

If surviving sources like *Faenza, Buxheim, Pesaro, Zorzi,* and *Spinacino*, are indeed representative of fifteenth-century instrumental practice, the stylistic continuum of the repertory spans from composed music on one side, including dances, songs, and motets, to improvisation on the other, which could be applied to whatever repertory was required by the context and is most responsible for the great adaptability of instrumental music during this period. Reconstructing the improvisational practice of any

---

[21] In fifteenth-century Ferrarese court records, lutenists are often listed as "pulsator," as in the "cantor et pulsator eccelentissimo" Niccolò Tedesco, cited by Lockwood, *Music in Renaissance Ferrara*, 47. A century later in the same city, the title "musico" had become the general term applied to instrumentalists at the court – see Anthony Newcomb, *The Madrigal at Ferrara 1579–1597* (Princeton, 1980), I, 164–6.
[22] See Gambassi, *Il Concerto Palatino*, 619–20.

tradition of the past is a formidable task, particularly one for which there is no continuous "living" tradition, as we know exist in some folk or world musics. On the other hand, we are fortunate to possess a handful of sources that offer a surprisingly close look at how improvisation might have been accomplished. The most detailed are the theoretical treatises, especially those by Tinctoris. In addition, a few practical sources such as the *Fundamenta* in *Buxheim* reveal that instrumentalists followed procedures very close to those outlined by Tinctoris and other traditional theorists.

Musical practice was usually determined by context. For dance music the number of dancers influenced the choice and size of the instrumentation, and often only a melody was needed; for small groups, chamber musicians playing lute or various combinations of soft instruments worked well. For larger groups and outdoor events, the shawm band was the usual choice. Regional tastes also played a role. In the north (France, the Low Countries, and England), dances were of the Burgundian type, with the basse dance being central. In this type of dance the melody consisted of a string of long notes of equal value, and around this tune the performers would invent lively counterpoints. If the dance melodies themselves were more elaborate, as they were in Italy, creating an appropriate counterpoint was a more complex process. For the nobility, elaborate solo dances might be expected; these could be created for the individual occasion, were highly complex, and demanded extensive preparation on the part of the dancers and musicians. For the urban classes dancing was largely a social recreation. The dance patterns were not uncomplicated, but for the musicians providing the music it was more a matter of routine – one evening of dancing was probably like the others. Naturally, the lower classes and peasants also danced. We know that bagpipes or combinations of shawms and bagpipes were favored by the rustic community, but we know almost nothing of their actual music.

The performance of songs was similarly influenced by context. Banquets with an audience of aristocrats called for a high-art, international repertory with sophisticated instrumental combinations. Here, chamber musicians were prominently displayed, and this was one setting that characteristically involved performance with singers. Shawm bands could be another option, though for this kind of performance the players might choose to play on recorders. Banquets in urban settings normally involved the elite stratum, requiring some prominent items of the international song repertory, but there would also be emphasis on local favorites. German songs, for example, never yielded completely to foreign intrusions. Still, the high-art song repertory everywhere was based on the French chanson. This audience would most often call on the civic musicians, almost always a wind band, to provide the music as this was the ensemble most likely to provide the highest caliber professional performance. The top-level professional ensembles, both civic and at court, knew an ample body of pieces from memory, something in the range of 200 pieces. Chansons by Dufay and Ockeghem could be played just as they were composed. This may seem like a large amount, but we should also bear in mind that their entire repertory was "contemporary." They could also use the tenor of one of those chansons as a basis for an improvisatory version. In other words, the song repertory represented a mixture of composed pieces and improvisations based on tunes from existing models.

To say that instrumentalists performed "motets" carries with it a quite flexible understanding of the term (a conventional definition of which during the Renaissance would be "a polyphonic, sacred piece usually on a Latin text"). To begin, a purely instrumental performance conveys, obviously, no text at all. Still, it is quite clear that for all instrumentalists, lutenists, keyboardists, chamber musicians, and those in wind bands, performing sacred music was a regular part of their performance options. In civic processions, for example, the carrying of the city's most precious relic was accompanied by instruments, and the players were constrained to perform "sacred" music. Archival and visual evidence from around 1480 to the middle of the sixteenth century reveal that lutenists regularly appeared in the processions organized by the Venetian confraternities of the *Scuole Grandi*, sometimes in concert with a lira (or viola) da braccio and a harp, an ensemble that is depicted with faithful accuracy in Gentile Bellini's painting of a procession in Piazza San Marco from 1496 (Galleria dell' Accademia), which was commissioned for the Venetian *Scuola* of St. John the Evangelist.[23]

Other occasions for which sacred music was apt were ceremonies marking special events. An example was that held on one of the main squares in Bruges in 1488, to mark the signing of an agreement between the city and Maximilian of Habsburg, marking the end of Maximilian's imprisonment in the city. To emphasize the solemnity of the occasion, the Bruges civic wind band performed versions of *Alma redemptoris mater* and

---

[23] The complete archival documentation and a detail of Bellini's painting showing the ensemble are given in Jonathan Glixon, "Lutenists in Renaissance Venice: Some Notes from the Archives," *JLSA* 16 (1983), 15–26.

Ave regina celorum; Strohm suggested that both of these works were composed by Obrecht.[24] But it is also possible that on this occasion and others like it, the musicians improvised polyphonic versions on the sacred melodies, resulting in derivative pieces that can be broadly defined as "instrumental motets."

Instruction, composition, and performance in the sixteenth century

Two fundamental changes impacted how instrumental music was taught, learned, and executed in the sixteenth century. The first involved the acquisition of new contrapuntal skills, which required a definitive change in pedagogy and style around 1480. It is a well-known fact that through much of the fourteenth and fifteenth centuries the basic approach to composition was through the addition of successive layers of newly composed voices, one by one, to an existing, borrowed melody. For instrumentalists, as we have shown, this normally involved improvising lines, sometimes highly embellished, *super librum*, of which our tangible evidence for this practice is almost entirely from *post facto* sources like *Spinacino*, which contains lute duets written in this style. This technique was replaced by the concept of a texture based on imitative counterpoint, which required all the voices to be conceived more or less at the same time – *simultaneously*, as is often said (not without quibbles), rather than *successively*. Since improvising anything more than very simple, formulaic, imitation in four and five parts was impossible for all but the most skilled improvisers, the result was that instrumentalists writing in the new contrapuntal style now either committed most of their art to notation or performed pre-existing pieces that they had committed to memory. Improvisation after 1500, in short, assumed a less important role in the making of compositions, but this shift was not absolute. For young apprentice professionals, the art of improvisation remained as a requisite skill that had to be mastered since there were many types of variation-style pieces based on chordal patterns, accompaniment roles, and embellishment practices that required it.

The second change involved the rapid, inevitable, and unstoppable impact of music printing on pedagogy; simply put, with the advent of printed books, written pieces were much more available to play, to own, to

---

[24] Strohm, *Music in Late Medieval Bruges*, 87, 145.

study, to memorize, and in what becomes crucial, to *adapt*. As the printed tradition took hold, books, manuals, and treatises began to fill the space between teacher and student, and the availability of performance instructions allowed amateurs to learn many rudimentary musical skills by themselves instead of simply being taught note-by-note where to place their fingers. For professional musicians, too, a much broader range of repertory now became available for study and adaptation, leading to compositions and arrangements of increasing complexity that demanded a much broader level of technique and pedagogy.

These two developments of the early sixteenth century – the rise of imitative counterpoint and its collateral impact on pedagogy, and the impact of printed music – coincide with a flood of treatises providing instruction on a variety of instruments. While aimed primarily at the new market of non-professionals, these treatises reveal a great deal about how both amateurs and professionals learned and performed. They show that despite the differences in writing counterpoint and in overall style, the fundamental approach to composition was similar to the previous century and may be discussed through the same three categories of (1) acquiring basic skills, (2) learning to play the instruments, and (3) adapting the repertory.

Learning the basics

In the sixteenth century essentially all student musicians, whether of amateur or professional status, received a more systematic and formalized training of basic skills due to the accessibility to information brought about by printing and notation. Amateur lutenists who had been dependent on rote learning now had printed tutors available to them, which responded to the task with simple language, elementary illustrations of basic rhythmic values and notation, and non-scientific but clear explanations of stringing and tuning. The pedagogical benefits of printing were realized early on by the Spanish courtier and vihuelist Luys Milán, whose 1536 book is appropriately titled *El maestro*, since the book essentially acts as a proxy for a real teacher. Indeed, Milán organized his book in "the same manner and order that a teacher would bring to a beginning student," and it therefore provides a close look at what constituted a systematic pedagogy for an instrumentalist during the early sixteenth century.[25] The preface to Pierre

---

[25] See John Griffiths, "Juan Bermudo, Self-instruction, and the Amateur Instrumentalist." In *Music Education in the Middle Ages and the Renaissance*, ed. Russell E. Murray, Jr., Susan Forscher Weiss, and Cynthia J. Cyrus, 126–37.

Phalèse's *Des chansons reduictz en Talature de Lut...* (Louvain, 1545₃) offers another typical example. The instructions propose "A short introduction to learn by yourself the art and customs of the lute," with succeeding chapters headed (1) "To learn to find the notes" followed by (2) explanations "of durations or measures and rests," and then tackling technical issues such as (3) "To know where to place the fingers," and finally, (4) "to know how to stretch and tune the strings."[26] Even the inclusion of topics like string care imparts to the student the "home maintenance," do-it-yourself knowledge that was once the prized and private domain of the master.[27] In general, these instruction manuals seem to take nothing for granted with regard to previous training on the part of the student.

What *was* taken for granted, however, was the adoption of lute tablature as the standard notational orthography for the lute, a development that undoubtedly stimulated the widespread commerce of the instrument in sixteenth-century Europe at every level connected to performance, publication, and pedagogy. Although regional variants of tablature proliferated throughout the period, namely Italian, French, German, Spanish, and Neapolitan, the principle remained the same: unlike staff notation, which represents actual pitches on a staff line, tablature is essentially a "picture" of the lute neck that shows players visually where to place their fingers on the frets of the instrument.[28] There is no question that because of its

---

[26] "Brefve introduction pour apprendre de soy mesme l'art & usance du Lutz," with succeeding chapters headed (1) "Pour scavoir trouver les tons" and (2) "Sensuit du temps ou des mesures et pauses," before moving on to purely technical issues: (3) "Pour scavoir mettre les doitz," and finally, (4) "Pour scavoir tender et accorder les cordes." Reprinted in Joël Dugot, ed., *Luth: Méthodes – Dictionnaires et Encyclopédies – Ouvrages generaux*, Méthodes & Traités 19, vol. 1 (Bressuire, 2004), 20–3.

[27] The importance of string choice and their qualities were central concerns of players during the sixteenth century. See Mimmo Peruffo, "Balance on the Lute: The Role of the Strings." In *The Music Room in Early Modern France and Italy*, ed. Deborah Howard and Laura Moretti (Oxford, 2012), 135–44.

[28] The regional varieties of tablature can sometimes be confusing since they often crossed international boundaries. For example, Italian tablature (which uses numbers to indicate the frets with "0" designating the open string) was used in Italy but also in Spain, Lyons, and Southern Austria. French tablature (which uses letters, rather than numbers, to indicate the frets, with "a" designating the open string), was employed in France, but also England, and seventeenth- and eighteenth-century Germany; German tablature (which uses an assortment of lower-case letters to designate each individual string and fret on the lute fingerboard, was used exclusively in Germany, while Spanish tablature (like Italian but reversed) was used sparingly in Spain as well as England (the Edward Paston lutebooks, for example), but has become the standard version of tablature used by contemporary guitarists in folk, rock, blues, and country. Neapolitan tablature, used almost exclusively in Naples, is like Italian tablature except that the number "1" indicates the open string rather than "0".

accessibility and flexibility – one could use instruments tuned at different pitches without changing the fingering of the piece – tablature became, to apply Elizabeth Eisenstein's famous words about printing, an "agent of change." By providing a completely idiomatic notational format, tablature was both integral to how lutenists acquired the formalized pedagogy needed to learn imitative counterpoint, and critical to the wide dissemination and circulation of music through the print medium. By 1546–47, a significant watershed year for the publication of lute music, the base of players was demographically broad and geographically vast. Lute, guitar, and vihuela tablatures circulated widely in Europe among both new and experienced players; through the self-help tutors contained in the prefaces to many of these collections, players quickly learned the rudiments of the technique, contributing directly to the production of an ever-growing notated repertory that amounted to thousands of pieces and over 100 printed books by the end of the sixteenth century.

Beyond providing instruction in fingering and reading tablature, some lute books, in particular by the Germans Judenkünig (1523_2), Gerle (1532_2, 1546_9), and Newsidler (1536_6), extended the discussion to the finger-plucking technique that was replacing plectrum-style during this period. Similar to *Spinacino*, which locates a point of transition between improvisation and notation, these German accounts testify not to a sudden "game-changing" shift in playing technique, but rather to an important period of flux between the decline (and persistence) of one style and the emergence of another. The rules contained in Newsidler's lutebook are far more detailed than Petrucci, and contain detailed instruction on fingering, notation, and rhythm, as well as several etudes that provide the beginning player with an actual context for the practicing of these techniques.[29] Continuing this German interest in detailed lute pedagogy, Matthaeus Waissel (c. 1540–1602), a theology student at the University of Königsberg in the 1560s, and later a teacher, published one of the most comprehensive sets of instructions in his lute book of 1592_{12}. Stating that his information was collected from famous masters in France and Italy, he intended for his book to take the place of a teacher for students who could not find one, but could also assist more experienced players. Indeed, the chapters contain examples dealing with many contemporary idioms of the late sixteenth century that would be of

---

[29] A useful translation of Newsidler's rules is in Marc Southard and Suzana Cooper, "A Translation of Hans Newsidler's *Ein newgeordent künstlich Lautenbuch...* (1536)" *JLSA* 11 (1978) 5–25.

particular interest to players with some ability, such as highly embellished diminutions, ornaments, small rhythmic subdivisions, full 4-voiced chords, and rapid scales in both the high and low registers of the instrument.[30]

Composition and arrangement

In describing the change in compositional process – that is, the procedures by which composers *composed* – that took place at the beginning of the sixteenth century it is useful to begin with a fundamental aesthetic observation. For fifteenth-century instrumentalists, creating a "finished" composition was not the end game; their musical results, improvised, adapted, and largely unpreserved, were all process, a work in progress that did not have a central *Urtext*. For instrumentalists during the sixteenth century, changes in practice and pedagogy revise the notion of what constitutes a musical work, and with notation and the printed book becoming increasingly important, a clearer sense emerges of what constitutes a "finished piece."

In tracing the change, we can begin with the rise of lute tablature notation in the late fifteenth century, which introduced a new pedagogical efficiency (tablature showing finger position, not notes) as well as flexibility (it had many regional variants and could be adapted to changes in the size and tuning of the instrument).[31] By extension, it had several important effects on compositional process. At the fundamental level, tablature allowed for the preservation of improvised music and a resulting codification of style and repertory. More importantly, tablature became lute, vihuela, and guitar players' new workbench for assembling – *intabulating* – polyphonic vocal parts into a single instrumental arrangement of vocal music. Intabulations allowed instrumentalists to make the jump from two or three players improvising one or two parts against a tenor, to a single player composing and performing complete four- and five-voice polyphony.

Comprising by far the largest category of sixteenth-century lute music, intabulations can be seen historically as yet another example of the dependency, forged already in the fifteenth century, of instrumentalists on vocal music. In practice, however, sixteenth-century instrumentalists

---

[30] Waissel's rules are translated in Douglas A. Smith, "The Instructions in Matthaeus Waissel's *Lautenbuch*," *JLSA* 8 (1975), 49–79.

[31] Tablature was used by keyboardists as well, however, the focus in this section will be primarily on lute tablatures.

approached the making of these arrangements in a very different way, and tablature notation was central to this change. Where fifteenth-century lutenists or wind players arranged vocal music by borrowing a melody (usually the tenor) and improvising a highly decorated line above it (as in the lute duet) or counterpoints above and below, sixteenth-century instrumentalists were counseled by most writers on the subject to be faithful to the vocal model and to include as many of the original parts as possible, preserving, in essence, the integrity of the original contrapuntal texture.[32] In the instructions given by Adrian Le Roy, Bartolomeo Lieto, and others, the lutenist or vihuelist is shown how to transfer (and sometimes transpose) the notes of the vocal model into tablature through the use of charts, resulting in an intra-semiotic translation between two notational systems. Not only did tablature allow lutenists to adapt any kind of vocal music to their instrument, the entire process of making intabulations was used as a method to learn counterpoint, with the theoretical rules that governed the writing of polyphony taught "in real time" through the arranging of vocal music into tablature. Thus, a second, equally important by-product of intabulations was their role not just as compositions in themselves, but as a middle-ground process leading to the making of a *fantasia* or *ricercar*. These are the goals of the most comprehensive Renaissance treatise on intabulation, Vincenzo Galilei's *Fronimo* of 1568_2 (rev. 1584_5; see SBS 12), which explains in detail how the practice of intabulation leads to the acquisition of contrapuntal skill but is also a procedure towards writing *fantasie*, a process also described by Adrian Le Roy in $1567_2/1568_3$ and in systematic detail by Juan Bermudo in 1555_1(see CS 1).

Intabulations and the musical text

Scholarly debates about the importance of intabulations in the study of Renaissance music touch on three of the central themes in this book: (1) the acknowledgment of a shared repertory between Renaissance instrumental and vocal music; (2) the need to validate arrangements and alternate readings of pieces played by instrumentalists; and, (3) how, consequently, to accept the notion of "fluidity" in this repertory, as was clearly understood by players and listeners during the Renaissance.

---

[32] For a survey of lute treatises dedicated to this topic, see Hiroyuki Minamino, "Sixteenth-Century Lute Treatises with Emphasis on Process and Techniques of Intabulation," PhD diss., University of Chicago (1988).

Unfortunately, our understanding of these pieces has been restricted by their having been studied, for the most part, as purely derivative works within the same analytical, philological, and historical parameters used for study of vocal music. Consequently, and with few exceptions, intabulations have been treated as subsidiary to their vocal originals. In arbitrating differences between the vocal model and its arrangement, analysis almost always defers to the *model* as the textual authority; the interpretive license earned by intabulators to *transform* a vocal source revoked by theoretical judgments on the grounds of voice-moving violations with respect to the model or disputes about the intabulator's application of sharps and flats, which are, of course, unequivocal in tablature notation.

But, intabulations surely introduce perspectives beyond what they tell us about the model. As Vaccaro wrote, intabulations "succeed through a new arrangement of the materials in the model and a complete re-organization of its structure, which result in the creation of an entirely new object in sound."[33] First of all, "intabulations" must be understood as a generic category that covers a range of approaches towards arranging a vocal model, comprising: (1) faithful renderings of the model – basically transcription; (2) glosses and highly ornamented renderings as seen, for example, in the arrangements made by the Petrucci lutenists, in which the contour of the model is, as Howard Brown has (somewhat dismissively) described it, "obscured beneath an avalanche of endless and directionless scale fragments," or through *bastarda*-style figuration or divisions; (3) paraphrase, in which motives from the model are revised and reorganized; (4) quotation, in which only themes (or parts thereof) are borrowed and integrated with new material, resulting in a fantasia; (5) the lute duet (sometimes called *contrapunto*) in which the lower parts of a model are scored for one lute, while the other plays a highly ornamented version of the superius;[34] (6) the polyphonic duet, in which a cantus firmus motet, secular vocal work, or instrumental canzona, is separated into two polyphonic vihuela or lute parts;[35] (7) the *fantasia* or *ricercar sopra*..., in which a new imitative work is created out of an intabulation of the model, drawing on certain subjects only, and often not in their original order;[36]

---

[33] Jean-Michel Vaccaro, *La musique de luth en France au XVIe siècle* (Paris, 1981), 131.
[34] See Ivanoff, "Das Lautenduo."
[35] For an example of the cantus firmus motet type, see Coelho, "Revisiting the Workshop." Some excellent examples of polyphonic lute duet arrangements of chansons, madrigals, and instrumental canzonas are contained in Giovanni Terzi's *Intavolatura di liutto* (Bergamo, 1593_7), 19–56.
[36] A discussion of this category of intabulation is in Vaccaro, "The *Fantasia sopra*," 18–36.

and (8) the accompanied lute song, in which one voice (either soprano or bass) is sung while the other voices of the model are intabulated.[37] In view of these techniques it seems overly simplistic to assume that intabulations were ideally meant to stay close to or reflect upon the model.

As with translation, the motives of intabulators are fundamentally determined by the audience, or *target*. Some demonstrate, by their choice of model and approach to arranging, a regional or cultural practice, or even a performance context. In this case, the target audience is fairly well defined. Other intabulations, such as those based on popular vocal models, reveal an interest in the economics of the market – that is, the popularity of the work or composer – and therefore reach out to a broader and more diverse audience; still others are dedicated to pedagogical ends. In other words, there are several goal-oriented strategies influencing how and why intabulations are made, a point that suggests examining the practice of intabulation within the broader context of literary translation and imitation. The sixteenth-century French literary theorist Jacques Pelletier du Mans asserts in his *Art Poétique* of 1555 that translation is the "truest kind of imitation," which develops skills that can be used to approach other forms of imitation.[38] The composition of ricercars or fantasias can be understood in this manner. Many of them are based on subjects from vocal works and are probably mediated by an intabulation – acting in the manner of a literal translation – of the parent work, similar to the way a modern treatment of a classic foreign text, whether it is a libretto or screenplay, is dependent first on its translation.

Until now, the traditional procedure for studying intabulations has been to begin with the vocal source as a model, examine the intabulation derived from it, and then work from the intabulation *back* to the model in order to assess differences and similarities. In truth, however, the intabulation occupies a middle ground between model and target, and the flow moves in the opposite manner. Rather than mirroring (or distorting) its model, an intabulation suggests instead the presence of a newer readership to which it is aimed. The intabulation does not lead back to the model any more than Charles Singleton's famous prose translation of the *Divine Comedy*, which dispenses with *terza rima* structure and rhyme, should invite further

---

[37] For discussions of this type of intabulation, see Palisca, "Vincenzo Galilei and Some Links," and Coelho, "Raffaello Cavalcanti's Lutebook." In *Le concert des voix et des instruments*, ed. Jean-Michel Vaccaro; and Mason, *"Per cantare e sonare."* In *Performance on Lute, Guitar, and Vihuela*, ed. Victor Coelho.

[38] Quoted in André Lefevere, ed., *Translation/History/Culture: A Sourcebook* (London and New York, 1992), 52.

comparisons with Dante's original.³⁹ Singleton's edition proposes a new projection of Dante intended to reach new readers, and as Singleton himself admits almost apologetically in his notes about why another English version is needed, "The answer must be that translation is interpretation, and that the version in prose here presented is but one more answer to the perennial question: How do we read this verse, this tercet, this canto? What do we conceive its essential meaning to be?"⁴⁰ Clearly, the traditional understanding of intabulations as merely derivative works of limited value to editors of texts is unsatisfactory to account for the diversity of approaches.⁴¹ In a powerful critique of the historical exclusion of arrangements, Vaccaro sees musicology's resistance to valorizing intabulations as an "almost Manichean" process, in which music originally conceived naturally in the mind of the composer subsequently devolves into an abstraction of new notational characters, to finally being incarnated as an instrumental realization. In this conceptual model, writes Vaccaro, importance is placed only on the original composition, not the sound – *la forme sonore*, as the French say – or performance adaptation(s) of the piece; "the instrument is regarded as constraining" the work, the arrangement limiting the natural freedom of the musical imagination.⁴² Similar to translations of classical texts, intabulations, on the contrary, demonstrate both flexibility *and* fidelity with respect to the model, and they deserve to assume a more autonomous, rather than a merely derivative, role.

---

³⁹ Dante, *The Divine Comedy*, translated with commentary by Charles Singleton, 6 vols. (Princeton, 1970)

⁴⁰ Ibid., *Inferno*, I: Text, 372.

⁴¹ A traditional musicological argument against the use of intabulations as "texts" concerns the application of *musica ficta*, an editorial problem that tablature actually helps to ameliorate, since it shows exact pitch and probably conveys the way singers performed their works. As Haar and Lockwood write in the *New Josquin Edition*: "[T]he instrumental intabulations of portions of the Mass [Josquin's *Missa Hercules Dux Ferrarie*] found in the publications of Narvaez, de Vaena, Pisador, and Fuenllana are important as later evidence of the widespread reception of the Mass but their value as textual sources for an edition of this *or any other vocal work of the period* [emphasis ours] is extremely limited. It is true that their notation is unequivocal with respect to accidentals, but they represent the practices of solo instrumentalists operating within the digital practicalities of their instruments [an argument one simply cannot make with respect to the faithful intabulations of Gailiei, to cite just one example], thus operating on premises quite different from those that must have governed the judgments about unwritten accidentals in vocal ensembles of Josquin's time." See James Haar and Lewis Lockwood, ed., "Critical Commentary to *Missa Hercules Dux Ferrarie*." In *Josquin des Prez: Masses based on Solmisation Themes*, in *New Josquin Edition* 11.1 (Utrecht, 2002), 44. A persuasive account, based on Renaissance theorists that challenges this devaluation of intabulations is in Robert Toft, *Aural Images of Lost Traditions: Sharps and Flats in the Sixteenth Century* (Toronto, 1992).

⁴² Vaccaro, *La musique de luth*, 129.

Renaissance translations

A theoretical model that can inspire this type of work is found in the field of translation studies. Such are the connections between intabulations and their destination that they can be understood as a sub-category of translation, an area that was already addressed in the sixteenth century in such relevant texts as Etienne Dolet's *De la manière de bien traduire d'une langue en autre* of 1540, which is contemporary with a large body of intabulations. Given the variety of approaches to arrangement we have already cited, we might also pursue Singleton's idea of linking translation to *interpretation*. Recent work by Umberto Eco does just that, freeing translation completely from the doctrinaire notions of philology and authority.[43] Eco's placing of translation within the larger category of "interpretation" is a crucial and even brilliant distinction, if not altogether original, and it opens the door to an overdue consideration of how "interpretation" might be acknowledged in Renaissance music. As a text in one language (tablature) adapted from a text in another language (vocal notation) and then interpreted through performance, intabulations can provide a variety of answers to some of the fundamental questions posed in this book.

Translation studies is an old area of scholarship covering a much older practice, the Renaissance being a period of unprecedented growth in the field.[44] Its specific roots as a discipline probably begin with the study of Biblical translations, but the awareness that translations can be politically and culturally motivated, as well as a powerful tool for expressing ideology, begins with the transference of the sacred into the vernacular from about the time of the Carolingian Renaissance. The shift from Latin to the vernacular through translation was an important process in the rebalancing of power, and while Latin continued to be accepted as an authority of the past, translations into the vernacular often served to undermine that power and authority. Dante's *De vulgari eloquentia* was written in Latin as the language that united Europe; but at the same time Dante celebrated the various dialects he encountered in his years of exile, effectively displacing Latin.[45] Similarly, variants encountered in intabulations serve the same purpose in molding exclusive sacred music for inclusive domestic

---

[43] Umberto Eco, *Experiences in Translation* (Toronto, 2001).
[44] An earlier version of the material in this section was presented by Victor Coelho in "Crossing the Sacred: Intabulations as Translations," paper presented at the 69th Annual Meeting of the American Musicological Society, Houston, Texas, 2003.
[45] For this discussion we have relied on Lino Pertile, "Dante." In *The Cambridge History of Italian Literature*, ed. Peter Brand and Lino Pertile (Cambridge, 1996), 39–69, esp. 46–50.

consumption. The result is that the language is expanded idiomatically. As motets and Mass movements cross into secular, domestic environments, soloistic figuration, cadential ornaments, occasional parallel intervals, unprepared dissonance, and truncations of the original usually prohibited in the writing of sacred music are permitted, producing a new "vernacular" in translation that is not limited by language or religion.

During the Renaissance, translation played a central role in the recovery and deliberation of ancient texts, and many theorists, including Gaffurio, Zarlino, and Galilei, relied exclusively on translations in order to study the original sources of ancient theory and bridge them with modern practice. Vincenzo Galilei's crucial correspondence with Girolamo Mei was instigated by Galilei's dissatisfaction with available translations of Ptolemy and Aristoxenus. And if we date Galilei's interest in translations to the years just prior to the beginning of his correspondence with Girolamo Mei in 1572, it coincides with the publication of the first edition of his intabulation treatise, *Il Fronimo,* in 1568.[46]

Translation, then, is both a rhetorical undertaking and an act of modernization; its goal was usually *not* to reproduce an original with faithful accuracy, but to adapt the text to a reader's cultural and linguistic universe. Other than Galilei, whose contrapuntal orthodoxy stands out, neither translators nor intabulators felt bound to replicate a text word-for-word, or note-for-note. In holding this view, lutenists, like translators of Latin texts, seem to be aware that the source-model might itself be a translation, perhaps of some live performance as part of the compositional process of the work, rendering the translator as justified in adapting his translation. Adaptation is particularly noticeable if the source and the target are incommensurable, as is the case with some of the larger sacred works intabulated in lute books. In this instance, the main interest is in the "effect" of the translated text on the target culture.[47]

Intabulations can be thus regarded as essentially translations of motets, Mass movements, chansons, and madrigals into instrumental works that replace text with figuration or repetitions, add new voices or voice movement, and in the absence of text, occasionally rewrite or revise certain passages. It is not in the same category as parody – in the way that we generally understand the term in musicology – since as an intralinguistic process, parody operates within the same natural language system.

---

[46] On this dating, see Claude V. Palisca, *Girolamo Mei (1519–1594): Letters on Ancient and Modern Music to Vincenzo Galilei and Giovanni Bardi* (Stuttgart, 1960), 7–8.

[47] Eco, *Experiences in Translation,* 20–2.

Intabulation, like translation, is a bilingual exercise, and within translation theory, belongs to an intersemiotic category in which verbal signs (text, and music/text relationships) are translated into signs of non-verbal systems, meaning that alteration is almost inevitable.

It is therefore surprising that there has been so little exploration of the connection between intabulation and translation, given that "translation" has been used to describe the way modern editions alter the original notational premises of early music through editorial convention and concessions to modern tastes, what Margaret Bent has termed "The Dilemma of Translation." According to Bent, "all transcription translates," "a transcribed and scored version is no longer the original text," and that "We shall have taken a large step forward when, as editors, we recognize that we are translating, not merely transcribing."[48] Lastly, she correctly affirms that "Tablature is at least in part instrument-specific and is intended to show the performer where his fingers should go, though in practice it may fall short of his goal and itself reveal a translation process."[49]

If modern editions are indeed translations, sixteenth-century intabulations can be considered in a like manner given their almost identical methods: like a modern edition, they involve the transcription of one notational style (mensural), whose rhythmic values are determined by a proportional relationship, to another, in which every unit is rhythmically autonomous; like the modern edition, tablatures assemble partbooks into score (tablature is, of course, a score in which all the voice parts are arranged vertically on a single plane); and like the modern edition again, tablatures almost always impose barlines, which divide the original into measures or perfections. Intabulations are truly the modern editions, or translations, of sixteenth-century vocal music, intended for new performers and changing performance conventions.

The relationship between intabulations and their users is bonded within the new print culture of the sixteenth century, in which intabulations of Mass, motet, chanson, and madrigal circulated widely, targeting audiences not only by the choice of pieces, but through the way they were adapted for lute. Sacred music becomes re-contextualized and re-written for domestic settings; the original polyphonic vocal writing is adapted and secularized as it is filtered through intabulation, transposition, and the player's ability. In adapting a model, particularly one from a previous generation – Francesco da Milano's setting of *O bone Jesu* by Loyset Compère, for

---

[48] Margaret Bent, "Editing Early Music: The Dilemma of Translation," *EM* 22 (1994), 390–1.
[49] Ibid., 389.

example, whose presence in Milan and Rome predates Francesco's birth in 1497 – the intabulator is faced with bringing two musical cultures, preserved in different notations, into contact. Practically everything else depends on the destination of the intabulation. We remain unclear about the function of many intabulations, but we can at least propose five main purposes, ones that are largely commensurate with the destinations of French translations of classical texts made during the sixteenth century (see CS 13): (1) pedagogical: to learn counterpoint and as part of the didactic process to compose fantasias; (2) to become familiar with classic sources or canonized works; (3) to edit the original and redact it for sake of comprehension or facility; (4) to be faithful to the original through a literal transcription; and, (5) to reach new audiences by making some distinct original mark on the source (extensive ornamentation, creating a duo or ensemble version, or adapting it as an accompaniment for solo singing).

Case study 13

Intabulations as translations: Etienne Dolet's *De la manière de bien traduire d'une langue en autre* (1540)

The connection between Renaissance intabulations and translations can be more firmly established through a consideration of the famous Renaissance French translator Etienne Dolet's five precepts of translation, dated 1540.[1] Dolet (1508–46) was a printer and humanist who studied in Italy, a firm believer in classical languages but also secular values. He received a privilege from Francis I to set up a printing press in Lyons, where he published the works of Rabelais and made translations of the Psalms into French. His defense of Ciceronian Latin was seen to be heretical. He was convicted by theologians at the Sorbonne of being an atheist, and subsequently burned at the stake in Place Maubert in 1546.

Dolet's "method to translate well one language to another" is contained in five points, of which two overall considerations stand out: the translator must aim to be faithful to the sense of the source text, and at the same time express himself elegantly in the destination language. This might be understood in musical terms as the intabulator assuring that the model's rhythmic, cadential, and rhetorical function is maintained, while allowing for its expression through the particular idiomatic possibilities of the instrument.

Briefly, Dolet's first point alludes to the underlying thrust of his rules – that the translator should be primarily obligated to the target rather than the source.[2] The first rule stipulates that an accurate translation requires that the translator act as an interpreter – *entendre*, meaning to seek out the meaning of the text, rather than merely find equivalent words – and that he remove difficulties or obscurities from the source. For the musician, this might imply an understanding of the musical text and the clarification of certain textual problems (*ficta* for example); Dolet does not set limits for the translator's interference with the source text and seems to allow the possibility that the translation may well distort the original.

Applying Dolet's second point to intabulations – that the translator should possess an unequivocal knowledge of both the original and the destination language – is important in the implicit requirement that the lutenist is a rounded musician with full knowledge of contrapuntal rules as well as contemporary styles.[3] The intabulation, then, like the translation, should be stylistically excellent; it should not be for mere virtuoso display. The translator must understand the differences between the idiom of the source and the target language. For Dolet, the translation is in no way inferior to the model but it may and can improve upon it. The third point is expressed in the negative to warn first against a direct, literal transcription followed by a most interesting sentence that permits the translator to ignore word order in the original and criticizes the practice of starting the translation at the beginning of a sentence.[4] Here, like the Fantasia that is built out from an intabulation of the vocal model, like a *fantasia sopra*, Dolet advocates the reading of the entire sentence first, then deriving a freer translation of the general meaning irrespective of the original word order.

This thought continues in Dolet's fourth point, which states that the translation should draw from common idioms in order to aim the source directly to its target audience, which constitutes a modernization, or at least a vernacularization of the source.[5] Finally, Dolet's last point pleads for a readable translation on aesthetic grounds and that it is attractive to the senses, rather than simply defer to a classical model in a doctrinaire fashion.[6] Dolet expressed his ideas with brilliant clarity, and as is often the case, he in effect crystallized in his five points ideas that were part of a deep undercurrent of contemporary thought. That those currents also acted on musicians is clear from the transformative intabulations of such varied figures as the Italian lutenist Francesco da Milano and the Spanish organist Antonio de Cabezón.

Notes

1 Etienne Dolet, *De la manière de bien traduire d'une langue en autre* (Lyons, 1540).
2 *La premiere reigle:* Or saiche donques qu'il est besoing et necessaire à tout traducteur d'entendre parfaictement le sens de l'autheur, qu'il tourne d'une langue en autre. Et sans cela il ne peut traduire seuerement et fidelement [14].
3 *La seconde reigle:* ... que le traducteur ait parfaicte congnoissance de la langue de l'autheur qu'il traduit: et soit pareillement excellent en la langue en laquelle il se met à traduire [14–15].
4 *La tierce reigle:* Le tiers poinct est qu'en traduisant il ne se fault pas asservir jusques à la que l'on rende mot par mot [15] ... Et par ainsi, c'est superstition trop grande (diray je besterie ou ignorance?) de commencer sa traduction au commencement de la clausule. Mais si, l'ordre des mots perverti, tu exprimes l'intention de celuy que tu traduis, aucun ne t'en peult reprendre [15–16].
5 *La quarte reigle:* Il te fault garder d'usurper mots trop approchans du Latin, et peu usitez par le passé: mais contente toy du commun, sans innover aucunes dictions follement, et par curiosité reprehensible [16–17].
6 *La cinquiesme reigle:* Venons maintenant à la cinquiesme reigle... C'est assçavoir une liaison et assemblement des dictions avec telle doulceur, que non seulement l'ame s'en contente, mais aussi les oreilles en sont toutes ravies [17–18].

* * *

To this point, the focus in this section has been on the pedagogy embedded in intabulations, but this is not to ignore the variety of instructional methods that became available in prints that showcased the range of the new mentality of the sixteenth century. This was a particular fascination in German regions, beginning with Sebastian Virdung's *Musica Getutscht* of 1511_3, which provided an illustrated survey of the instruments in common use at the time. In the same year Arnolt Schlick published his *Spiegel der Orgelmacher und Organisten*, which presented rich detail on the construction of organs. In 1529_1, Martin Agricola, with *Musica instrumentalis deudsch*, published a sequel to Virdung's volume, one that was written particularly to instruct young boys in the Protestant schools in his region. This was reprinted three times, and was such a success that he revised and expanded it in 1545_1. Michael Praetorius furnished the capstone of these German Renaissance prints in his *Syntagma musicum* II and III (1619–20), which gave meticulously detailed drawings of all the instruments in common use in the late sixteenth century. The Italians tended to be more interested in instructional, rather than encyclopedic, material. Silvestro Ganassi produced two remarkably informative works: the *Opera*

Intitulata Fontegara (1535$_1$) gave in-depth information for beginning players of the recorder on such matters as fingering and how to use the tongue, followed by an extensive set of examples providing guidance in applying decorations to melodic lines; the *Regola Rubertina* (1542$_2$/1543$_2$) comprised two volumes of instructional material for playing the viol. Ganassi discussed the various sizes of the viol, how to tune them, gave a veiled description of how to transpose music that was in awkward ranges, and in addition provided examples of solo music for the instrument.[50] Italians also provided multiple manuals on the art of melodic decoration; perhaps the most comprehensive was *Il vero modo di diminuir* (two volumes, 1584$_2$) by the Udinese virtuoso and *Capo de concerti delli stromenti da fiato* in Venice, Girolamo Dalla Casa (*c*.1530–1601).[51] Some of the Spanish and French contributions have been discussed above, and in fact, essentially all regions contributed to the production and the consumption of pedagogical prints. By the mid-sixteenth century beginning players throughout Europe could draw upon a broad base of instructional material that both provided basic information and introduced them to advanced techniques as well.

The sustaining of improvisational skills notwithstanding, there is no question that the rise of tablature, the inevitable codification of practice brought about by increasing reliance on written music and performance manuals, and instrumentalists' deeper knowledge of contrapuntal rules, in part through the making of intabulations, slowly eroded the role of improvisation as part of the act of composition. For fifteenth-century instrumentalists, improvisation was a central condition for the creation of counterpoint. In the sixteenth century, improvisation no longer occupied the same role, which was taken over by a dependence on studying and arranging written polyphonic models: for soloists, intabulation (which became theorized by Bermudo, Galilei, and others as a curriculum in

---

[50] All of the sixteenth-century sources mentioned here are inventoried in Brown, *1600*. Still valuable as a concise introduction to diminution is Howard Mayer Brown, *Embellishing Sixteenth-Century Music* (Oxford, 1976); see pages x–xiv for a survey of the theoretical sources. A useful practical guide is Bruce Dickey, "Ornamentation in Sixteenth-Century Music." In *A Performer's Guide*, ed. Jeffery Kite-Powell, 300–24. For a discussion of Ganassi's tuning and transposition instructions for viols, see Herbert W. Myers, "The Sizes and Tunings of Early Viols: Some Questions (and a Few Answers)," *Journal of the Viola da Gamba Society of America* 38 (2001), 5–26, with a follow up in the same journal, 40 (2003), 75–9. This updates the treatment in Woodfield, *The Early History*, 140–54.

[51] For a short but informative documentary/cultural study of Dalla Casa, see Franco Colussi, David Bryant, and Elena Quaranta, *Girolamo Dalla Casa detto da Udene e l'ambiente musicale veneziano* (Clauzetto, 2000). A translation of Dalla Casa's *Il vero modo...* is in Jesse Rosenberg, "*Il vero modo di diminuir* – Girolamo Dalla Casa: A Translation," *HBSJ* 1 (1989) 109–14.

counterpoint), occupied a crucial place in compositional process, leading to the derivation of fantasias and ricercars. The situation was somewhat different for sixteenth-century ensemble musicians, at least prior to the 1580s, for whom autonomous composition was not a central activity. They shared the same scores as singers, sometimes performing them as written, but more often adapting them through melodic ornamentation or variation. Improvisation, for them, was in the main limited to melodic decoration or variation, or the occasional addition of a single part to a pre-existing composition. Indeed, decoration and variation, even if extemporized, must be considered apart from those improvisational practices that form an important background element to compositional process, such as adding improvised counterpoints to an existing voice or improvising an entire polyphonic texture. The elaborately ornamented instrumental versions of madrigals, such as those on Cipriano's "Anchor che co'l partire" made by Dalla Casa (1584_2), Bassano (1591_2), Rogniono (1592_{10}), Bovicelli (1594_3), and others, should not be seen as reflecting improvised practice, but rather as highly decorated, derivative *compositions* in which the concept of virtuosity is validated on aesthetic grounds.[52] In these works one sees the principle of transforming and contemporizing canonic works, with publications like Arcadelt's *Primo Libro di Madrigali*, first published in 1538, achieving classic status by the end of the sixteenth century and used frequently as a source for elaborate instrumental readings into the period of Frescobaldi.

Convergence of instrumentalist and composer

By the end of the sixteenth century, it is clear that compositional process was no longer divided into discrete tracks of instrumental and vocal techniques. Rather, an important reconciliation of musical pedagogy is noticeable in the convergence of vocal and instrumental training received by composers. Andrea and Giovanni Gabrieli, Merulo, Tallis, Byrd, Dowland, and Monteverdi to name just a few, were all trained equally as instrumentalists and singers, and their musical output reflects professional competency in both areas. Whatever rigid taxonomies existed in the fifteenth century with regard to instrumental and vocal music largely

---

[52] A comparative edition of these versions appears in Richard Erig and Veronika Gutmann, ed., *Italienische Diminutionen: die zwischen 1553 und 1638 mehrmals bearbeiteten Sätze* (Winterthur, 1979), 187–210.

disintegrated. Up to around 1500, the instrumentalist was not included within the rank of a "composer" (for that matter, trumpeters were almost never listed under the rubric of "musicians" until the late seventeenth century). For composer/instrumentalists of the late sixteenth century, like Dowland, instrumental music had been finally theoretically validated; it had developed distinct identifiable idioms, and a high proficiency in instrumental training was part of the composer's fundamental musical education. Howard Brown's often-quoted observation about the "emancipation of instrumental music" may finally apply here in the late sixteenth century.[53]

---

[53] "The emancipation of instrumental from vocal music is one of the most important developments in the history of music between 1400 and 1600." Howard Mayer Brown, *Music in the Renaissance* (Englewood Cliffs, 1976), 257.

6 | Renaissance instruments
Images and realities

Audiences and musicians in the early fifteenth century viewed instruments as falling into two classes of loud (*haut*) and soft (*bas*), distinguished by timbre. The categories were not rigid, as professional musicians were constantly pressed to be flexible, but in general players of soft instruments formed one distinctive class, those of loud ones another.[1] These understandings gradually broke down over the course of the century with the arrival around 1500 of quite different concepts. Players of trombone, a loud instrument, might also play lutes or viols, as we know was the case with the Schubingers;[2] players of the shawm, also in the loud class, might have played cornett and performed with singers, something that would not have been possible a century earlier. Lasocki documents an amusing, but telling, instance of this kind involving the Anjou court musician Faillon, who began in 1476 as a pipe and tabor player but also doubled on other instruments, so that only two years later he is listed as playing a variety of loud instruments prior to assuming, in another two years, the position of court fool. The relevance of this story for our purposes is that, as Lasocki concludes, "Clearly, Faillon the fool was no fool, for he seems to have begun as a pipe or fife and tabor player, then rapidly expanded his instrumental ability sufficiently to join the court minstrels on the bagpipe, *doucaine*, shawm, and trombone."[3] By 1511 a new frame of reference of categorizing instruments was signaled by Virdung who divided instruments not into soft and loud, but into strings, winds, brass, and percussion.

---

[1] See Bowles, "Haut and Bas," and Polk, *German Instrumental Music*, 13–86. In terms of terminology, the two categories, loud and soft, are most clearly distinguished in French sources, where the words *haut* and *bas* occur with some frequency. The terms are less common in English documents, and quite rare in those from Germany and the Low Countries.

[2] On the Schubingers and their abilities on a variety of instruments, see Keith Polk, "The Schubingers of Augsburg: Innovation in Renaissance Instrumental Music." In *Quaestiones in musica. Festschrift für Franz Krautwurst*, ed. Friedhelm Brusniak and Horst Leuchtmann (Tutzing, 1989), 495–503.

[3] See David Lasocki, "Tracing the Lives of Players and Makers of the Flute and Recorder in the Renaissance." In *Musicque de Joye: Proceedings of the International Symposium on the Renaissance Flute and Recorder Consort, Utrecht 2003*, ed. David Lasocki (Utrecht, 2005), 380.

Challenges to invention

The disintegration of the loud/soft distinction was the inevitable result of an evolving mentality among musicians that can be traced throughout the Renaissance. Seeking to improve the capabilities of the instruments they had in their hands or under their fingers, performers constantly sought out new designs, makers, and solutions – a search that is clearly revealed by the astonishing number of improvements or completely new instruments produced during this time. To synchronize their instruments with new compositional demands and techniques, players needed instruments that played lower, higher, or enabled more chromatic alterations. They desired instruments, too, that could "imitate as much as possible the human voice," as Girolamo Dalla Casa writes about the cornett, which in some instances would blend better, and in others could project with more strength.[4] Professionals wanted instruments that matched the variable contexts of performance and the conditions of their employment, while amateurs preferred those that were adaptable to their more polyvalent needs.

Professional instrumentalists, as we have noted, often constructed and modified their own instruments, but there is no better example of the drive for technical and stylistic improvements than that of instrument makers, who struck out in myriad directions, artistically and commercially, to respond to these needs.[5] In an early example from the middle of the fourteenth century, pairs of shawms (then both playing in the soprano range) began to turn from a purely ceremonial – even decorative – function to one that involved more musical substance. As this took place, it became desirable to have one of the two instruments play in a lower register to provide contrast and support. The mechanical obstacle to this, though, was that finger holes for a shawm-like instrument larger than the discant size would be too far apart for the normal hand. The answer to the problem was to provide a key for the lowest hole, a simple, but completely novel invention, arrived at around 1350. The resulting instrument, usually termed a *bombard* at the time, allowed for a highly successful companion playing tenor to the discant shawm. This duo provided the core of the wind ensemble until well after 1500. The concept of the key continued to develop, and is now a basic feature of all modern woodwind instruments.

---

[4] Girolamo Dalla Casa, *Il vero modo di diminuir*, translated by Rosenberg, "*Il vero modo*," 112.

[5] For some examples of performers involved in instrument construction during the sixteenth century, see Lasocki, "Tracing the Lives of Players," 377–8.

Another response to a technological challenge arose with the same core unit of discant and tenor shawm. By the early fifteenth century ensembles capable of three parts became increasingly the norm; thus, an instrument was needed to expand the discant/tenor duet of the shawm and bombard – that is, to add a bass size to that duet (or "contratenor" in the terminology of the time). The solution was to add a slide mechanism to a trumpet-like instrument, resulting, in other words, in the trombone. Iconography suggests that in the early stages of this, shortly after 1400, evidently only one tube would slide, but the double slide appeared by around 1450 or shortly thereafter. In either case, a slide mechanism, with one metal tube gliding within another, demanded a very high level of technical skill on the part of the maker. This invention was the unique product of European craftsmen, and even within Europe, the making of trombones was a highly specialized skill, with Nuremberg becoming a renowned center in the production of the instrument.

As a final example, over the last two decades of the fifteenth century, noble amateurs and wealthy urban elites became significantly more engaged in music making. As they did so they required instruments appropriate to their interests and, more crucially, abilities. In addition, the prevailing textures of music at this time had shifted to four parts from the three of the previous generation, requiring instruments capable of reaching deeper into the bass register. In other words, there was a more pronounced demand for instruments that were relatively easy to master, but could also cover all registers, from soprano to bass. One popular response was the viol, which first appeared about 1480 in more or less its modern form. While a new instrument, the viol did not require an entirely original technology. Its features resembled the medieval fiddle, and other elements may have drawn upon the large Spanish bowed vihuela, as suggested by Ian Woodfield.[6] What was new was the concept of a *family* of bowed string instruments with frets, which made it especially suitable for amateurs. The success of the viol was immediate, and within a decade or two it had spread to all corners of Europe. Whether by invention or adaptation, makers and musicians in the Renaissance constantly pressed on the borders of what was possible.

Economics, distribution, and ownership

The conventional historical narrative about instruments has focused mainly on the genealogical legacy of makers and the supply side of the

---

[6] Woodfield, *The Early History of the Viol*, 61–79.

production and design of their instruments. For example, scholars have assembled important archival information on families of wind and brass instrument makers such as the Rauchs, Schnitzers, and Neuschels, and recent scholarship has also produced fascinating details concerning Italian lute makers – or, to be precise, German lute makers active in Italy.[7] We must bear in mind, however, that all this activity was dependent on the demand side as well, for given what we know about the enormous production and inventory of these shops, there must have been a ravenous appetite for music making on the part of the Renaissance public to support the range of instrument makers plying their trade and their active supply lines. Unfortunately, we know very little about how these makers connected to their clients.

What is clear is that by the middle of the sixteenth century, people knew where the finest instruments by type could be found – recorders and lutes from Venice and Padua, violins and other bowed strings from Brescia and Cremona, recorders and cornetts from Germany, and instruments by makers such as the Tieffenbrucker and Bassano families were especially coveted. Large courts usually amassed a considerable inventory of instruments that were used by their court musicians for both performing and teaching duties. From what evidence we have, these instruments were often purchased directly from the maker, as with the case of the court at Stuttgart purchasing around sixteen flutes in 1585 from the *pfeiffenmacher* Ulrike Schniepp of Wiesensteig, who regularly provided instruments to the court.[8] Brokers were also employed as middlemen between patrons (or commissioning committees) and makers in order to find quality instruments of a specific type, particularly larger, installed instruments like organs. We have evidence of this type from Pistoia, where a broker, the organist Andrea di Nanni from Prato, sold an organ to the Pieve of Sant' Andrea in Pistoia in the 1490s.[9]

Some instrument makers had a foot in both the supply and demand sides of the equation. Hans Neuschel, the most prominent maker of trombones in the early sixteenth century, was himself a fine performer on the

---

[7] See Giulio M. Ongaro, "The Tieffenbruckers and the Business of Lute-Making in Sixteenth-Century Venice," *GSJ* 44 (1991), 46–54, and Bonnie J. Blackburn, "'Il magnifico Sigismondo Maler thedescho' and His Family: The Venetian Connection," *LSJ* 50 (2010), 60–86. On the diffusion of northern lute makers in Italy, with particular reference to Padua, see Francesco Liguori, *L'arte del liuto: le botteghe dei Tieffenbrucker prestigiosi costruttori di liuti a Padova tra il Cinquecento e il Seicento* (Padua, 2010).
[8] See Lasocki, "Tracing the Lives of Players," 377.
[9] Stephen J. Milner, "Organ Culture and Organ Contracts in Renaissance Pistoia," *Recercare* 12 (2000), 82.

instrument; he was both a member of the civic ensemble in Nuremberg and on call with the wind band of Maximilian I. Similarly, members of the Rauch family, an important name in recorder manufacture in the era, were performers as well, both in the civic ensemble in Augsburg and at the court of Bavaria in Munich. In his treatise *Fontegara* of 1535, Silvestro Ganassi included illustrations of three recorders for the purpose of showing fingering charts, of which each recorder was branded with a different maker's mark. Lasocki has revealed two of these instruments to derive from the Rauch and Schnitzer families.[10] Strategically placed in prominent positions, Rauch and the Schnitzers, along with the Neuschels, were firmly connected to circles of performers and thus had intimate knowledge of the demand side while they were themselves part of the supply-side chain of production.[11]

Given the enormous repertory and popularity of the lute, it is not surprising that the most detailed information of both supply and demand sides are to be found in sixteenth-century lute-making operations.[12] These shops testify to a vibrant manufacturing and artisanal infrastructure, which like the expanding print industry of the time, was both artistically connected to performers and commercially motivated. As cited in Chapter 3, lute making was dominated for many decades by long-established legacy operations in resource-rich and heavily forested Bavaria, centered mainly in Füssen and Augsburg, with supply and trade routes connecting to Venice. By the middle of the sixteenth century, many of these family-run lute makers had relocated to Italy, where the exploding commerce of printed music and the subsequent rise in amateur lute players created a profitable commercial opportunity in Venice and in the university towns of Bologna and Padua. The most famous makers were Laux Maler and his cousin Marx Unverdorben, who relocated to Bologna, and Laux's brother Sigismund, who settled in Venice. The great Tyrolean maker Magno Tieffenbrucker also set up shop in Venice, while his cousin Wendelin, known as Vendelio Venere, settled in Padua. One of the finest German lute makers, Hans Frei, worked out of Bologna.

---

[10] Lasocki, "Tracing the Lives of Players," 374–5.
[11] The pairing of the function of player and maker was noted by Martin Kirnbauer, "Die Nürnberger Trompeten- und Posaunenmacher vor 1500 im Spiegel Nürnberger Quellen." In *Musik und Tanz zur Zeit Kaiser Maximilian I*, ed. Walter Salmen (Innsbruck, 1992), 136.
[12] The subsequent discussion of lute manufacture is indebted principally to the following studies: Douglas Alton Smith, *A History of the Lute*, 62–78 and 308–25, Stefano Toffolo, *Antichi strumenti Veneziani* (Venice, 1987), Ongaro, "The Tieffenbruckers," and Blackburn, "Il magnifico Sigismondo."

Inventories of lute-making shops in Venice and Bologna list hundreds of instruments in various stages of construction, with stockpiles of materials – barrels of necks, soundboards, strings, bridges – that could produce hundreds more, but we have almost no idea of how those makers sold, exported, marketed, or otherwise moved that inventory. Were these instruments ordered, individually customized, or available *prêt-à-jouer*? Who, or what forces, drove innovation in manufacture and design? Did makers have wholesale as well as retail operations for their instruments? What were the relative costs of the instruments they sold? And finally, who bought these instruments, and why these and not others?

Some preliminary answers concerning the demand side are offered by Stefano Toffolo's examination of sixteenth-century Venetian notarial documents, listing the possessions, including musical instruments, held by a range of Venetians from various social strata.[13] Organized according to the tripartite demographic classification of *nobili*, *cittadini*, and *popolani* that is well known to historians of Venice, the records clearly show that persons of noble class were twice as likely to own instruments than the much larger (and bourgeois) group of *cittadini*, and three times as likely as the *popolani*. The data offered by specific instruments tell the story more clearly. Lutes – by far the most frequently cited instrument in the inventories – are distributed among all three classes but clearly concentrated in the category of *nobili*; harpsichords, however, are spread throughout the classes fairly evenly, with recorders owned almost exclusively by members of the two upper classes. References to wind instruments other than recorders are scarce, numbering only eighteen out of a total of 274 references.

Although the sample size is small and concentrated in a single city – albeit one that is among the most important musically of the period – the documents provide valuable information about the owners of these instruments. We find members of the Querini, Gritti, Contarini, Priuli, and Venier – in short, Venice's most noble families – owning instruments of unusually high quality or exhibiting special details of craftsmanship. For example, in 1533 it is noted that Francesco Priuli owned "an old black

---

[13] Stefano Toffolo, *Strumenti musicali a Venezia* (Cremona, 1995), 47–67. For a classic discussion of the Venetian class structure of *nobili, cittadine,* and *popolani,* see Edwin Muir, *Civic Ritual in Renaissance Venice* (Princeton, 1986), 34–55. More recent analyses have revised the notion of a strict tripartite demographic classification in favor of a more fluid structure, particularly within the class of *cittadini*, as in James S. Grubb, "Elite Citizens." In *Venice Reconsidered: The History and Civilization of an Italian City-State, 1297–1797*, ed. John Jeffries Martin and Denis Romano (Baltimore and London, 2000), 339–64.

lute [perhaps referring to one made with ebony or possibly detailed with African blackwood] and another large good lute"; in 1559, "a harpsichord with its case decorated in gold" is listed as belonging to Luca Contarini, and it is common to find belonging to *nobili* instruments as having keys of ivory or decorated with carved or inlaid designs, costly aesthetic upgrades that are not alluded to in the instruments owned by the two other classes.[14] In the category of *cittadini*, instrument owners include the great Venetian painter Giacomo Palma (Palma il Vecchio, c.1480–1528), who left "a large lute," the famous music theorist and former *maestro di cappella* at San Marco, Gioseffo Zarlino, who owned a "broken lute, a chromatic harpsichord, and a clavichord," the San Marco singer Pietro da Piombino, who left "a lute with its case," and various priests, notaries, and government members. Finally, found among the *popolani* who owned instruments are a jeweler (lute), bookseller (viola and cornetto), perfumist (harpsichord), cheesemonger (lute), haberdasher (harpsichord and guitar), cloth dyer (harpsichord), a barber (two broken lutes and a harpsichord), and an unnamed professional musician whose possessions at his death in 1557 included a curtal, flutes, a trombone, and three trumpets.[15]

* * *

An image-based history

The following discussion is designed to illuminate the use of Renaissance instruments in the manifold cultural settings in which purely instrumental music was heard, and to convey technical and performance-related information through surviving instruments and images of identifiable professional musicians. Broadly speaking, we have given priority to images for which at least some of the following conditions could be established:

- where performances can be connected to eyewitness accounts
- when participation of either amateur or of professional performers is clear
- where salient features of instruments can be confirmed
- when images are discussed and embedded in theoretical works

---

[14] The use of ivory for construction and decoration of sixteenth-century Venetian instruments is corroborated by Ongaro's archival research into the lute production of the Tieffenbrucker family of Venice, whose inventories include references to many high-priced lutes (*liuti da pretio*) made with ivory or inlaid with ivory coat-of-arms; see Ongaro, "The Tieffenbruckers," 49.

[15] Toffolo, *Strumenti*, 64.

- where the configuration of the performers can serve as a guide to instrumentation or context
- when regional variants can be revealed
- when dating can be established with reasonable accuracy

This methodology, while logical, does not come without hazards. Contemporary illustrations, even portraits or still-lifes, were not photographs, and depicted instruments were part of the overall harmony and form of a painting, often requiring compromises on exactitudes of proportion and position. Moreover, many external factors could intrude, ranging from particular details in the commission between painter and patron to the reliance on the conventional iconology associated with such instruments as trumpets (Jericho), harp (David), and lute (Orpheus). Scriptural conventions also play a determining role: images of the Coronation of the Virgin almost always include string instruments (following *Psalms* 45.8, for example), but the presence of the musicians in this setting was clearly more important than the precision of what they played; similarly, David was often shown playing a harp, but in many surviving illustrations apparently anything that looked vaguely similar to a harp would suffice. More often than not, artists were unfamiliar with precisely those details of instruments – hand position, shape of bridges, number of strings, proportions, and playing posture – that are critical for a precise organological examination. Regional variants must also be taken into account, particularly concerning plucked-string and keyboard instruments. Nonetheless, when coupled with information from other sources such as archival documents, theoretical writings (some themselves illustrated) by figures such as Tinctoris, Virdung, Agricola, and Praetorius, surviving instruments, and the demands of the music itself, illustrations drawn from contemporary art works, with all their potential shortcomings, provide an efficient means of demonstrating the variety of the Renaissance *instrumentarium*.

I. Plucked-string instruments

The largest surviving instrumental repertory of the Renaissance is for plucked-string instruments, amounting to several thousand works preserved mainly in sixteenth-century printed and manuscript tablatures for lute, vihuela, and guitar. Of these, the lute assumed a position of prominence, equal, it is fair to say, to that of the piano in the nineteenth century – a versatile solo, ensemble, and accompanying instrument played by amateurs and professionals, and a visible symbol of culture, class, and erudition. Prior to the sixteenth century, it is of course difficult to ascertain the extent of this repertory since lutenists and other plucked-string practitioners improvised or memorized their music. But given the sizeable iconographic evidence from the fifteenth century, there is clear visual testimony to the preponderance not only of bowed instruments like the vielle, but to those that are plucked, such as the lute, gittern, quintern, and citole. Unfortunately, there is neither now – nor, in particular, was there *then* – a completely consistent and agreed-upon nomenclature for which to distinguish all of these instruments. In court documents and in literature, classical allusions were often employed, so that lutes are embellished as lyres or citharas; depending on the rank, region, and purpose of other informants, the same instrument is given another name. An example of this variability (or, indeed, inconsistency) in terminology can be seen with the various names used to refer to the great lutenist Pietrobono of Ferrara. In the Ferrara payrolls of 1446 and 1449, he is normally described as "Pietrobono dal Chitarino"; in 1459 Cornazzano refers to his instrument as a "cetra," and him as "cythariste," Tinctoris (1481–3) as "lyricen" (i.e., player of the lyre), and both Caleffini (1484) and the King of Naples (1476) describe him as a player of the "leuto" or "liuto."[16] Indeed, it is possible that Pietrobono's main instrument was more specifically the quintern or gittern ("dal chitarino"), a small lute played with a plectrum that is shown in paintings of the period as having three strings (Figure 6.1), but later illustrated by Virdung as having as many strings as a six-course lute.

Gittern

The modern viewer with some knowledge of the central place of the lute in the High Renaissance might well categorize the pear-shaped instrument in Figure 6.1, painted by Fra Angelico, as a small lute. The instrument, however, is a gittern, which had its own distinctive construction and playing traditions. Most importantly the body was carved from one piece; it did not have the more delicate (and more resonant) ribbed construction of the lute nor a body/neck joint. One significant result was a "thinness of its sound" noted by Tinctoris.[17] The gittern was consistently

---

[16] Lockwood, *Music in Renaissance Ferrara*, 316, 102, 100, 103.
[17] On gittern construction and use, see Crawford Young, "Lute, Gittern, & Citole." In *A Performer's Guide*, ed. Ross Duffin (2000), 356–8 and 367–8.

Figure 6.1 Gittern: *Coronation of the Virgin* (detail), Fra Angelico, c.1450–3. Paris, Musée du Louvre. ©RMN-Grand Palais/Art Resource, New York

a smaller instrument than the lute and was most useful for playing melodic lines in the soprano register. It was fretted, played with a plectrum, and in about 1400 usually designed with only three or four courses (later instruments had five). The peg box was made in a sickle shape, not in the lute's well-known flat form bent at roughly eighty degrees to the neck.

Figure 6.2 Three-string lute (or gittern): Francesco del Cossa, detail from *The Triumph of Apollo, the Month of May* (1469–70), Ferrara, Palazzo Schifanoia. Scala/Art Resource, New York

Both archival and iconographical sources reveal that the gittern was a more favored instrument than the lute up to about 1420, though they were often paired in that era. In fact, as the lute duo began its ascent in about 1430 in many of the earlier pairings the soprano part was undoubtedly taken by the gittern. At some point in the fifteenth century the gittern gave way to a similarly high-pitched lute; one of these transitional three-string instruments is seen in Figure 6.2, from the Palazzo Schifanoia, Ferrara, executed around 1469–70, making this detailed fresco exactly contemporaneous with Pietrobono's last years of service under Duke Borso d'Este of Ferrara. There were probably some national preferences at work; the soprano lute could have taken over earlier in Germany than Italy, for example, but the precise chronology of this transition remains murky. A lute pair illustrated in the *The Triumph of Maximilian I* clearly shows a small and large lute duo – but the quintern (i.e., gittern) illustrated by Virdung still retained the sickle-shaped peg box.[18] The two illustrations are from almost exactly the same time, illustrating practice of about 1510.

[18] For the *Triumph* text and illustrations, see Stanley Appelbaum, ed. *The Triumph of Maximilian I* (New York, 1964); the two lutes are shown in Plate 24.

Lute: fifteenth century

Theoretical and documentary sources containing information about the fifteenth-century lute are remarkably consistent in describing a five-course instrument tuned in fourths with the interval of a third between the third and fourth strings. Most sources give the highest string as pitched at g', making the lowest string a c.[19] Occasional variants in pitch reveal that lutes were not standardized in overall size and could have different string lengths – the distance calculated between the bridge and the nut – resulting in larger instruments tuned a third or fourth lower. The strings, as described by Virdung (1511) and others, "are made from the gut or from the intestines of sheep," and were strung in pairs throughout until the late fifteenth century, when the first string was usually single. The first, second, and third string pairs were tuned in unison, while the fourth and fifth could be tuned in octave or in unison, a registration that is sometimes discernible in later notated lute music through a careful examination of the voice leading. Numerous sources testify to the superiority of strings from Germany and Italy, particularly Munich and Aquila, respectively, but also from Siena and Florence.[20]

Visual evidence prior to around the middle of the fifteenth century shows that lutenists played with a plectrum – usually a quill – that was held between the index finger and thumb. This was the technique used by lutenists like Pietrobono, with which he embellished, using up-and-down strokes, the top lines of polyphonic songs "with wondrous decorative figures," as described by Tinctoris, or else improvised elaborate melodies over an existing tenor or drone.[21] Even though plectrum technique, in combination with the use of the fingers, can be (and certainly was) used for playing music in two and sometimes three parts, as we can clearly see in the Wolfenbüttel tablature fragments from around 1460, by the 1470s it is clear that finger technique was slowly replacing the use of the plectrum as

---

[19] See Christopher Page, "The 15th-Century Lute: New and Neglected Sources," *EM* 9 (1981), 11–21. Naturally, these pitches are approximate and should not be considered equal to the pitch of modern A=440. On this topic, see Bruce Haynes, *A History of Performing Pitch: The Story of "A"* (Lanham, MD & Oxford, 2002).

[20] In Adrian Le Roy's, *Breve et facile instruction... sur le luth* (Paris [1567]) preserved only in an English translation as *A briefe and easye instruction...* (London, 1568; expanded in 1574), he writes (f. 60v) that the best strings "come to us of Almaigne, on this side the toune of Munic, and from Aquila in Italie"; modern edition in Adrian Le Roy, *Les Instructions pour le luth* (1574), I, ed. Jean Jacquot, Pierre-Yves Sordes, and Jean-Michel Vaccaro (Paris, 1977), 47.

[21] Page, "The 15th-Century Lute," 13.

lutenists began to play and arrange more complex works in three and even four parts.[22] The pace of this change was gradual but resolute; Tinctoris writes in the 1480s that both techniques were in use, and we know from Sanudo and from other sources that lutenists continued using plectrum technique into the second decade of the sixteenth century.[23] Interestingly, the precise entry in Sanudo's *Diarii* of 1523 mentions that it was the lutenist "Zuan Maria zudio [Gian Maria Giudeo or Alemani] with his three companions, and they all played lute à 4, he himself with the plectrum wonderfully."[24] What is intriguing about this passage is that Gian Maria was the author of Petrucci's now-lost third book of tablature, published in 1508, raising the possibility that some or all of the music in this book may have been intended for the plectrum lute. In the end, however, there is no extant source in tablature after the Pesaro manuscript (*c*.1490) that is intended for plectrum lute, and as we have noted elsewhere, there remains some debate as to whether any of the pieces in *Pesaro* were even written for a plectrum player.[25]

Both the transition of playing techniques during the late fifteenth century and the characteristics of the instrument are clearly captured in Lorenzo Costa's *Concert* of *c*.1492–5 (Figure 6.3), executed in Ferrara, in which the lutenist, still positioning his plucking hand horizontally across the lute as if he were using a plectrum, now plays entirely with his fingers. The rounder shape of the five-course lute, when compared to the almond and pear shapes that begin to emerge after 1480, conforms to the characteristic design and cross-section drawings of the instrument contained in a short treatise written around 1440 by Henri Arnaut de Zwolle, the doctor and astrologer to King Charles VII of France and Philip the Good of Burgundy.[26] With a geometric design that can be drawn entirely with a compass, the fifteenth-century "Gothic" lute represented by Costa also has a deeper, "tubbier" body and a thin neck.

---

[22] On Wolfenbüttel, see Martin Staehelin, "Norddeutsche Fragmente mit Lautenmusik um 1460 in Wolfenbüttel." In *Kleinüberlieferung mehrstimmiger Musik vor 1550 in deutschem Sprachgebiet* (Berlin, 2012), 67–88 & 141–44.," and Marc Lewon, "An Assessment of the Wolffenbüttel Lute Tablature", <https://mlewon.wordpress.com/2014/03/28/assessment/> accessed 19 December 2015.

[23] See *SBS* 6.   [24] Cited in Pirrotta, "Music and Cultural Tendencies," 158.

[25] See *SBS* 6, n. 41.

[26] Paris Bibliothèque Nationale, Lat. 7295, f. 132; see G. le Cerf and E. R. Labande, *Les traités d'Henri-Arnaut Zwolle et de divers anonymes* (Paris, 1932). For an analysis of these pages, see Vaccaro, *La musique de luth*, 53–6.

Figure 6.3 Fifteenth-century lute: *Concert*, Lorenzo Costa (*c.*1485–95). London, National Gallery/Art Resource, New York

Lute: sixteenth-century

In the immediate decades after 1500, and again in the decade before 1600, the lute underwent significant changes in construction and size, including new designs, materials, and thinner soundboards. (Earlier plectrum lutenists, like modern *oud* players, required instruments with thicker soundboards, otherwise all that would be heard is the percussive sound of the pick.) These new lutes responded to the acoustical demands of the new finger-playing technique, and in general there is ongoing adaptation of the instrument to different uses and evolving musical styles. The majority of the music from the first half of the century calls for a six- (tuned g′, d′, A, F, C, G, or a step higher), or seven-course instrument (seventh course tuned to F or D). But because of the canonization and frequent anthologizing of certain repertories from this period – intabulations of chansons and motets by Josquin, madrigals by Arcadelt, a couple of dozen widely circulated chansons by Crecquillon, Sermisy, Clemens, and Lasso, and lute music by Francesco da Milano, for example – these lutes continued to be played by amateurs into the early seventeenth century. Indeed, in the famous and much-studied Caravaggio painting of "The Lute Player," executed around 1595–6, the subject holds a seven-course lute and he is playing and singing from Arcadelt's *Primo Libro di Madrigali* published in 1539.[27] By the second third of the century, the lower range of the lute is extended in Italy and England with the addition of an eighth course, and by the early seventeenth century, players in France and the Lowlands were writing for an instrument of ten or eleven courses, on which an entirely new repertoire was created with little carryover from the past.[28]

Annibale Carracci's exquisite portrait of his professional lute-playing friend Giulio Pedrizzano, known as "Mascheroni," is an ideal representation of the late sixteenth-century lute. Mascheroni served as lutenist of the Concerto Palatino of Bologna from 1589 to 1602, succeeding his more famous father Cesare Mascarone, who was employed from 1526 to 1571.[29] Executed by Carracci around 1593–4 – a full century after Costa's painting, though the two artists were neighbors geographically – the painting shown in Figure 6.4 clearly shows a seven-course, pear-shape lute characteristic of the Füssen–Bologna instruments that dominated lute design in the sixteenth century, the new right-hand position as it descends at an angle to the strings as opposed to the old horizontal plectrum position, and, importantly, the lutenist recognized as a professional composer, given the presence of the manuscript paper and inkwell.

Like viols and many wind instruments, sixteenth-century lutes were constructed in families, comprising soprano, alto, tenor, and bass sizes, surviving instruments of which date mostly from after 1550. Although only a small repertory of ensemble lute music (Pacolini [$1564_7/1587_6$], Adriansen [1584_6], Terzi [1599_{11}], and Piccinini [1623]) survives, documentary and visual evidence testify to the frequent presence of multiple lutes playing together, often with voices or sometimes viols, in both private and

---

[27] An accurate and detailed study of the painting and its musical themes is in Keith Christiansen, *A Caravaggio Rediscovered: The Lute Player* (New York, 1990).
[28] For a useful chart on lute sizes used in Italian sources of the seventeenth century, see Coelho, *The Manuscript Sources*, 34–5.
[29] Pedrizzano is one of the few lutenists represented in art from which we have actual surviving music. A dance setting entitled "Una corente del Pedrizzano" appears in Berkeley, University of California Music Library, Ms. 757, fol. 29, a manuscript of Bolognese provenance dated c.1615–30. See Coelho, *The Manuscript Sources*, 53. Concerning the employment of the father in Bologna, see Gambassi, *Il Concerto Palatino*, 616–28, and for the son, ibid., 634–8.

Figure 6.4 Seven-course lute: Annibale Carracci, *Portrait of the lute player, Giulio Mascheroni*, c.1593–4, Dresden, Staatliche Kunstsammlungen/Art Resource, New York

courtly settings as well as in large public contexts.[30] Ensembles of lutes are especially well documented in Florentine festivals of the late sixteenth and early seventeenth centuries, particularly the celebrations staged for the 1608 wedding of Cosimo II Medici to Maria Magdalena of Austria.[31] Carefully programmed within the allegorical backdrop of these events, lutes were used not only on stage for *intermedi*, but at banquets and on floats, boats, clouds, and mythical monsters, employed as much for their classical allusions to Orphic lyres as for their acoustical and mobile attributes.[32]

---

[30] On the presence of lute consorts at the English court and a summary of the concerted lute repertory, see Spring, *The Lute in Britain*, 157–9.

[31] The ensemble lutes used in the Florentine celebrations for the 1608 marriage of Cosimo II Medici and Maria Magdalena of Austria are described in Coelho, "Public Works and Private Contexts," 121–32.

[32] For a summary of these events based on contemporary descriptions and containing reproductions of the iconographical testimony, see Nagler, *Theatre Festivals*.

Although seven- and eight-course lutes continue to be used throughout the late sixteenth and early seventeenth centuries, three developments around 1600 disrupt both the future design of lutes and the manner in which they were used, forcing radical changes onto the instrument and effectively bringing to an end the history of the "Renaissance" lute: (1) the rise of the basso continuo, which shifted the pedagogical fundamentals of lutenists towards accompanying, rather than solo playing or intabulating vocal music;[33] (2) the subsequent rise of larger, extended-neck lutes of 11–14 strings like the *chitarrone, arciliuto,* and *liuto attiorbato,* as well as the rise of the guitar;[34] (3) and in France, and soon thereafter in Germany, the introduction of new lute tunings in order to enlarge the harmonic vocabulary and broaden the playing textures, which could only result in a definitive break with the sixteenth-century "Renaissance" repertory. One might say that the Renaissance lute occupies the same position in instrumental music as the Renaissance polyphonic Mass, madrigal, or motet: it is representative of a cohesive stylistic period, a *prima prattica* affirmation of balanced polyphony, counterpoint, and reserved but sublime expression – all qualities that are at the center of the disputes about musical aesthetics at the turn of the sixteenth century.

Vihuela

The origins of the European lute are, as is well known, found in the Arabic instrument *al-ud* (= *l'ud* = lute). It was brought into Europe by the Moors from northern Africa through Spain, and possibly through Arabic connections in southern Italy as well, where it flourished from the late thirteenth century, as attested by iconographical and documentary sources. A prevailing theory is that with the expulsion of Arabic and Jewish peoples from Spain in 1492, the lute, with its powerful symbolic, musical, and physical associations

---

[33] See Coelho, "The Players of Florentine Monody."

[34] By the 1580s, Medici inventories already list an instrument called the "chitarrone," a large lute that was augmented with a second neck that normally held seven additional bass strings, thus extending the lower range of the lute to almost that of the keyboard. The chitarrone's origins are found at the Medici Court in Florence in the circle of Giulio Caccini and Medici lutenist Antonio Naldi, and its first documented use was in the 1589 Florentine *intermedi*. Developed as an accompanying instrument, the chitarrone was much larger than a lute and employed a different tuning and technique, thus severing any possibility of an interchangeable repertory between the two instruments; see Coelho, *The Manuscript Sources*, 38. For a full study of the instrument and its origins, see Kevin Mason, *The Chitarrone and its Repertoire in Early Seventeenth-Century Italy* (Aberystwyth, 1989).

with the Arabic instrument, was also deported.[35] This explanation should not be totally rejected, for there is indeed no extant music specifically for lute from sixteenth-century Spain, though late sixteenth-century inventories of Spanish nobility do list lutes along with vihuelas, and the term "vihuela," was probably also used to designate the lute.[36] Nevertheless, it is the guitar-shaped vihuela *de mano* (that is, a viola played with "the hand" as opposed to *de arco*, "with the bow") that emerges at the end of the fifteenth century as the main plucked instrument used in sixteenth-century Spain, even though this instrument, too, had connections to – though perhaps not ancestry with – Moorish culture.[37] Tinctoris made note of the instrument's Spanish origins and its narrow hips, describing the lute as shaped like "a tortoise-shell," and the vihuela "curved inward on each side."[38]

Through the presence of the Aragonese court in Naples (fl. 1443–1503) and the papacy of the Borgia Pope Alexander VI (*reg.* 1492–1503), who as a young man was educated in Valencia, the vihuela also became well known in Italy, where a version of it was known as the *viola da mano*. Identical to the lute in tuning and playing technique, the *viola* was used interchangeably with the lute in many Neapolitan sources. In 1536, printer Joannes Sultzbach published in Naples two of the earliest editions of lute music by Francesco da Milano, specifying on the title page that they were for "viola *or* lute," and Bartolomeo Lieto's intabulation treatise (Naples, 1559) is similarly intended for players of both instruments.[39] A large Neapolitan manuscript known as the Barbarino Lutebook (*c.*1580–1611), a central source for the music of the great Neapolitan lutenist Fabrizio Dentice, was probably intended for either lute or vihuela, and it testifies to the use of the instrument in Italy up to around 1600.[40] The earliest

---

[35] On the close cultural connections between the *ud* and lute, see Vladimir Ivanoff, "Eros and Death: The Lute as a Symbol in Oriental and Occidental Art and Music," *Luths et luthistes en Occident*, 31–41. For one account of the decline of the lute connected to the expulsion of Arabs from Spain, see Smith, *A History of the Lute*, 221–3.

[36] Some of these inventories are briefly summarized in John Griffiths, "La vihuela en la época de Felipe II." In *Políticas y prácticas musicales en el mundo de Felipe II*, ed. John Griffiths and Javier Suárez-Pajares (Madrid, 2004), 420–3.

[37] See Griffiths, "The Vihuela." In *Performance on Lute, Guitar, and Vihuela*, ed. Victor Coelho, 160.

[38] Quoted in Laurence Wright, "The Medieval Gittern and Citole: A Case of Mistaken Identity," *GSJ* 30 (1977), 21. On the Italian viola da mano, see Hiroyuki Minamino, "The Spanish Plucked Viola in Renaissance Italy, 1480–1530," *EM* 32 (2004), 177–92.

[39] Francesco da Milano, *Intavolatura de viola overo Lauto... Libro Primo della Fortuna e Libro Secondo* (Naples, 1536); facsimile rpt. (Geneva, 1988); Bartolomeo Lieto, *Dialogo quarto di musica...* (Naples, 1558), facsimile rpt. with commentary, ed. Patrizio Barbieri (Lucca, 1993).

[40] The manuscript is Cracow, Biblioteca Jagiellonska Mus. Ms. 40032. For a study of the manuscript and partial edition of the Neapolitan repertory, see John Griffiths and Dinko Fabris, ed., *Neapolitan Lute Music: Fabrizio Dentice, Giulio Severino, Giovanni Antonio Severino,*

Figure 6.5 Vihuela: frontispiece to Luys Milán, *El Maestro* (Valencia, 1536)

surviving music for the instrument may be an Italian fragment in "Neapolitan" tablature dating from the late fifteenth to early sixteenth century, preserved in the University Library in Bologna.[41]

The large bulk and stylistic core of the vihuela repertory, however, is concentrated within a relatively short forty-year period and contained in seven distinguished Spanish publications, beginning with Luys Milán's *El Maestro* in 1536$_5$ (see Figure 6.5) and culminating with Esteban Daza's *El*

Francesco Cardone (Madison, 2004). For a complete inventory, see Dieter Kirsch & Lenz Meierott, ed., *Berliner Lautentabulaturen in Krakau* (Mainz, 1992), 1–53.

[41] For a transcription, see Minamino, "The Spanish Plucked *viola,*" 179. Curiously uncited in Minamino's 2004 study (which is largely derived from Fallows, "15th-Century Tablatures") is the description of an early sixteenth-century fragment in London by Antonio Corona-Alcalde, "The Earliest Vihuela Tablature: A Recent Discovery," *EM* 20 (1992), 594–600, which though clearly postdating the Bologna fragment, should be considered as an important source for the vihuela prior to Milán (1536$_5$).

Parnasso of 1576₁. As an instrument whose music was almost entirely conditioned by the venerable contrapuntal tradition of the sixteenth century – dances make up only a small fraction of a repertory that is overwhelmingly dedicated to fantasias, intabulations of the Josquin and post-Josquin generation, songs, and variation sets – the vihuela was not subject to the extreme modifications in size, tuning, and the number of strings that were forced on the lute to assure its adaptability to the new styles of accompaniment and solo playing of the seventeenth century. By the beginning of the seventeenth century the vihuela, fundamentally attached to an older repertory, is eclipsed in Spain by the guitar, and in Italy, by both the guitar and extended-neck lutes.

Renaissance guitar

Etymologically, the Renaissance guitar, a small four-course instrument of Spanish origin that enjoyed a burst of popularity in mid-sixteenth-century France, Italy, and Spain, would seem to have a direct ancestral line to earlier instruments known variously as *gittern, quintern*, and *chitarino*. Unfortunately, in the history of early plucked-string instruments, nothing is ever that simple. More complicated and fragmented a story than perhaps that of any other instrument described here, the origins of the guitar have been further traced to the vihuela, viol, and a variety of instruments portrayed in art, and there does not seem to have been a common terminology for describing it until the instrument itself was standardized around the first third of the sixteenth century. To further complicate matters, while in the fifteenth century the terms *gittern, quintern*, and *chitarino* refer not to a guitar but to a small treble lute, by the mid-sixteenth century they refer unequivocally to the guitar, as seen in Figure 6.6.[42] To explain how and why these designations evolved after 1500 is to understand how instrumentalists and theorists understood a new affinity between like instruments and how they are grouped – no longer the result of a cleaved binary classification according to dynamic range (loud/soft), but rather through a carefully trimmed taxonomy in which instruments were part of

---

[42] "Guiterne" is used, for example, in the treatise attributed to Bonaventure des Periers, *Discours non plus melancoliques que divers... & a la fin La maniere de bien & justement entoucher les Lucs & Guiternes* (Poitiers, 1556), Ch. 21, 96, in which the author writes that "as far as the name, I know that there are people who call it *Guiterre*, others *Quinterne*, for what reason I do not know." A facsimile of the treatise is in Joël Dugot, ed., *Luth: Méthodes*, 25–53. The surviving leaves of Adrian Le Roy's *Instruction to the Gitterne* also testify to the use of the term in England. See Page, *The Guitar in Tudor England*, 79–108.

LE
PREMIER LIVRE DE
CHANSONS, GAILLARDES, PAVANNES,
Branſles, Almandes, Fantaiſies, reduictz en tabulature de Guiterne
par Maiſtre Guillaume Morlaye ioueur de Lut.

A PARIS.
De l'Imprimerie de Robert GranIon & Michel Fezandat, au Mont
S. Hylaire, à l'Enſeigne des Grandz Ions.
1552.
Auec priuilege du Roy.

Figure 6.6 Renaissance guitar: frontispiece to Guillaume Morlaye, *Le premier livre de chansons, gaillardes, pavanes . . . reduictz en tabulature de Guiterne* (Paris, 1552)

larger cognate families (strings, winds, etc.). This new classification, already introduced by Virdung, underscores the evolving rise of ensembles composed of like instruments, the homogeneity of imitative textures found in the contemporary madrigal, Mass, motet, and chanson, and, lest we forget, to the purely practical marketing need of sixteenth-century music publishers for consistency in the names given to instruments. Even so, it remained elusive to arrive at a standardized nomenclature for the guitar and lute, two instruments that are on an accelerated rate of physical change after around 1550.

The earliest music published for the four-course Renaissance guitar consists of six pieces grouped together at the end of Book 1 in Mudarra's *Tres libros* of 1546 (see *SBS* 10), a book otherwise intended for solo vihuela and songs with vihuela accompaniment, and indicative of players competent on both instruments. With only four courses, the Renaissance guitar was often subject to different tunings, particularly in the lower strings, to increase its range. Mudarra includes pieces in two tunings, a single fantasia in the old *temple viejos* and the remainder in the new *temple nuevos*, which corresponds to the standard tuning of the Renaissance guitar. It has the identical intervals as the highest four strings of the modern guitar, or as

Bermudo described it in his *Declaracion* of 1555, like a vihuela without the outer strings, giving the intervals from lowest to highest of 4th–3rd–4th, with the lowest string tuned normally in G or A.[43]

The image on the frontispiece in Figure 6.6 accurately shows the small size of the guitar in proportion to a book of music – the instrument is not much longer than the width of a full opening of a lute or guitar tablature. The image clearly shows four courses, the first single, and the remaining three doubled; the lowest course was usually doubled at the octave. Like the lute and vihuela, the guitar is plucked with the fingers, and the technique is almost identical. The guitar found considerable popularity in France during the 1550s, so much that Bonaventure des Periers in 1556 claimed that "since twelve or fifteen years, everyone has started to *guiterner*, the lute being almost forgotten ...."[44] The last decades of the century witness the meteoric rise in Spain and Italy of the 5-string Spanish guitar, along with a new strumming technique (*rasgueado*). Florentine sources of the late sixteenth century testify to the importance of this instrument early on in the history of monody, and it develops a large and influential repertory in Italy and France during the seventeenth and eighteenth centuries.[45]

Harp

As seen with the elegant instrument depicted by van Eyck in Figure 6.7, the Renaissance harp was composed of three parts: body, neck, and forepillar. The body was hollowed out (usually from one piece of wood) to provide a resonating chamber, and this was held closest to the player. The neck held the tuning pins, and the forepillar functioned as a brace from the end of the neck to the bottom of the body. During the fifteenth century the bass register of the instrument was extended, resulting in a lengthened body and a more straightened forepillar than was the case with earlier medieval harps. Smaller harps had only eight strings, but larger harps, which were quite common, had as many as twenty-five or twenty-six (Figure 6.7, remarkably detailed, shows twenty-four). Still, the pitches on the fifteenth-century instrument were

---

[43] For an excellent general history of the early guitar, see James Tyler and Paul Sparks, *The Guitar and Its Music from the Renaissance to the Classical Era* (Oxford, 2002).

[44] Bonaventure des Periers, *Discours*, 96: "mais despuis douze ou quinze ans en ça, tout nostre monde s'est mis a Guiterner, le Luc presque mis en obly...."

[45] Even with the rise of the 5-course instrument, the 4-course guitar was still used in the late sixteenth and early seventeenth centuries, as testified by Florence, Biblioteca Nazionale Centrale, Cl. XIX. 29, described in Giovanna Lazzi, ed., *Rime e suoni per corde spagnole: fonti per la chitarra barocca a Firenze* (Florence, 2002), 49–50.

Figure 6.7 Harp, fiddle, and positive organ: Jan and Hubert van Eyck, detail from *Ghent Altarpiece*, 1432. Ghent, Cathedral of St. Bavo. Scala/Art Resource, New York

generally limited to the diatonic notes. As discussed in Chapter 2, the late fifteenth-century Spanish harpist Ludovico developed a technique of placing his finger against the string in order to make leading tones at cadences (see *SBS* 10). The range of the larger instruments was wide, some three octaves, with the bottom note being described as either F or G (as Myers points out, this probably actually sounded a C). The European harp was evidently plucked with the thumb and fleshy part of the fingers, and with skilled players both hands could have been used, allowing for the playing of two distinct parts.[46]

---

[46] For a well-informed discussion of the harp, see Myers, *A Performer's Guide*, ed. Jeffery Kite-Powell, 187–93. Myers (188) points out that the fifteenth-century harp had an inefficient resonator due to the choice of hardwood for the belly of the instrument, and suggested that

The harp was often illustrated or mentioned in contemporary sources, but a vast majority of those sources have little bearing on actual performance practices, because in most the harp appeared as a symbol (associated in many illustrations with King David, for example). Nonetheless, from the early fifteenth century the harp was popular as both a solo and ensemble instrument. Baude Cordier and Richard de Locqueville were both harpists as well as composers, and as harpists they were probably considered more as soloists than ensemble players; they are never listed, at any rate, in payments with players of other instruments.[47] Yet at about the same time, the court at Baden apparently supported an ensemble that consisted of gittern and harp, while a duo of lute and harp performed a bit later at the court of Holland.[48] As performers they were of professional rank, but prominent amateurs also played the harp, including the Queen of France, Charles of Orléans, and Philip the Good of Burgundy.[49] Sources document the appeal of the harp in all regions of Europe, especially in England.

The technique for playing the harp was demanding and required a considerable degree of specialization. The lute/fiddle pair at the Burgundian court, for example, can be considered as generalists, but they were never indicated as playing harp. One notable exception in this regard was Conrad Paumann, for the harp was one of the instruments he was alleged to have played – but his particular range of his skills was quite extraordinary for the time. Another factor was that contracted patronage for harpists was available only from the nobility, and from the very high nobility at that. Civic payrolls from Flanders, Bavaria, and Italy almost exclusively document players of loud instruments. On even the rare instances of contracted positions for soft instruments in the fifteenth century, these were not allotted to harpists.[50]

Though the harp continued to have an appeal as a solo instrument in the late fifteenth century, its ensemble use seemed to have declined. In the sixteenth century came demands for a wider range and for more extended

---

builders offered a compensation for this by the use of "bray pins," which added a buzzy quality to the sound, therefore adding to the carrying quality.

[47] For the harpist at the court of Burgundy, see Wright, *Music at the Court of Burgundy*, 31–2; for discussion of harpists at the French court, see André Pirro, *La musique à Paris sous la règne de Charles VI (1380–1422)* (Strasbourg, 1930, reprint Geneva, 1973), 12 and 26.

[48] Information on the court of Holland is given in Lingbeek-Schalekamp, *Overheid en muziek*, 183, 194.

[49] See Pirro, *La musique à Paris*, 26, and Wright, *Music at the Court of Burgundy*, 48.

[50] A rare exception was that in Bologna from 1503 onward, an "arpista" is listed among the civic musicians; see Gambassi, *Il Concerto Palatino*, 612 ff.

use of chromatic pitches. These demands placed the traditional harp, especially with its very limited ability to negotiate beyond the diatonic pitches, at a distinct disadvantage. Various approaches were taken to resolve the deficiencies: additional strings, perhaps with colors for chromatic pitches, or double sets of strings.[51] Still, in most regions the bipolar existence continued – that is, popular to some degree as a solo instrument, but not regularly included in ensemble practice. No harpist was included in the Munich wedding performance of 1568, for example, nor was a harpist on the extensive payrolls of instrumentalists during the reign of Henry VIII. Italy was something of an exception. Rinaldo dall'Arpa was a performer esteemed at the court of Ferrara in the 1590s, and harps were included in several ensembles performing in the Medici festivals of 1589.[52]

Psaltery and dulcimer

The psaltery and dulcimer share several features. Both were essentially wooden boxes with flat tops and bottoms and were relatively small, which limited the number of strings and restricted them to diatonic pitches. This restriction may have been a factor in their decline in use after about 1450. Neither disappeared completely, as the dulcimer experienced a resurgence in the nineteenth century and is also very prominent in contemporary folk music. Archival sources suggest that both were instruments played by professionals, though the technique of the psaltery does not pose a barrier for an amateur skilled on the harp. The players of these instruments do not seem to have been included into the upper tier of performers; in no instance, in any of the sources we have consulted, were players of the psaltery or dulcimer taken on as regular members of courtly or civic ensembles. None had the stature of Pietrobono in Ferrara or Paumann in Munich.

The psaltery was played either with the fingers or with a plectrum, often with one string provided for each pitch, though multiple strings were possible. Because of its modest size, the psaltery was usually

---

[51] Myers, "Harp." In *A Performer's Guide*, ed. Jeffery Kite-Powell, 187–93; for a useful discussion of the features of the harp, see Roslyn Rensch, *Harps and Harpists* (Bloomington, 1989, rev. ed., 2007).

[52] Concerning Rinaldo dall'Arpa at Ferrara, see Newcomb, *The Madrigal at Ferrara*, vol. I, 159. Newcomb also notes that Laura Peverara, one of the singers in the famous *Concerto delle Donne* at the court, was a harpist, ibid., 66. On harps in the Medici festivals, see Brown, *Sixteenth-Century Instrumentation*, 93–105.

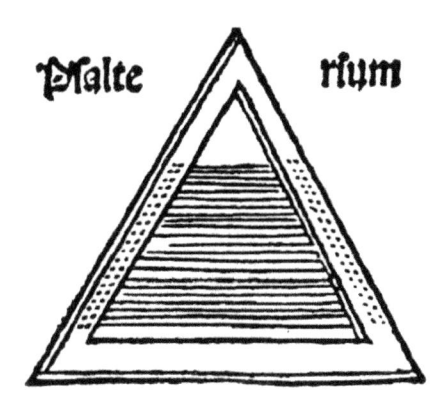

Figure 6.8 Psaltery from Sebastian Virdung, *Musica getutscht* (Basel, 1511), sig. B2v

restricted to the soprano register; it was normally held in the lap or on the chest. String length determined pitch, with the result that higher notes had much shorter strings than the lowest ones. Instrument makers produced various shapes reflecting this feature, the simplest solution being triangular, as seen in the Virdung woodcut (Figure 6.8).

Some instruments were made in trapezoidal form; another favored form was the so-called "pig snout," a roughly rectangular shape for the longer strings, with parallel sides curving in to the narrowest point. The psaltery reached a high point in esteem in the fourteenth and early fifteenth century, both as a solo and ensemble instrument. Thereafter it yielded to the lute and keyboard instruments that were better able to meet the more chromatic demands of the later Renaissance.

As shown in Figure 6.9, the dulcimer was played with two wooden sticks shaped to meet this purpose. As Myers pointed out, striking the strings in this manner was inefficient; to compensate, the dulcimer was routinely fitted out with multiple strings for each pitch.[53] A distinctive feature of the dulcimer was the bridge (or even multiple bridges) that ran across the soundboard. With a single bridge (the type illustrated by Virdung) the strings would be divided into two pitches (most often a fourth or fifth apart), which allowed fewer strings to produce more pitches. The evolutionary curve of the dulcimer came somewhat later than that of the psaltery. It seems to have appeared around 1350, flourished in the early decades of the fifteenth century, and then faded from view.

---

[53] Herbert W. Myers, "Psaltery & Dulcimer." In *A Performer's Guide*, ed. Ross Duffin, 441–2.

Figure 6.9 Dulcimer: Hans Memling, *Angel Musicians*, c.1480, Antwerp, Koninklijk Museum voor Schone Kunsten. Scala/Art Resource, New York

II. Bowed string instruments

Fiddle

The fiddle (shown above in Figure 6.7) aptly illustrates the variance that is characteristic of Renaissance music. In 1400, it was used by amateurs and professionals in a wide variety of contexts, with a matching, broadly varied repertory. The "workhorse among musical instruments," in the words of Howard Mayer Brown, the fiddle was illustrated, as he pointed out, far more often than any other instrument.⁵⁴ Within two or three decades, however, its prominence was challenged, followed by a sharp decline. The fiddle was equipped with three to six strings, held on the shoulder, and played with a bow. Beyond this, little else was standard for the instrument. In descriptions, fiddles, fall into two subgroups. One type was used as a melodic instrument, the other for accompaniment. The melodic type was gently waisted, usually with from three to five strings, unfretted, with the strings running over the fingerboard. An arched bridge allowed all strings to be played individually. The other could have a waisted, rounded, or a squared shape usually with five strings, four running over the fingerboard, the fifth not. This fifth string functioned as a drone to be played either with the thumb of the left hand (assuming the bow held in the right hand) or perhaps with the bow.⁵⁵ The bridge was more often flat, with the result that the instrument was largely restricted to playing drone accompaniments, though the example shown in the Ghent altarpiece clearly shows a curved bridge with strings of a different height over the fingerboard.⁵⁶ The two types had quite different lines of development. That of the accompaniment type was by far the more complex. Around 1400, everywhere in Europe were singers who performed narrative poetry or improvised texts to match their audience or the occasion; they did this either singing alone, or with the support of an instrument, the preferred choice then being the fiddle. This type of performance, however, rapidly fell out of favor by 1440 in France and in the Low Countries, replaced by a vogue for text settings as heard in chansons by such composers as Dufay and Binchois. The older style was sustained in German regions, with solo singers such as Michel Behaim still prominent well after 1450. This changed only in about 1470, with the increasing taste for polyphonic German songs as well as for imported French chansons. In Italy the

---

⁵⁴ Howard Mayer Brown, "The Trecento Fiddle and Its Bridges," *EM* 17 (1989), 309.
⁵⁵ Sometimes a sixth string, also off the fingerboard, was present, constituting a drone. For an illustration, see Anne-Emmanuelle Ceulemans, *De la vièle médiévale au violon du xviie siècle: Étude terminologique, iconographique et théorique* (Turnhout, 2011), 45. No specific information is available concerning fifteenth-century tunings for either type. See also Timothy J. McGee, "The Medieval Fiddle: Tuning, Technique, and Repertory."
In *Instruments, Ensembles, and Repertory*, ed. Timothy J. McGee and Stewart Carter, 31–56. For details on the structure of fiddles, see Ceulemanns, *De la vièle médiévale*, 69–87.
⁵⁶ Mary Remnant, *English Bowed Instruments from Anglo-Saxon to Tudor Times* (Oxford, 1986), 25–6, pointed out that a flat bridge could be notched in such a way that some strings could be placed deeper into the bridge than others, meaning that it might be possible to play some strings independently. This suggestion is expanded in McGee, "The Medieval Fiddle." In *Instruments, Ensembles, and Repertory*, ed. Timothy J. McGee and Stewart Carter, 34–6. Nonetheless, the instrument with a flat bridge was generally used for simple drone-type accompaniments.

tradition of the solo singer lasted much longer, kept in vogue with strong support from Italian humanists who viewed French polyphony with antipathy. Only as native polyphonic forms such as the frottola and especially the madrigal arrived did the older tradition give way.[57] As the older vocal style died out successively in each region, so did the accompaniment fiddle also fade from view. The melodic type fared better, at least for a time, as the fiddle was not yet completely displaced. In the earlier fifteenth century, fiddles were combined with a wide variety of soft instruments, especially the portative organ, harp, or lute. In fact, the combination of lute and fiddle was heard frequently until at least the 1480s. The viol arrived on the scene in the 1490s however, followed by the violin in the early decades of the next century, a combination that acted as a double menace. The viol displaced any further attraction of the fiddle for amateurs, and the violin was more effective for professionals. In sum, by the early sixteenth century both forms were rapidly fading from view. An explicit demonstration of their decline was that neither Virdung (1511) nor Agricola (1529) even bothered to discuss or illustrate the fiddle.

Rebec

As seen in Figure 6.10 by David (1509), the rebec was a small bowed string instrument, with a quasi-pear-shaped body. It was most often used as a discant instrument, though slightly larger sizes are sometimes shown in contemporary illustrations, suggesting that it was used for alto parts as well. Rebecs were constructed from a single piece of wood, including body and fingerboard, usually with a bent or curved peg box, and pegs perpendicular to the fingerboard (this in contrast to the pegs of the fiddle). It was usually fretless, with three strings probably tuned in fifths.[58]

Well-established in musical practice by about 1300, the rebec retained a firm place within the performance options of players in the early fifteenth century. It was an instrument for professionals, and was well suited for the decorative, elaborate discant parts (both written and improvised) of the time. It found its most prominent use in ensembles. Toward the end of the fifteenth century, as bowed string instruments started to appear in consorts, the rebec shrugged off any such normalizing concepts and continued on its own resolute path. It remained

[57] Ibid., 52–3.
[58] Sterling Jones, "Rebec." In *A Performer's Guide*, ed. Ross Duffin, 317–24, provides a useful overview. See also Remnant, *English Bowed Instruments*, 29–41, which includes an excellent survey of the capabilities and uses of the rebec.

Figure 6.10 Rebec: Gerard David, *Virgin among the Virgins* (detail), c.1509, Rouen, Musée des Beaux-Arts. Erich Lessing/Art Resource, New York

consistently (if anything was consistent about the instrument) small – in fact, often very small – and its usual role was for playing parts in the soprano range. Virdung mentioned the instrument in the plural (*Geigen*), but illustrated only one instrument. Agricola (1529$_1$) illustrated it as a family, but not one iconographical source aware to us shows such a family as existing in practice. In a period marked by incessant experimentation and change, the exceptional resilience of the rebec stands out, especially in contrast to the rapid alteration in the fortunes of its close cousin, the fiddle. The rebec in various guises continued to hold some place in musical practice almost to the end of the Renaissance, its final decline coming only with the surge in popularity of the violin toward the end of the sixteenth century.

Viols

This woodcut (Figure 6.11), though crude stylistically, provides the essential details of the viols. It was placed on the title page of the *Regola Rubertina* (Venice, 1542$_2$), a method book for the viol written by Silvestro Ganassi, then a member of the Doge's instrumental ensemble in

Figure 6.11 Viol: Silvestro di Ganassi, frontispiece to *Regola Rubertina* (Venice, 1542–3)

Venice. The woodcut is particularly appropriate, for not only was Venice at this time the leading center of music publishing in Europe, but instrument makers there were at about this time producing viols of such stature that they helped to define the shape and construction of what became the dominant form of the instrument.

Ganassi shows three viols: one bass and two smaller instruments that are probably tenors (the instrument on the left is partially obscured, but it is in any case not as large as the bass in the center). A fourth musician, a male singer holding a single sheet of music, fills out the quartet. No soprano instrument is present, and as Woodfield has shown, at mid-century Italian viol consorts, usually four in number, often consisted of two tenors and two basses (or even one tenor and three basses).[59] Although Ganassi described three sizes of viols, soprano, tenor, and bass, the soprano size was less favored, as suggested by its absence from this woodcut, as the viol consort at mid-century had a distinct bias for the deeper timbres of the tenor and bass instruments. The tenor instrument, moreover, had a wide enough range to cover soprano parts in most music of the period, and when that part might exceed the range, viol ensembles had a regular

---

[59] See Woodfield, *The Early History*, 185–6.

procedure in place (described by Ganassi) for simply transposing such pieces downward.

All three instruments in the illustration were played held downward, which remained the characteristic position for playing viols of all sizes from the late fifteenth century onward. The players are seated, and this, too, continued and became a defining feature of viol performance (distinguishing viols from violins, which were played while standing). The frets and the bows, held underhand, are clearly visible.[60]

The viol emerged in the early 1490s and the courts of Ferrara and Mantua were early and influential centers. From there it spread rapidly throughout Europe.[61] Subsequently, through the first half of the sixteenth century two opposing concepts of viol construction struggled for supremacy. One was Italian, with Venice as a center; instruments there were usually made with six strings and with the sloping (or slightly rounded) shoulders, as shown on the instrument to the right.[62] The German tradition called for instruments of five strings with more incut shoulders. Oddly, the large bass instrument in the center shows quite definitely only five strings and distinctly incut shoulders. The situation is laced with irony; here is a Venetian musician, in a Venetian publication, who plays on an instrument of distinctly German character. It should be noted, however, that like lute makers, several of the outstanding viol makers in the Veneto were, in fact, German speakers from north of the Alps. In any case, the illustration of this "foreign" instrument suggests only a minor anomaly in what was an overwhelming trend. Within one or two decades after Ganassi's publication, the Venetian form of the viol became the standard everywhere. After about 1550, matters become complex as enthusiasm for the viol was partially diluted by the growing popularity of the violin. This varied significantly from region to region, though, with a decline more noticeable in Italy than elsewhere. In England, by contrast, the end of the century witnessed a stream of compositions of astonishing quality calling for performance by viols.

Throughout the late sixteenth century viols were played by both professionals and amateurs. This often took place in whole consorts, that is, with

---

[60] For details on holding the bow, see ibid., 161–2.
[61] Ibid., 80–98, argues for the influence of the Spanish viol, which would have reached Ferrara and Mantua through the links with the Spanish court of Naples.
[62] On the other features that defined the Venetian viol, see ibid., 124–5. The strings of the viols were tuned in fourths, with a third in the middle. On the tunings, see ibid., 140–54, and Herbert W. Myers, "Renaissance Viol Tunings: A Reconsideration," *Journal of the Viola da Gamba Society of America* 44 (2007–8), 13–40.

viols alone without any other instruments. Some professional ensembles could include up to eight players, resulting in a marked increase in the number of sizes. To Ganassi's three (soprano, tenor, and bass), there could be added a small soprano, an alto, and a large bass.[63] Still, as in the woodcut, combining other timbres with viols continued throughout the century. Thomas Morley's *First Booke of Consort Lessons* (1599$_8$/1611) called for bass and treble viol combined with a mix of four other instruments. One further distinctive use was that of a single viol serving as the bass for an ensemble that otherwise included no other viols (an example can be seen in the illustration of the Bavarian court string ensemble in 1568, Figure 6.13).

Violins

The early history of the violin is muddled. No instruments from before 1550 survive, and contemporary terminology was ambiguous, as terms such as *violi* were applied to both viols and violins. Moreover, the violin was consistently an instrument for professionals and was not generally played by amateurs, who preferred the viol. Professional players, on the other hand, played both viols and violins. Further, it is unclear from surviving court payment records what string instruments might have been played in a particular performance. Thankfully, visual images have been helpful in providing clarity to the violin's early history. Drawing upon illustrations from the time, David Boyden and, more recently, Peter Holman, have assembled a reasonable chronology.[64] The first violins emerged by about 1510 and were readily adopted, becoming widespread by the 1520s. The instrument had a thinner body than the viol, and was unfretted. Earlier, it was fitted with three strings, tuned in fifths (in contrast to the basic tuning in fourths of the viol); a fourth string was added about 1550. It was from its inception a consort instrument in a variety of sizes, with its central role as performing for dancing. This context was reserved for professionals; while amateurs might play dance music for recreation, it would have been demeaning for them to have played a dance job. The violin was played while standing, again in contrast to the viol, it had a much more powerful sound than the viol, and it provided an attractive alternative to the winds for dancing.

[63] Woodfield, *The Early History*, 194.
[64] David D. Boyden, *The History of Violin Playing from Its Origins to 1761* (London, 1965), which has been updated by Holman, *Four and Twenty Fiddlers*, 1–52.

Figure 6.12 Violin: anonymous, Marguerite de Valois ("La Reine Margot"), 1553–1615, dancing *la Volta* at the Valois Court, late sixteenth century. Rennes, Musée des Beaux-Arts. Erich Lessing/Art Resource, New York

The anonymous painting given as Figure 6.12, though late in the century, clearly underlines these features. A pair – the woman being identified as Marguerite de Valois – is shown on the right, accompanied (on the left) by a small dance band of a violin, two violas, and a bass string instrument, either a tenor/bass violin or a small bass viol.[65] The violinist and players of viola are standing, with their instruments at the shoulder (not under the chin as is the modern manner), bowed overhand. The player of the bass instrument is seated, bracing it on his left leg, and is bowing

---

[65] It is difficult, though, to be absolutely accurate in judging size given the relatively poor level of detail; the configuration might also be two violins, viola, and bass instrument.

Figure 6.13 Violins playing for a banquet, from Hanns Wagner, *Kurtze doch gegründte Beschreibung* [of the Munich Court Wedding, 1568] (Munich, 1568)

underhand. Although we would like more precision, the fingerboard appears rather thick, suggesting that this is likely a small bass viol. This reinforces the point that one function of the bass viol was as the only viol mixed with other instruments.

The wedding banquet at the Bavarian court in 1568, illustrated in Figure 6.13, reveals that dancing was by no means the only context for violin performance. In fact, in Troiano's detailed description of the event, his response to the question "when do the court violinists perform?" was "during the time I was at the court I only heard them play for dining." Evidently during his extended stay in Munich the violins were never employed to accompany dancing; that task must have been assigned to the wind players. Troiano was specific that for dining it was the violins ("viole da Brazzo") that played, not viols. He added that for some other occasions, such as afternoon serenades, the string band did occasionally play on viols ("con viola di gamba") as well as with other instruments.[66]

[66] [Troiano], *Die Münchner Fürstenhochzeit*, 104–5.

We can be usually secure in matching the illustration with the events of the banquet, as Troiano is specific. During the third course of the meal "various six-part motets were played on six violins ('viole di braccio') including a work of Cipriano da Rore."[67] This was the only course that involved the violins by themselves. In Figure 6.13, we see those exact numbers: four violins of various sizes (again precision concerning sizes is impossible due to instruments being obscured), and two large bass instruments. The basses, of course, were not played *a braccio* and while the nature of the print makes it impossible to be certain, these two may well have been bass viols.

III.1 Keyboard instruments

Renaissance keyboard instruments can be divided into two groups; organs, activated by wind, and keyboard string instruments. Organs in turn were of four main types, the organ proper, positive organs, portative organs, and the regal. Descriptions and sources concerning the string types are more ambiguous, but these nonetheless can be divided into three main classifications: clavichord, harpsichord, and virginal.

Organ

"Let it be clear right from the start that the church organ, with its ingenious bellows, wind chests, pipework, tracker systems, keyboards, and so on, is among the peaks of medieval technology. Regrettably, walls between separate academic disciplines are so high, and the history of organ building, which is known in great and fascinating detail, has been so compartmentalized within the domain of musicology, that it has apparently never occurred to anyone to study the pre-baroque church organ as one, incredibly sophisticated, specimen of medieval technology. Yet that is where it belongs, too, on a par with the mechanical clock, with gothic architecture, the compass, the printing press, the stirrup, and all those other inventions which, whether or not they originated on West European soil, already in the Middle Ages lent to the cultivation of technology in Western Europe an unmistakably distinct character."[68]

Our modern inventions, especially those associated with technology, saturate all aspects of our lives. For those in the Renaissance the impact of innovation was every bit as powerful though certainly less invasive in

---

[67] Ibid., 142–3.
[68] H. Floris Cohen, "Beats and the Origins of Early Modern Science." In *Music and Science in the Age of Galileo*, ed. Victor Coelho (Dordrecht, 1992), 21–2.

that the most impressive and intricate mechanical marvel that they knew was the organ. Some were massive with over two thousand pipes and mechanisms of phenomenal complexity. In fact for citizens of cities such as Delft or Leiden in the Low Countries, Nördlingen in southern Germany, or Bologna in Italy, the technological device that they would point to with most civic pride was the organ in their most prominent church. Not incidentally, the Renaissance organ was also by far the most expensive musical instrument of the era.

By the end of the fourteenth century the organ had developed most of its basic features: numerous ranks of pipes, a sufficient wind chest to power the air flow through those pipes, and an adequate system of bellows. It remained primitive in certain aspects; in most, all the pipes played all the time and many organs were not yet outfitted with anything like a modern keyboard. Definitive changes soon arrived. Keyboards became regular features, with a division into diatonic notes and chromatic ones similar to the modern keyboard. Pipes were of two kinds: flue pipes (with the air directed over a sharp edge as with recorders), and reed pipes (with air activating a fixed, flexible strip of metal), with considerable experimentation to develop varied timbres within each type. Crucially, systems were developed to allow the player to select individual ranks of pipes. This was accomplished by shutting off, or *stopping*, the ranks that weren't desired.[69] The range of the organ earlier in the fifteenth century was from B to f'', but by the end of the century some instruments were capable of F or G to a'', that is, more or less matching the common vocal ranges. A few instruments in the sixteenth century expanded in both directions, to C, or perhaps even lower in the bass, and to c''' in the soprano.[70]

The large organ was almost always installed in a church, and the association with sacred services gave the instrument a profile unlike any other. As the centerpiece of the church, towns large and small throughout Europe spent large sums to commission an appropriately grand instrument. Perhaps it was this very popularity that emphasized regional differences, for there was a sufficient market everywhere to sustain numerous local centers of organ building. Highly skilled craftsmen in widely

---

[69] For a general survey of the history of the organ, see Peter Williams, *A New History of the Organ* (Bloomington and London, 1980), which updates his still valuable *The European Organ 1450–1850* (London, 1966).

[70] The notes required in the lowest few keys of the organ were largely diatonic. Some builders would then use the so-called "short octave," in which black keys might be used for diatonic pitches. On a keyboard that apparently ends with E, for example, the E key would sound C, and the $F\#$ and $G\#$ keys, respectively, would sound D and E.

separated locations came up with varied solutions to the challenges of expanding the potential of the organ – so much so that even a summary of organ history would demand a chapter unto itself. What can be said is that by 1500 organ makers everywhere were making instruments that combined a variety of ranks, each with a distinctive timbre. The ranks could be combined, or played individually. Northern organs had at least two manuals – players in Italy preferred single manual instruments – and all large organs were also equipped with foot pedals. Refinements would follow, but in essence the organ as it would be known for the next three centuries was in place.

Through most of the Renaissance the organ existed in splendid isolation, and until late in the sixteenth century it almost never performed with any other instruments. Similarly, combined performances with voices were not at all frequent, as the organist's task usually focused on either providing an occasional solo piece (a prelude, postlude, or some insertion such as a motet-like piece at the Elevation during the Mass), or performing in alternation (*alternatim*) with the choir. The latter was by far the more common assignment, and *alternatim* performances could take place in Office services (particularly at Vespers), during the Mass, or in paraliturgical services such as the *Salve*. The isolation broke down only in the last decades of the century as seen in the striking multi-choir works of Andrea and Giovanni Gabrieli, which called for dramatic combinations of voices and instruments, now including the organ (see *SBS* 15).

Portative organ

The portative organ (hereinafter, the portative), as seen in Figure 6.14 and as its name suggests, was a truly portable instrument, usually carried by a strap over the player's shoulder. One hand (usually the right) played while the other pumped the bellows located at the back of the instrument. Some were small with one rank of pipes, while others had two ranks. The range varied between one and two octaves, but as the instrument by definition was relatively small, it was used primarily for playing in the soprano register. No instruments survive, but its frequent presence in illustrations clearly attests to its popularity. These reveal that in the early fifteenth century it was sometimes built with push buttons, sometime with a small keyboard, which by late in the century became more standard. Both iconographic and archival sources underline the fact that the portative was common in chamber ensembles during the early Renaissance, often combined especially with lutes and fiddles. Its subsequent history ran

Figure 6.14 Portative organ: Marcellus Coffermans, *Maria with Child* (detail), c.1560. Antwerp, Museum Mayer van den Bergh, MM. 0021

curiously parallel to that of the fiddle. It, too, was in common usage in the early Renaissance and then gradually faded from use, disappearing almost completely in the early sixteenth century.

Positive organ

The positive organ (seen in Figure 6.7) was a somewhat hybrid instrument. It was not small enough to be carried by a player, but it was movable (note the handle shown on the left side of the instrument in the Van Eyck painting), which allowed for a more flexible use that was impossible for larger fixed-position instruments. Unlike the portative, it was played with both hands, usually had two or more ranks of pipes, and someone other than the player operated the bellows. Sizes varied, but larger instruments had a roughly three-octave range (probably from *G* to about *g″*.) Its use was more in line with the large organ rather than the portative, and was rarely, it seems, combined with other instruments. Its main use was probably as an instrument that could be moved to the various chapels within a church or even in secular contexts, such as at banquets and in processions. (One of the scenes in *The Triumph of Maximilian I*, not shown here, illustrates a positive on a carriage, the organist almost certainly being Hofhaimer.) The positive was also available for music in private chambers, which was probably one of the main performance contexts for the secular repertory in sources such as *Faenza*. Unlike the portative, the positive organ remained an important option for organists throughout the Renaissance.

Regal

Players requiring an easily available organ for performance at processions or at banquets faced problems. The positive organ was moveable, but its weight made the transportation of the instrument problematic. At the same time, the potential utility of the portative organ was compromised since it was played by only one hand. The regal (which apparently arrived on the scene in the late fifteenth century) offered a solution. It was sometimes quite a small instrument – as illustrated (Figure 6.15) almost identically by Virdung and Agricola, it was about the size of a very large book. Some were certainly larger. The instrument illustrated by Praetorius had a keyboard of more than three octaves, but even the larger organs could be moved, if necessary, by one person. The keyboard, intended for two hands, was on one of the long sides of the instrument with the bellows placed opposite. The reed pipes produced a sharp, nasal timbre, which Ashworth has described accurately as "something of a cordial snarl."[71] Contrary to the

Figure 6.15 Regal organ: Martin Agricola, *Musica instrumentalis deudsch* (Wittemberg, 1529), fol. 18v, sig. C2v

---

[71] Jack Ashworth, "Keyboard Instruments." In *A Performer's Guide*, ed. Jeffery Kite-Powell, 209, where he provides the illustration by Praetorius on 210.

approach of the larger organs, the regal found its central role in working with other instruments or with voices as a foundation instrument. This is how it was used, in any case, at three notable events where sources noted its presence: at the Bavarian wedding of 1568, at the fabled Medici wedding festival of 1589, and specified as a continuo instrument for some of the underworld scenes in Monteverdi's *Orfeo* of 1607.[72]

III.2 Keyboard string instruments

From our present-day perspective, the historical development of keyboard string instruments seems clear. There were three basic instruments, the clavichord, the harpsichord, and the virginal, with the strings either struck (as with the clavichord) or plucked (as with the other two). This clarity, however, comes with hindsight, as what seems obvious now was not at all evident at the time. The developmental strands of the keyboard's history are difficult to untangle, partially because through much of the fifteenth century these instruments were most often played in private chambers and left little record of their presence. Another contributing factor was that terminology was notoriously shifting and unstable. In addition we have only one detailed theoretical treatment of these instruments in the fifteenth century, again by Henri Arnaut of Zwolle, and even with this source the connection to actual musical practice is unclear. Exacerbating the problem is the complete absence of surviving instruments from the fifteenth century except for one from around 1480.

Typical of a period of intense creativity, instrument makers tried a great variety of mechanisms to activate strings from a keyboard, many of these being conceptual dead ends. While the Renaissance organ could draw upon traditions stretching back for many centuries, the notion of connecting a keyboard to a string instrument sprang from the imaginations of late fourteenth-century European makers and players unable to draw on any ancestry to pre-existing models. No shred of iconographical or archival evidence suggests such an innovation before that time. The first indication we have comes with a few documents in the 1360s that refer to an instrument called the chekker (or *eschiquier*). Iconographical sources from a later date seem to show the instrument as rather small, something on the order of perhaps a foot or slightly more wide, and twice as long. The illustrations

---

[72] In his description, Troiano referred to the regal as the "regale dolce," suggesting that at least on this occasion the tone quality of the regal was more refined (see *Die Münchner Fürstenhochzeit*, 144). On the instrumentation including the regal at the Medici wedding, see Brown, *Sixteenth-Century Instrumentation*, 133–5.

do not offer enough detail to be sure of the mechanism involved, but these were probably early versions of the clavichord.

As seen in so many other instrumental types, once the concept of a keyboard instrument took root, the ferment of players and makers produced rapid growth. A contemporary observer credited the unfortunate physician, Hermann Poll, with the invention of some kind of harpsichord.[73] By the 1440s Henri Arnaut could provide detailed drawings and descriptions of advanced types of both the clavichord and harpsichord; he even included discussion of what he called the *dulce melos* – in fact, what could have been a predecessor of the modern piano, though, like Leonardo's flying machines, this was apparently an unrealizable project.

Clavichord

The defining characteristic of the clavichord action is that when the player pressed down on a key, it activated a lever on the end of which was a brass tangent. The tangent struck the strings, but then stayed in contact with those strings, which vibrated as long as the key remained depressed. When the key was released, the strings dampened and ceased vibrating. With this action performers achieved subtle gradations of volume, but at its loudest the instrument was still very quiet. Because the key remained in contact with the string, another nuance possible is, with gentle action on the key, players could alter the sound with a subtle vibrato, a technique that was known as the *Bebung*. Probably to add a bit more resonance, clavichords were typically made with doubled strings tuned in unison, running parallel to the keyboard (or at a right angle to the keys).

The Renaissance clavichord (as shown in Figure 6.16) was a relatively small instrument, usually rectangular in shape, sometimes with no more than ten doubled strings. The keyboard was placed on the long side of the instrument. To achieve a wider range, the instrument was often built with an elaborate system of fretting and bending of levers by which each string was called upon to play three or four pitches – with the drawback, of course, that only one of those three or four pitches could be played at

---

[73] In a letter dated 1397, the instrument was called a *clavicembalum*; see Reinhard Strohm, *The Rise of European Music 1380–1500* (Cambridge, 1993), 92–3. In 1400, Poll was thirty-one at the time of his death, which would place the date of his reported invention to no earlier than about 1395.

Figure 6.16 Clavichord: Italian, end of the sixteenth or early seventeenth century, Boston, Museum of Fine Arts, Lesley Lindsey Mason Collection, 17.1796

any one time. By careful calculation of which pitches would be assigned to each key, though, the player could usually negotiate around any potential problems. And, of course, the contemporary harmonic system did not call for complicated chromatic combinations. The range varied considerably from instrument to instrument, but was usually at least three octaves (from F to f″, often with a short octave), with a four-octave range not at all exceptional.

With its sharply limited sound volume the clavichord found no consistent place in ensemble practice. It was versatile, on the other hand, for teaching and for practicing. Performers found the instrument appealing, as within its limited range it was highly responsive and capable of great expression. Given this capability, the clavichord could function effectively as a solo instrument in small spaces. Patrons, such as the duke of Bavaria, may well have called upon their keyboard players (Conrad Paumann, in this case) to perform in this way, but if they did, no documentary evidence of this has yet surfaced. Indeed, we know that Paumann played a variety of instruments – several are specifically mentioned – but in not a single instance was he recorded as playing the clavichord. If the instrument is indeed synonymous with references to the "manacordo" – and it is often translated as such – it appears prominently among the possessions of sixteenth-century amateur musicians.[74]

---

[74] See, for example, the many references to "manacordo" in the Venetian inventories listed by Toffolo, *Strumenti*, 55–63.

Harpsichord

The harpsichord usually had a winged shape with a characteristic "tail," and worked on an entirely different principle than the clavichord. When the player depressed a key it raised a wooden rod, the end of which activated a jack, which was fitted with a quill (or some other material). As the jack was levered upward, this quill plucked the string. The jack continued upward a short distance until it met a slot in a rail provided to halt and cushion its upward motion. When the key was lifted, the jack dropped (due to gravity), but the plucking device was designed to shift slightly to avoid plucking the string as it returned to its original position. At this point a damper stopped the vibration and silenced the string. Henri Arnaut had described and illustrated a different playing system, which may have achieved some currency in the earlier fifteenth century, but then fell out of use – probably because that system was quite complicated and would not have stood up well under severe playing circumstances.[75]

A distinctive characteristic of the playing mechanism, one that was by the eighteenth century seen as a disadvantage, is that the sound volume was uniform; the player could not vary the dynamic level by pressing harder or softer on the keys. Some instruments were built with only one set of strings. Other harpsichords were fitted with a second set of strings, which could be coupled to add volume or duplicate the note at the octave – but even here the additional strings were either on or off; no gradations of dynamic level were possible. Instruments in the earlier fifteenth century were small, with perhaps a range of two and a half octaves. By the end of the century, instruments of slightly more than three octaves (from F or G to a'') or even four octaves (from C to c''') were the norm. With these larger instruments the bottom fourth or fifth was built with the short octave (i.e., when F was the bottom note, $G\#$ and Bb would be omitted).

Assessing the place of the harpsichord in musical practice is particularly difficult for the fifteenth century as it was almost exclusively an instrument for private music making. For instruments central to ceremonial and public use we have a great deal of information. German civic records, for example, provide literally thousands of mentions of individual trumpeters, shawm players and lutenists. From these we can reasonably trace the arcs of development for these instruments and their ensemble combinations. By contrast, there are no more than a handful of German citations

---

[75] For Arnaut's text on harpsichords, see Herbert W. Myers, "String Keyboards." In *A Performer's Guide*, ed. Ross Duffin, 432–6. For a survey of Renaissance keyboard instruments, see Ashworth, "Keyboard Instruments." 206–21.

regarding keyboard string instruments. Italian records reflect the same bias; in D'Accone's massive study of music in Siena, there is not a single reference to the use of the harpsichord in the fifteenth century. Court and individual records, on the other hand, do allow at least occasional glimpses of harpsichords: a *magno cimbalo novit* was purchased at the court of Savoy in 1432;[76] an inventory of the household of Lorenzo de'Medici of 1492 listed eight harpsichords of various sizes;[77] Ferrara court documents mention harpsichords from time to time, though not until 1494 do the payrolls include a "maestro de clavicembalo."[78] The few references, taken along with ample iconographical examples and discussions of the harpsichord by theorists such as Henri Arnaut, point to the conclusion that the harpsichord was indeed a popular choice for private music making. Some instruments were reasonably large by early in the century (as the Savoy entry from 1432 suggests), and were thus capable of performing one or two lines within ensembles, or a solo repertory, such as that in *Faenza*.

The evolutionary pace of the harpsichord quickened in the sixteenth century, and by mid-century two distinct types had emerged, one Italian (as seen in Figure 6.17), the other Flemish. Italian instruments had thinner construction for their cases, were generally one-manual, and had a refined, elegant, and pleasingly dry tone quality. The cases of Flemish instruments were thicker, could be made with two manuals, and their tone was more assertive and robust.[79] Members of the Ruckers family of Antwerp were the preeminent makers of the Flemish instrument, which found a ready international market. In fact, an ample sampling of Ruckers instruments has survived into modern times. Both Italian and Flemish instruments were made in various sizes, with the larger instruments capable of ranges up to about four octaves. By the mid-sixteenth century the instrument began to challenge the primacy of the lute as a solo instrument. Gardane published a collection of music for harpsichord in 1551_5, and several other Italian publications followed in subsequent decades. More dramatic was the outpouring of music for solo harpsichord (or virginals) by English composers toward the end of the century. The harpsichord also became

---

[76] Robert John Bradley, "Musical Life and Culture at Savoy, 1420–1450," PhD diss., City University of New York (1992), 443.

[77] McGee, *Ceremonial Musicians*, 182, who also notes (208) that Giovanni Cellini, father of Benvenuto, was credited by his son as being a builder of harpsichords.

[78] Lockwood, *Music in Renaissance Ferrara*, 325. In 1461, though, there had been an individual payment for a performance by two Germans, one on *viola* the other on *cembalo*; see Kämper, "Studien zur instrumentalen Ensemblemusik des 16. Jahrhunderts in Italien," 89.

[79] For a concise discussion of the qualities of the two types, see Ashworth, "Keyboard Instruments," 216–19.

Figure 6.17 Harpsichord: Neapolitan, c.1550, Boston, Museum of Fine Arts, Arthur Tracy Cabot Fund, 1986.518

more prominent in ensemble performances, especially as the continuo concept of instruments providing a foundation function came into play. The incorporation of the harpsichord into large ensembles was especially clear in festival performances in Ferrara and Florence, but was also a feature seen in the Bavarian court wedding in 1568.[80] Finally, the instrument was favored by both amateurs and professionals. Concerning amateurs, a striking feature was the stature of those involved. Two harpsichords are listed in a 1503 inventory of the goods of Isabella, Queen of Spain. Margaret of Austria had been trained on the instrument in her youth, and as regent for the children of Philip the Fair after his death, she arranged for keyboard instruction for all the royal children, including Charles (later Charles V), Eleanor (later Queen of Portugal and then France), and Mary (queen of Hungary, later regent in the Netherlands). The star among the monarchs was Henry VIII who in his youth had immense enthusiasm for music, and was described in a 1516 report as "an excellent musician [who] plays well upon the harpsichord."[81] It hardly

---

[80] For instances of harpsichords in ensembles in Ferrara, see Newcomb, *The Madrigal at Ferrara*, I, 32–3; in Florence, see Brown, *Sixteenth-Century Instrumentation*, 94–102. For the Bavarian wedding, see Troiano, *Die Münchner Fürstenhochzeit*, 316.

[81] Ashbee, *Records*, VIII, 46.

needs saying, but whatever was fashionable among the royals would soon become fashionable everywhere else, but this prestige did not translate to the professional sphere. Certainly more musicians specialized in the harpsichord than had been the case earlier, but the celebrity keyboard players remained the organists. This had been the case from early in the sixteenth century, with Paul Hofhaimer and Arnolt Schlick as examples, to the end of the Renaissance, with such figures as Andrea and Giovanni Gabrieli. Only in the Baroque era could harpsichordists begin to match the stature of their organist colleagues.

Virginals and other string keyboards

"Virginal" is another of those exasperating terms that meant different things to different people. To a sixteenth-century German it meant a small rectangular harpsichord (as seen in Figure 6.18); to an Englishman at the

Figure 6.18 Virginals, title page from *Parthenia* (1612)

same time it was a generic term applied to all types and sizes of harpsichord. For our purposes we will suggest a flexible version of the former usage. That is, for most of Europe after about 1500, the virginal was a relatively small instrument similar in sounding mechanism to a harpsichord. One common form was rectangular with one set of strings running at right angles to the player, but just as likely were instruments with strings running at an oblique angle, with more complex polygonal shapes to accommodate that layout of the strings. Virginals were more often illustrated in contemporary art than were harpsichords, one reason being that virginals were smaller, less expensive, and thus more accessible than harpsichords, making the instrument more appropriate for the amateur musician. A further conclusion to be drawn is that a substantial market existed everywhere for virginals, and makers throughout Europe, especially in Italy, Germany, and Flanders, flourished in the sixteenth century. One result was that this relatively simple instrument came in a great structural variety – some with thin cases, others thicker, some with the keyboard placed in the center, others with the keyboard to the right or to the left. All of these variants gave the instrument an appealing versatility as well as a distinct effect on the sound.

The term spinet (*éspinette* in French, *spinetta* in Italian) assumed in the seventeenth century a rather specific meaning describing an instrument with a single set of strings running at an oblique angle from the keyboard. In the sixteenth century, however, the term was more likely much more general, probably a rough cognate of virginal. In any case, it was likely in most cases a small form of harpsichord. The *clavicytherium* was an upright harpsichord. It had the advantage of taking less horizontal space in a room, with the disadvantage that the jacks could not return to their resting position by gravity and needed to be assisted by a spring action of some sort. The *claviorganum* was an instrument that combined the harpsichord and organ – it was noted in a few documents, but evidently had little impact on actual musical practice.

IV. Wind instruments

Shawm and bombard: early fifteenth century

This illumination from the sumptuous Bible commissioned by Borso d'Este reveals the shawm band performing one of its primary functions: providing music for dancing, in this case for an elegant group of courtiers engaged in a round dance. The player on the far left is playing a shawm, the

Figure 6.19 Courtly dancing with wind band of shawm, bombard, and slide trumpet: Bible of Borso d'Este, executed under the direction of Taddeo Crivelli, 1455–61, Modena, Biblioteca Estense, Ms. VG 12 lat. 422–3, fol. 280 (detail). Alfredo Dagli Orti/ Art Resource, New York

one next to him a bombard. The shawm was a double-reed instrument, playing in the discant register. It had seven playing holes placed in the upper half of the instrument, as can be discerned by the hand positions in the illumination. What the image does not show is that with shawms eight holes were actually drilled, but the bottom hole was duplicated on the right and left side, allowing the player to choose to play it with either hand; the unused hole was then plugged with wax. The shawm was complex acoustically, and its sophisticated fingering system allowed it to play all the chromatic tones demanded by contemporary music. The bombard, pitched roughly a fifth lower was equipped (as discussed above) with a key for the lowest hole. This key mechanism, as shown in the illustration, was provided with a protective covering, the fontanelle.[82] Although this illustration is quite small and the details are unclear – the right hand of the bombard player is not visible, nor can we see anything of the reeds – the scene gives a very clear impression of the reed component of the ensemble.

[82] On the background and structure of the shawms, see Herbert W. Myers, "Reeds & Brass." In *A Performer's Guide*, ed. Ross Duffin, 386–90. Concerning the construction of the various sizes of shawms, including a survey of surviving instruments, see Frank P. Bär, *Holzblasinstrumente im 16. und frühen 17. Jahrhundert* (Tutzing, 2002).

A slide trumpet?

The third player is shown playing on what appears to be some form of trumpet. The left hand firmly grasps the mouthpiece between the index and second finger while the right hand is shown holding the body of the instrument, with the arm fully extended. The most striking feature here is the very long straight section between the mouthpiece and the curved tubing of the main body of the instrument. Heinrich Besseler argued years ago that this feature indicates that this instrument (and similar trumpets in numerous other contemporary illustrations of wind bands) was equipped with a single slide.[83] While most scholars accept this theory, it was questioned by Peter Downey. He argued that the first slide instrument was the trombone (that is, an instrument with two sliding tubes) and that there was no intermediate stage of a slide trumpet.[84] Downey suggests that the instrument shown here is a natural trumpet – one not equipped with a slide – and then only capable of the few notes of the harmonic series, like the modern bugle. Such an instrument could not have provided the full range of notes necessary for sophisticated counterpoint. Admittedly, the visual sources do not allow for certainty, as Renaissance artists lacked the modern cartoonist's clever technique of being able to show motion – in this case, of a slide moving back and forth. Still, scores of fifteenth-century illustrations show ensembles with two or three shawms performing with a trumpet-like instrument. In most of these, we can clearly discern that the player is holding the instrument with one hand near the mouthpiece, and the other further down on the instrument in just the manner we would expect from a slide trumpet (an instrument with a single slide). In fact, a surprising number of these can be dated after 1480, well after the principle of the double slide was unquestionably known. Moreover, the date of the image places it during the period when performers on the instrument played contrapuntal lines, thus requiring a slide. In sum, the archival, iconographical, and theoretical sources still lean towards the conclusion that a slide trumpet in some form was developed by about 1420.

---

[83] Heinrich Besseler, *Bourdon und Fauxbourdon* (Leipzig, 1950), 85 and 189; the illumination is given between pages 88 and 89.

[84] Peter Downey, "The Renaissance Slide Trumpet: Fact or Fiction," *EM* 12 (1984), 26–33; see, however, the responses in *EM* 17 (1987) by Duffin (397–402), Myers (382–9), and Polk (389–96). See also Myers, "Reeds & Brass." In *A Performer's Guide*, ed. Ross Duffin, 390–2.

The bagpipe, pipe and tabor, and douçaine

The bagpipe's characteristics set it distinctly apart from other winds. With this instrument, air was blown through a blowpipe into a leather bag (equipped with a flap that trapped the air between breaths). Air pressure was then applied by an elbow pressing on the bag, which supplied air to the double-reed chanter and to the drone pipe. Once the performer started the airflow it was continuous, meaning that variations in dynamics were not possible, nor were articulations.[85] The only way to create the effect of breaks was to apply "graces" – that is, short, embellishment-like figures. Moreover, because the instrument could not overblow, its range was limited by the number of finger holes, usually seven, or roughly an octave, on the chanter. It was primarily a diatonic instrument, and the performer was unable to make any adjustments in intonation once the airflow was in progress.

The bagpipe had a considerable vogue in the late fourteenth century, often providing the third voice to the duet of shawm and bombard or, indeed, as a companion to a single shawm. The bagpipe then fell out of favor in that role – due no doubt to its limitation of range, inflexibility with regard to dynamics, and inability to provide articulations – and the slide trumpet/trombone took over within the shawm band. However, it by no means disappeared, and it continued to be popular as a rustic instrument, as attested by the vivid images by Brueghel (Figure 6.20), and was affectionately imitated in lute and keyboard music in drone pieces entitled "Piva."[86] The sound of the bagpipe is unique, and even in more elevated circles it was called upon from time to time; German courts had a particular fondness for the instrument.[87] After its fourteenth-century vogue, however, it was only rarely combined with other instruments.

The pipe and tabor (*tambourin* in French) occupied a unique niche in the Renaissance – it was a one-person band, in which the musician manipulated both a pipe (a three-hole duct flute) with one hand and a tabor (a small two-headed drum) with the other. The pipe, designed to overblow easily, had a range of a twelfth or perhaps a bit more, enough to play whatever melody might be needed for dancing, which was its primary function. The *tambourin* was ubiquitous in European court life throughout the fifteenth and early sixteenth centuries (Margaret of Austria, for example, had a player attached to her modest court), probably because it was so handy. This musician could be called upon at a moment's notice to provide a perfectly satisfactory

---

[85] For a particularly well-informed treatment of the bagpipe, see Adam Gilbert, "Bagpipe." In *A Performer's Guide*, ed. Ross Duffin, 399–411.
[86] See *SBS* 6.   [87] See Polk, *German Instrumental Music*, 54–6.

Figure 6.20 Peasants dancing to bagpipes: Pieter Brueghel the Elder (1568), Vienna, Kunsthistorisches Museum. Erich Lessing/Art Resource, New York

accompaniment to any dance desired. For all its popularity, though, the pipe and tabor almost never performed with other instruments – it existed in a musical world of its own.

The douçaine remained until recently one of the most maddeningly inscrutable instruments of the Renaissance, mentioned often enough to take notice of its presence, but almost never with enough substance to understand exactly what this mysterious instrument was. Working from the brief description by Tinctoris, along with the fortuitous survival of an instrument from the sixteenth-century shipwreck of the *Mary Rose*, Myers suggests that this was a cylindrical bore, double-reed instrument.[88] Because of this characteristic, the range of the douçaine was limited to those notes possible by the single set of finger holes (evidently seven holes on the front, with a thumb hole on the reverse, thus yielding one note more than an octave). Despite its narrow range, it evidently possessed a gentler timbre than the shawm and, as a result, seemed to have had a consistent, if understated appeal, especially in the fifteenth century. It was evidently an instrument for professionals and usually played in consorts.

---

[88] Myers, "Reeds & Brass." In *A Performer's Guide*, ed. Ross Duffin, 393–5, summarizes his views on the instrument. See also Charles Foster, "Tinctoris' Imperfect Dulcina Perfected: The Mary Rose Still Shawm," *GSJ* 58 (2005), 46–50, 214.

The wind band c.1500

We have two witnesses to the music played for the coronation of Francesco Todeschini Piccolomini as Pope Pius III in 1503: one is Pinturicchio's fresco in the Piccolomini Library in the Siena Duomo, a detail of which is shown in Figure 6.21; the other is a written description by Simone (?) Borghesi. Borghesi stated that in a ceremony held in Siena immediately following the coronation in Rome, a polyphonic *Te Deum* was sung with a choir alternating with an ensemble consisting of one shawm ("tibia una") and three trombones ("tribus ... trombones").[89] Pinturicchio, on the other hand, chose to portray a more conservative trio of shawm, bombard, and trombone. The subject of the fresco (completed a year or two after the events concerned) was presumably of the coronation itself, held in Rome. In any case, these two testimonies reveal the diverging forces acting on the

Figure 6.21 Ceremony with wind band of shawm, bombard, and trombone: coronation of Pope Pius III, Bernardino Pinturicchio (*c*.1504), Siena, Libreria Piccolomini. Scala/Art Resource, New York

---

[89] For a translation of the Borghesi text, see Carter, *The Trombone in the Renaissance*, 126.

wind ensemble in the sixteenth century. The core unit shown by Pinturicchio remained essentially the same as shown in the Borso Bible in Figure 6.19: a trio of shawm, bombard, and a slide instrument, the latter being most probably a tenor trombone, held much as the modern instrument with the instrument grasped firmly by the left hand while the right hand manipulates the slide. The first hints of the double slide are to be found around 1450, but the trombone did not find more widespread use until about 1475.[90] In any case, the forces of the wind band shown in the fresco had been relatively stable for almost a century with a core unit of three instruments – a shawm, bombard, and a brass instrument. Borghesi's description, however, with one shawm and multiple trombones, is just one symptom of the forces that would upend established traditions. Shortly after 1500, wind players played in groups of six or even eight, and with this came an expansion of range, especially into the bass register. With the desire for a greater variety of color, wind players combined routinely in ways that were unthinkable two or three decades earlier. Until the end of the fifteenth century, the wind ensemble continued to work in isolation. But within a breathtakingly short time, that isolation broke down and wind performers became an integral part of the larger community of performers. All these changes deeply affected their performance practices.

Cornetts and trombones

Of the newer timbres acquired by wind players, the most important were those produced by the cornett, a soprano instrument made in two main forms. The standard cornett, most often curved, was made of wood, with six finger holes and a thumb hole. With a conical bore, it was played with a small mouthpiece inserted in the upper end, and in the sixteenth century had a range from g to a''. The mute cornett was of about the same size, though straight, and the mouthpiece was built in to the instrument, which produced a softer sound. By mid-century there were attempts to make cornetts in larger sizes, but in the Renaissance only a slighter larger size (a tenor instrument) found any significant use – the development of a bass form, the serpent, came later.[91] The cornett burst on the scene shortly before 1500 and quickly found three main uses, as a soprano in the shawm band, as a solo instrument joined to a vocal choir, or with one or two cornetts in combination with trombones.

---

[90] On the fifteenth-century iconography of the trombone, see ibid., 17–59.
[91] For a brief description, see Myers, "Reeds & Brass." In *A Performer's Guide*, ed. Ross Duffin, 395; for a more extensive discussion, see Douglas Kirk, "Cornet." In *A Performer's Guide*, ed. Jeffery Kite-Powell, 106–25.

Figure 6.22 Cornett and trombone with vocal ensemble: Hans Burgkmair and others, *The Triumph of Maximilian I*, c.1518, plate 26

This latter combination became a standard ensemble when instruments were combined with voices. Indeed, one of the greatest of the sixteenth-century cornettists, Girolamo Dalla Casa (c.1530–1601), wrote in his *Il vero modo di diminuir* (1584_2) that "Among wind instruments, the most excellent is the cornetto for imitating the human voice ... This instrument can play *piano et forte* and in all manner of tone, as with the voice."[92]

As early as about 1515 Hans Burgkmair showed a cornett and trombone performing with Maximilian's choir, and while he only showed one of each in the final version of his woodcut, according to the text of the program, "On the cart should be the choir, and also cornett players and trombonists."[93] In Figure 6.22 Burgkmair clearly ran into space limitations; he was unable to show an adult choir of more than a dozen singers on the float and still have room for five or six instrumentalists, particularly for the trombonists who needed extra room to extend their slides. His solution was to include just the leaders of each contingent, Augustine Schubinger

---

[92] Girolamo Dalla Casa, *Il vero modo di diminuir* (Venice, 1584), "Del Cornetto," fol. 2v.
[93] Appelbaum, ed., *The Triumph of Maximilian I*, in the unpaginated introduction, see item number 26.

on cornett and Georg Stewdlin on trombone, to stand in for the entire ensemble. The full ensemble would probably have been in five parts, with two cornetts and three trombones.

Recorders

The recorder was a great favorite among wind players in the Renaissance. While this instrument is played with a mouthpiece inserted in the lips, as a member of the duct flute family the sound is actually produced by the air passing through an aperture that is then directed across a fixed sharpened edge, as is clearly seen in the detail from Titian's *The Three Ages of Man* (Figure 6.23).[94] That is, the player's lips do not control the pitch or volume. As a result (and as with the crumhorn, described below), the control of

Figure 6.23 Recorder: detail from *The Three Ages of Man*, Titian, c.1512–14, Edinburgh, National Galleries of Scotland. Erich Lessing/Art Resource, New York

---

[94] Howard Mayer Brown, "The Recorder in the Middle Ages and Renaissance." In *The Cambridge Companion to the Recorder*, ed. John Mansfield Thomson (Cambridge, 1995), 1–25, provides a useful overview. For further on the recorder in the fifteenth century, see Herbert W. Myers, "Flutes." In *A Performer's Guide*, ed. Ross Duffin, 378–82; for the sixteenth century, see Myers, "Recorder." In *A Performer's Guide*, ed. Jeffery Kite-Powell, 55–70. Details of construction, including a discussion of surviving instruments, are treated in Bär, *Holzblasinstrumente*.

intonation and volume is restricted. Because the recorder did not require highly developed muscular control of the embouchure (as was necessary for the cornett, shawm, and trombone), the instrument was popular with amateurs during the Renaissance, as it is today. While relatively simple to play, the internal design of the recorder was very complex. Some were made with more cylindrical bores, other were conical. Perhaps the most common type was one with seven finger holes and a thumb hole that gradually constricted from the upper tone holes to the lowest, with a modest flare to the end.[95] The instrument was capable of an ample range; by overblowing at least an octave and a sixth was possible, with some instrumental designs allowing slightly more, perhaps as much as two octaves.[96] It was from the early fifteenth century onward a consort instrument, but two sizes, soprano and tenor, sufficed for much of the fifteenth century, and even into the early sixteenth century apparently three sizes, soprano, tenor, and bass, were all that were needed for most musical configurations. After 1500, however, a larger choice of other sizes was added, and indeed, recorders were commonly available in more sizes than was the case for any other wind instrument.[97]

Crumhorns

Another popular alternative timbre for wind players from about 1500 was the crumhorn. The instrument had limitations; its double reed was enclosed in a windcap, which meant that the reed did not come into direct contact with the player's lips, resulting in intonation being more difficult to control and the range of volume restricted. With seven finger holes, a thumb hole, and a narrow bore (basically cylindrical), the range was limited to barely more than an octave. Still, the distinctive buzzing quality of the crumhorn had a wide appeal. It had two uses, either as a complete consort (it was commonly made in soprano, alto, tenor, and bass sizes), or

---

[95] For a simple explanation of this see Myers, "Recorder," 58–9. For a more extensive treatment, see Adrian Brown, "An Overview of the Surviving Renaissance Recorders." In *Musicque de Joye*, ed. David Lasocki, 79–85.

[96] For the ranges possible, based essentially on the bore design (whether predominantly conical or cylindrical), see Peter Van Heyghen, "The Recorder Consort in the Sixteenth Century: Dealing with the Embarrassment of Riches." In *Musicque de Joye*, ed. David Lasocki, 244–53.

[97] Some idea of the sizes of instruments available can be gleaned from surviving inventories. The Antwerp civic ensemble in 1532, for example, had twenty-nine recorders available (and only two trombones), while an inventory of the English court in 1542 listed well over 100 recorders of all sizes. See David Lasocki, "A Listing of Inventories and Purchases of Flutes, Recorders, Flageolets, and Tabor Pipes, 1388–1630." In *Musicque de Joye*, ed. David Lasocki, 429–30 and 435–6. See also Polk, *German Instrumental Music*, 75.

Figure 6.24 Consort of crumhorns: Hans Burgkmair and others, *The Triumph of Maximilian I*, c.1518, plate 20

with one or two crumhorns inserted into the shawm band, as seen in Figure 6.24, with two bombards, two crumhorns, and one trombone. As with the shawms, trombones, and cornetts, the crumhorn in the sixteenth century was principally an instrument for professionals; it is, however, a great favorite of amateur players in modern times.[98]

Flute

The story behind the use of the transverse flute is unusually complex and layered. The flute was made with a cylindrical bore and only six finger holes (there was no thumb hole), but because of the ease of overblowing had an unusually large range of two octaves or more. It had been a fairly popular instrument in the fourteenth century, but seems mysteriously to have vanished from use after about 1400. Around 1470 it began to reemerge, but in a distinctly limited context in which it was paired with a field drum, a musical tandem that was particularly identified with Swiss military units.

---

[98] On the history and structure of the crumhorn, see Barra Boydell, *The Crumhorn and other Renaissance Windcap Instruments* (Buren, 1982).

Figure 6.25 Flute, with lute and singer: Master of the Female Half Lengths, first half of the sixteenth century, St. Petersburg, the Hermitage Museum. Scala/Art Resource, New York[99]

As the Swiss infantry was the most feared of the time the identification brought with it a certain cachet. Soon thereafter, flute and drum pairs were attached to many courts of high nobles of the late fifteenth century. At some point early in the sixteenth century larger groups of flutists came into fashion, and by about 1530 ensembles of flutes, now played by courtly or civic wind players, were more commonly heard. The flute consort consisted of three sizes, with frequent sounding bottom pitches of G, d, and a, with other configurations possible; while called bass, tenor, and discant, the "bass"

---

[99] For an iconographical study of this painting and its musical inscription, see H. Colin Slim, "Paintings of Lady Concerts and the Transmission of 'Jouissance vous donneray.'"
In *Painting Music in the Sixteenth Century: Essays in Iconography*, ed. H. Colin Slim (New York, 2002), VII.

was more or less the equivalent of the modern alto flute, the tenor the modern flute, and the discant about halfway between the flute and the modern piccolo. With these bottom pitches, the consort of course played the contemporary repertory an octave higher than written.[100]

The flute enjoyed a considerable vogue as an amateur instrument, as two of Attaingnant's first ensemble publications included some pieces specifically designated for transverse flutes. These prints were clearly intended for an amateur, not a professional, market.[101] Through much of the first half of the sixteenth century flutes were more usually played in consorts, but by the late sixteenth century a flute was quite often incorporated into mixed ensembles.

Wind band with shawms: late sixteenth century

Beginning around 1550, challenges to the preeminent status of the shawm band intensified, but this ensemble nonetheless retained its artistic vitality well beyond the turn of the next century. In Figure 6.26, Denijs Alsloot provided a late example, from about 1615, of a six-part ensemble with a shawm, cornett, two tenor shawms, a trombone, and a curtal. By 1540, as the ranges expanded to accommodate six and more parts, the search for an adequate bass instrument for the wind ensemble became a serious issue. The tenor-size trombone, of which the instrument drawn by Alsloot is an example, is limited in its ability to reach into the bass register by the length of the player's arm; the lowest practical note for use in counterpoint is about F or G at the bottom of the bass clef. A bass size of the shawm was known, but was so long that it could not have been carried by a player for such occasions as the procession shown here. Similarly, instrument makers developed a bass trombone, made possible by a lever attached to the slide that permitted the player to extend the slide beyond the normal reach. The instrument was, however, also cumbersome to play, and was unstable in terms of its construction, handicaps that made its use in processions (a common demand on wind players at the time) problematic. In short, neither the bass shawm nor the bass trombone, while useful in certain contexts, was completely satisfactory.

A solution that did meet the requirements of wind band performance was to fold two halves of the bass shawm upon itself, as we see with the

---

[100] This is a highly simplified explanation of a complex, multifaceted subject; see Myers, "Renaissance Flute." In *A Performer's Guide*, ed. Jeffery Kite-Powell, 72–5.

[101] The two (*Chansons musicales a quatre parties* and *Vingt & sept chansons musicales a quatre parties*) were both published by Attaingnant in Paris, 1533_2 and 1533_3.

286   *Renaissance instruments: images and realities*

Figure 6.26 Wind band with shawms, trombone, cornett, and curtal: procession in Brussels in Honor of Archduchess Isabella (1615), Denijs Alsloot, 1616, Madrid, Prado Museum. Album/Art Resource, New York

curtal illustrated above; this is, of course, also the form of the modern bassoon. The instrument then became easily portable, and after about 1550 it was widely adopted. The move into the bass range created a kind of torsion internally within the ensemble. The traditional bombard, which was the tenor instrument in the fifteenth century, was not capable of low tenor parts, and a new, larger size was developed. As Ross Duffin suggested, by about 1550 "a fully equipped shawm band might consist of one or two trebles, one or two altos, one or two sackbuts, and one basset or bass shawm."[102] And, of course, a cornett or two might be an alternative in the treble range, and the curtal increasingly functioned as the bass, as we see in the Alsloot painting.

Trumpets: early fifteenth century

The illustration of the month of May in the *Très riches heures du duc de Berry*, executed around 1415, presents the most sumptuous illustration of wind

---

[102] Ross W. Duffin, "Shawm and Curtal." In *A Performer's Guide*, ed. Jeffery Kite-Powell, 86–7. For an extended treatment of technical features of the shawms, see Bär, *Holzblasinstrumente*.

Figure 6.27 Trumpets heading a procession of nobles: the Limbourg brothers, 1412–16, "May" from the *Très Riches Heures du Duc de Berry*, Ms. 65, fol. 5v (detail). Chantilly, Musée Condé. ©RMN-Grand Palais/Art Resource, New York

musicians of the entire century. The artist of Figure 6.27, probably one of the Limbourg brothers, was attempting to give an accurate portrayal of an elegant outing and procession of the ducal court. At the point illustrated, a mixed group of men and women of the court are being led by musicians evidently on their return toward Paris, the towers of which are shown in the distance. Still, however spectacular, it is a work of art and is in fact only accurate up to a point. The numbers of instrumentalists are approximately correct: two trumpets are shown, the normal number supported by the high nobility at this time. One of the instruments is a straight herald trumpet with the other in the folded form of the modern natural trumpet. The folded form verifies the fact that by the late fourteenth century (sometime between about 1370 and 1400) metal workers had mastered the intricacies of bent tubing, but the illustration also reveals that this more modern form did not supplant the straight outline that had been known since antiquity. Both types of instrument are largely cylindrical with the bell segment made more conical, ending in a final flare at the bell. Three players of shawms are also present, again the numbers appropriate for a ducal household. The trumpets were placed at the front of the procession where they would be most effective, particularly to announce the arrival of the noble party as the procession made its way back into the city.

Some details are slightly awry, however. The banners of the trumpets – only the trumpets have them, not the shawms – are shown without a coat of arms, which is curious given the lavish detail of the clothing of the courtly men and women. In addition, trumpets at this time were constructed in several pieces, held together by clearly defined joints, called *ferrules*; these joints are not shown. Further, the bells of the three shawms are all clearly illustrated, and none are equipped with a fontanelle that would cover and protect the key mechanism needed for a larger size of shawm. In other words, no tenor instrument is present if the artist is to be believed, which would be highly unlikely for musical reasons. More important, the folded trumpet is shown performing with the shawms while the other trumpeter holds his instrument at rest over his shoulder. As shown above, 1415 was the time archival documents began to mention a new kind of musician, the player of "minstrel trumpet" who was added to the shawmists, one evidently playing a trumpet now equipped with a slide mechanism. What the scene reveals is that during this early period of transition, as a slide instrument was incorporated into the wind band, the player of the brass instrument sometimes shifted back and forth between the wind band and the trumpet grouping. A probable explanation for this scene is that at the moment shown, the assembly is still outside the city walls and the wind band (with the slide trumpet) is playing a kind of afternoon serenade. As the procession entered the city, that trumpet player would have joined his herald trumpet colleague and begun to play appropriate fanfares. In any case, the illustration shows two forms of the trumpet and further adds iconographic evidence that indicate that two trumpets formed a normal unit in noble households of the time.

Figure 6.28 Trumpets in procession: Hans Burgkmair and others, *The Triumph of Maximilian I*, c.1518, plate 117

Trumpets: sixteenth century

During the course of the fifteenth century, the trumpet became ever more central to the projection of noble image. While two trumpets sufficed for even the highest nobility at the beginning of the century, by c.1450 prominent nobles had expanded their trumpet bands to five or six. The growth continued to the end of the century, and by 1500, nobles of this stature, with Maximilian I providing an example, could call on ensembles of a dozen, backed up by several players of large kettledrums. When these trumpet bands appeared in force in front of their lord on entering a city, they were undoubtedly capable of an awesome racket.

While Maximilian's career in political affairs was littered with failures, his forays in the artistic sphere (as embodied in the *The Triumph of Maximilian*) were a smashing success. *The Triumph* was envisioned by Maximilian as a representation of the aspirations and accomplishments of his reign as seen through a vast procession. Though the project was left unfinished on his death, 137 magnificent woodcuts were completed. Among these were three with images of "The Imperial Trumpeters."[103] Shown in Figure 6.28 are twenty-five trumpeters accompanied by five

---

[103] Appelbaum, ed., *The Triumph of Maximilian I*, plates 115–17.

players of kettledrums. While those numbers were grossly exaggerated, Maximilian's intent with this publication was to establish a legacy. As he himself said, "Whoever prepares no memorial for himself during his lifetime has none after his death and is forgotten along with the sound of the bell that tolls his passing."[104] "Accuracy," in other words, was not a priority. The illustrations nonetheless tell us a great deal. All the trumpets are decorated with banners, and all appear to be of about the same size and shape. While there were quite possibly some players who specialized in the higher register, they would have done so without resorting to smaller instruments. The trumpet band continued throughout the sixteenth century in roughly the same configuration as with Maximilian. Henry VIII maintained between a dozen and fifteen players, while the illustration of the trumpet ensemble present at the funeral procession of Charles V in Brussels shows thirteen players with two kettledrums.[105]

Two parallel tracks can be discerned concerning trumpet performance practice in the sixteenth century. One continued the complete separation of trumpets from other instrumentalists. In this tradition the isolation of trumpeters was exaggerated, in that to maintain their stature their techniques continued to be passed down from one player to another in a deliberately secretive way. No sixteenth-century sources of trumpet music have survived. Not until the seventeenth century, with the further development of the clarino register, did trumpeters begin to join mainstream music making.[106]

Pragmatic considerations were at the root of the second track. Maintaining separate ensembles of shawms and of trumpets was very costly. Yet apprentice wind players were trained to double in a general training that included instruction on the trumpet. It was obvious that one way a patron could save considerable expense was to combine the functions of the wind band and trumpet ensembles. This was the approach

---

[104] Ibid., Introduction (unpaginated).
[105] For the illustration, see Tom L. Naylor, *The Trumpet & Trombone in Graphic Arts, 1500–1800* (Nashville, 1979), plate 140.
[106] In one notable exception, Cesare Bendinelli, a trumpeter at the Munich court from 1580, prepared a manuscript trumpet method that he presented to the Accademia Filarmonica in Verona in 1614, which contains pieces dated 1584, 1587, and 1588. See Edward Tarr, *The Trumpet* (London, 1988), 70–4. On the development of the specialization in various registers (particularly that of the clarino register) in the sixteenth century, see ibid., 68–79. Tarr's volume is also useful for the discussion of surviving instruments from the Renaissance; see ibid., 79–84.

taken, for example, at the Danish royal court. In fact the extensive ensemble manuscripts prepared there at mid-century were compiled by a court trumpet player – but when he and his colleagues performed that repertory they would have played them on various wind instruments, not on the trumpet.[107]

---

[107] These manuscripts (*Copenhagen* and *Copenhagen 1873*) are discussed in *SBS* 9.

Epilogue: function and fantasy

In this book, we have explored the contributions of instrumentalists to the culture, daily life, and sound of the Renaissance, as well as the broad infrastructure – institutional, domestic, commercial, and artisanal – that supported their activity. For the listener, instrumental music could be either diffuse or focused, depending on the function, and through the various techniques players used to adapt, arrange, and improvise, their music was heard along a continuum of being familiar, merely recognizable, to unfamiliar. Even in situations where their music was formulaic or functional – the musicians playing "on the fences," as we have quoted Galilei earlier in the book, or the trumpeter signaling – nowhere should we apply the modern term "background music" to the contributions of Renaissance instrumentalists. When bells sounded the hours of work and rest, an instrumentalist was responsible; when soldiers marched to battle, flute players and drummers guided their formation; and when arrivals of nobility were announced by trumpet fanfares, those instrumentalists defined class, rank, and conveyed a sense of awe. In all these cases, Renaissance musicians were responsive to the spaces in which they played, creating an important connection between location, function, and sound: loud and soft were not merely categories of amplitude and instrumentation, but evoked distinct social and cultural settings.

If the presence of instrumental music was considered an essential element in Renaissance daily life, what instrumentalists actually played is one of the main questions this book has hoped to answer. A painting shows a civic ensemble standing on a tower: what were the musicians playing? A document of 1483 from the Low Countries indicates that the ensemble in Kampen was expected to play written pieces, *twe gesette stucken*.[1] That task might seem similar to performance in our time; when an orchestra programs a Brahms symphony the musicians play the notes on the page staying as close to the written document as they are able. Playing a "written piece" in the Renaissance, however, merely opened up a range of possibilities. As we have documented in several case- and source-based

---

[1] Polk, *German Instrumental Music*, 122.

studies, an ensemble could indeed defer to the written notes of the original text. But more often one of a number of creative possibilities would enter. The players could add decorative embellishments to individual lines; they might improvise an additional part onto the written structure; or they might dispense with an original part or two and substitute new ones. For them the idea of a fixed, privileged text didn't exist. Soloists, controlling the entire structure themselves, had an even greater range of options. The lutenist Francesco da Milano or vihuelist Alonso Mudarra could take a chanson, motet, or Mass section, intabulate it close to the original, adapt it through embellishment, or extract from it various motives and weave those into a new *fantasia sopra* or *glosa*. Some of these "pieces" were ultimately written out, but it was clear that these and other instrumentalists could provide them on the spot. In short, for Renaissance instrumentalists a "piece" was more a fluid concept than a fixed object, a process not a product. And this idea introduces a fundamental challenge to a prevailing orthodoxy that an *Urtext* edition is a representative text that would have been recognized. Indeed, it is likely that a person in the Renaissance heard a chanson by Crecquillon or Clemens more often in decorated instrumental arrangements than as a texted chanson.

Not only was the approach to the musical text quite fluid, so was the notion of musical genres. By the eighteenth century, purely instrumental genres such as the symphony, sonata, and concerto dictated formal and musical structures. In the Renaissance, vocal forms, particularly the chanson and motet, formed the backbone of the instrumental repertory. Instead of idiomatic features being inherent in the structure of the piece, as is the case of a Beethoven symphony, for much of the Renaissance the basic outline of a work for instruments was vocal in concept. Idiomatic features – decorations, diminutions, transpositions – were to be added in, but even then, instrumental teachers stressed that their students should model their performance on the human voice. Throughout the era there was a commonality between what was sung and what was played, and one of the central points in this book has been to stress this fundamental connection between vocal and instrumental music.

In other ways, however, we have noted how the worlds between singers and players were very different. This began with their training. Singers were educated in church choir schools; instrumentalists were trained as apprentices in the system characteristic of guilds. Choirboys learned not only how to sing counterpoint, but to read and write music, and they also received at least a basic general education, enough that in many cases they were prepared to enter into a university when they reached maturity. Training for instrumentalists, especially before the advent of printing, was an aural process. Instrumentalists may have been literate, but that was not an essential part of their pedagogical program. And, of course, the career path for singers was not at all like that of instrumentalists. One often-overlooked difference had particular impact: since most singers took religious orders and were therefore required to be celibate, father–son networks, which, as we have noted, were sustained among instrumentalists, were nipped in the proverbial bud for singers. Finally, we have mapped the different national profiles of singers and instrumentalists. Singers (and singer/composers) from the Low Countries and northern France dominated the important court and cathedral choirs in Europe, and particularly Italy, from early in the fifteenth century to at least 1550. In instrumental music, two different tendencies can be identified: German musicians achieved a kind of preeminence from about 1400 to 1520, yet local traditions remained strong in every region. Florence often imported German players in the civic ensemble; Venice, on the other hand, maintained an ensemble without drawing on any foreigners at all. Ensembles in the Low Countries drew on players from northern France at least as often as from Germany – though there, too, a vast majority of the players were regional if not local.

Finally, where and how does instrumental music fit in with the great human developments – the "highlight reel" – traditionally identified with the Renaissance: perspective, Humanism, Gutenberg, Copernicus, Leonardo, exploration, counterpoint? For instrumentalists, we can view this at the macro as well as micro level. At the former came critical technical and compositional changes in the way instrumentalists operated, and the end of the fifteenth century marked a breaking point almost as definitive as any in the history of the field. At that defining moment, the nature of the raw material changed as imitation became a common compositional approach and more parts were added to the texture. This resulted in an entirely new sound, as instrumentalists shifted from a previous emphasis on improvisation to one that was more dependent on a composed text. At the micro level, we could cite crucial improvements in the manufacture of instruments and the invention of new ones. Instruments were constantly being adapted and modified in response to changing compositional developments, requiring more strings, greater range, more resonant materials, and, in the sixteenth century, the creation of "offspring" in order to form instrument families to match the ranges and styles of ensemble vocal music. Once again, there was a distinct tipping point, with a flood of new instruments and techniques arriving, not surprisingly, at about 1500.

In this sense, the Renaissance represents a study in opposites. In some areas, conditions for instrumentalists were utterly transformed; nothing makes this clearer than their "status." Around 1400 they were tagged as minstrels and considered among the lower rungs within the hierarchy of musicians. Not a single major composer in the mid-fifteenth century was listed on the payrolls as an instrumentalist. By 1600 the change could not have been greater – by then *all* major composers began their careers as players. Still, there were elements of unity throughout the period. The shawm remained a basic ingredient of the wind ensemble into the seventeenth century; the lute, once it rose to prominence in the early fifteenth century, remained a premier instrument for more than two centuries. In some areas, providing music for dancing, particularly improvisation, was as essential a tool for players in 1580 as it was in 1420. Transformation and tradition were twin forces cutting across all levels of music making throughout the era.

Bibliography

Primary theoretical and secondary sources

Agricola, Martin. *Musica instrumentalis deudsch*. Wittemberg, 1529. Translated and edited by William E. Hettrick. *Musica instrumentalis deudsch: A Treatise on Musical Instruments (1529 and 1545) by Martin Agricola*. Cambridge, 1994.

Anglés, Higinio. *La Música en la corte de Carlos V*. Monumentos de la Música Española II. Revised 2nd edition. Barcelona, 1984.

[Anonymous]. *Het Boeck van al 't gene datter geschiet es binnen Brugge sichtent Jaer 1477, 14 Frebuarii, tot 1491*. Maatschappy der Vlaemsche Bibliophilen. Ed. Charles Carton. Ser. 2, no. 2 Ghent, 1859.

Apel, Willi. *Keyboard Music of the Fourteenth and Fifteenth Centuries*. Corpus of Early Keyboard Music, I, n.p., 1963.

Appelbaum, Stanley, ed. *The Triumph of Maximilian I*. New York, 1964.

[Arnaut de Zwolle, Henri]. *Instruments de musique du XVe siècle; les traités d'Henri-Arnaut de Zwolle et de divers anonymes (Ms. B.N. latin 7295*. Ed. G. Le Cerf and E.-R. Labande. Paris, 1932.

Arnold, Denis. *Giovanni Gabrieli and the Music of the Venetian High Renaissance*. Oxford, 1979.

Ashbee, Andrew, ed. *Records of English Court Music, Volume VII, 1485–1558*. Aldershot and Brookfield, Vermont, 1993.

Ashworth, Jack. "Keyboard Instruments." In *A Performer's Guide*. Ed. Kite-Powell, 206–21.

Atlas, Allan. *Renaissance Music: Music in Western Europe, 1400-1600*. New York, 1998.

Baines, Anthony. *Brass Instruments: Their History and Development*. New York, 1976, reprint, 1993.

Woodwind Instruments and their History. 3rd edition. New York, 1967.

Banks, Jon. *The Instrumental Consort Repertory of the Late Fifteenth Century*. Aldershot and Burlington, Vermont, 2006.

Bär, Frank P. *Holzblasinstrumente im 16. und frühen 17. Jahrhundert*. Tutzing, 2002.

Ballester, Jordi. "An Unexpected Discovery: The Fifteenth-Century Angel Musicians of the Valencia Cathedral," *Music in Art* 33 (2008), 11–29.

Barblan, Guglielmo. "Vita musicale alla corte sforzesca." *Storia di Milano* 9 (1961), 787–852.

Baroncini, Rodolfo. "Zorzi Trombetta and the Band of *Piffari* and Trombones of the *Serenissima*: New Documentary Evidence." Trans. Hugh Ward-Perkins, *HBSJ* 14 (2002), 59–82.

"Zorzi Trombetta da Modon and the Founding of the Band of *Piffari* and *Tromboni* of the *Serenissima*." *HBSJ* 16 (2004), 1–17.

Bassano, Giovanni. *Ricercare, Passaggi et Cadentie* (Venice, 1585). Ed. Richard Erig. Zürich, 1976.

[Beck, Sidney]. *The First Book of Consort Lessons for Treble and Bass Viols, Flute, Lute, Cittern and Pandora Collected by Thomas Morley, 1559–1661.* Reconstructed and edited by Sidney Beck. New York, 1954.

Bent, Margaret. *Counterpoint, Composition and Musica Ficta*. New York and London, 2002.

"Editing Early Music: The Dilemma of Translation." *EM* 22 (1994), 372–92.

"The Musical Stanzas in Martin Le Franc's *Le Champion des Dames*." In *Music and Medieval Manuscripts, Paleography and Performance: Essays Dedicated to Andrew Hughes*. Ed. John Haines and Randall Rosenfeld. Aldershot and Burlington, Vermont, 2004. 91–127.

"*Resfacta* and *Cantare Super Librum*." *JAMS* 36 (1983), 371–91.

Berger, Anna Maria Busse. *Medieval Music and the Art of Memory*. Berkeley and Los Angeles, 2005.

"The Problem of Diminished Counterpoint." In *Uno Gentile et Subtile Ingenio, Studies in Renaissance Music in Honour of Bonnie J. Blackburn*. Ed. Jennifer Bloxam, Gioia Filocamo, and Leofranc Holford-Strevens. Brepols, 2009, 13–27.

Bermudo, Juan *Declaración de instrumentos musicales*. Osuna, 1555.

Bernstein, Jane A. *Music Printing in Renaissance Venice: The Scotto Press (1539–1572)*. New York and Oxford, 1998.

Besseler, Heinrich. *Bourdon und Fauxbourdon*. Leipzig, 1950.

Biordi, Paolo and Vittorio Ghielmid, ed. *Viole de gambe: Méthodes, traités, dictionnaires et encyclopédies, ouvrages généraux*. Courlay, France, 2004.

Birkendorf, Rainer. *Der Codex Pernner*. Collectanea Musicologica 6, Augsburg, 1994.

Blackburn, Bonnie J. "'Il magnifico Sigismondo Maler thedescho' and His Family: The Venetian Connection." *LSJ* 50 (2010), 60–86.

"On Compositional Process in the Fifteenth Century." *JAMS* 40 (1987), 210–84.

Blades, James. *Early Percussion Instruments from the Middle Ages to the Baroque*. Oxford, 1976.

Bodig, Richard D. "Ganassi's Regola Rubertina." *JLSA* 18 (1966), 13–66.

Boorman, Stanley. *Ottaviano Petrucci: Catalogue Raisonné*. Oxford and New York, 2006.

Borg, Paul. "The Polyphonic Music in the Guatemalan Music Manuscripts of the Lilly Library." PhD diss., Indiana University, 1985.

Bouckaert, Bruno and Eugeen Schreurs. "Hans Nagel, Performer and Spy in England and Flanders (c.1490–1531)." In *Tielman Susato*. Ed. Keith Polk. Hillsdale, New York. 63–102.

Bovicelli, Giovanni Battista. *Regole, passaggi di musica*. Venice, 1594. Facsimile edition. Ed. Nanie Bridgman. Kassel, 1957; English trans. Jesse Rosenberg, *HBSJ* 4 (1992), 27–44.

Bower, Calvin M. *Fundamentals of Music [by] Anicius Manlius Boethius*. New Haven, 1989.

Bowles, Edmond. "Haut and Bas: The Grouping of Musical Instruments in the Middle Ages." *MD* 8 (1954), 115–40.

Boydell, Barra. *The Crumhorn and other Renaissance Windcap Instruments*. Buren, 1982.

Boyden, David D. *The History of Violin Playing from Its Origins to 1761*. London, 1965.

Bradley, Robert John. "Musical Life and Culture at Savoy, 1420–1450." PhD diss., City University of New York, 1992.

Brand, Peter and Lino Pertile, ed. *The Cambridge History of Italian Literature*. Cambridge, 1996.

Bray, Roger. "Music and the Quadrivium in Early Tudor England." *ML* 76 (1995), 1–18.

Brennecke, Wilfried. *Die Handschrift A. R. 940/41 der Proske-Bibliothek zu Regensburg. Ein Beitrag zur Musikgeschichte im zweiten Drittel des 16. Jahrhunderts*. Schriften des Landesinstituts für Musikforschung, Kassel, 1953.

Brennecke, Wilfried, ed. *Carmina Germanica et Gallica*. Hortus Musicus, vols. 137–8. Kassel, 1965.

Brett, Philip. "The English Consort Song, 1570–1625." *PRMA* 88 (1961–1962), 73–88.

Brett, Philip, ed. *Consort Songs*. Musica Britannica, Vol. XXII. London, 1967.

The Consort Songs for Voice and Viols. The Collected Works of William Byrd, Vol. 15. London, 1970.

Brinzing, Armin. "Bemerkungen zur Hofkapelle Herzog Wilhelms IV, mit einer provisorischen Liste der Hofmusiker." *Die Münchner Hofkapelle des 16. Jahrhunderts im europäischen Kontext*. Bayerische Akademie der Wissenschaftern, Philosophisch-Historisch Klasse, Abhandlungen, Neue Folge, Heft 128. Ed. Theodor Göllner and Bernhold Schmid, with assistance from Severin Putz. Munich, 2006, 20–46.

Studien zur instrumentalen Ensemblemusik im deutschsprachigen Raum des 16. Jahrhunderts. Abhandlungen zur Musikgeschichte. Ed. Martin Staehelin. Göttingen, 1998.

Bromberg, Carla and Ana Maria Alfonso-Goldfarb. "Vincenzo Galilei and Music: Some Socio-Cultural and Acoustical Discussions." *Circumscribere: International Journal for the History of Science* 6 (2009), 1–11. Accessed July 11, 2015. <revistas.pucsp.br/index.php/circumhc/article/download/1939/1195>.

Brown, Adrian. "An Overview of the Surviving Renaissance Recorders." In *Musicque de Joye*. Ed. David Lasocki, 79–85.

Brown, Alan. "England." In *Keyboard Music Before 1700*. Ed. Alexander Silbiger. New York, 1995, 23–89.

Brown, Alan, ed. *William Byrd, Keyboard Music*. 3rd revised edition. Musica Brittanica, 27 and 28. London, 2004.

Brown, Howard Mayer. *Embellishing Sixteenth-Century Music*. Oxford, 1976.
  Instrumental Music Printed Before 1600. Cambridge, MA, 1965, reprint, 1967.
  Music in the French Secular Theater, 1400–1550. Cambridge, MA, 1963.
  Music in the Renaissance. Englewood Cliffs, 1976.
  "The Recorder in the Middle Ages and Renaissance." In *The Cambridge Companion to the Recorder*. Ed. John Mansfield Thomson. Cambridge, 1995, 1–25.
  Review of *The Castle of Fair Welcome*, Gothic Voices dir. Christopher Page (1985), *EM* 15 (1987), 77–8.
  Sixteenth-Century Instrumentation: The Music of the Florentine Intermedii. Musicological Studies and Documents 30. Rome, 1973.
  "The Trecento Fiddle and Its Bridges, "*EM* 17 (1989), 308–29.
  "Vincenzo Galilei in Rome: His First Book of Lute Music (1563) and Its Cultural Context." In *Music and Science in the Age of Galileo*. Ed. Victor Coelho. Dordrecht, 1992, 153–84.

Brown, Howard and Keith Polk. "Instrumental Music, *c*. 1300–*c*. 1520." In *Music as Concept and Practice in the Late Middle Ages*. Ed. Reinhard Strohm and Bonnie Blackburn. Oxford, 2001, 97–161.

Burke, Peter. *Popular Culture in Early Modern Europe*. 3rd edition. Farnham and Burlington, Vermont, 2009.

Byrd, William. *Psalmes, Sonets and Songs (1588)*. Ed. Jeremy Smith. *The Byrd Edition* 12. London, 2004.

Canguilhem, Philippe. Fronimo *de Vincenzo Galilei*. Paris, 2001.

Canguilhem, Philippe, and Alexander Stalarow. "Singing Upon the Book According to Vicente Lusitano." *EMH* 30 (2011), 55–103.

Capra, Marco, ed. *Claudio, Musico: Le arte molteplici di Claudio Merulo da Correggio (1533–1604) tra Venezia e Parma*. Venice, 2006.

Carter, Stewart. *The Trombone in the Renaissance; A History in Pictures and Documents*. Hillsdale, NY, 2012.

Carter, Tim. "A Florentine Wedding of 1608." *AcM* 55 (1983), 89–107.

[Castiglione, Baldasar]. *Baldesar Castiglione, The Book of the Courtier*. Trans. George Bull. New York, 1976,

Cazaux, Christelle. *La musique à la cour de François Ier*. Paris, 2002.

Ceulemans, Anne-Emmanuelle. *De la vièle médiévale au violon du xviie siècle: Étude terminologique, iconographique et théorique*. Turnhout, 2011.

Chapman, Catherine Weeks. "Printed Collections of Polyphonic Music Owned by Ferdinand Columbus." *JAMS* 21 (1968), 34–84.

Charteris, Richard, ed. *Giovanni Gabrieli, Opera Omnia*. Corpus Mensurabilis Musicae, vol. 12. Neuhausen, 1998.

Giovanni Gabrieli (ca. 1555–1612): a Thematic Catalogue of his Music with a Guide to the Source Materials and Translations of his Vocal Texts. New York, 1996.

Christiansen, Keith. *A Caravaggio Rediscovered: The Lute Player.* New York, 1990.

Coclico, Adrian Petit. *Compendium musices.* (Nuremberg, 1552). Facsimile edition. Ed. Manfred Bukofzer. Kassel, 1954. Translated by Albert Seay. Colorado Springs, 1973.

Coelho, Victor. "Bronzino's *Lute Player*: Music and Youth Culture in Renaissance Florence." In *Renaissance Studies in Honor of Joseph Connors.* Ed. Machtelt Israëls and Louis A. Waldman. I Tatti Studies in the Renaissance. Milan, 2013, 650–59 and 734–35.

"Francesco Canova da Milano." *Die Musik in Geschichte und Gegenwart.* Personenteil 6. Ed. Ludwig Finscher. Kassel, 1994, 1571–1575.

The Manuscript Sources of Seventeenth-Century Italian Lute Music. New York, 1995.

"Old Worlds and New." In *The Cambridge History of Seventeenth-Century Music.* Ed. Tim Carter and John Butt. Cambridge, 2005, 88–110.

"Papal Tastes and Musical Genres: Francesco da Milano 'Il Divino' (1497–1543) and the Clementine Aesthetic." In *The Pontificate of Clement VII: History, Politics, Culture.* Ed. Kenneth Gouwens and Sheryl Reiss. Aldershot and Burlington, Vermont, 2005, 277–92.

"The Players of Florentine Monody in Context and in History, and a Newly Recognized Source for *Le Nuove Musiche.*" *JSCM* 9 (2003), 48–67. Accessed June 3, 2015. http://sscm-jscm.org/v9/no1/coelho.html#AuthorNote.

"Public Works and Private Contexts: Lorenzo Allegri and the Florentine *Intermedi* of 1608." In *Luths et luthistes en Occident.* Ed. Joël Dugot, 121–32.

"Raffaello Cavalcanti's Lute Book and the Ideal of Singing and Playing." In *Le concert des voix et des instruments.* Ed. Jean-Michel Vaccaro, 423–42.

"Revisiting the Workshop of Howard Mayer Brown: [Josquin's] *Obsecro te Domina* and the Context of Arrangement." In *"La musique de tous les passetemps le plus beau": Hommage à Jean-Michel Vaccaro.* Ed. Henri Vanhulst and François Lesure. Paris, 1998, 47–65.

Coelho, Victor, ed. *Music and Science in the Age of Galileo.* Dordrecht, 1992

ed. *Performance on Lute, Guitar, and Vihuela: Historical Practice and Modern Interpretation.* Cambridge Studies in Performance Practice. Cambridge, 1997.

Coelho, Victor and Keith Polk. "Instrumental Music, 1520–1640." In *European Music, 1520–1640.* Ed. James Haar. Woodbridge, 2006. 527–55.

Cole, Janie. *Music, Spectacle and Cultural Brokerage in Early Modern Italy: Michelangelo Buonarroti il Giovane.* Florence, 2011.

Colussi, Franco, David Bryant, and Elena Quaranta. *Girolamo Dalla Casa detto* da Udene *e l'ambiente musicale veneziano.* Clauzetto, 2000.

Conforto, Giovanni Luca. *Breve et Facile Maniera di essercitarsi . . .* Rome, 1593. Edited and translated by Murray C. Bradshaw. Rome/Holzgerlingen, 1999.

Conklin, Rosalind. "Medieval English Minstrels, 1216–1485." PhD diss., University of Chicago, 1964.
Corona-Alcalde, Antonio. "The Earliest Vihuela Tablature: A Recent Discovery." *EM* 20 (1992), 594–600.
Craig-McFeely, Julia. "English Lute Manuscripts and Scribes, 1530–1630." PhD diss., University of Oxford, 1994.
Crane, Frederick. *Materials for the Study of the Fifteenth-Century Basse Dance.* Brooklyn, 1968.
Cummings, Anthony. "Gian Maria Giudeo, *Sonatore del Liuto*, and the Medici." *FAM* 38 (1991), 312–18.
  The Lion's Ear: Pope Leo X, the Renaissance Papacy, & Music. Ann Arbor, 2012.
  The Politicized Muse: Music for Medici Festivals, 1512–1537. Princeton, 1992.
Cuyler, Louise. *The Emperor Maximilian I and Music.* Oxford, 1973.
D'Accone, Frank A. *The Civic Muse: Music and Musicians in Siena during the Middle Ages and the Renaissance.* Chicago and London, 1997.
Dalla Casa, Girolamo. *Il vero modo di diminuir* (Venice 1584). Facsimile edition. Ed. Giuseppe Vecchi. Bologna, 1970; *Viole de gambe: Méthodes, traités, dictionnaires et encyclopédies, ouvrages généraux.* Ed. Paolo Biordi and Vittorio Ghielmid. Courlay, France, 2004.
Damman, Rolf. "Die Musik im Triumphzug Maximilians I." *AMw* 36 (1974), 245–289.
Danner, Peter. "Before Petrucci: The Lute in the Fifteenth Century." *JLSA* 5 (1972), 4–17.
Dean, Jeffrey J. "Josquin's Teaching: Ignored and Lost Sources." In *Uno Gentile et Subtile Ingenio.* Ed. Jennifer Bloxam, Gioia Filocamo, and Leofranc Holford-Strevens. 741–50.
Devillers, Léopold. *Essai sur l'histoire de la musique à Mons.* Mons, 1868.
Dickey, Bruce. "Ornamentation in Sixteenth-Century Music." In *A Performer's Guide.* Ed. Jeffery Kite-Powell. 300–24.
Dimutrescu, Theodor. *The Early Tudor Court and International Relations.* Aldershot and Burlington, Vermont, 2007.
Diruta, Girolamo. *The Transylvanian*: Il Transilvano. Ed. Murray C. Bradshaw and Edward J. Soehnlein. Henryville, PA, 1984.
Doe, Paul, ed. *Elizabethan Consort Music.* Musica Britannica 44. London, 1979.
Dolata, David. *Meantone Temperaments on Lutes and Viols.* Bloomington, 2016.
Downey, Peter. "The Renaissance Slide Trumpet: Fact or Fiction." *EM* 12 (1984), 26–33.
Drake, Stillman. "Vincenzio Galilei and Galileo." In *Galileo Studies: Personality, Tradition, and Revolution.* Ann Arbor, 1970, 43–62.
Duffin, Ross W. "*Contrapunctus Simplex et Diminutus*: Polyphonic Improvisation for Voices in the Fifteenth Century." *BJhM* (2007), 73–94.

"Ensemble Improvisation in the Fifteenth-Century Mensural Dance Repertoire." In *Instruments, Ensembles, and Repertory*. Ed. Timothy J. McGee and Stewart Carter. 195–233.

How Equal Temperament Ruined Harmony (And Why You Should Care). New York, 2007.

"Shawm and Curtal." In *A Performer's Guide*. Ed. Kite-Powell. 85–92.

"The *trompette des menestrels* in the 15th-century *alta capella*." *EM* 17 (1989), 397–402.

Duffin, Ross W., ed. *A Performer's Guide to Medieval Music*. Bloomington, Indiana, 2000.

Dugot, Joël, ed. *Luths et luthistes en Occident*. Paris, 1999.

——— ed. *Luth: Méthodes – Dictionnaires et Encyclopédies – Ouvrages généraux*. Méthodes & Traités 19, vol. 1. Bressuire, 2004.

Durán, Domingo Marcos. *Súmula de canto de organo: contrapunto y composición vocal y instrumental: practical y speculative*. Salamanca, c1507.

Eberlein, Roland. "The Faenza Codex: Music for Organ or Lute Duet?" *EM* 20 (1992), 460–66.

Eco, Umberto. *Experiences in Translation*. Toronto, 2001.

Edwards, Rebecca. "Claudio Merulo, l'altro gioiello nella corona di Correggio." In *A Messer Claudio, Musico*. Ed. Marco Capra, 15–29.

——— "Claudio Merulo: Servant of the State and Musical Entrepreneur in Late Sixteenth-Century Venice." PhD diss., Princeton University, 1990.

El-Mallah, Issam. *Die Pass'e mezzi und Saltarelli aus der Münchner Lautenhandschrift von Jacomo Gorzanis*. Tutzing, 1979.

——— *Ein Tanzzyklus des 16. Jahrhunderts für Laute von Giacomo Gorzanis*. Tutzing, 1979.

Elders, Willem. *Josquin des Prez and His Musical Legacy: An Introductory Guide*. Leuven, 2013.

Elliott, Kenneth, ed. *Consort Music*. In *The Collected Works of William Byrd* 17. London, 1971.

Erig, Richard, ed. (with the collaboration of Veronika Gutman). *Italienische Diminutionen: die zwischen 1553 und 1638 mehrmals bearbeiteten Sätze*. Zurich, 1979.

Espinosa, Dawn Astrid. "Juan Bermudo: 'On Playing the Vihuela ("De tañer vihuela")'." *JLSA* 28–29 (1995–96).

Estaire, Luís Robledo, Tess Knighton, Cristina Bordas Ibáñez, Juan José Carreras. *Aspectos de la cultura musical en la corte de Felipe II*. Madrid, 2000.

Evans, Edward G., ed. *Johannes Martini: Secular Pieces*. Recent Researches in Music of the Middle Ages and Early Renaissance, I. Madison, 1975.

Fabris, Dinko. "Lute Tablature Instructions in Italy: A Survey of the *Regole* from 1507 to 1759." In *Performance on Lute, Guitar, and Vihuela*. Ed. Victor Coelho. 16–46.

"Le prime intavolature italiane per liuto: 1500–1540." In *Venezia 1501: Petrucci e la stampa musicale / Venice 1501: Petrucci, Music, Print and Publishing*. Ed. Giulio Cattin and Patrizia Dalla Vecchia. Venice, 2005, 473–90.

Fallows, David. *A Catalogue of Polyphonic Songs 1415–1480*. Oxford, 1999.

"The Early History of the Tenorlied and its Ensembles." In *Le Concert des voix et des instruments*. Ed. Jean-Michel Vaccaro. 199–206.

"15th-Century Tablatures for Plucked Instruments: A Summary, a Revision, and a Suggestion." In David Fallows. *Songs and Musicians in the Fifteenth Century*. Aldershot and Burlington, Vermont, 1996, XII (also in *LSJ* 19 (1977), 7–33).

Josquin. Turnhout, 2009.

Fallows, David, ed. *The Songbook of Fridolin Sicher*. Peer, Belgium, 1996.

Fallows, David, general editor. *Harmonice Musices Odhecaton A: One Hundred Songs of Harmonic Music*. Revised edition. Watertown, MA, 2003.

Fenlon, Iain. "Merulo and State Ceremonial: The Visit to Venice of Henry III." In *A Messer Claudio, Musico*. Ed. Marco Capra, 261–75.

Music and Culture in Late Renaissance Italy. Oxford, 2002.

Ferand, Ernst T. *Die Improvisation in der Musik*. Zurich, 1938.

"What is Res Facta?" *JAMS* 10 (1957), 141–50.

Ferer, Mary Tiffany. *Music and Ceremony at the Court of Charles V: The* Capilla Flamenca *and the Art of Political Promotion*. Woodbridge, 2012.

Fiala, David. "Les musiciens étrangers de la cour de Bourgogne à la fin du XVème siècle." *Revue du Nord* 345–346 (2002), 2–19.

Finck, Hermann. *Practica musica*. Wittenberg, 1556. Facsimile edition. Bologna, 1969, and Hildesheim, 1970.

Fitch, Fabrice. "'Virtual' Ascriptions in Ms. AugS 142a: A Window on Agricola's Late Style." *Journal of the Alamire Foundation* 4 (2012), 114–42.

Forney, Kristine. "New Insights into the Career and Musical Contributions of Tielman Susato." In *Tielman Susato*. Ed. Keith Polk. 1–10.

Foster, Charles. "Tinctoris' Imperfect Dulcina Perfected: The Mary Rose Still Shawm." *GSJ* 58 (2005), 46–50, 214.

Fraser Jenkins, A.D. "Cosimo de'Medici's Patronage of Art and the Theory of Magnificence." *Journal of the Warburg and Courtauld Institutes* 33 (1970), 162–70.

Fuller Maitland, J.A. [John Alexander] and W. [William] Barclay Squire, ed. *The Fitzwilliam Virginal Book*. Leipzig, 1899; reprint, New York, 1979.

Galilei, Vincenzo. *Discorso intorno all'opere de M. Gioseffo Zarlino*. Venice, 1589.

Galilei, Vincenzo. *Il Fronimo*. Venice, 1568/1584. Facsimile edition. Bologna [n.d.].

Gallo, F. Alberto. *Music in the Castle: Troubadours, Books, and Orators in Italian Courts of the Thirteenth, Fourteenth, and Fifteenth Centuries*. Chicago, 1996.

Gambassi, Osvaldo. *La cappella musicale de S. Petronio*. Florence, 1987.

Il Concerto Palatino della Signoria di Bologna. Florence, 1989.

Ganassi, Sylvestro. *Opera Intitulata Fontegara*. Venice, 1535. Ed. Hildemarie Peter, *La Fontegara, Schule des kunstvollen Flötenspiels und Lehrbuch des Diminuierens*. Berlin-Lichterfelde, 1956.

Regola Rubertina. Venice, 1542-3. Ed. Hildemarie Peter. Berlin-Lichterfelde, 1972.

Gásser, Luis. *Luis Milán on Sixteenth-Century Performance Practice*. Bloomington, 1996.

Gilbert, Adam. "Bagpipe." In *A Performer's Guide*. Ed. Duffin. 399-411.

"Reverse Engineering Fifteenth-Century Counterpoint: *Es solt ein man kein mole farn* and *Cançon de pifari dco. el Ferrarese*." In *Instruments, Ensembles, and Repertory*. Ed. Timothy J. McGee and Stewart Carter. 173-194.

Gilliodts-Van Severen, Louis. *Les Ménestrels de Bruges*. Essais d'archéologie brugeoise, vol. 2. Bruges, 1912.

Girard, Sharon, ed. *Renaissance Wind Band Music of Guatemala*. Berkeley, CA, 1981.

Glahn, Henrik, ed. *Music from the Time of Christian III*. Dania Sonans, vols. IV-V. Copenhagen, 1978-86.

Glixon, Jonathan. *Honoring God and the City: Music at the Venetian Confraternities, 1260-1807*. Oxford and New York, 1993.

"Lutenists in Renaissance Venice: Some Notes from the Archives." *JLSA* 16 (1983), 15-26.

Goldberg, Randall E. "Where Nature and Art Adjoin: Investigations into The Zarlino-Galilei Dispute, Including an Annotated Translation of Vincenzo Galilei's *Discorso Intorno All'opere Di Messer Gioseffo Zarlino*." PhD diss., Indiana University, 2011.

Gombosi, Otto. ed. *Compositione di Meser Vincenzo Capirola: Lute-Book (circa 1517)*. Neuilly-sur-Seine, 1955.

Gómez Muntané, María del Carmen. "El manuscrito M 971 de la Biblioteca de Catalunya (Misa de Barcelona)." *Butlletí de la Biblioteca de Catalunya* 10 (1982-84) [1986], 159-317.

Grafton, Anthony. "The Humanist and the Commonplace Book: Education in Practice." In *Music Education in the Middle Ages and the Renaissance*. Ed. Russell Murray, Jr., Susan Forscher Weiss, and Cynthia J. Cyrus. Bloomington, 2010, 141-57.

Graziano, Stefano A. "From Language to Music: Mapping the History of the Italian Lute Vocabulary." PhD diss., Boston University (2011).

Greve, Werner. *Braunschweiger Stadtmusikanten*. Braunschweig, 1991.

Griffiths, John. "At Court and at Home with the *Vihuela de mano*: Current Perspectives on the Instrument, its Music and its World." *JLSA* 22 (1989), 1-28.

"La 'Fantasía que contrahaze la harpa' de Alonso Mudarra: estudio histórico-analítico." *Revista de Musicología* 9 (1986), 29-40.

"Improvisation and Composition in the Vihuela Songs of Luis Milán and Alonso Mudarra." In *Gesang zur Laute. Trossingen Jahrbuch für Renaissancemusik* 2. Ed. Nicole Schwindt. Kassel, 2002, 111–32.

"Juan Bermudo, Self-Instruction, and the Amateur Instrumentalist." In *Music Education in the Middle Ages and the Renaissance*. Ed. Russell E. Murray, Jr., Susan Forscher Weiss, and Cynthia J. Cyrus, 126–40.

"Printing the Art of Orpheus: Vihuela Tablatures in Sixteenth-Century Spain." In *Early Music Printing and Publishing in the Iberian World*. Ed. Iain Fenlon and Tess Knighton. Kassel, 2006.

"Spinacino's Twelve-Tone Experiment." *JLSA* 40 (2011), 47–76.

"La vihuela en la época de Felipe II." In *Políticas y prácticas musicales en el mundo de Felipe II*. Ed. John Griffiths and Javier Suárez-Pajares. Madrid, 2004, 415–48.

"The Vihuela Fantasia: A Comparative Study of Forms and Styles." PhD diss., Monash University, 1983.

"The Vihuela: Performance Practice, Style, and Context." In *Performance on Lute, Guitar, and Vihuela*. Ed. Victor Coelho. 158–79.

Griffiths, John, and Dinko Fabris, ed. *Neapolitan Lute Music: Fabrizio Dentice, Giulio Severino, Giovanni Antonio Severino, Francesco Cardone*. Recent Researches in the Music of the Renaissance 140. Madison, 2004.

Grojean, Ardis. "Tielman Susato and Sweden; The Swedish Evidence, 1555–1570." In *Tielman Susato*. Ed. Keith Polk, 45–59.

Grubb, James S. "Elite Citizens." In *Venice Reconsidered: The History and Civilization of an Italian City-State, 1297–1797*. Ed. John Jeffries Martin and Denis Romano. Baltimore, 2002, 339–64.

Haar, James and Lewis Lockwood, ed. "Critical Commentary to *Missa Hercules Dux Ferrarie*." In *Josquin des Prez: Masses based on Solmisation Themes. New Josquin Edition* 11.1. Utrecht, 2002.

Haggh, Barbara. "Music, Litrugy, and Ceremony in Brussels, 1350–1500." PhD diss., University of Illinois. 1988.

Harmon, Roger. "'Musica laetitiae comes' and Vermeer's *Music Lesson*." *Oud Holland* 113 (1999), 161–6.

Harms, Benjamin. "Early Percussion." In *A Performer's Guide*. Ed. Jeffery Kite-Powell, 194–205.

Haynes, Bruce. *A History of Performing Pitch: The Story of "A."* Lanham, Maryland and Oxford, 2002.

Heartz, Daniel. "The Basse Dance, Its Evolution circa 1450 to 1550." *Annales Musicologiques* 6 (1958–63), 287–340.

"Hoftanz and Basse Dance." *JAMS* 19 (1966), 13–36.

Preludes, Chansons and Dances for Lute. Neuilly-sur-Seine, 1964.

"Sources and Forms of the French Instrumental Dance in the Sixteenth Century." PhD diss., Harvard University, 1957.

Henning, Uta. *Musica Maximiliana. Die Musikgraphiken in den bibliophilen Unternehmungen Kaiser Maximilians I*. Neu-Ulm, 1987.

Herbert, Trevor. *The Trombone*. New Haven and London, 2006.

"The Trombone in England before 1800. " PhD thesis, Open University. 1984.

"Susato's Colleagues: The Trombonists of the Tudor Court." In *Tielman Susato*. Ed. Keith Polk, 117–32.

Hewitt, Helen, ed. *Harmonice musices Odhecaton A*. Cambridge, MA, 1942; reprint, New York, 1978.

Heyghen, Peter van. "The Recorder Consort in the Sixteenth Century: Dealing with the Embarrassment of Riches." In *Musicque de Joye*. Ed. David Lasocki, 244–53.

Holman, Peter. *Four and Twenty Fiddlers: The Violin at the English Court 1540–1690*. Oxford, 1993.

Horsley, Imogene. "Improvised Embellishment in the Performance of Renaissance Polyphonic Music." *JAMS* 4 (1951), 3–19.

Horst, Walter. *Musikgeschichte der Stadt Lüneburg*. Tutzing, 1967.

Hubbell, Leslie Chapman. "Sixteenth-Century Italian Songs for Solo Voice and Lute." 2 vols. PhD diss., Northwestern University, 1982.

Ivanoff, Vladimir. "An Invitation to the Fifteenth-Century Plectrum Lute: The Pesaro Manuscript." In *Performance on Lute, Guitar, and Vihuela*. Ed. Victor Coelho. 1–15.

"Eros and Death: The Lute as a Symbol in Oriental and Occidental Art and Music." In *Luths et luthistes en Occident*. Ed. Joël Dugot. 31–42.

Das Pesaro-Manuskript. Ein Beitrag zur Frühgeschichte der Lautentabulatur. Tutzing, 1988.

Eine zentrale Quelle der frühen italienischen Lautenpraxis. Edition der Handschrift Pesaro, Biblioteca Oliveriana, Ms.1144. Tutzing, 1988.

"Das Lautenduo im 15. Jahrhundert." *BJhM* 8 (1984), 147–62.

Janse, Antheunis. "Het Muziekleven aan het Hof van Albrecht van Beieren (1358–1404)." *TVNM* 36 (1986), 136–57.

Janssen, Carole Ann. "The Waytes of Norwich in Medieval and Renaissance Civic Pageantry." PhD diss., University of New Brunswick. 1977.

Jonas, Luise, ed. *Das Augsburger Liederbuch*. Berliner musikwissenschaftliche Arbeit, vol. 21. Munich-Salzburg, 1983.

Jones, Sterling. "Rebec." In *A Performer's Guide*. Ed. Ross Duffin. 317–24.

Kämper, Dietrich. "Studien zur instrumentalen Ensemblemusik des 16. Jahrhunderts in Italien." *AM* 10 (1970).

Kendrick, Robert. *Celestial Sirens: Nuns and their Music in Early Modern Milan*. Oxford, 1996.

The Sounds of Milan, 1585–1650. Oxford, 2002.

Kieffer, Paul. "An Approach to Reconstructing the First Lute Intabulations." *Lute Society of America Quarterly* 49 (2014), 7–15.

Kimball, Roger. "The Fortunes of Permanence." *The New Criterion* 20/10 (2002), 4–16.

Kirk, Douglas K, "Churching the Shawms in Renaissance Spain: Lerma, Archivo de San Pedro Ms. Mus. 1." PhD diss., McGill University, 1993.

"Cornett." In *A Performer's Guide*. Ed. Jeffery Kite-Powell. 79–96.

Music for the Duke of Lerma; Canciones and Motets of Four, Five, and Six Voices; The Music of Archivo de San Pedro de Lerma ms. Mus. 1. Watertown, MA, 2003.

"Rediscovered Works of Philippe Rogier in Spanish and Mexican Instrumental Manuscripts." In *Encomium Musicæ: Essays in Memory of Robert J. Snow*. Ed. David Crawford and Grayson G. Wagstaff. Hillsdale, NY, 2002, 47–74.

Kirkendale, Warren. *The Court Musicians in Florence during the Principate of the Medici*. Florence, 1993.

Kirkman, Andrew. *The Cultural Life of the Early Polyphonic Mass: Medieval Context to Modern Revival*. Cambridge, 2010.

Kirnbauer, Martin. "Die Nürnberger Trompeten- und Posaunenmacher vor 1500 im Spiegel Nürnberger Quellen." In *Musik und Tanz zur Zeit Kaiser Maximilian I*. Ed. Walter Salmen. Innsbruck, 1992.

Kirsch, Dieter and Lenz Meierott, ed. *Berliner Lautentabulaturen in Krakau*. Mainz, 1992.

Kite-Powell, Jeffery. "Capped Double Reeds." In *A Performer's Guide*. Ed. Jeffery Kite-Powell, 82–3.

"Crumhorn." In *A Performer's Guide*. Ed. Jeffery Kite-Powell, 63–8.

"Racket." In *A Performer's Guide*. Ed. Jeffery Kite-Powell, 93–5.

Kite-Powell, Jeffery T., ed. *A Performer's Guide to Renaissance Music*. 2nd edition. New York, 2007.

Kmetz, John. *Die Handschriften der Universitätsbibliothek Basel: Katalog der Musikhandschriften des 16. Jahrhunderts. Quellenkritische und historische Untersuchung*. Basel, 1988.

"Singing Texted Sounds from Untexted Songbooks: The Evidence of the Basel Liederhandschriften." In *Le Concert des voix et des instruments*. Ed Jean-Michel Vaccaro, 141–3.

Koch, Klaus-Peter. "Studentische Lauten- und Claviertabulaturen im Ostseeraum des 16. und 17. Jahrhunderts und ihre Bedeutung für die Vermittlung eines europäischen Repertoires." In *Universität und Musik im Ostseeraum*. Ed. Ekkehard Ochs, et al. Berlin, 2009, 117–32.

Krautwurst, Franz. "Konrad Pauman." *Fränkische Lebensbilder*. Veröffentlichungen der Gesellschaft für fränkische Geschichte. Ed. G. Pfeiffer and A. Wendenburg, Series VII A, 7 (1977) 33–48.

Kreitner, Kenneth. "The Cathedral Band of León in 1548, and What it Played." *EM* 30 (2003), 41–62.

"Minstrels in Spanish Churches, 1400–1600." *EM* 20 (1992), 533–46.

"Music in the Corpus Christi Procession of Fifteenth-Century Barcelona." *EMH* 14 (1995), 153–204.

"The Repertory of the Spanish Cathedral Bands." *EM* 37 (2009), 267–86.

Kurtzman, Jeffrey and Koldau, Linda Maria. "*Trombe, Trombe d'argento, Trombe squarciate, Tromboni*, and *Pifferi* in Venetian Processions and Ceremonies of the Sixteenth and Seventeenth Centuries." *JSCM* 8 (2002), Accessed June 4, 2015. http://sscm-jscm.org/v8/no1/kurtzman.html.

Lasocki, David. *The Bassanos: Venetian Musicians and Instrument Makers in England, 1531–1665*. Aldershot and Brookfield, Vermont, 1995.

"Tracing the Lives of Players and Makers of the Flute and Recorder in the Renaissance." In *Musicque de Joye*. Ed. David Lasocki. 363–405.

Lasocki, David, ed. Musicque de Joye: *Proceedings of the International Symposium on the Renaissance Flute and Recorder Consort, Utrecht 2003*. The Hague, 2005

Layer, Adolf. *Musik und Musiker der Fuggerzeit*. Augsburg, 1959.

Lazzi, Giovanna, ed. *Rime e suoni per corde spagnole: fonti per la chitarra barocca a Firenze*. Florence, 2002.

Le Roy, Adrian, *Breve et facile instruction . . . sur le luth*. Paris [1567]. English translation as *A briefe and easye instruction . . . .* London, 1568; expanded in 1574.

Les Instructions pour le luth (1574). Ed. Jean Jacquot, Pierre Yves Sordes and Jean-Michel Vaccaro. Paris, 1977.

Leech-Wilkinson, Daniel. "Il libro de appunti di un suonatore di tromba del quindecesimo secolo." *RIM* 16 (1981), 16–39.

Liguori, Francesco. *L'arte del liuto: le botteghe dei Tieffenbrucker prestigiosi costruttori di liuti a Padova tra il Cinquecento e il Seicento*. Padua, 2010.

Lingbeek-Schalekamp, C. *Overheid en muziek in Holland tot 1672*. n.p., 1984.

Litterick, Louise. "Chansons for Three and Four Voices." In *The Josquin Companion*. Ed. Richard Sherr. Oxford, 2000, 335–91.

"Performing Franco-Netherlandish Secular Music of the Late Fifteenth Century." *EM* 8 (1980), 474–85.

Lockwood, Lewis. *Music in Renaissance Ferrara, 1400–1505*. Cambridge, MA, 1984.

Lockwood, Lewis, ed. *A Ferrarese Chansonnier, Roma Biblioteca Casanatense 2856*. Lucca, 2002.

Maier, Ralph "Josquin's Mass Settings for Vihuela, with a Critical Edition of Diego Pisador's Intabulations of *Faysant regretz* (1552)." PhD diss., University of Calgary, 2011.

Marincola, Federico. "The Instructions From Vincenzo Capirola's Lute Book: A New Translation." *The Lute* 23, pt. 2 (1983), 23–8.

Marix, Jeanne. *Histoire de la musique et des musiciens de la cour de Bourgogne sous le règne de Philippe le Bon*. Strasbourg, 1939; reprint, Geneva, 1972.

Marlow, Richard, ed. *Giles and Richard Farnaby, Keyboard Music*. Musica Brittanica, 24. London, 1965.

Mason, Kevin. *The Chitarrone and its Repertoire in Early Seventeenth-Century Italy*. Aberystwyth, 1989.

"*Per cantare e sonare:* Accompanying Italian Lute Song of the Late Sixteenth Century." In *Performance on Lute*. Ed. Victor Coelho, 72–107.

McCarthy, Kerry. "Josquin in England: An Unexpected Sighting." *EM* 43 (2015), 449–54.

McCoy, Stewart. "Edward Paston and the Textless Lute-Song." *EM* 15 (1987), 221–7.
McGee, Timothy J. *The Ceremonial Musicians of Late Medieval Florence.* Bloomington, 2009.
  "Dinner Music for the Florentine Signoria, 1350–1450." *Speculum* 74 (1999), 95–114.
  "Giovanni Cellini, Piffero of Florence." *HBSJ* 12 (2000), 210–25.
  "Instruments and the Faenza Codex." *EM* 14 (1986), 480–90.
  "The Medieval Fiddle: Tuning, Technique, and Repertory." In *Instruments, Ensembles, and Repertory*. Ed. Timothy J. McGee and Stewart Carter, 31–56.
McGee, Timothy J. and Stewart Carter, ed. *Instruments, Ensembles, and Repertory, 1300–1600: Essays in Honour of Keith Polk*. Turnhout, 2013,
McGinnis, Kathryn Tucker. "Your Most Humble Subject, Cesare Negri Milanese." In *Dance, Spectacle, and the Body Politick*. Ed. Jennifer Nevile, 211–28.
Memelsdorff, Pedro. *The Codex Faenza 117: Instrumental Polyphony in Late Medieval Italy; Introductory Study and Facsimile Edition*. Lucca, 2012/2013, vol. I, Introductory Study; vol. 2, Facsimile Edition.
  "The Filiation and Transmission of Instrumental Polyphony in Late Medieval Italy: The Codex Faenza 117." PhD diss., University of Utrecht, 2010.
  "*Motti a motti*: Reflections on a Motet Intabulation of the Early Quattrocento." *Recercare* 10 (1998), 39–68.
Milner, Stephen J., "Organ Culture and Organ Contracts in Renaissance Pistoia." *Recercare* 12 (2000), 77–94.
Minamino, Hiroyuki. "Conrad Paumann and the Evolution of Solo Lute Practice in the Fifteenth Century." *JMR* 6 (1986), 291–310.
  "Sixteenth-Century Lute Treatises with Emphasis on Process and Techniques of Intabulation." PhD diss., University of Chicago, 1988.
  "The Spanish Plucked *Viola* in Renaissance Italy, 1480–1530." *EM* 32 (2004), 177–92.
Morehen, John, ed. *Claudio Merulo: Ricercari d'intavolatura d'organo*. Madison, 2000.
Moser, Hans Joachim. *Die Musikergenossenschaften im deutschen Mittelalter*. Rostock, 1910.
  Paul Hofhaimer. Revised edition. Hildesheim, 1966.
Muir, Edwin. *Civic Ritual in Renaissance Venice*. Princeton, 1981.
Myers, Herbert W. "Flutes." In *A Performer's Guide*. Ed. Jeffery Kite-Powell, 378–82.
  "Harp." In *A Performer's Guide*. Ed. Jeffery Kite-Powell, 187–93.
  "Psaltery & Dulcimer." In *A Performer's Guide*. Ed. Ross Duffin, 441–2.
  "Recorder." In *A Performer's Guide*. Ed. Jeffery Kite-Powell, 41–55.
  "Reeds & Brass." In *A Performer's Guide*. Ed. Ross Duffin, 386–90.
  "Renaissance Flute." In *A Performer's Guide*. Ed. Jeffery Kite-Powell, 56–60.

"Renaissance Viol Tunings: A Reconsideration." *Journal of the Viola da Gamba Society of America* 44 (2007–8), 13–40.

"The Sizes and Tunings of Early Viols: Some Questions (and a Few Answers)." *Journal of the Viola da Gamba Society of America* 38 (2001), 5–26 [with a follow up in the same journal, 40 (2003), 237–9].

"String Keyboards." In *A Performer's Guide*. Ed. Ross Duffin, 431–9.

Nagler, Alois. *Theatre Festivals of the Medici, 1539–1637*. New York, 1964, reprint 1976.

Naylor, Tom L. *The Trumpet & Trombone in Graphic Arts, 1500–1800*. Nashville, TN, 1979.

Neighbour, Oliver. *The Consort and Keyboard Music of William Byrd*. Berkeley and Los Angeles, 1978.

Nelson, Bernadette. "The Chansons of Thomas Crecquillon and Clemens non Papa in Sources of Instrumental Music in Spain and Portugal, and Sixteenth-Century Keyboard Traditions." In *Beyond Contemporary Fame: Reassessing the Art of Clemens non Papa and Thomas Crecquillon*. Ed. Eric Jas. Turnhout, 2005, 167–89.

"Music Treatises and 'artes para tanger' in Portugal Before the 18th Century: An Overview." In *Tratados de Arte em Portugal*. Ed. Rafael Moreira and Ana Duarte Rodrigues. Lisbon, 2011.

Ness, Arthur. "The Herwarth Lute Manuscripts at the Bavarian State Library, Munich: A Bibliographical Study with Emphasis on the Works of Marco dall'Aquila and Melchior Newsidler." PhD diss., 2 vols. New York University, 1984.

Ness, Arthur, ed. *The Lute Music of Francesco Canova da Milano, 1497–1543*. Cambridge, MA, 1970.

Nevile, Jennifer, ed. *Dance, Spectacle, and the Body Politick*. Bloomington, 2008.

The Eloquent Body: Dance and Humanist Culture in Fifteenth-Century Italy. Bloomington, 2004.

Newcomb, Anthony. *The Madrigal at Ferrara, 1579–1597*. Princeton, 1980.

Nijsten, Gerard. *Het Hof van Gelre: Cultuur ten tijde van de hertogen uit het Gulikse en Egmondse huis (1371–1473)*. 2nd edition. Kampen, 1992.

Nordstrom, Lyle. "Albert de Rippe: *Joueur de luth du Roy*." *EM* 7 (1989), 378–85.

Nösselt, Hans-Joachim. *Ein ältest Orchester 1530–1980. 450 Jahre Bayerisches Hof- und Staatsorchester*. Munich, 1980.

Oettinger, Rebecca. *Music as Propaganda in the German Reformation*. Aldershot and Burlington, Vermont, 2001.

Ongaro, Giulio. "The Chapel of St. Mark's at the time of Adrian Willaert (1527–1562), A Documentary Study." PhD diss., University of North Carolina, 1986.

"Sixteenth-Century Venetian Wind Instrument Makers and their Clients." *EM* 13 (1985), 391–7.

"The Tieffenbruckers and the Business of Lute-making in Sixteenth-Century Venice." *GSJ* 44 (1991), 46–54.

Ortiz, Diego. *Tratado de glosas sobre clausulas y otros generos de puntos en la musica de violones*. Rome, 1553. Ed. Max Schneider. Kassel, 1936; facsimile edition, Florence, 1984.

Owens, Jessie Ann. *Composers at Work: The Craft of Musical Composition, 1450–1600*. Oxford, 1997.

Owens, Jessie Ann, ed. *Kraków, Biblioteka Jagiellónska, Glogauer Liederbuch*. Renaissance Music in Facsimile. Ed. Howard Mayer Brown, Frank A. D'Accone, and Jessie Ann Owens, vol. 6. New York and London, 1986.

Page, Christopher. "David Fallows and the Performance of Medieval Music." In *Essays on Renaissance Music in Honour of David Fallows: Bon jour, bon mois et bonne estrenne*. Ed. Fabrice Fitch and Jacobijn Kiel. Woodbridge, Suffolk, 2011, 2–8.

"The 15th-century Lute: New and Neglected Sources." *EM* 9 (1981), 11–21.

The Guitar in Tudor England: A Social and Musical History. Cambridge, 2015.

Palisca, Claude. *Girolamo Mei: Letters on Ancient and Modern Music to Vincenzo Galilei and Giovanni Bardi*. 2nd ed. American Institute of Musicology, 1977.

"Vincenzo Galilei and Some Links Between Pseudo-Monody and Monody." *MQ* 46 (1960) 344–6.

"Vincenzo Galilei's Arrangements for Voice and Lute." In *Essays in Musicology in Honor of Dragan Plamenac*. Ed. Gustave Reese and Robert J. Snow. Pittsburgh, 1969, 207–32.

"Was Galileo's Father an Experimental Scientist?" In *Music and Science in the Age of Galileo*. Ed. Victor Coelho. 143–51.

Pavan, Franco. "Francesco da Milano (1497–1543)." Tesi di Laurea, Università di Milano, 1996–97.

Pearsall, Eileen Sharpe. "Tudor Court Musicians, 1485–1547: Their Number, Status and Function." PhD diss., New York University, 1986.

Pérez García, María del Carmen. *Los ángeles músicos de la catedral de Valencia*. Valencia, 2006.

Peruffo, Mimmo. "Balance on the Lute: The Role of the Strings." In *The Music Room in Early Modern France and Italy*. Ed. Deborah Howard and Laura Moretti. Oxford, 2012, 135–44.

Peters, Gretchen. *The Musical Sounds of Medieval French Cities: Players, Patrons, and Politics*. Cambridge, 2012.

Pirro, André. *La musique à Paris sous le règne de Charles VI (1380–1422)*. Strasbourg, 1930; reprint, Geneva, 1973.

Pirrotta, Nino. "Music and Cultural Tendencies in 15th-Century Italy." *JAMS* 19 (1966), 127–61.

Music and Theatre from Poliziano to Monteverdi. trans. Karen Eales. Cambridge, 1982.

Plamenac, Dragan, ed. *Keyboard Music of the Late Middle Ages in Codex Faenza 117*. n.p., 1972.

Polk, Keith. "Augustein Schubinger and the Zinck: Innovation in Performance Practice." *HBSJ* 1 (1989), 83–92.

"English Instrumental Music in the Fifteenth Century." In *Uno Gentile et Subtile Ingenio*. Ed. Jennifer M. Bloxam, Gioia Filocamo, and Leofranc Holford-Strevens. 659–67.

"Ensemble Instrumental Music in Flanders-1450–1550." *Journal of Band Research* 11 (1975), 12–27.

"Foreign and Domestic in Italian Instrumental Music of the Fifteenth Century." In *Musica Franca: Essays in Honor of Frank A. D'Accone*. Ed. Irene Alm, Alyson McLamore, and Colleen Reardon. Stuyvesant, NY, 1996, 323–32.

German Instrumental Music in the Late Middle Ages: Players, Patrons and Performance Practice. Cambridge, 1992.

"Instrumental Music in the Urban Centres of Renaissance Germany." *EMH* 7 (1987), 159–86.

"The Schubingers of Augsburg: Innovation in Renaissance Instrumental Music." In *Quaestiones in musica. Festschrift für Franz Krautwurst*. Ed. Friedhelm Brusniak and Horst Leuchtmann. Tutzing, 1989. 495–503.

"Susato and Instrumental Music in Flanders in the 16th Century." In *Tielman Susato*. Ed. Keith Polk. 63–102.

"Voices and Instruments: Soloists and Ensembles in the 15th Century." *EM* 18 (1989), 179–98.

Polk, Keith, ed. *Tielman Susato and the Music of His Time*. Hillsdale, 2005.

Poulton, Diana. *John Dowland*. Revised edition. Berkeley and Los Angeles, 1982.

Pozniak, Piotr. "Problems of Tonality in the Ricercars of Spinacino and Bossinensis." *JLSA* 23 (1990), 64–80.

Prizer, William. "The Frottola and the Unwritten Tradition." *Studi Musicali* 15 (1986), 3–37.

"Instrumental Music / Instrumentally Performed Music ca. 1500: The Genres of Paris, Bibliothèque Nationale, Ms Rés.Vm.⁷ 676." In *Le concert des voix et des instruments*. Ed. Jean-Michel Vaccaro. 185–7.

Rastall, Richard. "The Minstrels of the English Royal Households, 25, Edward I – 1 Henry VIII: An Inventory." *Royal Music Association Research Chronicle* 4 (1964), 1–41.

Minstrels Playing Music in Early English Religious Drama. Woodbridge, Suffolk, 2001.

"Secular Musicians in Late Medieval England." PhD diss., Manchester University, 1968.

Remnant, Mary. *English Bowed Instruments from Anglo-Saxon to Tudor Times*. Oxford, 1986.

Rensch, Roslyn. *Harps and Harpists*. Revised edition. Bloomington, 2007.

Rifkin, Joshua. "Franco-Netherlandish Repertory in an Early 16th-Century German Manuscript." Unpublished paper presented at the New England

Chapter Meeting of the American Musicological Society, Yale University, 10 April 1971.

"Munich, Milan, and a Marian Motet: Dating Josquin's *Ave Maria ... virgo serena.*" *JAMS* 56 (2003), 239–350.

Robinson, Thomas. *The Schoole of Musicke (1603)*. Edited and transcribed by David Lumsden. Paris, 1971.

Robledo Estaire, Luís. "La estructuración de las casas reales: Felipe II como punto de encuentro y punto de partida." In *Aspectos de la Cultura musical en la corte de Felipe II*. Ed. Luís Robledo Estaire, Tess Knighton, Cristina Bordas Ibáñez, and Juan José Carreras, 1–34.

Rogniono, Richardo. *Passagi per potersi essercitare nel diminuire terminatamente con ogni sorte d'instromente*. Venice, 1592.

Rosenberg, Jesse. "*Il vero modo di diminuir* – Girolamo Dalla Casa: A Translation." *HBSJ* 1 (1989), 109–14.

Rubsamen, Walter. "The Earliest French Lute Tablature." *JAMS* 21 (1968), 286–99.

Ruhnke, Martin. *Beiträge zu einer Geschichte der deutschen Hofmusikkollegien im 16. Jahrhundert*. Berlin, 1963.

Ruiz Jiménez, Juan. "The Mid-Sixteenth-Century Franco-Flemish Chanson in Spain: The Evidence of Ms. 975 of the Manuel de Falla Library." *TVNM* 51 (2001), 25–41.

"Power and Musical Exchange: The Dukes of Medina Sidonia in Renaissance Seville." *EM* 37 (2009), 401–15.

Sachs, Klaus-Jürgen. "Arten improvisierter Mehrstimmigkeit nach Lehrtexten des 14. bis 16. Jahrhunderts." *BJhM* 7 (1983), 166–83.

De modo compenendi: Studien zu musikalischen Lehrtexten des späten 15. Jahrhunderts. Olms, 2002.

Der Contrapunctus im 14. und 15. Jahrhundert. Beihefte zum Archiv für Musikwissenschaft, vol. 13. Wiesbaden, 1974.

Sadie, Stanley, ed. *New Grove Dictionary of Music and Musicians*. 29 vols. 2nd edition. London, 2001.

Salmen, Walter. *Der Spielmann im Mittelalter*. Innsbruck, 1983.

Sandberger, Adolf. *Beiträge zur Geschichte der bayerischen Hofkapelle unter Orlando di Lasso*. Leipzig, 1894–5, reprint, Walluf b. Wiesbaden, 1973.

Schmidt, Henry Louis, III. "The First Printed Lute Books: Francesco Spinacino's *Intabulatura de Lauto, Libro primo and Libro secondo*." PhD diss., University of North Carolina, Chapel Hill, 1969.

Schubert, Peter. "From Improvisation to Composition; Three 16th-century Case Studies." In *Improvising Early Music*, Geschriften van het Orpheus Instituut/ Collected Writings of the Orpheus Insitute. Ed. Dirk Moelants. Leuven, 2014, 93–130.

Schure, Steffen. *Die Geschichte des Stadtmusikantentums in Ulm (1388–1840)*. Ulm and Stuttgart, 2007.

Schwab, Heinrich W. *Die Anfänge des weltlichen Berufsmusikertums in der mittelalterlichen Stadt. Kieler Schriften zur Musikwissenschaft* 24. Kassel, 1982.

Schwindt, Nicole. "Hans Mielichs bildliche Darstellung der Münchner Hofkapelle von 1570." *AM* 68 (1996), 48–85.

Selfridge-Field, Eleanor. *Venetian Instrumental Music from Gabrieli to Vivaldi*. Oxford, 1975.

Silbiger, Alexander. "Music and the Crisis of Seventeenth-Century Europe." In *Music and Science in the Age of Galileo*. Ed. Victor Coelho, 35–44.

Silbiger, Alexander, ed. *Keyboard Music Before 1700*. 2nd edition. New York, 2004.

Slim, H. Colin. "Gian and Gian Maria, Some Fifteenth- and Sixteenth-Century Namesakes." *MQ* 57 (1971), 562–74.

"Musicians on Parnassus." *Studies in the Renaissance* 12 (1965), 134–63.

Painting Music in the Sixteenth Century: Essays in Iconography. New York, 2002.

Slootmans, C. J. F. *De Heilig Kruis Ommegang van Bergen op Zoom*. Bergen op Zoom, 1946.

"De Hoge Lieve Vrouw van Bergen op Zoom." II, *Jaarboek van de Oudheidkundige Kring "de Ghulden Roos"* 25 (1965), 193–233.

Smijers, Albert. *De Illustre Lieve Vrouwe Broederschap te 's-Hertogenbosch*. Uitgave der Vereeniging voor Nederlandsche Muziekgeschiedenis, I. Amsterdam, 1932.

Smith, Anne. *The Performance of 16th-Century Music: Learning from the Theorists*. New York, 2011.

Smith, David J. "A Legend? Francis Tregian the Younger as Music Copyist." *The Musical Times*, 143 (Summer, 2002), 7–16.

Smith, Douglas A. *A History of the Lute*. n.p., 2002.

"The Instructions in Matthaeus Waissel's *Lautenbuch*." *JLSA* 8 (1975), 49–79.

Smith, Jeremy, ed. *William Byrd, Psalmes, Songs and Sonnets (London: Thomas East, 1588)*. The Byrd Edition 12. London, 2004.

Smits van Waesberghe, Josef. "Een 15de eeuws muziekboek van de stadsministrelen van Maastricht?" In *Renaissance-Muziek 1400–1600. Donum Natalicium René Bernard Lenaerts*. Ed. Jozef Robijns. Leuven, 1969, 247–73.

Snyder, Kerala, ed. *The Organ as a Mirror of its Time: North European Reflections, 1610–2000*. Oxford, 2002.

Soehnlein, Edward J. "Diruta on the Art of Keyboard-Playing: An Annotated Translation and Transcription of *Il Transilvano*, pts. I (1593) and II (1609)." PhD diss., University of Michigan, 1975.

Southard, Marc and Suzana Cooper. "A Translation of Hans Newsidler's *Ein newgeordent künstlich Lautenbuch* ... (1536)." *JLSA* 11 (1978) 5–25.

Spencer, Robert. "Dowland's Dance Songs: Those of his Compositions Which Exist in Two Versions, Songs and Instrumental Dances." In *Le Concert des voix et des instruments*. Ed. Jean-Michel Vaccaro, 587–99.

Spiessens, Godelieve. "De Antwerpse stadsspeellieden Deel I: 15e en 16e eeuw." *Noordgouw* 10 (1970), 1–53.
De Antwerpse stadsspellieden (ca. 1411–1749). Deel I, Antwerp, 2014.
Spitzer, John and Neal Zaslaw. *The Birth of the Orchestra: History of an Institution, 1650–1815*. Oxford and New York, 2004.
Spring, Matthew. *The Lute in Britain: a History of the Instrument and its Music*. Oxford and New York, 2001.
Staehelin, Martin. "Norddeutsche Fragmente mit Lautenmusik um 1460 in Wolfenbüttel." In *Kleinüberlieferung mehrstimmiger Musik vor 1550 in deutschem Sprachgebiet*. Berlin, 2012, 67–88 and 141–4.
Steele, John and Francis Cameron, ed. *John Bull, Keyboard Music*. Revised edition. Musica Brittanica 14. London, 1967.
Stevens, John. *Music and Poetry in the Early Tudor Court*. Revised edition. Cambridge, 1979.
Stevens, John, ed. *Music at the Court of Henry VIII*. Musica Britannica XVII. London, 1973.
Stevenson, Robert M. "European Music in 16th-Century Guatemala." *MQ* 50 (1964), 341–52.
Spanish Music in the Age of Columbus. The Hague, 1960.
Straeten, Edmond Vander. *Les Ménestrels aux Pays-Bas du XIIIe au XVIIIe siècle*. Brussels, 1878.
Strohm, Reinhard. *Music in Late Medieval Bruges*. Oxford, 1985.
The Rise of European Music 1380–1500. Cambridge, 1993.
Tarr, Edward. *The Trumpet*. London, 1988.
Thompson, Glenda Goss. "Music in the Court Records of Mary of Hungary." *TVNM* 34 (1984), 132–51.
Thompson, Ruby Reid. "Francis Tregian the Younger as Music Copyist: A Legend and an Alternative View." *ML* 82 (2001), 1–31.
Tinctoris, Johannes. *The Art of Counterpoint*. Translated and edited by Albert Seay. n.p., 1961.
Toffolo, Stefano. *Antichi strumenti Veneziani*. Venice, 1987.
Strumenti musicali a Venezia. Cremona, 1995.
Towne, Gary. "*Tubatori e Piffari*: Civic Wind Players in Medieval and Renaissance Bergamo." *HBSJ* 9 (1997), 175–95.
Toulouse, Michel de. *L'art et instruction de bien dancer*. Paris, 1488–96.
Treadwell, Nina. "She Descended on a Cloud 'From the Highest Spheres': Florentine Monody 'alla Romanina'." *Cambridge Opera Journal* 16 (2004), 1–22.
Troiano, Massimo. *Dialoghi*. Munich, 1568. Mod. ed. in *Die Münchner Fürstenhochzeit von 1568: Massimo Troiano*. Ed. Horst Leuchtmann. Munich-Salzburg, 1980.
Tyler, James and Paul Sparks. *The Guitar and its Music from the Renaissance to the Classical Era*. Oxford, 2002.

Urquhart, Peter and Heather de Savage. "Evidence Contrary to the *a cappella* Hypothesis for the 15th-Century Chanson." *EM* 39 (2011), 359–78.

Vaccaro, Jean-Michel. "The *Fantasia sopra*... in the Works of Jean-Paul Paladin." *JLSA* 23 (1990), 18–36.

La musique de luth en France au XVIe siècle. Paris, 1981.

Vaccaro, Jean-Michel, ed. *Le Concert des voix et des instruments à la Renaissance.* Paris, 1995.

ed. *Œuvres d'Albert de Rippe: II. Motets / Chansons (première partie).* Paris, 1974.

ed. *Œuvres d'Albert de Rippe: I. Fantaisies.* Paris, 1972.

Vaughan, Richard. *Valois Burgundy.* London, 1975.

Vente, Maarten Albert, ed. *Bouwstenen voor een geschiedenis der toonkunst in de Nederlande,* 3. Utrecht and Amsterdam, 1980.

Virdung, Sebastian. *Musica getutscht.* Basel, 1511. Modern edition in *Musica getutscht: A Treatise on Musical Instruments.* Translated and edited by Beth Bullard. Cambridge, 1993.

Warburton, Thomas, ed. *Keyboard Intabulations of Music by Josquin des Prez.* Recent Researches in the Music of the Renaissance 34. Madison, 1980.

Wallner, Berta Antonia, ed. *Das Buxheimer Orgelbuch.* Das Erbe Deutscher Musik, vols. 37–39. Kassel-Basel-London, 1958.

Wegman, Rob C. "From Maker to Composer: Improvisation and Musical Authorship in the Low Countries, 1450–1500." *JAMS* 49 (1996), 409–79.

"The State of the Art." In *Renaissance? Perceptions of Continuity and Discontinuity in Europe, c.1300-c.1550.* Ed. Pit Péporté and Harry Schnitke. Leiden, 2010, 129–60.

Weiss, Susan F. "Bologna Q18: Some Reflections on Content and Context." *JAMS* 41 (1988), 63–101.

Welker, Lorenz. "'Alta Capella' zur Ensemblepraxis der Blasinstrumente im 15. Jahrhundert." *BJhM* 7 (1983), 150–61.

"Wind Ensembles in the Renaissance." In *Companion to Medieval and Renaissance Music.* Ed. Tess Knighton and David Fallows. New York, 1992, 146–53.

Williams, Peter. *The European Organ 1450–1850.* London, 1980.

A New History of the Organ. Bloomington and London, 1980.

Wilson, Blake. *Music and Merchants: The Laudesi Companies of Republican Florence.* Oxford, 1992.

Wilson, David R. "The Basse Dance c.1445-c.1545." In *Dance, Spectacle, and the Body Politick.* Ed. Jennifer Nevile, 174–8.

Wolff, Christoph. "Conrad Paumanns Fundamentum organisandi und seine verschiedenen Fassungen." *AMw* 25 (1968), 196–222.

Woodfield, Ian. *The Early History of the Viol.* Cambridge, 1984.

Woodfill, Walter L. *Musicians in English Society from Elizabeth to Charles I.* Princeton, 1953, reprint, New York, 1969.

Wright, Craig. *Music at the Court of Burgundy.* Henryville-Ottawa-Binningen, 1979.

Wright, Laurence. "The Medieval Gittern and Citole: A Case of Mistaken Identity." *GSJ* 30 (1977), 9–42.

Wustmann, Rudolf. *Musikgeschichte Leipzigs,* vol. 1: *Bis zur Mitte des 17. Jahrhunderts.* Leipzig and Berlin, 1909.

Yong, Kwee Him. "Sixteenth-Century Printed Instrumental Arrangements of Works by Josquin des Prez. An Inventory." *TVNM* 22 (1971), 43–66.

Young, Crawford. "The King of Spain: una bassadanza troppo forte." *Lute Society of America Quarterly* 48 1 & 2 (2013), 40–61.

"Lute, Gittern, & Citole." In *A Performer's Guide.* Ed. Ross Duffin (2002), 355–75.

"Zur Klassifikation und ikonographischen Interpretation mittelalterlicher Zupfinstrumente." *BJhM* 8 (1984), 67–103.

Young, Crawford and Martin Kirnbauer, ed. *Frühe Lautentabulaturen im Faksimile.* Winterthur, 2003.

Zacconi, Ludovico. *Prattica di musica.* Venice, 1592, reprint, Hildesheim, 1982.

Zak, Sabine. *Music als 'Ehr und Zier' im mittelalterlichen Reich.* Neuss, 1978.

Index of primary sources

I. Manuscript Sources

Augsburg, Staats, Kreis- und Stadtbibliothek MS 142a [*Augsburg*], 85–9, 94–5
Basel, Universitätsbibliothek, F IX 23, 162 (n. 2)
Basel, Universitätsbibliothek, F IX 70 [*Wurstisen*], 159–62
Basel, Universitätsbibliothek, F X 5–9, 95 (n. 70)
Basel, Universitätsbibliothek, F X 11, 162 (n. 2)
Berkeley, University of California Music Library, Ms. 757, 240 (n. 29)
Berlin, Staatsbibliothek Preussischer Kulturbesitz, Mus.ms.40613 (*olim* Wernigerode, Fürstlich Stolbergsche Bibliothek, Zb 14) [*Lochamer*], 69–70
Berlin, Staatsbibliothek theol. lat. quart. 290 [*Windsheim*], 70, 184
Bloomington, Indiana University, Libby Library, Stevenson Mss. 1–15, 42–6
Bologna, Biblioteca Universitaria, MS 596. HH.2/4, 244
Bologna, Civico Museo Bibliografico Musicale, MS Q16, 76 (n. 25)
Bologna, Civico Museo Bibliografico Musicale, MS Q17, 76 (n. 25)
Bologna, Civico Museo Bibliografico Musicale, MS Q18, 144 (n. 1 and 2)
Brussels, Bibliothèque Royale de Belgique, MS 9085, 101 (n. 79)
Brussels, Bibliothèque Royale de Belgique, MS II 275 [*Cavalcanti*], 157, 159–62
Cambridge, Fitzwilliam Museum, Music MS 168 [*Fitzwilliam*], 123–5, 129
Cambridge, Fitzwilliam Museum, Ms. Mus. 689, 130
Chicago, Newberry Library, MS 107501 [*Capirola*], 10, 90, 111, 162
Coimbra, Biblioteca Geral da Universidade, MS M. 48, and MS M. 242, 114 (n. 107)
Copenhagen, Kongelige Bibliotek, Gl.Kgl. Sml.1872-4° [*Copenhagen*], 10–11, 94–6, 113, 115–7, 291
Copenhagen, Kongelige Bibliotek, Gl.Kgl. Sml.1873-4° [*Copenhagen 1873*], 95–6, 291
Cracow, Biblioteca Jagiellońska Mus. Ms. 40032, 243 (n. 39)
Cracow, Biblioteka Jagiellońska, Ms. Mus. 40098 [Glogauer part books], 38, 72
Dublin, Archbishop Marsh's Library, Ms Z3.2.13, 126–7
Faenza, Biblioteca comunale 117 [*Faenza*], 37, 64–6, 68, 70–1, 83, 193, 205, 265, 270
Florence, Biblioteca Nazionale Centrale, Cl. XIX. 29, 247 (n. 45)
Florence, Biblioteca Nazionale Centrale, MS Banco Rari 229 [*Florence 229*], 9, 76 (n. 25), 89 (n. 56)
Florence, Biblioteca Nazionale Centrale, MS Magl. XIX. 176 [*Florence 176*], 72, 76 (n. 25)
Florence, Biblioteca Nazionale Centrale, MS Magl. XIX. 178, 76 (n. 25)
Florence, Biblioteca Nazionale Centrale, Fondo Anteriori di Galilei 6 [*Galilei 1584*], 82, 105
Florence, Biblioteca Riccardiana, MS 2356, 76 (n. 25)
Florence, Biblioteca Riccardiana, MS 2794, 76 (n. 25)
Florence, Museo Bardini, MS 967 [Elena Malvezzi MS], 155
Granada, Biblioteca de Manuel de Falla, Ms. 975, 114 (n. 107)
Lerma, Archivo de San Pedro Ms. Mus. 1 [*Lerma 1*], 11, 49, 113–7
London, British Library, Additional MS 31922, 29
London, British Library, Cotton MS Titus A. xxvi [*Zorzi*], 66–8, 71, 73–4, 88, 204–5
London, British Library, Egerton MS 2046 [Jane Pickeringe lute book], 154
London, British Library, MS Mus. 1591 [My Lady Nevells Book], 123

Index of primary sources 319

London, Royal Academy of Music, Robert Spencer Collection [Margaret Board lute book], 154
Maastricht, Rijksarchief van Limburg, MS without ms number, 85 (n. 46)
Madrid, Biblioteca de Palacio Real, MS II-1335 (formerly 1-I-5) [*Cancionero de Palacio*], 101 (n. 80)
Munich, Bayerische Staatsbibliothek, Mus. MS 1511a (Gorzanis [1567]), 82
Munich, Bayerische Staatsbibliothek, Mus. MS 1516, 95 (n. 70)
Munich, Bayerische Staatsbibliothek, Cim. 352b [*Buxheim*], 38, 66, 69–71, 193, 196, 205–6
Munich, Universitätsbibliothek, 4°Cod. ms. 718, 94
Paris, Bibliothèque nationale, f.fr 15123 [*Pixérécourt*], 72, 76 (n. 25)
Paris, Bibliothèque nationale, Lat. 7295, 238
Paris, Bibliothèque nationale, Rés. Vma ms. 851, 111
Paris, private collection, 'Ileborgh Tablature,' 69–70
Perugia, Biblioteca Comunale Augusta, MS 431, 101 (n. 80)
Pesaro, Biblioteca Oliveriana, Ms 1144 [*Pesaro*]. 79–80, 80 (n. 29), 193, 205, 238
Puebla, Archivo de Música Sacra de la Catedral, Ms. XIX, 45–6
Regensburg, Bischöfliche Zentralbibliothek (Proskesche Musikbibliothek), Ms. A.R. 775–777, 116
Regensburg, Bischöfliche Zentralbibliothek (Proskesche Musikbibliothek), Ms. A.R.940/41, 115
Regensburg, Thurn und Taxissche Hofbibliothek, Ms. F.K. Mus. 3/I, 116
Rome, Biblioteca Casanatense, MS 2856 [*Casanatense*], 9, 14 (n. 5), 71–6, 78, 96, 193, 198
Rome, Vatican City, Biblioteca Apostolica Vaticana, Cappella Giulia, XIII.27, 76 (n. 25)
St. Gallen, Stiftsbibliothek Cod. Sang. 461, 85 (n. 46), 87
Trent, Castello del Buonconsiglio, Monumenti e Collezioni Provinciali, MS 89 [now 1376]), 72 (n. 14)
Utrecht, Universiteitsbibliotheek, Ms. 3.L.16 [*Lerma 2*], 11, 49, 114, 116–17
Vienna, Österreichische Nationalbibliothek, MS 2856, 72 (n. 14)

Wolfenbüttel, Niedersächsisches Landesarchiv-Staatsarchiv, cod. VII B Hs Nr. 264, 257–6

II. Printed Sources

148?$_1$ Michel de Toulouse (pub.), *L'art et instruction de bien dancer* (Paris), 101
1496 Franchino Gaffurio, *Practica musicae* (Milan), 190
1501$_1$ Ottaviano Petrucci (pub.), *Harmonice musices Odhecaton A* (Venice), 9, 76–9, 81, 83, 85–7, 95
1504$_1$ Ottaviano Petrucci (pub.), *Canti C* (Venice), 9
1507? Domingo Marcos Durán, *Súmula de canto de organo* (Salamanca), 199
1507$_2$ Francesco Spanacino, *Intabulatura de Lauto Libro primo / Libro secondo* (Venice), 4, 9, 12–14, 78–85, 89–90, 111, 189, 194, 205, 208, 211
1508$_1$ Giovan Maria, *Intabulatura di Lauto* (Venice, lost), 84, 89, 238
1508$_2$ Joan Ambrosio Dalza, *Intabulatura de lauto* (Venice), 84, 93, 100
1509$_1$ Franciscus Bossinensis, *Tenori e contrabassi intabulati col sopran ... Libro primo* (Venice), 89
1511$_1$ Franciscus Bossinensis, *Tenori e contrabassi intabulati col sopran ... Libro secundo* (Venice), 89
1511$_2$ Arnolt Schlick, *Spiegel der Orgelmacher und Organisten* (Speyer), 222
1511$_3$ Sebastian Virdung, *Musica Getutscht* (Basel), 95, 222, 226, 233–4, 236–7, 246, 251, 254–5, 265
1523$_2$ Hans Judenkünig, *Ain schone kunstliche Underweisung* (Vienna), 89, 211
1529$_1$ See 1545$_1$
1532$_2$ Hans Gerle, *Musica Teusch* (Nuremberg), 89, 94, 211
1533$_2$ Pierre Attaingnant (pub.), *Chansons musicales a quatre parties* (Paris), 285
1533$_3$ Pierre Attaingnant (pub.), *Vingt & sept chansons musicales a quatre parties* (Paris), 62, 285
1535$_1$ Silvestro Ganassi, *Opera intitulata Fontegara* (Venice), 59, 163, 223, 230
1536 Francesco da Milano, *Intabolatura de viola o vero Lauto* (Naples), 85, 94, 243
1536$_3$ Francesco da Milano, *Intabulatura di liuto* (Venice), 94

1536_5 Luys Milán, *Libro de música de vihuela de mano intitulado El maestro* (Valencia), 91, 97, 209, 244

1536_6 Hans Newsidler, *Ein newgeordent künstlich Lautenbuch* (Nuremberg), 91, 211

1536_9 Giovanni Antonio Casteliono, *Intabolatura di Leuto de diversi autori* (Milan), 85, 89–94, 103, 158

1538_1 Luis de Narváez, *Los seys libros del Delphin de musica* (Valladolid), 11, 97–8, 216

1538_2 Hieronymus Formschneider (pub.), *Tenor trium vocum Carmina* (Nuremberg), 95

1539 Jacques Arcadelt, *Il primo libro di madrigali* (Venice, 1539 [1538, lost]), 240

1539 Georg Forster, *Frische teutsche Liedlein* (Nuremberg), 94

1540_3 Andrea Arrivabene (pub.), *Musica nova* (Venice), 62, 111, 113, 117

1542_2 Silvestro Ganassi, *Regola. Rubert[i]na* (Venice), 223, 255–6

1543_1 Girolamo Cavazzoni, *Intavolaltura cioe recercari, canzoni, himni, magnificati* (Venice), 111

1543_2 Silvestro Ganassi, *[Regola Rubertina] Lettione Seconda* (Venice), 223, 255–6

1545_1 Martin Agricola, *Musica instrumentalis Deudsch* (Wittemberg), 95, 222, 233, 254–5, 265

1545_3 Pierre Phalèse, *Des chansons reduictz en Talature de Lut . . .* (Louvain), 86, 210

1546_9 Hans Gerle, *Musica und Tabulatur* (Nuremberg), 211

1546_{14} Alonso Mudarra, *Tres libros de música en cifras para vihuela* (Seville), 11, 97–100, 246

1547 Heinrich Glarean, *Dodecachordon* (Basel), 190

1547_1 Jacques Buus, *Ricercari* (Venice), 62, 117

1547_5 Enriquez de Valderrábano, *Libro de música de vihuela* (Valladolid), 11–13, 97

$154?_6$ Jacques Moderne (pub.), *Musicque de Joye* (Lyon), 113

$154?_4$ Francesco da Milano, *Intabolatura da leuto* (Venice?), 94

1551_5 Antonio Gardane (pub.), *Intabolatura nova* (Venice), 270

1551_8 Tielman Susato, *Het derde musyck boexken . . . danserye* (Antwerp), 100–4, 124–5, 158

1552_5 Guillaume Morlaye, *Le premier livre de chansons, gaillardes, pavanes . . . reduictz en tabulature de Guiterne* (Paris), 245–6

1552_7 Diego Pisador, *Libro de música de vihuela* (Salamanca), 11, 97

1553_5 Diego Ortiz, *Trattado de Glosas* (Rome), 111

1554_3 Miguel de Fuenllana, *Libro de música para Vihuela* (Valladolid), 97

1555_1 Juan Bermudo, *Comiença el libro llamado declaracion de inst[r]umentos musicales* (Osuna), 11–14, 99, 213, 247

1558 Gioseffo Zarlino, *Le istitutioni harmoniche* (Venice), 190

1558_6 Albert de Rippe, *Sixiesme livre de tabulature de leut* (Paris), 12

1559_5 Bartolomeo Lieto, *Dialogo quarto di musica* (Naples, 1559), 213

1563_7 Vincenzo Galilei, *Intavolature de Lauto* (Rome), 104–7 (also 1584_5)

1564_7 [Joannis Pacoloni] Frederic Viaera, *Nova et elegantissima in cythara ludenda carmina* (Louvain), 240

1567_2 Claudio Merulo, *Ricercari d'intavolatura d'organo* (Venice), 109–13

1568_2 Vincenzo Galilei, *Fronimo Dialogo* (Venice), 108–9, 213, 218

1568_3 Adrian Le Roy, *A briefe and easye instru[c]tion to learne the tableture* (London), 127, 213, 237 (see also 1574_2)

1571_5 Pierre Phalèse, *Leviorum Carminum* (Louvain), 102

1574_3 Claudio Merulo, *Il primo libro de ricercari* (Venice), 117

1574_5 Melchior Newsidler, *Teutsch Lautenbuch* (Augsburg), 10

1576_1 Esteban Daza, *Libro de música en cifras para Vihuela initulado el Parnasso* (Valladolid), 98, 244

1584_2 Girolamo Dalla Casa, *Il vero modo di diminuir* (Venice), 223–4, 227, 280

1584_5 see 1563_7

1584_6 Emanuel Adriansen, *Pratum Musicum* (Antwerp), 240

1584_{10} Fiorenzo Maschera, *Libro primo de canzoni da sonare* (Brescia), 117

1587_3 Andrea and Giovanni Gabrieli, *Concerti di Andrea et di Gio Gabrieli* (Venice), 118

1587_6 Giovanni Pacolini, *Tabulatura tribus testudinibus* (Milan), 240 [lost]

1588_2 William Byrd, *Psalmes, Sonets, & songs . . . made into Musicke of five parts* (London), 120–5

1589_3 Andrea Gabrieli, *Madrigali et ricercari* (Venice), 117

1589_6 Jacob Paix, *Thesaurus Motetarum* (Strasbourg), 10

1591_2 Giovanni Bassano, *Motetti, Madrigali et Canzoni Francese* (Venice), 224

1592_{10} Richardo Rogniono, *Passaggi per potersi essercitare nel diminuire* (Venice), 224

1592_{12} Matthäus Waissel, *Lautenbuch Darinn von der Tabulatur* (Frankfurt on the Oder), 211–12

1593_3 Girolamo Diruta, *Il Transilvano* (Venice), 113

1594_3 Giovanni Battista Bovicelli, *Regole, passaggi di musica* (Venice), 224

1596_4 William Barley, *A new booke of Tabliture for the Orpharion* (London), 127–8

1597_4 John Dowland, *The First Booke of Songes or Ayres* (London), 127–8

1597_5 Giovanni Gabrieli, *Sacrae symphoniae* (Venice), 116–19, 263

1599_8 Thomas Morley, *First Booke of Consort Lessons* (London), 122, 258

1599_{11} Giovanni Antonio Terzi, *Il Secondo Libro de Intavolatura di Liuto* (Venice), 240 (*see also* p. 214, n. 35, above, concerning Terzi 1593_7)

1600 John Dowland, *The Second Booke of Songs or Ayres* (London), 127

1600 Antoine Francisque, *Le Trésor d'Orphée* (Paris), 130

1603 Jean-Baptiste Besard, *Thesaurus Harmonicus* (Cologne), 128, 160

1603 Thomas Robinson, *Schoole of Musicke* (London), 128

1604 John Dowland, *Lachrimæ or Seaven Tears* (London), 127

1607 Claudio Monteverdi, *L'Orfeo, favola in Musica* [1607] (Venice, 1609), 181, 266

1608 Giovanni Gabrieli, *Canzoni per sonare con ogni sorti di stromenti* (Venice), 119

1609 Philip Rosseter, *Lessons for Consort* (London), 122

1610 Robert Dowland, *A Varietie of Lute Lessons* (London), 126–8, 160

1611 Robert Ballard, [*Premier livre de luth*] (Paris), 130

[1612] *Parthenia or the Maydenhead* (London), 272

1614 Robert Ballard, *Diverses piesces mises sur le luth* (Paris), 130

1619 Michael Praetorius, *Syntagma musicum* (Wolfenbüttel), 222

1623 Alessandro Piccinini, *Intavolatura di liuto, et di chitarrone* (Bologna), 240

General index

Aachen, 166
Abondante, Julio, 106
Adriansen, Emanuel, 240
Agricola, Alexander, 10, 73, 81, 87, 187
    [*Dulces exuviae*], 87
    "Fortuna desperata," 87
Agricola, Martin, 95, 222, 233, 254–5, 265
Agricola, Rudolph, 25
Alamire, Petrus, 18, 27, 56
Albert IV, Duke of Bavaria, 151
Albert V, Duke of Bavaria, 148, 169–71
Albutio, Jacob, 92
Alexander VI (Borgia), 243
Alfons, Nicolas, 137
Alighieri, Dante, 215–17
Alkmaar, 57
Allegri, Lorenzo, 183
Alonzo de Avila, 45
alternatim performance, 37, 65, 115, 184, 263
Alvise, Giovanni, 185
Amsterdam, 57
Anna "canterina Anglica," 25
Anne Duc de Joyeuse, 179
Antwerp, 55–8, 61, 100–1, 103, 118, 123, 135, 147, 168, 172–3, 186, 270
Aquila, 237
Aragon (House of), 21, 99, 243
Arbeau, Thoinot, 101
Arcadelt, Jacques, 92, 96, 224, 239–40
Archilei, Vittoria, 156
Arezzo, 25
Aristoxenus, 218
Armani, Vincenza, 156
Arnaut de Zwolle, Henri, 238, 266–7, 269–70
Assisi, 25
Attaingnant, Pierre, 62, 85, 89, 102, 117, 163, 285
Augsburg (also the source *Augsburg*), 3, 25, 51, 59–60, 85, 86–9, 94–5, 118, 133, 135–8, 147, 149, 151, 154, 230
Austria, 24–5

Bach, Johann Sebastian, 77, 111
Bacheler, Daniel, 126, 129
    "Mounsieurs Almaine," 129
Baden, 249
Ballard, Robert, 130
banquets, 1, 6, 20, 22, 136, 140, 164, 169, 171, 173–4, 177, 206, 241, 265
Barcelona, 54
Bargagli, Girolamo, 183
Barley, William, 127–8
Basel, 24, 159, 161
Bassano family, 30, 134, 229
    Giovanni ("Anchor che col partire"), 224
Behaim, Michel, 253
Bellini, Gentile, 207
Bent, Margaret, 198, 219
Bergamo, 47
Bermudo, Juan, 11–12, 99, 109, 213, 223, 247
Bergen op Zoom, 48, 55, 168, 172–3, 186
Besard, Jean-Baptiste, 128, 160 (*Thesaurus Harmonicus*)
Besseler, Heinrich, 275
Beverly, 53
Biel, 161
Binchois, Gilles, 21, 153, 159, 175–6, 189, 253
    "Je ne vis onques," 175
Board, Margaret, 154
Boethius, 108, 190–1
Bologna, 3, 25, 47 (San Petronio), 50–1, 58–9, 61, 142, 144, 155, 205, 230–1, 240, 244
Bonaventure des Periers, 247
Boorman, Stanley, 83, 85, 91
Borghesi, Simone (?), 278
Borrono, Pietro Paolo, 92–3
Boyden, David, 258
Brabant, 51, 167
Brandenburg, 24, 149
Brandolino, Lippo, 75
Braunschweig, 47
Brauwere, Nicasius de, 186
Bredemers, Henry, 157
Brescia, 229
Brinzing, Armin, 95

Bristol, 53
broken consort, 36, 122, 170, 258
Bronzino, Agnolo, 161
Brown, Howard Mayer, 2, 11, 35–6, 62–3, 88, 107, 180, 214, 225, 252
Brueghel the Elder, Pieter, 2, 179, 277
Bruges, 39–40, 52, 55, 133, 135–40, 147, 149–50, 164–9, 173, 181, 186, 194, 207
   St. Donatian, 167–8
   St. Saviour, 39, 187
Brumel, Antoine, 26
   "Una maistres," 81
Brumel, Giaches, 111–12
Brussels, 60, 106, 286, 290
Bull, John, 123–5
   Galiard to the Quadran Paven, 125
   Passamezzo moderno (Quadran Pavan), 125
   Quadran Pavan, 125
   Ut, re, mi, fa, sol, la, 124
   Variation of the Quadran Pavan, 125
Buonarroti, Michelangelo, 92
Buonarroti "il giovane," Michelangelo, 184
Burgkmair, Hans, 280, 283, 289
Burgundy (Duchy of), 18–19, 22–4, 26, 37, 51–2, 134, 136–7, 145, 151, 157, 164, 166, 174, 238, 249
Busnoys, Antoine, 10, 13, 150
Buus, Jacques, 62
Byrd, William, 110, 120–5, 127, 224
   The Bells, 124
   Carmens Whistle, 124
   Galiarda, 125
   Lachrymae Pavan, 125
   Miserere, 124
   "O Sidney, prince of fame," 121
   Pavana, 125
   Quadran Paven with (Galiard), 124
   Tregian's Ground, 124
   "Why do I use," 121

Cabezón, Antonio de, 33, 221
Caleffini, Ugo, 234
Calvin, John, 48, 160, 188
Cambrai, 189
Cambridge, 53, 60, 174
Canterbury, 48, 53
Capirola, Vincenzo, 10, 90, 111, 162
Caravaggio, Michelangelo Merisi da 240
Caroso, Fabrizio, 101, 180
Carracci, Annibale, 240–1
Casteliono, Giovanni, 85, 89–94, 103, 158
Castiglione Baldesar, 107, 156
Cavalcanti, Raffaello, 157, 159–62
Cavazzoni, Girolamo, 111

Cavazzoni, Marc Antonio, 157
Cellini, Benvenuto, 133, 140–4, 188
   Giovanni, 141
Cesena, 143
chanson, 29, 56, 62, 85, 87–9, 92, 143, 154, 174–5, 194, 253
   chanson performance with instruments, 7–9, 18, 65, 67–8, 71–83, 95–7, 115–18, 155, 159–60, 163, 170, 176–7, 193, 205, 207, 210, 218–19, 239–40, 246, 293
Charteris, Richard, 119
Clemens non Papa, Jacob, 97, 115–17, 159–60, 240, 293
Coburg, 178
Coclico, Adrianus, 189–90
Colchester, 53
Cologne, 50, 56, 147, 178
Compère, Loyset, 10, 77, 219
   "Nous sommes de l'ordre de Saynt Babuyn," 77–8
   O bone Jesu, 219
Copenhagen (also the source *Copenhagen*), 10–11, 36, 94–96, 113, 115–17
Concerto Palatino, 240
confraternities, 40–1, 48, 56, 138, 185, 207
Conklin, Rosalind, 53
convents, 38, 155
Copernicus, Nicolaus, 294
Cordier, Baude, 249
Cordoval [Jehan], *see* Fernandez and Cordoval
Cornaz[z]ano, Antonio, 101 (n.78), 234
Corrado d'Alemagna, 25, 136
Costa, Lorenzo, 238–40
Coventry, 60
Crecquillon, Thomas, 97, 116–17, 240, 293
Cremona, 229
Cummings, Anthony, 164
Cutting, Francis, 127

D'Accone, Frank, 270
Dalla Casa, Girolamo, 47, 223–4, 227, 280
   "Anchor che co'l partire," 224 (setting of madrigal by Cipriano de Rore)
Dalza, Joanambrosio, 84, 93, 100
   Piva, 84
   "Tastar de corde," 84
Dance (dance settings, dancing), 2–3, 6, 18, 20, 22, 29, 30, 38, 63, 66, 68, 71, 81–2, 84–5, 88–91, 93, 95–6, 98, 100–1, 106, 109, 113, 115–17, 120–2, 124–5, 129, 136, 138, 155, 157, 159–61, 163, 164–6, 169–72, 176–80, 178–82, 184, 192–3, 205–6, 240, 245, 258, 259–60, 273–4, 276–7, 295

Dance (dance settings, dancing) (cont.)
  Allemaigne, 103, 128–9
  Basse dance, 85, 102
  Bergerette, 102–3
  Bergerette sans Roch, 102–3
  Branle, 101, 103–4
  Courant, 128, 130
  Der Calvinisten dantz, 160
  Deutscher Tanz, 103
  Fagot, 104
  Folia, 107
  Gaillarde, Galliard, 101, 103, 125, 128–9, 160
  German Dance, 160
  Greensleeves, 104
  Hoboeken dans, 104
  La Barriera, 178
  La Cara Cosa, 178
  La Spagna, 101, 178
  La Traditora, 178
  Moresca, 103
  Passamezzo, 96, 105, 107, 160, 178
  Passamezzo antico, 103–4, 124
  Passamezzo moderno, 104, 124
  Pavane, 84, 101, 103, 125, 128–9, 160, 246
  Pavana alla Ferrarese (or alla Venetiana), 178
  Lachrymae Pavan, 125
  Pavane La Bataille, 103
  Piva, 84, 276
  Romanesca, 99, 105, 107
  Ronde, 103
  Saltarello, 84, 93, 101, 103, 105, 160
  Spagnoletta, 178
  Volta, 128–30, 259
David, Gerard, 254–5
Daza, Esteban, 98, 244
del Cossa, Francesco, 238
de la Torre, Francisco, 101
Della Viola family, 25–6, 74
  Andrea, 25
  Zampaulo, 75 (n. 23)
Dendermonde, 55, 172–3
Denmark, 129, 291
Dentice, Fabrizio, 243
Deventer, 50
Dewes, Anthony, 30
Dinant, Jean de, 137
Dinkelsbühl, 50
Diruta, Girolamo, 113
Doe, Paul, 122
Dolet Etiennne, 217, 220–2

Domenico da Piacenza, 101 (n. 78)
Dowland, John, 110, 125–30, 147, 224–5
  "Can she excuse my wrongs," 129
  "Flow my tears," 127
  galliard (Earl of Essex, King of Denmark), 129
  Lachrymae ("Lachrimae Pavan"), 125, 127
  Most Sacred Queen Elizabeth, her Galliard, 129
Dowland, Robert, 126–30, 160
Downey, Peter 275
Dufay, Guillaume, 11, 13, 21, 68, 74, 150, 153, 159, 175, 207, 253
  "Je ne vis onques," 175 (Binchois?)
Dunstable, John, 67–8
  "Puisque m'amour," 67–8
Durán, Domingo Marcus, 198
Durham, 48

Eco, Umberto, 217
Edward IV (York), 18, 23, 27, 133
Eisenstein, Elizabeth, 211
England, 9, 18–19, 23, 27, 30–3, 36, 38, 41, 43, 48, 50, 52–3, 56, 60, 67, 120, 123, 127–8, 134, 136, 157, 188, 206, 240, 249, 257
Escobar, André de, 54
Este family
  Borso, 236, 273–4
  Ercole, 25–6, 74
  Isabella, 154, 157, 182, 271
Evans, Thomas, 30
Exeter, 53

Fallows, David, 72–3, 78
fantasia (*fantasia sopra*; see also ricercar), 11, 12, 18, 70, 92–4 (*Casteliono*), 95, 97–100 (*Tres libros*), 106, 108–9 (*Fronimo*), 117 (for ensemble), 121–2, 125, 127, 129, 160, 213–15 (rel. to intabulations), 220–1, 224, 245–6, 293
Farnaby, Giles, 125
  Farnaby's Conceit, 125
  Giles Farnaby's Dreame, 125
  Lachrymae Pavan, 125
Farrant, Richard, 120
Farnese (Parma), 92 (Pope Paul III), 110
Ferand, Ernst, 196
Ferdinand II of Aragon, 98
Fernandez [Jehan] and Cordoval (duo), 20–1, 23, 54, 151, 153–4, 195
Ferrabosco, Alfonso, 129

Ferrara, 4, 9, 21, 24–7, 30, 73, 75, 109, 111–12, 136–7, 149–50, 152, 156, 182, 234, 236, 238, 250, 257, 270–1
Fézendat, Michel, 85
Flanders, 27, 30, 43, 50–2, 54, 57–8, 67, 132, 139, 148–9, 167, 172–3, 187, 240
Florence, 4, 50–1, 59, 76, 133–4, 136, 140–2, 148–9, 154, 156, 160, 164–5, 178–183, 185, 194, 237, 271, 294
Formschneider, Hieronymus, 95
Forster, Georg, 94
Fossombrone, 90
Fountains Abbey, 36
Fra Angelico, 16, 234–5
France, 10, 18–19, 22–3, 27, 30, 36, 41, 50, 53–4, 81, 129, 150, 166, 206, 211, 238, 240, 242, 245, 247, 249, 253, 271, 293–4
Francesco da Milano, 90–1, 93–4, 106–7, 111–12, 126, 219–21, 240, 243, 293
   Fantasia 20, 92–3
   O bone Jesu, 219 (intabulation of Compère)
   Tochata, 94
Francis Xavier, 45
Francisque, Antoine, 130
Frei, Hans, 230
Frescobaldi, Girolamo, 110–224
frottola, 89, 157, 159, 234
Fuenllana, Miguel de, 97
Füssen, 139, 230, 240

Gabrieli, Andrea, 34–5, 109–10, 112, 116, 118, 224, 263, 272
   Ricercar del Duodecimo Tuono 118
   Ricercar del Sesto Tuono, 118
Gabrieli, Giovanni, 34–5, 62, 110, 117–19, 224, 263, 272
   Canzon in echo, 119
   Canzon Septimi Toni a 8, 118–19
   Canzona III, 118
   Sonata pian' e forte, 119
Gaffurio, Franchino, 190
Galilei, Galileo, 104–5
Galilei, Vincenzo, 11, 17, 82, 104–9, 160, 213, 218, 223, 292
Gans, Wolff, 60
Ganassi, Silvestro, 59, 142, 163, 222–3, 230, 255–8
   Fontegara (1536), 223, 230
   Regola Rubertina (1542–3), 255–7
Gardano, Antonio, 85, 270
Gerle, Hans, 89, 94, 211

Germany, 3, 9, 10, 22, 24, 41, 50, 52–4, 60, 69, 89, 129, 137, 147, 150, 229, 236–7, 242, 262, 273, 294
Ghent, 52, 135, 137, 145, 147, 149, 167, 248, 253
Ghiselin, Johannes
   "La alphonsina," 77
Ghizeghem, Hayne van, 77
   "De tous biens playne," 80
Gian Maria Giudeo [Alemani, Ebreo], 80, 84, 89, 107, 157, 238
Gibbons, Orlando, 121, 125
Giovanni dall'arpa Inglese, 25
Glarean, Heinrich, 190
Goa, 45
Gombert, Nicolas, 11, 96, 117
Gonzaga, Francesco, 39, 185
Gorzanis, Giacomo, 82, 106
Griffiths, John, 82
Groos, Jan de, 167
Grundherr, Ulrich and Paul, 151
Guadalajara, 43
Guami, Gioseffo, 35
Guatemala, 42–3, 45–6
Guerrero, Francisco, 100, 115
Guido d'Arezzo, 190
Guglielmo Ebreo da Pesaro, 101 (n. 78)
Gutenberg, Johannes, 294

Haarlem, 48
Habsburg (House)
   Charles V, 11, 157
   Eleanor of Austria, 157
   Frederick III, Emperor, 152, 166
   Margaret of Austria, 56, 154, 157, 271, 276
   Maria Magdalena, 179, 183, 241
   Mary of Hungary, 60, 271
   Maximilian I, 23, 25–7, 30, 52, 59, 86–7, 135, 137, 146, 149, 154, 157, 166–8, 187, 207, 230, 236, 265, 280, 283, 289–90
   Philip II, 33
   Philip the Fair, 56, 157
Herbert, Trevor, 188
Herbert of Cherbury, Lord, 130
Hofhaimer, Paul, 26, 86–7, 203, 265, 272
Holborne, Anthony, 129
Holland, 21–2, 52, 57, 167, 249
Holman, Peter, 120, 122, 157, 258
Hurlacher family, 35, 147
   Endries & Sebastian, 60
   Jacob, 86, 89

improvisation, 5, 16, 44, 63, 80, 90, 104, 112, 143, 162, 193–4, 196–9, 202, 204–8, 211, 223–4, 294–5
India, 45
instruments (also players of instruments, i.e. trumpeters, and ensembles)
  arciliuto, 242
  bagpipe, 5, 181, 206, 277
  bassoon, 286
  bells, 171, 186, 288, 292
  bombard, 20, 227–8, 273–4, 276, 278–9, 283
  cembalo, *see* harpsichord
  chekker, 266
  chitarino, 75, 234 (*see also* gittern)
  chitarrone, 242
  cittern, 122
  clavichord, 5, 159, 232, 261, 266–9
  clavicytherium, 273
  claviorganum, 273
  cornett, 17, 26, 32, 35–6, 43, 47–8, 51, 59–61, 86, 96, 118–19, 141–3, 170, 181, 183, 187–8, 226–7, 229, 232, 279–83, 286
  crumhorns, 35, 96, 176, 282–3
  curtal, 232, 285–6
  dulcian, 170, 175
  douçaine, 226, 276–7
  drum (kettledrum), 1, 26, 33, 49, 58, 172, 276, 283–4, 289–90, 292
  fiddle, 20, 38, 63, 65, 138, 152, 172, 180, 185, 192, 228, 248, 249 (w/lute), 252–5, 263–4
  fife, 26, 33, 181, 226
  flute, 26, 35–6, 62, 122, 155, 170, 175, 184, 229, 232, 276, 281, 281–5, 292
  gittern (quintern), 234–35
  guitar, 30, 97–9, 155, 184, 211–12, 232–3, 242–3, 245–67
  harp, 20, 23, 25–6, 58, 79, 83, 99, 138, 154, 157, 159, 172, 185, 207, 233, 247–50, 254
  harpsichord, 5, 15, 30, 36, 123, 159, 231–2, 261, 266–7, 269–73
  lirone, 183
  liuto attiorbato, 242
  lute (lutenist), 1, 5, 6, 8, 10, 12, 16, 18, 20–1, 24–6, 28, 30, 32, 45, 59, 62–5, 78, 80–6, 89–95, 98–100, 102, 104–109, 111–12, 117, 122, 124–31, 136, 138, 147, 152, 154–62, 170, 175, 178–82, 185, 189, 191, 193, 203–7, 209, 218–19, 221, 226, 230, 232–43, 245–7, 251, 269–70, 276, 293, 295
    lute (with plectrum), 75, 80, 82, 84, 89, 211, 234, 237–9

  lute ensembles (and duos), 2, 12, 24, 35, 38, 74, 151, 153, 172–3, 179, 182, 184, 192, 194, 208, 241, 249, 254, 263, 284
  manacordo, 268
  mandola, 183
  organ (organist), 5–7, 11, 18, 20, 24–7, 30, 33–7, 44–5, 48–9, 62, 64–5, 69–71, 79, 86, 109–12, 114, 118–19, 151–2, 155, 157, 169–70, 173–5, 181, 184–6, 189, 190, 196, 198–9, 203, 221, 222, 229, 248, 254, 261–6, 272–3
    regal organ, 36, 170, 261, 265–6
  pandora, 122
  pifferi, 3–4, 50, 72–3, 134, 146
  pipe-and-tabor, 27, 33, 180, 226, 276–7
  psaltery, 183, 250–1
  quintern, 234, 236, 245
  rebec, 30, 154, 185, 254–5
  recorder, 5–6, 20, 28, 30, 35–6, 59, 62, 74, 141, 152, 156, 159, 163, 170, 175–6, 206, 223, 229–31, 262, 281–2
  sackbut, 27, 29–30, 43–4, 48, 61, 118, 175, 188, 286
  shawm (shawmists), 1, 6, 20, 61, 65, 69, 74, 86, 115, 143, 146, 149, 158, 168, 172, 175, 182, 185, 188, 203–4, 226, 269, 273–4, 277, 282, 295
    shawm band, 2, 24–6, 28, 46, 49, 50, 58, 67, 169, 176, 180, 206, 227–8, 275–6, 278–9, 283, 285–6, 288, 290
  spinet, 273
  trombones, 5, 17, 20–1, 26, 28, 35–6, 47, 49–51, 56, 58, 60–1, 67, 74, 96, 119, 169–70, 172, 176, 182–5, 187–8, 226, 228–9, 232, 275–6, 278–83, 285–6
  trumpets (trumpeters), 1, 5, 20, 23–8, 29, 31–3, 35–7, 40–1, 51, 58–9, 61, 65, 67, 132, 143, 158–9, 164, 167–71, 174–5, 183, 225, 228, 232–3, 269, 274–6 (slide trumpet), 286–92
  tympani, 26, 33, 36, 169–70
  vielle, 234
  vihuela, 8, 10–11, 13, 91, 97–100, 112, 211–12, 214, 228, 233, 242–7
  viol, 6, 8, 18, 36, 45, 56, 94, 111, 120, 122, 154–9, 172, 180–2, 184, 226, 228, 240, 245, 254, 257–8, 260
    viol ensembles, 26, 30, 35, 117, 121–2, 127, 150, 170, 183, 256
  viola (*viola da mano,* viola da gamba), 35, 107, 119, 207, 232, 243, 259–60

violin, 32, 34–6, 47, 58, 63, 119–20, 122, 139, 155, 170, 172–3, 177, 179–80, 182–4, 229, 254–5, 257–61
virginals, 123, 161, 261, 266, 270, 272–3
intabulation (intabulating), 11–12, 62–3, 66, 81–4 (*Spinacino*), 93, 97–100 (Mudarra), 106–9 (Galilei), 111, 113, 127, 160, 162, 189, 212–23 (as translations), 239, 242–3, 245
intermedio, 181–4, 241
Isaac, Heinrich, 26, 42, 76–7, 87, 96, 117, 148, 184, 189, 194, 200
  "Et qui la dira," 77
  "Helas," 77
  La mi la sol, 200
  "La morra," 77, 87, 117
Isabel of Portugal, 23
Isabella, Queen of Spain, 271
Italy, 3, 7, 10, 24, 30, 41, 43, 47, 50, 52–4, 58–9, 61, 65, 76, 78–9, 81, 85, 89, 91, 106, 109, 119–20, 129, 137, 143, 149–50, 162, 173, 188, 206, 211, 220, 229–30, 236–7, 240, 242–3, 245, 247, 249–50, 253, 257, 262–3, 273, 294
Ixcoy, 43
Ixtatán, 43

[Jacopo da Bologna]
  "Sotto l'imperio," 66
Jehan de la Court, 23
Johnson, John, 126
Johnson, Robert, 126
Jonson, Ben, 129
Josquin des Prez, 8–14, 11, 26, 42, 77–8, 81, 83, 87, 92, 96, 98, 116–17, 162–3, 189, 239, 245
  "Adieu mes amours," 9, 78
  Ave Maria, 10, 72
  Benedicta es, 10, 12
  "Bergerette savoyene," 78
  "Cela sans plus," 77
  "Comment peult avoir joye," 81
  "Faulte d'argent," 87
  "Fors seulement," 87
  "La plus des plus," 9, 77
  "La Bernardina," 9, 12, 83, 117
  Missa de Beata Virgine, 13
  Missa Faysans regres, 98
  Missa Pange Lingua, 10
  Obsecro te Domina, 13
  Pater noster, 10
  Stabat Mater, 10
Judenkünig, 89, 211

Kampen, 39, 186, 292
Kempten, 149
Kendrick, Robert, 1
Kimball, Roger, 198
Krumsdorfer, Nicholas (Niccolo Tedesco), 25
Kuffer, Wolfgang, 115–16

La Rue, Pierre de, 56, 187
  "Por quoy non," 78
Lancaster (House of)
  Henry IV, 18
  Henry V, 31
Landshut, 151
Lasocki, David, 30, 226, 230
Lasso, Orlando di (Lassus), 4, 34, 58, 97, 115–16, 124, 148, 159–60, 170, 177, 240
[Laufenberg = Henrici de Libero Castro; see Fallows, *Catalogue*, 376]
  "Souvent m'espas [mes pas]," 66, 68
Le Franc, Martin, 21
Le Roy, Adrian, 127–8, 213
Leipzig, 47, 60, 134, 178
Leonardo da Vinci, 267, 294
Lepanto, 117
Lerma (Church of San Pedro), 11, 49, 113–17
Lieto, Bartolomeo, 213, 243
Lille, 54, 154, 174, 181
Lincoln, 60
Lobo, Alonso, 115
Lockwood, Lewis, 72–4, 150, 195
Locqueville, Richard de, 249
Lof (*Salve*) celebrations, 39, 48, 168, 186
London, 52–3, 57, 60, 120–1
  Chapel Royal, 171
  St. Paul's Cathedral, 120
  Westminster Abbey, 120
Lorraine (House), 67, 169, 183
  Christine, 183
  Renata, 169
Louvain [Leuven], 86, 147, 210
Low Countries, 10, 19, 27, 39, 48–50, 53, 56–7, 60, 85, 103, 132, 134, 147, 150, 157, 166, 168, 186–7, 206, 253, 262, 292, 294
Lucca, 143
Ludovico el del Arpe, 99, 248
Ludwig II of Bavaria, 171
Lüneberg, 47
lute making, 139–40, 145, 229, 231, 257
lute song, 15, 79, 98, 100, 107, 109, 215
Luzzaschi, Luzzasco, 110
Lyons, 113, 182, 220

Maastricht, 147
madrigal, 92, 96, 115–7, 121, 170, 177, 183, 242, 246, 254
   intabulations / arrangements of, 106–8, 155, 160, 218–19, 224, 239–40
Malacise, Francesco, 74–5
Maler, Laux, 230
Maler, Sigismund, 230
Malvezzi, Cristofano, 182–3
   "O quale, O qual risplende nube," 182
   Sinfonias, 184
Malvezzi, Elena, 155
Mantua, 30, 32, 39, 59, 73, 88, 92, 137, 146, 149, 150, 152, 156, 185, 257
Marco dall'Aquila, 89–94, 111
Marcolini, Francesco, 85, 89
Marguerite de Vaudémont, 179
Martini, Johannes, 73–6
   "La martinella," 74, 95
   "Tout joyeux," 74–5
Mascarone, Cesare, 240
Maschera, Florentio 117
Mass, 56, 92, 113, 188, 194, 242, 263
   instrumental performance of, 8, 10–12, 37, 40–1, 47–8, 65, 113, 115, 122, 162, 184–5, 187, 218–19, 246, 293
Maximilian I, *see* Habsburg
McGee, Timothy, 83
Mechelen, 48, 52, 56, 147, 187
Medici family, 84, 144, 157, 164–5, 182, 250, 266, 277
   Alessandro, 107
   Clement VII (Giulio de'Medici), 91, 111, 142–3
   Cosimo I, 4
   Cosimo II, 179, 183, 241
   Ferdinando I, 4, 183
   Francesco, 4
   Giulio, 142
   Leo X, 91, 111
   Lorenzo the Magnificent, 4, 51, 89, 143, 146, 148, 270
Mei, Girolamo, 108, 218
Memling, Hans, 252
memory (memorization)
   copying from, 161, 204
   pedagogy, 44
   performance from, 63, 65, 143, 152, 162, 176, 192–3, 196, 207–8
   singing from, 95, 197
Memo, Dionysius, 30
Merlo, Alessandro, 106

Merulo, Claudio, 109–13, 117–18, 224
   Ricercari, 109–13
Mexico, 42–5
Mexico City, 44
Middelburg, 172
Milan, 32, 89–93, 142, 152, 155, 179
Milán, Luys, 91, 97, 209, 244
minstrels, 22–3, 27–8, 31, 38, 44, 52, 64–5, 71, 131, 133, 137, 167, 186, 199, 204, 226, 295
Moderne, Jacques, 85, 113, 117
Monson, Craig, 155
Montepulciano, 25
Monteverdi, Claudio
   L'Orfeo, 181, 266
Morales, Cristóbal, 11, 42, 100, 115
Morari, Antonio, 177
Morlaye, Guillaume, 85, 246
Morley, Thomas, 122
   Lachrymae Pavan, 125
motet, 8, 56, 174–5, 194, 242, 246
   motet (instrumental performance of), 10–12, 38–40, 65, 71, 87–8, 92, 96, 108, 113, 115–17, 143, 154–5, 160, 168–170, 177, 186–8, 192, 205, 207–8, 214, 218–19, 239, 261, 263, 293
Mouton, Jean, 42
Mudarra, Alonso, 11, 97–100, 246, 293
   Conde claros, 99
   Fantasia de pasos largos para desenbolver las manos, 98
   Fantasia facil, 98
   Fantasia que contrahaze la harpa en la manera de Ludovico, 99
   Missa faysan regres (intabulation of Josquin), 99
   Tiento, 100
Munich, 4, 21, 24, 34–6, 59, 61, 69–72, 148–9, 151, 173, 176–7, 230, 237, 250, 260
Myers, Herbert W., 248, 251, 277

Nagel, Hans, 27, 33, 56
Namur, 147
Naples, 109, 152, 234, 243
Narváez, Luys de, 11, 97–8
Negri, Cesare, 101, 179–80
Nepotis, Govard, 157
Neuschel, Hans, 26, 229–30
Newsidler, Hans, 91, 211
Newsidler, Melchior, 10
Nicaragua, 43
Nördlingen, 134, 149, 178, 262

Norwich, 48–9, 53, 60
Nuremberg, 3, 50–1, 70, 140, 149–51, 178, 181, 228, 230

Oaxaca, 43
Obrecht, Jacob, 39, 186, 194
  Alma redemptoris mater, 207
  Ave regina celorum, 168, 208
  Salve regina, 168
  "Tsat een meskin," 78
Ockeghem, Johannes, 81, 150, 207
Öglin, Erhard, 87
Oisterwijk, Gommar van, 57–8
Orto, Marbriano de
  Ave Maria, 77
Orléans, 161
Ottoman Empire, 116–17
Ovid, 100
Oxford, 174

Pacolini, Giovanni, 240
Padovano, Annibale, 109–11, 169–7
  Battaglia, 169
Padua, 169, 229–30
Paix, Jacob, 10
Paladin, Jean-Paul, 14
Palma, Giacomo (Palma il Vecchio), 232
Parabosco, Giovanni, 109
Paris, 9, 18, 85, 89, 92, 95, 130, 287
Parma, 110
Parsons, Robert, 120
Passau, 178
Paston, Edward, 127
patronage, 2–3, 16–17, 18–22 (Burgundy), 31–4, 36–7, 39–41, 43, 48–56, 59–61, 146–7, 160
Paumann, Conrad, 6, 24, 64, 69–71, 80–1, 150–3, 173, 195–6, 198, 203, 249–50, 268
  "Bekenne myn klag," 71
  Fundamenta, 69–71, 153, 196, 198, 203, 206
  "Wiplich figur," 71
Pedrizzano, Giulio, 240
Peler, John de, 27
Pelken, Segher, 57–8
Pelletier du Mans, Jacques, 215
Peters, Gretchen, 54, 138
Petrarch, Francesco 100, 155
Petrucci, Ottaviano, 4, 9, 76, 78–81, 83–5, 89–90, 92, 111, 189, 193, 200, 205, 211, 214, 238
Phalèse, Pierre, 85–6, 102, 210
Philips, Peter, 123
Piccinini, Alessandro, 240

Piccolomini, Francesco Todeschino (Pope Pius III), 278
Pickering, Jane, 154
Pietrobono de Burzellis, 25–6, 74–5, 79, 83, 136, 150, 152–3, 173, 195, 234, 23–7, 250
Pinturicchio (Bernardino di Betto), 278–9
Piombino, Pietro da, 232
Pirrotta, Nino, 66, 181–2
Pisa, 142
Pisador, Diego, 11, 97
Poliziano (Angelo Ambrogini), 181
Poll, Hermann, 267
Praetorius, Michael, 222, 233, 265
Ptolemy, 218
printing (*see also* Attaingnant, Casteliono, Gardano, Marcolini, Morlaye, Petrucci, Phalèse, Scotto), 3–5
  by Petrucci, 76, 80, 83
  for amateur musicians, 131–2
  impact of, 162, 194, 208–9, 211, 261, 294
  in Paris, 85, 220
  in Louvain, 86
  keyboard music, 109–10
  lute music, 89–90, 94
  of Josquin's music, 10
processions, 6, 20, 22, 25, 40, 138, 150, 164–7, 171–3, 181, 207, 265, 285, 287–90
Prosdocimus de Beldemandis, 196
Puebla, 45
Pyrot, John, 30

Rastall, Richard, 53
Rauch family, 35, 147, 149, 229–30
  Claus, 149
  David, 149
  Hans, 60
Regensburg, 24, 115–16, 151–2
Reggio, Claudio, 110
Reimerswaal, 173
Res facta, 194, 196–9
ricercar (*see also fantasia*), 12, 18, 80, 81–4 (*Spinacino*), 89–90, 92, 105–7 (Galilei), 109–13 (Merulo), 117–18 (for ensemble), 122, 170, 194, 213–15 (rel. with intabulations), 224
Richard III (York), 18, 28–9
Rifkin, Joshua, 72–3
Rinaldo dall'Arpa, 250
Rippe, Albert de 12, 32, 93–4, 111, 128
  Fantasia XII, 93
Robinson, Thomas, 128
Rogier, Philippe, 115

Rogniono, Richardo
   "Anchor che co'l partire," 224 (setting of madrigal by Rore)
Rore, Cipriano de, 155, 170, 261
   "Anchor che co'l partire," 224
Rosenplüt, Hans, 152
Rosseter, Philip, 122
Ruckers (instrument makers), 270

Sachs, Klaus-Jürgen, 198
Salve, see Lof
Santa Eulalia, 43
Sanudo, Marin, 80, 238
Schlick, Arnolt, 222
Schnitzer family of musicians, 35, 147, 149, 229–30
Schrattenbach, 149
Schubinger family, 147, 226
   Michel Schubinger, 4, 25, 74, 137
   Augustine Schubinger, 26, 51, 56, 59, 86, 137, 148, 187, 280
   Ulrich the Younger, 137, 147–8
Scotto, Girolamo, 85
Senfl, Ludwig, 87
   "Ich klag denn tag," 96
Sermisy, Claudin de, 29, 95, 117, 240
Severnake, John, 30
's-Hertogenbosch, 185
Seville, 9, 44, 49, 97–9
Siena, 47, 50–1, 59, 142, 164–5, 173, 237, 270, 278
Singleton, Charles, 215–17
Snyder, Kerala, 69
Spain, 10, 11, 21, 32–4, 41, 43–4, 46, 49–50, 53–4, 98, 100, 113, 148, 188, 242–3, 245, 247, 271
Spataro, Giovanni/Aaron, Pietro correspondence, 142
Spinacino, Francesco, 4, 9, 12–13, 79–85, 89–90, 111, 189, 194, 205, 208, 211
   Recercare di tutti le toni, 82
Stefano ("da Savoia"), 25
Stewdlin, Georg, 26, 187, 281
Stockholm, 9
Strasbourg, 50
Striggio, Alessandro, 115, 170
Strohm, Reinhard, 168, 208
Stuart (House of), 130
   Princess Elizabeth, 125
Sultzbach, Joannes, 85, 243
super librum, 194, 196–9, 208
Susato, Tielman, 55–8, 85, 100–4, 117, 124–5, 158, 163
   Allemaigne, 103
   Basse dance, 102–3
   Bergerette, 102–3
   Bergerette sans Roch, 102–3
   Branle, 101, 103
   Fagot, 104
   Gaillard, 103
   Hoboeken dans, 104
   Moresca, 103
   Pavane, 103
   Pavane La Bataille, 103
   Passamezzo antico, 103–4
   Ronde, 103
   Saltarello, 103
Sweden, 57
Sweelinck, Jan Pieterszoon, 124
   Psalm 140, 124
Sydney, Sir Philip, 121

tablature, 9, 11, 79–83 (emergence of), 90, 97, 99, 102, 106, 109, 113, 126–7, 160–2, 189, 191, 193, 205, 210–14, 217, 219, 223, 237–8, 244, 247
Tallis, Thomas, 127, 224
Taverner, John, 121
   Benedictus (from the *Missa Gloria tibi Trinitas*), 121–2
Terzi, Giovanni Antonio, 240
Tieffenbrucker, Magno, 230
Tieffenbrucker, Wendelin (Vendelio Venere), 229–30
Tinctoris, Johannes, 13, 77, 150, 152–3, 173, 190, 194, 196–9, 202, 206, 233–4, 238, 243, 277
Toffolo, Stefano, 230
Toledo, 187
Torre, Francisco de la
   Alta, 101
Tregian the Younger, Francis, 123–4
Troiano, Massimo, 34–6, 169–70, 174, 176–7, 260–1
Tromboncino, Bartolomeo, 4
Tudor (House of)
   Edward VI, 48
   Elizabeth I, 48, 57, 120, 126, 129, 157
   Henry VII, 18, 25–27
   Henry VIII, 18, 27–32, 34, 48, 55, 61, 120, 133, 145, 156–7, 187, 250, 271, 290
   Mary I, 48, 157

Ulm, 24, 47
Unverdorben, Marx, 230
Utrecht, 37, 39, 114, 168, 172, 186